W9-CKU-512

DATE DUE

GAYLORD

PRINTED IN U.S.A.

The United States, the European Union, and the "Globalization" of World Trade

Allies or Adversaries?

THOMAS C. FISCHER

Foreword by Sir David Williams

QUORUM BOOKS
Westport, Connecticut • London

Library of Congress Cataloging-in-Publication Data

Fischer, Thomas C. (Thomas Covell)
    The United States, the European Union, and the "globalization" of
world trade : allies or adversaries? / Thomas C. Fischer ; foreword by
Sir David Williams.
        p. cm.
    Includes bibliographical references and index.
    ISBN 1-56720-037-0 (alk. paper)
    1. United States—Foreign economic relations—European Union
countries.   2. European Union countries—Foreign economic relations—
United States.   3. Free trade—United States.   4. Free trade—
European Union countries.   5. Free trade—Asia.   6. Competition,
International.   I. Title.
HF1456.5.E8F57   2000
337.7304—dc21   99–40351

British Library Cataloguing in Publication Data is available.

Library of Congress Catalog Card Number: 99–40351
ISBN: 1–56720–037–0

First published in 2000

Quorum Books, 88 Post Road West, Westport, CT 06881
An imprint of Greenwood Publishing Group, Inc.
www.quorumbooks.com

Printed in the United States of America

The paper used in this book complies with the
Permanent Paper Standard issued by the National
Information Standards Organization (Z39.48–1984).

10 9 8 7 6 5 4 3 2

History, according to Karl Marx, is economics in action—the contest, among individuals, groups, classes, and states, for food, fuel, materials, and economic power. . . . The past leaves little doubt that every economic system must sooner or later rely on some form of the profit motive. . . . [Alt]hough men cannot be equal, their access to . . . opportunity can be made more nearly equal.

—Will and Ariel Durant, THE LESSONS OF HISTORY

Contents

Foreword by Sir David Williams, QC   ix

Preface   xi

Acknowledgments   xiii

Acronyms   xv

I. What in the World Is Happening (to World Trade)?   1

  1. The "Globalization" Process   3

  2. Regulating Global Trade   8

II. New Trade Paradigms   17

  3. An Economic Map of the World   19

  4. Four Economic "Models"   30

  5. Global Trade and Global "Government"   32

III. Three Trading Giants? (and Their Spheres of Influence)   41

  6. The United States   43

  7. Afta' NAFTA: The Free Trade Area of the Americas (FTAA) 58

  8. The European Union: Can It Compete?   75

  9. The European Union Program   93

  10. Widening the European Community   136

11.   Japan: Asia's Disintegrating Colossus   145

12.   China: The Middle Kingdom in the Middle   160

13.   Asia's Emerging Economies: "Miracle," Myth or Neither?   178

IV.   "Globalizing" Trade   **199**

14.   Metamorphosing the GATT: The World Trade Organization
      (WTO)   201

15.   A New Era in World Trade   223

Appendix   245
Notes   255
Selected Bibliography   325
Index   333

Foreword

This is an adventurous and imaginative study of the "globalization" of world trade. The author delves deeply into complex areas, and he presents his material with both lucidity and a lightness of touch.

Professor Fischer emphasizes that there no longer is, or can be, a national economic policy unaffected by global pressures, and he looks in detail at the emergence of three powerful and expanding trading blocs (America, Europe and the Asia/Pacific Rim). In the course of his wide-ranging consideration of so many interlocking areas of economic activity, he examines (for instance) the North American Free Trade Agreement (NAFTA) and the Free Trade Area of the Americas (FTAA).

Considerable attention is given to the European Union, with a sensitive awareness of the problems of "federalization" evolving either by design or otherwise. He accepts that "there continue to be divisions among the heads of state about the pace and direction of European integration," and he is fully aware of the differences of political and social philosophy, of culture, history and language. Moreover, he is fully aware of critical developments of the last decade, and he recognizes the continuing pressure for expansion of the Community. There is great unpredictability in the process of absorption, and it is difficult to formulate a timetable for developments in the new millennium.

There is a predictably somber note in the treatment of Japan ("Asia's Disintegrating Colossus"), of China ("the greatest enigma of all") and of the varying fortunes of other economies including Hong Kong, Singapore, South Korea, Taiwan and Thailand, but Professor Fischer is not pessimistic about the future.

The final part of the book, on the subject of "globalizing" trade, brings together the themes and perceptions of the earlier parts of the book. Professor Fischer is anxious that the World Trade Organization (WTO) should continue to develop, since few international organizations "have as much potential to harmonize world trade as the WTO." Fischer emphasizes "that trade globalization is a powerful and complicated force in today's world, beyond the ability of any single nation to control." His approach, throughout the book and in the concluding sections, is consistently constructive, realistic and cautiously optimistic.

This is a book of undoubted scholarship, and it is undoubtedly timely in its identification and explanation of so many of the competing forces in world trade. There are economic, institutional,, social, environmental, political and legal challenges to be faced, and Professor Fischer has provided an invaluable guide.

> Professor Sir David Williams, QC
> Vice Chancellor Emeritus
> University of Cambridge, England

Preface

In certain ways, this book is like the second voyage of Columbus to the new world. An earlier excursion of mine into the subject matter, THE EURO-PEANIZATION OF AMERICA (1995), helped me to plot the course and to discover the most salient features of the landscape. Hence, it will not do for me to accomplish no more with this book than to plot a bit more of the terrain and to describe the natives and their behavior in greater detail.

Rather, I have taken as my task to try to make some holistic sense of what I have discovered; to place it in the context of much larger movements that I believe are overspreading this globe.

The subject is as vast, complex and intertwined as any I have addressed. For that reason, I have tried to present it in digestible chunks, even at the expense of some oversimplification. Armed with this outline and aware of the plentitude of uncertainties that surround it, perhaps my reader will be able to place new events into context as they occur.

That is to say that I do not seek merely to recount facts, but to estimate their impact on the evolving world order. What else is a voyage of discovery for?

Preface

Acknowledgments

So many people have influenced this book—from pub patrons in English villages to a cab driver in Canberra—that I could not possibly thank them all. They know who they are, and what their contributions were, and how grateful I am for them. I hope this knowledge will suffice.

However, some persons have figured so prominently in the project that they deserve to be thanked individually. I begin with Terence Daintith, former Director of the Institute of Advanced Legal Studies at the University of London (and now Dean of its Schools of Advanced Studies), and his successor as Institute Director, Barry A. K. Rider, of Jesus College, Cambridge. They had enough faith in my work to steer me into an Inns of Court Fellowship, where serious work on the book began. While I was resident at Lincoln's Inn, Treasurer Sir Maurice Drake, DFC; Under Treasurer Malcolm Carver; my "shepherd," Christopher McCall, QC; and the Inn librarian, Guy Holborn (and that of Middle Temple, Janet Edgell), did all in their power to accommodate and advance my work. Other exceptionally welcoming members of the Inn were Paul Heim, former Registrar of the European Court of Justice, David Lord Renton and Sir Robert "Ted" Megarry, to mention just a few.

Elsewhere in London I enjoyed the assistance of David Vaughan, QC, barrister of Brick Court Chambers, and his young colleague, Aidan Robertson; Peter Goldsmith, QC, of Fountain Court, Temple; Kate Timms, head of the U.K. Ministry of Agriculture, Fish and Food (MAFF); Clare Ede, Librarian of the EU Mission to London; Sir Raymond Whitney, OBE, and the Rt. Hon. David Heathcoat-Amory of the House of Commons; Baroness Elles (formerly a Member of the European Parliament); and Lords Wallace of Saltaire and Slynn of Hadley, who gave quite different perspectives on the EU. Dr. Christopher Kerse, Legal Advisor to the House of Lords Committee on the European Communities, and Francis Jacobs, Advocate General of the European Court of Justice, were invaluable sources of help.

My old mentor, Kurt Lipstein, Professor Emeritus of European Law at Clare College, Cambridge, is to be thanked for his continuing interest in my work, as is Cambridge Vice-Chancellor Emeritus, Professor Sir David Williams, QC, who first welcomed me there. Other Cambridge resources include Alan Dashwood, formerly Director of Legal Services for the European Council and now head of the Centre for European Legal Studies (CELS), Gordon Johnson and John Seagrave of Wolfson College, Vaughan Lowe of Corpus Christi and David Wills, Squire Law Librarian.

While I was in the South Pacific working on that segment of the book, I was aided by Aneurian Hughes, European Union Ambassador to Australia and New Zealand; Bruce Harris, Dean of the University of Auckland Faculty of Law; his colleague, Jane Kelsey; and Professors Ian Eagles and Robert Scollay of the Department of Commercial Law and APEC Studies Centre, respectively. I also was aided by the advice of Curtis Stewart, Economic Counselor to the U.S. Embassy, and the work of Professor Peter Drysdale of the Australia–Japan Research Centre at the Australian National University in Canberra.

Finally, I thank those "unseen" persons who provide the encouragement and practical support that help one through a project of this sort. Brenda, my wife, who set me on this stream of inquiry (but who sometimes regrets it); Nick Colannino, Information Officer of the EU Mission to the UN; Linda Muir, Librarian of the Craven County (NC) Library (where I did a lot of writing); my hearty research associates, Pheobe Jacobs, Jennifer Loeb-Cederwall, Ingrid Gude, Jon Lindemann and Wendy Skillman; hardworking reference librarians Barry Stearns, Brian Flaherty and Anne Acton; secretaries Patricia Gresham, Dawn Medford, Pamela Cole and Carol Palmer; and copyist Sue Roche.

This project has been an incredible trip, so I was grateful for their company.

Acronyms

ABAC	APEC Business Advisory Council
ACP	African, Caribbean and Pacific countries (former colonies of EC nations); parties to the Lomé Convention
ADB	Asian Development Bank
AFTA	ASEAN Free Trade Area
AGGF	Agricultural Guidance and Guarantee Fund of the EU
APEC	Asia Pacific Economic Cooperation forum (states include Australia, Brunei, Canada, Chile, China, Hong Kong, Indonesia, Japan, Malaysia, Mexico, New Zealand, Papua New Guinea, Peru, the Philippines, Russia, Singapore, South Korea, Taiwan, Thailand, the United States and Vietnam)
ASEAN	Association of Southeast Asian Nations (states include Brunei, Cambodia, Indonesia, Laos, Malaysia, Myanmar, the Philippines, Singapore, Thailand and Vietnam)
Benelux	Economic Union of Belgium, Luxembourg and the Netherlands
BTD	BNA International Trade Daily (Bureau of National Affairs)
CAP	Common Agricultural Policy
CCT	Common Customs Tariff
CDP	Common Defense Policy
CEES	Central and Eastern European states (formerly part of the Soviet Union)
CFI	Court of First Instance of the EU
CFP	Common Fisheries Policy; Common Foreign Policy
CFSP	Common Foreign and Security Policy

CMLR	Common Market Law Review
COREPER	Committee of Permanent Representatives (EU Council)
CSCE	Conference on Security and Cooperation in Europe (consists of 35 nations: all sixteen members of NATO, the former six members of the Warsaw Treaty Organization, plus Albania, Austria, Cyprus, Finland, Ireland, Liechtenstein, Malta, Monaco, San Marino, Sweden, Switzerland, the Vatican City and Yugoslavia)
DG	Directorate General
DM	Deutsche mark
DSB	Dispute Settlement Body (WTO)
EA	European Agreements
EAGGF	European Agricultural Guidance and Guarantee Fund
EBRD	European Bank for Reconstruction and Development
EC	European Community
ECB	European Central Bank
ECJ	European Court of Justice
Ecofin Council	Council of Ministers for Economic and Financial Affairs
ECR	European Court Reports
ECSC	European Coal and Steel Community
ECU	European Currency Unit (now the euro)
EDF	European Development Fund
EEA	European Economic Area
EEC	European Economic Community
EFTA	European Free Trade Association
EIB	European Investment Bank
EMI	European Monetary Institute
EMS	European Monetary System
EMU	Economic and Monetary Union
EP	European Parliament
EPC	European Political Cooperation
EPU	European Political Union
ERDF	European Regional Development Fund
ERM	Exchange Rate Mechanism
ESC	Economic and Social Committee
ESCB	European System of Central Banks
ESF	European Social Fund
EU	European Union
Euratom	European Atomic Energy Community (EAEC)

euro	The common currency for eleven EU states as of January 1, 1999
Europol	European Police Office
FDI	Foreign Direct Investment
FTA	Free Trade Agreement; Free Trade Area
FTAA	Free Trade Area of the Americas
G-7/G-8	Group of seven industrial nations (Canada, France, Germany, Italy, Japan, the United Kingdom, and the United States, now sometimes including Russia)
GATS	General Agreement on Trade in Services
GATT	General Agreement on Tariffs and Trade (successive "rounds")
GDP	Gross Domestic Product
GNP	Gross National Product
GSP	Generalized System of Preferences
ILO	International Labor Organization
IMF	International Monetary Fund
IPR	Intellectual Property Rights
ITA	Information Technology Agreement
ITR	International Trade Reporter (Bureau of National Affairs)
LDC	Less-Developed Country
MAI	Multilateral Agreement on Investment
MEP	Member of European Parliament
Mercosur	Southern Common Market (states include Argentina, Brazil, Paraguay and Uruguay, with Chile associated)
MFN	Most-Favored Nation (now, generally, Normal Trade Relations—NTR)
MRA	Mutual Recognition Agreement
NAFTA	North American Free Trade Agreement
NATO	North Atlantic Treaty Organization
NGOs	Non-Governmental Organizations
NICs	Newly Industrialized Countries
NIS	Newly Independent States (former states of the Soviet Union)
NTA	New Transatlantic Agenda (the United States and the EU)
NTB	Non-Tariff Barriers
NTR	Normal Trade Relations (replacing MFN—Most-Favored Nation)
OECD	Organisation for Economic Co-operation and Development
OJ	Official Journal of the European Communities
PECC	Pacific Economic Cooperation Council
PHARE	Poland and Hungary: aid for economic restructuring

Quad Four	Canada, the EU, Japan and the United States
R & D	Research and Development
SEA	Single European Act
SMEs	Small and Medium-sized Enterprises
TABD	Transatlantic Business Dialogue
TEP	Transatlantic Economic Partnership (the U.S. and the EU)
TEU	Treaty on European Union
TRIMs	Trade-Related Investment Measures Agreement
TRIPs	Trade-Related Aspects of Intellectual Property Rights
U.K.	United Kingdom
UN	United Nations
UNCTAD	United Nations Conference on Trade and Development
UR	Uruguay Round
U.S.	United States
USTR	United States Trade Representative (or Office of the U.S. Trade Representative)
VAT	Value Added Tax
WEU	Western European Union (European military alliance)
WIPO	World Intellectual Property Organization
WTO	World Trade Organization (successor to the GATT)

Part I

What in the World Is Happening (to World Trade)?

Chapter 1

The "Globalization" Process

GREAT LEAPS FORWARD

Change rarely occurs at a constant rate. Recently, physicians have discovered that children develop in a series of "growth spurts." I believe that world trade has developed in much the same way—long lulls punctuated by what I call "great leaps forward." Among the former would be the Middle Ages. Among numerous examples of the latter we might list: the voyages of the Phoenician traders, who exchanged goods and culture throughout the pre-Christian world; the opening of trade with the Orient in the age of Marco Polo; the discovery of the Americas by Columbus; and the subsequent circumnavigation of the globe and colonization of discovered lands and peoples, with their labor, resources and markets. The Industrial Revolution increased the speed and scope of the globalization process, and powered transport—by steam, gasoline and jet engines—accelerated it even more.

On the political side, there was World War I, which left the combatants wearied, but with new knowledge and capacities. An attempted League of Nations failed, and the world drifted into isolation characterized by protectionist tariffs. World War II once again pushed nations, their people and institutions to their limit. But, resolving not to make the punitive mistakes of the prior war, constructive multinational initiatives like the United Nations, the Marshall Plan, the World Bank, the International Monetary Fund (IMF) and the General Agreement on Tariffs and Trade (GATT) were pursued.[1] Any one of these events (and certainly the last group, collectively) can be considered a great leap forward. The reason is that they put trade, indeed *international* trade, on a whole new footing and changed it fundamentally for the future.

Although these last entries suggest the rapid evolution in world trade during the past 40 years, I believe we are at the threshold of yet another great leap forward. It is by no means guaranteed, because the process of trade liberalization is generally both collaborative and competitive. The choice between them can result in success or failure in today's highly complex trading world. If such opportunities are managed well, they can produce the breakthrough I anticipate. If poorly managed, they can produce stalemate, a lull, and worse: retrenchment and war.

"GLOBALIZATION" DEFINED

For lack of a better term, I call this new leap forward the "globalization" of world trade. It is a cliché of course to suggest that "the world is getting smaller" and that trade is increasingly internationalized or globalized. This process has been going on since the earliest of my examples. From the eighteenth century forward, there has been a growing emphasis on things international. After World War II, the emphasis gradually changed to multinationalism. Now the catchphrase is "globalization." But these terms need definition. They may have different meanings.

Whereas "international" trade almost literally implies the engagement of nations in their free-standing national capacities, "multinational" implies that actors from several nations are involved. There is a notion of shared responsibility, but not enough to suggest that nationhood is irrelevant. However, the concept of "globalization" suggests a substantial melding of interests across national borders so that "global" solutions are important but national perspectives are not. It suggests a solution that diminishes *national* interests for the good of all. It stresses interdependence at the expense of a potentially destructive independence. Of course, "globalism" can affect any area of affairs—culture, environment or finance. Our concern is trade or business, broadly speaking. To the extent that it is truly globalized, it is no longer one nation's concern.

Just as important as the *denationalization* of a truly global problem is the prospect that the *national* interests in its successful resolution (e.g., security) pale in comparison to its economic consequences (e.g., jobs, health and environmental protection). Thus, globalization also shifts attention from *public* interests to those that are essentially business related (traditionally described as *private* international law). Hence, the other aspect of "globalization" is the significant shift from *public* interests and actors to *private* interests and actors. In my opinion, the difference between public and private international law has all but disappeared today.

When the federal government enters a GATT or other negotiation (as opposed to an arms treaty) with the express goal of protecting business interests, creating jobs and stimulating exports, there is virtually no difference between public and private international law. The former becomes the servant of the latter. And because no national interest can long hold out against a contrary global interest, a purely national viewpoint becomes largely irrelevant. It is precisely this diminution of the national (public) interest by an increasingly interdependent (private) business economy that has altered the balance in the global marketplace.

This interdependence and denationalization has several profound impacts on national economies, both developed and developing. First, no large national market can suffer a significant shock without its impact being felt in other national markets.[2] Second, it is clear that not even the most powerful and wealthiest nation in the world can permanently influence market conditions on its own. No country can be exclusively responsible for its own problems, for they affect other nations. Conversely, every country cannot be equally responsible for both local and non-local problems. When a job is everyone's, it often is no one's in particular. Thus, the increasing globalization of the world marketplace calls for coordination and a division of responsibility. For example, the United States had the laboring oar in the Mexican financial crisis; the European Union was principally responsible in Bosnia; and Japan has done more for emerging Asian countries than has any other nation.

The sum of all this is that there no longer is, or can be, a national economic policy unaffected by global pressures. The interdependence of goods, capital, labor and services calls for more international coordination. What efforts there have been at internationalization (the UN, GATT, OECD, IMF) have been too loose. Efforts at regionalization (EU, NAFTA, APEC) have not been wholly successful and are under constant pressure to expand. Ultimately, they may threaten the success of more global efforts like the World Trade Organization (WTO).[3]

Meanwhile, a sort of "world government" is emerging from such groups as the WTO, G-7 and Quad 4. It is not a government in any traditional sense. It has no territory, constituents, voters or branches; no executive, legislative or judiciary. And yet, *de facto*, it has all these things and promises to develop as time passes. Competing national or regional initiatives interfere with this process. Conversely, there is substantial (and legitimate) disagreement about whether we should have a global trading system and, if so, how it ought to be structured. That is what this book is about.

Although the term "globalization" has been used for some time now, the process as I have defined it has begun only quite recently. It is typified by the emergence of three powerful and expanding trading blocs: America, Europe and Asia/Pacific Rim. Each is becoming better structured and is developing internal trade mechanisms. In this sense, these enterprises compete with international or multinational organizations such as the UN or World Bank. More important, each group embraces a somewhat different philosophy with regard to world trade. Eventually these will have to be reconciled.

Perhaps most remarkable, these undertakings to liberalize the world trade marketplace are made at the behest of businesses. That is, they are not just routine public law efforts in the international sphere, but collaborations between businesses and government to *globalize* world trade. In this way, they differ from past efforts to increase peace and security.

Trade expansion has always been a global integrator. But with the pace of private business integration so demonstrably exceeding the pace of public integration schemes, the engine of national policy seems to be business driven. This produces certain frictions among the three leading trading blocs because there are fundamental differences about their approach to trade. The arrangements they make during the next few years may well determine whether the globalizing process will be orderly or rife with conflict. The "internationalization" of world trade has been going on since the time of the Phoenicians. The "globalization" of world trade is recent. It has produced a different set of trading phenomena. Approximately, they are these:

1. The volume and value of world trade will continue to grow. That growth may be particularly swift in certain emerging and developing countries. It will be far slower in developed countries, but more predictable. It also will vary *considerably* by business sector. No matter that the volume of domestic trade will greatly exceed export trade, *growth* will be greatest in the latter sector.

2. A group of *world* organizations will assume an increasing share of the responsibility for stimulating, measuring and supervising the evolution of world trade. Individually and collectively, they will constitute something of a *de facto* "world government." The WTO should emerge as the most important of these.

3. The influence of large multinational corporations on the process of globalization and on the public institutions that oversee it will increase dramatically. As private entities establish themselves, merge, co-venture and license across national borders, they threaten to outrun public institutions and their ability to monitor/ regulate. The involvement of private actors in this previously public enterprise will hasten the pace and scope of globalization. It also will produce a situation in which nations or national businesses do not compete with one another as much as they collaborate; replacing the old win/lose paradigm with a joint win/ win, lose/lose situation.

4. Capital, technical know-how and natural resources are the coinage of the global economy. These are not evenly distributed in the world. Their scarcity and maldistribution could lead to conflicts between peoples and nations that feel excluded. Bipartisan institutions must ensure that weaker nations aren't ignored and marginalized.

5. Speculation in financial markets, including currency speculation, is increasing at a rapid pace. Uncontrolled, this can have a destablizing or even bankrupting effect on weaker economies. Consequently, harmonized standards of bookkeeping and disclosure and possible intervention will be needed to regulate currency flows and harmful speculation.

6. The economic influence of large industrialized entities like the United States,

the European Union (EU) and Japan will shrink as emerging economies grow to maturity. The former will have to develop new mechanisms to maintain a sufficient degree of influence on world trade issues.

7. There may be some finite limit to trade expansion, either political, economic or ecological.

8. Staggering social and environmental problems are being revealed as more becomes known about many of the world's economies. In many areas, fighting has broken out due to ethnic or religious antipathy. Just as often, there is conflict over access to scarce or desirable resources. Outside assistance in these circumstances cannot be left to chance or caprice. A comprehensive and coordinated assistance mechanism—perhaps regional—is needed to address these situations.

9. Despite the emergence of numerous regional trading blocs, there seems to be a consensus among them that their local arrangements should not interfere with global trade initiatives.

10. Unchecked capitalism can be exploitative, whereas too much regulation can dispirit innovation, as past events in the former Soviet Union and current ones in China and Europe suggest today. Clearly, an expanding, globalized trading system needs rules that are a hybrid of the competing systems and regulate neither too much or too little.

11. The size and value of the global market has attracted adventurers and criminals. Their behavior distorts and destablilizes the global economy, but is often beyond the capacity of any single nation to address. A unified, cooperative response of equal force and ingenuity is needed.

In sectors where market forces are free to operate, it makes more sense for trading nations to collaborate (in order to advance the pace and benefits of world trade) rather than compete. This is not a practice that has prevailed for much of human history, however, so it will take some adjustment. Those that are better off will not easily give up their preferred position. They will be protective of their markets. Conversely, those less well off will become envious and impatient. They also may turn protectionist. In sum, collaboration in the world trade arena requires a good deal of effort and foresight. National economies do not grow uniformly. If the advantaged or disadvantaged foreswear cooperation, then longer-term relationships cannot be forged. Cooperation is always at risk unless there is the appearance of fairness and stability. If international trade is to have a future, then people and businesses and nations will have to accept that world trade isn't necessarily a "zero-sum" game (I win only if you lose). But will they?

Chapter 2

Regulating Global Trade

In the past, the world looked to the United States to regulate world trade, and it was in a position to do so. Today it has lost its hegemonic position[1]— as have all other nations and trading blocs—so there is no clear leader to suggest a world trading system or to enforce it. The best candidate, undoubtably, is the WTO. But it is too large, and its membership still too diversified, for it to agree on a single system under which to coordinate world trade. The larger trading blocs are more cohesive and homogenous (the European Union [EU] being the most so), but none commands a majority of world traders and neither do they agree on a single trading model.[2] Moreover, one would not want one or another of these regional trading blocs to seize the upper hand and force its vision of trade on the world marketplace. That would undercut the one true global group—the WTO[3]—and would not reach more than one-half of global trade. In the absence of consensus, multinational businesses are left on their own to set the pace and objectives of global trade, a kind of global "economic imperialism" that could marginalize other important government concerns, such as the environment, human and labor rights and culture.[4]

Surely we don't want a trade world with no traffic cop, wherein the generators of wealth and well-being (capital, know-how and resources) move from venue to venue as opportunity arises with no concern for the consequences. That is not to suggest that a world market dominated by private players will dissolve in chaos. There are plenty of delimiting factors. But a world trade system without sufficient checks and balances is more prone to harmful consequences than one that is properly regulated. That is, an ideal system is neither totally free and capitalistic nor too heavily regulated, but a balance of the two.

However, because the world financial market is so large, speculative and volatile, it may already be beyond the best efforts of the G-7 or Quad 4 (Canada, the EU, Japan and the U.S.) to regulate. After all, the massive intervention of central banks in 1987 to support currency stabilization (the G-7's Louvre Accord) was ultimately a failure. Would it be otherwise today? I think not. Clearly it is beyond the capacity of any single sovereign. In 1995, $1.3 trillion in foreign exchange transactions were registered *every day*—a 50 percent rise since 1992. That is about one-fifth the *annual* budget of the United States.[5]

The Mexican peso crisis of 1994 and the sluggishness of the Japanese, Asian and European economies today suggest that free markets can punish economies that don't offer sufficient security and return. Fortunately, world monetary leaders and the grit of the Mexican people pulled them through their crisis. But, given the exchange levels just cited, one wonders whether concerted action or massive intervention can modulate the judgments of private traders.[6] As a result, capital often moves away from markets that are stable but offer poor returns and flows to areas that are less secure but offer higher returns.[7] Even these compete with one another.[8]

So the public-arena strategy has to be for developed nations to collaborate as closely as possible (bearing in mind that there will be political pressures on each of them to outperform the other) and to bring along developing and emerging countries (the developed nations' primary export markets) as rapidly as feasible. Ultimately, this probably means allowing the latter to manage their markets a bit more than the developed economies would like and to liberalize them more slowly.[9] Because so many countries, with different currencies and economic cultures, now participate (and compete) in the global marketplace and because the influence of developed nations is shrinking, it behooves the latter to work together to keep the market under control. Private forces could easily distort it. Of course, the coordination will never be perfect. But the forward growth of the global economy seems to depend in equal measures on stable economic fundamentals, improved labor and human conditions and avoidance of environmental degradation.[10]

Thus, the security and stability of the global economy and the *de facto* "world government" of which I spoke will depend on the development of some sort of well-coordinated (and possibly enforceable) understanding among developed nations. G-7 nations will try to set the standards for world trade, through their own accords and by using their collective leverage in world bodies like the WTO.[11]

No matter how the process is managed, however, "Western" influence is bound to shrink. Economic growth in emerging economies often exceeds 6 percent a year, whereas highly industrialized countries average only 2 to 3 percent (admittedly, on a much larger base). Assuming such trends continue (as seems likely), East Asia soon will have decreased its per capita GDP gap, compared to Western Europe, by one-half since 1970. In the early part of the new century, per capita purchasing power in South Korea and Singapore may approximate that of the U.S. Accordingly, the share of world GDP consumed by developing Asian countries (including China and India) could rise as high as 28 percent by 2010 (from 18 percent in 1990). Conversely, Western Europe's share of world GDP would fall from 22 percent in 1990 to 17 percent in 2010, and that of the U.S. from 23 percent to 18 percent.

Of course, it is no great "crisis" if the U.S., with about 5 percent of the world's population, shrinks its consumption to 18 percent of the world's production. The U.S. will still have a decidedly disproportionate impact on world trade. But this will require that it remain at the forefront of liberalization and competitiveness. After stumbling badly in the late 1980s, the U.S. seems to have recovered the high ground. Asia, as we have seen, has the potential, but has failed to adjust to the new paradigms.[12]

Europe is another matter. It should be America's closest ally in the process of global trade liberalization. At present, however, its sluggish economy does not make Western Europe a very attractive site for business and investment. Add to this its substantial bureaucratic red tape and high social costs (social security transfers in the EU in 1994 accounted for 21.5 percent of GDP), and it does not look as if Europe will participate fully in global expansion in the near term. High public spending—particularly on welfare—has strained budget deficits. Labor markets are too inflexible, and privatization is proceeding too slowly.[13]

If the U.S. has lost or will lose the hegemonic trade position it enjoyed in the 1950s,[14] and if the EU is an uncertain—and possibly ineffective—partner in world trade negotiations, it simply means that the U.S. government and domestic businesses will have to work harder and more creatively to forge the type of trade alliances we need in the twenty-first century. The fact that the United States is no longer preeminent in world trade does not mean it cannot be the opinion leader and consensus builder. To play this role, however, we will need allies. As our position of dominance ebbs, so will our ability to enforce unilateral positions. Hence, the prospect of the U.S. (or any other industrialized nation) "holding onto" its current share of world trade by erecting barriers to freer trade is ultimately doomed to failure. A much more coordinated and collaborative approach is needed. By being proactive about new trading relationships, however, the U.S. can maintain momentum and a degree of control.

This was the mistake of the early Clinton years. The president first elevated domestic issues over global trade issues and then pursued the latter chiefly on a unilateral basis. In both cases he was out of step with the evolving realities. First, America's domestic well-being increasingly depends on global trade (which falls uniquely to the executive under our Constitution). Second, bilateral and multilateral initiatives are much more likely to succeed in today's trade world than unilateral initiatives. The change in strategy on the part of the Clinton administration has been called a "GATT plus" agenda.[15] It employs the leverage of unilateral, bilateral and multilateral initiatives in the world trade sector,[16] while acclimating workers to the new trading environment.

To be credible in this new environment, the president needs "fast track" authority from Congress.[17] This is the type of authority the president had in the NAFTA and GATT treaties, both reasonably successful. Without this authority, our trading partners would have legitimate concern that a treaty negotiated by the executive (possibly containing many sophisticated, subtle and multilayered compromises) would be pulled apart on the public stage in Congress because one interest group or another objected. Generally, this is not a problem for our trading partners, because the head of state or government holds that position by virtue of his party's ability to control the majority of the votes in parliament. In the U.S., where the executive and legislative branches have distinct and coordinate treaty-making roles, there is no such guarantee. Fast-track authority can make this process more efficient and certain, as the GATT and NAFTA agreements proved. But the U.S. also has pursued bilateral deals (like the U.S.–Japan auto accord) that other trading nations would like to have joined and unilateral actions (such as Section 301 investigations, extraterritorial enforcement of the Sherman antitrust act and the Helms-Burton law regarding Cuba.)[18]

The last reason for our national schizophrenia about trade policy is that we as a nation have not cultivated much of a "worldview." In this last half-century, we have grown used to dominating. Just as often, our attention (and that of our politicians) is absorbed by *domestic* issues like jobs, wages, crime and schools. The impression given is that, if only we could solve these problems, the rest of the world would not matter. But this clearly is not the case. Our economy depends increasingly on the growth of exports. People must be *trained* for that world of the future. They must be *conditioned* to the problems it will cause.

For the strongest trading nation in the world to send mixed messages to its most important trading partners is very harmful to the development of world trade. We are seen to engage in narrow, bilateral skirmishes with trading partners, when an available multinational alternative like the WTO exists. As a consequence, we are perceived as a bully as much as a free trader. Perhaps the reason for this selfish provincialism is that the American people don't understand what is happening in the world trading system. Perhaps we don't feel we *need* allies, or that *our* vision of free trade is the best. In all this we are wrong.

Aggressive, unilateral behavior on the part of the U.S. naturally results in reciprocal actions by our trading partners. Among them are so-called clawback provisions in European law, criminalizing the release of information under their control that might assist the U.S. in an extraterritorial investigation.[19] The tension evident in these trade situations underscores the potential conflicts between national laws and a globalized trading system. No one would argue with the right of each sovereign to determine, within its borders, what acts are proper or improper. However, acts done elsewhere can have local impacts, and acts done locally can have effects elsewhere.

What sovereign's court should have jurisdiction of these cases, and what rule of law should apply? Global trade deals seldom are limited by national boundaries and may therefore be subject to the law and jurisdiction of several sovereigns. If the sector is covered by some international agreement and dispute-resolving system (like the WTO), then resolution ought to be achievable. However, many trade sectors and disputes are not covered by international arrangements, and the WTO system has been criticized as too political and slow. If each sovereign assumes that it can assert its national interests in these circumstances, then a great deal of conflict will result.

In times past, it may have been possible to erect barriers to immigration, to exclude unwanted goods or tax them heavily and to manage one's economy purely to suit national interests. That time is gone. Today, national borders are porous to persons and goods. Increments in economic well-being depend on foreign trade and external investment. Foreign business generally is welcomed because it creates jobs. But this is not a one-way street. If we seek (far less demand) access to foreign markets, it seems elemental that foreign producers are going to want access to ours. If that results in a loss of market share for U.S. businesses, or a loss of U.S. jobs (even though consumers may be benefitted through lower prices), elected officials are put under pressure to "do something." If they choose "protectionism," this simply spawns retorsion. This type of behavior led to the worldwide depression of the 1930s.

Until recently, Europe's experience with the globalization of trade has been different. They have been at it far longer than we have, and it is one of the principal reasons for Europe's speedy recovery from the devastation of World War II. But, whereas the U.S. has expanded its trade relations in three major regions—Europe, the Americas, and the Pacific Rim—the establishment of a "single" market in Europe has led to further business concentration there. From 1985 to 1995, intra-European trade increased from just over 61 percent to nearly 68 percent. Moreover, there was a discernable concentration of products in the market.[20] This would suggest that the EU's single market really is beginning to realize some of the gains claimed for it. It could easily stand to expand its market vision. Too much concentration on the European market could cost it dearly and deny the U.S. the ally it badly wants (or needs) to open other foreign markets.[21]

The European Union has been more careful about the alliances it has formed, however, and more reliable about executing them.[22] The Americans, by comparison, look like economic and political "cowboys." This seems to me to create an opportunity for China, India and other underdeveloped, emerging nations to play one off against the other. Whether due to haste, decision-making mechanisms or different interests, the U.S. and EU could end up as adversaries in the world scene. This could have considerable adverse affect not just on their trading relationship, but also on the pace of integration. It could push both capitalist trading groups into compromising alliances that could slow the progress of globalization and possibly devolve into regionalization.

Of course, one may well wonder why the "have" nations should be at "war" with one another over access to markets and the conditions thereof, when it is the "have-not" nations that pose the greatest threat to the peace and prosperity of developed nations. Given the more enlightened—and more globalized—nature of world trade integration at this time, it seems inherently wrong to talk about the process as if it was a economic "war" between nation states.[23] Businesses are so positioned globally that it is less and less a case of *one* nation's government or business versus another. It is hard to believe (in world-trade terms) that the U.S. would really want to "defeat" Japan and/or Europe in a trade "war." Wouldn't it be more sensible (as well as economic) to collaborate with them on the development of world trade?

When there is no general plan of support and financial assistance (foreign aid), there is a risk of duplication and omission. The large trading nations already are finding ways to allocate responsibility in order to avoid these consequences. The U.S. had the largest role in the Mexican rescue plan of 1994, while the EU took primary responsibility for resolving the conflict in Bosnia and has given the most aid to help newly independent states in Central and Eastern Europe. Japan invests most of its foreign aid in Asia. Thus, in a *de facto* manner, the great trading nations are collaborating in a scheme to develop emerging nations in a more-or-less coordinated way. There will be some crossover, of course, as perceptions of advantage and disadvantage emerge. But in the final analysis, this is the most equitable and efficient way to develop the world's economy.

We should remember that domestic well-being is inextricably linked to world trade.[24] Foreign nations' ability to sell us their goods and services stimulates growth in their economies, while our need to compete with them stimulates innovation and the quest for efficiency at home. To be certain, nearly 90 percent of U.S. goods and services are consumed at home. But, although that market is large, it is semisaturated. Growth was less than 2 percent in 1996. Whereas U.S. exports represent a much smaller percentage of our GDP, the export market has grown from 8 percent of U.S. GDP in 1980, to 11 percent in 1996.

This global competition for markets and market share can have the synergistic effect of reducing prices (good for consumers), while encouraging more efficiency and productivity (bad for workers) and resulting in lower profit margins (less tax income for social programs). At the present time, we are experiencing the "squeeze" put on the global marketplace by this drive for competitiveness (efficiency and productivity). In the U.S., it has resulted in corporate "downsizing" or "rightsizing." The same pressures are felt in Germany, Japan and elsewhere. Indeed, the need to reconcile the competing economic, political and legal influences on various types of trading systems has put pressure on them to coordinate. An astute economist argued some years back that neither a pure democracy nor a pure autocracy was a fit way to run an economy. The first was quite equal, but too inefficient. The latter was most efficient, but inherently unequal.[25] Obviously, the solution lies somewhere between these extremes. If governments intervene in the market it should be to ensure its fairness, not to distort it. This reflects a "economic Darwinism" in which the market can't be permanently destabilized.

That said, how is this likely to come about? My first observation is that it will take time. Too rapid a pace will be destabilizing in itself. If the U.S.— the most capitalistic of market models—has suffered so much pain in adjusting to the global marketplace, how much harder will it be for more-managed economies? Traditionally, they support government ownership and subsidies for "national heroes," even if they are inefficient. This is too costly in a world economy, but it will take time to privatize and make these enterprises self-sufficient. Meanwhile, the services they provide must continue. Over-managed economies can be a powerful drain on capital, slowing job creation and suppressing innovation. But they are not easy to reform.

Conversely, pure free-market systems reward efficiency but don't generally provide for society's neediest members. And only the hardiest capitalists are willing to do that. Presently we are struggling through a period in which there is pressure on all systems to converge into one that produces a more equitable balance. Capitalist systems will become more socialized. More-socialized systems will become more privatized and capitalistic (as the EU is becoming of late). State-managed systems, such as Japan, Russia and China, will open themselves increasingly to foreign capital, competition and collaboration. If they do not, they will face revolt from their own people. After all, there can be no *world* trade system without some unity of approach and policy. This means greater agreement on a market system, if not a *common* one. And capitalism, broadly defined, has clearly won the contest for the most productive system.[26]

That does not mean, however, that American capitalism will become the standard, any more than that English will become the uniform language or McDonald's hamburgers the uniform food. As "first among equals," America is likely to have more than its fair share of influence. But the whole point of introducing the various approaches to economic management is to suggest that ours is not the sole—and possibly not the best—system. A harmonizing approach to resolving global trade problems; one that "blends" the American approach with others, is likely to prevail.

It is clear that Americans consume too much (especially foreign goods) and save too little. The Japanese, it appears, save too much and consume too little (especially foreign goods). Europeans have recognized that they must shrink their social and agriculture programs, liberalize their labor market and become more competitive. Their social programs and business subsidies have created dangerous dependencies. The newly independent states—especially Russia—realize that freedom and capital don't necessarily create a capitalistic, free-market economy.

The issue then is what is the *proper* role of government and international institutions in this globalized world marketplace?[27] Clearly it would be best if the U.S. (or NAFTA nations) and the EU could collaborate on a master plan. After all, they are the most experienced capitalistic nations and represent over one-half of world GDP. Together they could incorporate developing nations into the world trading system.

These initiatives are better taken in *world* organizations like the WTO, however. Its agenda expands steadily, to include core labor standards, environmental protection, anti-dumping legislation, rules of origin, investment and competition law, to name just a sample.[28] Its first director, Renato Ruggiero of Italy, did a brilliant job in launching global trade cooperation. Other world groups—like the G-7—also have become more proactive as world convergence puts more and more emphasis on cooperation and coordination. Problems of international finance, communications, transport and crime require it.[29] The threads of world trade are numerous, interdependent and fluid. Hence allies and alliances are absolutely necessary, even if they are fluid and can be difficult. Ultimately there are no lasting solutions. There must be a willingness to negotiate about everything and compromise on anything. These are not inherent American traits. But, we are learning.

Part II

New Trade Paradigms

Chapter 3

An Economic Map of the World

The title of this chapter is admittedly pretentious.[1] There is not room here to give a thorough picture of the world's economic geography, nor would the average reader be interested. Furthermore, it would change as I wrote. However, it *is* necessary to describe briefly the landscape over which our trading drama is played out. I have been selective about the information shared, since it is merely to suggest the order of magnitude of the trends involved.

AMERICA'S TRADE PARTNERS AND BALANCE OF TRADE

Today's trading world is "open for business"; there is no doubt about that. From 1985 to 1994, U.S. exports and imports of goods and services more than doubled, from $382 billion to $833 billion (118%) in the case of goods and $484 billion to $954 billion in the case of services (97%). In that same period, the U.S. population increased only 7 percent.

However, U.S. investment abroad grew from $39 billion to $126 billion, while foreign direct investment in the U.S. grew from $141 billion to $315 billion. Most telling of all is the fact that U.S. gross domestic product grew at a rather slow 5.6 percent average year on year, while exports and imports grew at an average rate of 12.6 percent (over twice as fast) and exports alone averaged a 14.3 percent growth.[2] It is not difficult to see where the growth in America's economy lies today. While our domestic economy may be sluggish, foreign trade has been booming.

From 1990 to 1994 alone, U.S. exports to all countries grew from $394 billion to $513, billion, or 30 percent. In the same period, imports grew from $495 billion to $664 billion (34%), a negative balance of about $151 billion. This negative balance shrunk some during the 1991–1992 recession, but now has returned to record levels.

Whereas Canada is our largest single national trading partner; importing $113 billion in U.S. goods while exporting some $129 billion to us, the fifteen-state European Union (EU) is our largest regional trading partner (unless you include the North American Free Trade group). In 1994, the U.S. exported about $116 billion in goods to the EU, while importing some $121 billion. In the case of Canada and the EU, we enjoy a relatively balanced rate of trade.

Mexico, our other NAFTA partner, would have been our third largest export partner in 1994, except that it was narrowly edged out by Japan. In that year, we exported $51 billion to Mexico and $53 billion to Japan. There the similarity ends, however, for we *imported* only $49 billion in goods from Mexico (a positive balance), but imported $119 billion from Japan (for a negative trade balance of some $66 billion). Our trade with China is equally unbalanced, and has grown rapidly to a level approximating that with Japan; including the size of the negative balance.[3]

There should be no doubt then about the "natural" trading partners of the U.S. They are the other two large economies in North America (Canada and Mexico) and particularly the EU. The latter relationship has existed since colonial times and is based on links of history, culture, language and a tradition of cooperation, capitalism and democracy. The rest of Latin and South America might eventually be drawn into a Free Trade Area of the Americas (FTAA), but at present they collectively account for only about 18 percent to hemispheric GDP. Trade with other Latin and South American and Asian countries is bound to increase, however.

One reason for this is that these nations—and especially the Asians—have tended to play the trade game by a different set of rules; seeking access to Western markets, while limiting access to their own. It will take some time for them to reform. This may be just as well, given the chaotic experience of Russia with capitalism. In the meantime, whatever the size and potential of the rest of the Americas, the Pacific Rim has to be a major concern. All these nations are in need of Western capital and technology, but one wonders how it will be used. Their reliability as trading partners is still suspect and is reflected in their persistant trade imbalances with the U.S. One has to be cautious about these regions, compared with Europe, including Central and Eastern Europe and the Mediterranean basin.

I do not wish to leave the American side of this trade equation, however, before commenting on the growth of services in international trade. The service sector is the largest in the U.S. economy, but it is not easy to measure, particularly when those services are rendered abroad. Nevertheless, statistics reveal that U.S. exports in the services sector grew by 78 percent from 1988 to 1994 (from $109 to $195 billion). Trade in goods *and* services grew only 50 percent in the same period.[4] What is more, the balance of foreign trade in *services* favors the U.S., whereas our balance of trade in goods has long been in deficit.

Finally, it warrants saying that Europe has invested more heavily in the U.S. than all other nations combined. In 1993, EU investment in the U.S. amounted to about 61 percent of a total foreign investment of $445 billion. Japan was well behind at $96 billion (22%), and Canada still further at $38 billion (9%). In all, foreign operators with a 10 percent or greater stake in U.S. businesses, represent $1.8 trillion in assets, and employ nearly 5 million Americans.[5] In 1995, U.S. assets abroad ($280 billion) more than doubled the 1994 level (at $126 billion), and foreign assets in the United States reached an all-time high ($426.3 billion), 46 percent higher than in 1994.[6]

All this seems relatively rosy until one remembers that U.S. influence over world affairs is shrinking. As EU nations struggle with their public deficits in order to support a single currency, the U.S. trade deficit with the rest of the world continues to grow. Every time that we achieve some modest improvement, sluggish foreign markets, an excess of consumption and/or deficit spending widens the gap again.[7]

The North American Free Trade Agreement (NAFTA) simply made concrete what already was the *de facto* condition in cross-border trade. The U.S., Canada and Mexico have been long tied together by two-way export/import trade. NAFTA simply put the relationship on a firmer footing by inserting some labor and environmental understandings and a dispute-resolution mechanism.[8] Now that Mexico has weathered the "peso crisis" and repaid its emergency loan from the United States, its market should return to its pre-crisis health and expand steadily.[9] Hence, North America probably is the most stable and robust of the world's trading areas.

MAPPING TODAY'S TRADE WORLD

Global market presence is influenced by a variety of factors—social, economic and political. Specifically, trade is measured by current account balances, including comparative export/import statistics, foreign exchange rates and foreign direct investment. Let us not ignore other factors, however, such as long-term religious battles or government instability, when assessing a country or region's health in international trade terms.

In recent years, developed economies have enjoyed a prolonged period of growth. After expanding by around 4 percent in 1993, world trade grew by 10 percent in 1994 alone, or at nearly four times the rate of world gross domestic product (GDP).[10] By reaching beyond a narrow band of trading partners, post–World War II economies are approximating a "global" trade. A prime example is the leading regional trade bloc, the EU. These fifteen diverse European nations form the world's largest market today. Even outside the EU, however, in South America, Southeast Asia, and Central and

Eastern Europe, economic leaders are preaching the benefits of free trade. The world no longer looks to a single economic leader (the U.S.) as the sparkplug it needs to ignite economic engines. Indeed, America's fraction of world GDP has declined.[11] While there are many factors contributing to this, the largest factor has been the rapid growth of the global marketplace.[12]

Thanks to the postwar recovery of Europe and Japan, the world economic stage came to be occupied by "three superpowers": the United States, Japan and the EU. But, continued trade globalization has gradually eroded this once valid framework. Germany no longer maintains a trade surplus or a positive current account balance, and the influence of other EU members has increased immeasurably. Central and Eastern European states could save the EU or sink it. We don't hear about trade with the rest of Latin America as much as we do with our NAFTA partner, Mexico. But General Motors does not look to export simply to Argentina, but to the entire Mercosur (Brazil, Paraguay, Uruguay *and* Argentina). The 1990–1994 period saw 30 new regional integration agreements notified to GATT, compared to about a third of that number during the previous decade.[13] The notion that three superpowers still dominate the globalized trade world may be questioned.

First, consider the *United States*. Without question, the American taxpayer was fairly content in 1997, as President Clinton's reelection would testify. Gross domestic product increased by not less than 2 percent during his first three years in office. Inflation was at 2.1 percent, its lowest level in 30 years. Interest rates were low, and corporate profits, adjusted for inflation, soared in the 1990s.[14] Unemployment was at its lowest in some time,[15] and the stock market gained over 65 percent since the beginning of 1995.[16] The United States may *appear* to be the dominant world power, but is it really? How much of its growth can be attributed to the globalization process? Exports and imports now amount to 26 percent of our GDP.[17] Moreover, their *rate* of growth has been 14 percent since 1994, three times the rate of the economy.[18] How long will this prolonged strength last? Economists remind us that actual trade, that is, export and import figures, can be misleading. This is true because movements in a country's trade balance reflect differences in income growth rates between the country and its trading partners, and their exchange rates.[19]

Accordingly, a better figure to use is the current account balance. Trade in services, together with unilateral transfer payments, are *combined* with merchandise trade to compose this "comprehensive gauge" of a country's international competitive position.[20] For example, look at the American experience in the 1980s. In 1981, the United States had a current account surplus of $5 billion.[21] Then, in 1982 it fell into deficit, falling all the way to a negative balance of $166.3 billion in 1987. It shrank to only $7.4 billion in 1991 but expanded to new heights in the late 1990s.[22] What happened? An overvalued dollar in the first half of the decade resulted in a fall in global export volume and a rise in import volume. Accompanied by lower output in the traded-goods sector, it resulted in political pressure for protectionist measures. At the end of the 1980s, the dollar depreciated, reversing trade flows. There was less pressure for protectionism and a new level of U.S. participation in global markets.[23]

How does this affect the American taxpayer? Although a falling dollar may not affect living standards a great deal (a 5% fall in the value of the dollar raises consumer prices only 0.2%), a weaker dollar makes it more expensive for Americans to import foreign goods or travel abroad.[24] Fewer foreigners want to hold dollar assets, foreign investments become more expensive and foreign investment in the U.S. surges. A strong dollar reverses these trends. Remember, however, the United States has been here before. A weak dollar has done little to heal America's trade deficit. Several economists worry that the market boom of the late 1990s might open the door to inflation.[25] So far, Federal Reserve Chief Alan Greenspan, has been able to sustain growth *and* hold inflation in check. But, America's global leadership is increasingly collective. Monetary policy may be principally—but not solely—ours.

The second trader to examine is *Japan* and its influence on world trade. Japan is, after all, the second largest trading nation in the world. While a series of adjustments have been made, Japan still finds itself suffering from a national banking crisis that began in 1991 and has gotten steadily worse. Gross domestic product figures are dismal for 1992–1995. In those years, Japan's GDP growth was below 1 percent. The predictions from 1996 through 1998 were more optimistic, but they have proved wrong. By the late 1990s Japan was in recession. Japanese leadership has adopted numerous "recovery" plans since 1991 to try to alleviate some of these deflationary pressures, but with little or no success.[26] The negative impact on trade growth in 1994, however, was essentially caused by the strength of the yen. In nominal terms, it appreciated by 7 percent against the ecu and by 9 percent against the dollar.[27]

However, Japan has remained a world leader throughout these difficulties. First, in merchandise trade, it is no secret that Japan has maintained a large surplus with its trading partners since the early 1980s.[28] While starting near equilibrium in 1980, Japan reached a surplus of $90 billion in 1986, which skyrocketed to about $140 billion in 1992[29] and continued to grow.[30] In terms of world share of exports and imports, however, Japan's share is expected to shrink, as developing nations begin to compete. For example, Japan held at or near 10 percent of the world's exports from 1986 to 1988, but will have only about 8 percent from 1996 to 1998.[31] Japan's account surplus will eventually drop as well.[32] But this depends a great deal on reviving domestic demand and opening its markets to foreign goods. Japan's current economic troubles are not conductive to either. Regardless, Japan had the largest current account surplus on a world scale in 1997, with the EU close behind.[33]

Thus, while a much-touted model of efficiency in the 1980s and early 1990s, Japan's magical trading plan seems to have run out of gas. What must Japan do to remain one of the world's economic leaders? The answer is trade liberalization and adjusting to economic interdependence. The same seems to be true of the rest of the Asian Pacific, including China. Having aligned themselves with Japan and the Japanese model, they have suffered a similar fate in the late 1990s.

For most of the postwar period, the Japanese government discouraged inward foreign direct investment (FDI). As a result, FDI in Japan was much lower than in other industrialized countries. For example, less U.S. money was invested in Japan than in the Philippines or in any of the eight largest Latin American economies.[34] In 1955, however, Japan joined the GATT. In keeping with its trade requirements, Japan began liberalizing its investment regime. But in 1986, foreign firms still only had a 1 percent share of Japan's domestic sales, while they had 10 percent of domestic sales in the United States, 18 percent in Germany, and 20 percent in Great Britain.[35] This does not mean that the Japanese market is entirely closed to foreign corporations and their goods, however. American firms like Schick, Coca-Cola and Johnson & Johnson dominate their respective markets in Japan.[36]

While the exact purpose of cross-border investment is not always straightforward, for the most part it is usually based on cost advantage. That may be due to tariffs, cheap labor, lower taxes or perhaps simply to increase market share abroad. Put another way, foreign direct investment suggests that multinational companies consider cross-border transactions from the point of view of economics, not national allegiance. The share of multinational companies in total trade is quite high in both the United States and Japan. After having invested primarily in OECD countries until the late 1980s, Japanese companies have since directed a large part of the FDI to emerging economies of Asia.[37]

Overseas production by Japanese affiliates now represents 10 percent of their total production, compared with 4 percent in 1986.[38] "Reverse imports" from Japanese affiliates abroad also surged and now account for 14 percent of total imports compared with 4 percent in 1992.[39] Most of this new FDI was in Asia, which accounts for 16 percent of Japan's total outstanding FDI.[40] Furthermore, sales by Japanese firms in Asia accounted for 32 percent of Japan's total sales in 1992; about the same share that went to the United States.[41]

The second major trading bloc of which I spoke is the *European Union*, formerly the European Community (EC) or European Economic Community (EEC). Each of these titles was used at different stages of its development, and the EU continues to evolve. Many questions have been raised about whether it won't eventually *dissolve*, but that seems increasingly unlikely. Either way, with some 370 million people and a combined GDP of nearly $8 trillion (about equal to ours), the EU is a force to be reckoned with. Equally important is the fact that the EU is the other major, democratic, essentially capitalist trading bloc in the world.[42]

At its core, the fifteen-nation European Union is a customs union, with a great deal of internal legislation and an external tariff. But, with the Maastricht Treaty (officially, the Treaty on European Union), two new "pillars" were added and the project allegedly became a "union." As the EU adjusted to the global marketplace, its economy seemed locked in the starting gate. While the United States consistently maintained an unemployment rate in the low single digits, Europe's rate was 10 percent or higher.[43] A wave of privatization and the removal of government subsidies unnerved European workers, who had grown accustomed to job security and social security benefits that, in the view of employers, hindered business growth. In turn, European private enterprise has been starved for capital by high interest rates, high taxes and government borrowing.

An additional burden on the EU's recovery is the lingering effect of German unification. The move from communism to capitalism has proved to be no easy task for East Germany. One year after reunification, its industrial production was 40 percent below its pre-unification levels.[44] Two years later, it was 80 percent below those levels.[45] In the move away from communism, one-half of the East German labor force is likely to end up either unemployed or working part time.[46] Moreover, government subsidies to large domestic businesses across the EU certainly have not halted. Evidenced by the Credit Lyonnais debacle, the EU's program for curbing state aids often has been weak and politically motivated.[47]

That is, while in search of a competitive open market, the EU has not been completely adverse to allowing member states to protect their national "heroes." United Parcel Service of America Inc. (UPS) alleges that there is not an open market for package-delivery services in Germany and throughout Europe.[48] Another example is Sweden. Once the model socialist state in Western Europe, the Swedish government is desperately scaling back government expenditures that reached two-thirds of Sweden's total economic output in 1995.[49] This is serious government downsizing. But there is a reason. German businesses say they cannot compete in a global market with the labor and social costs they have to pay. Simply stated, EU governments are cutting spending to become more competitive and meet the criterion for a planned currency union in 1999.[50]

However, one can hardly label this transformation destructive. "The movement to privatize pension systems in Germany, Italy, and elsewhere will create a vast pool of capital in search of returns that beat the money markets. Also, as state-owned companies go private and as the banking and corporate sectors dismantle inefficient cross-holdings, many more people will have a chance to buy stocks." Europe remains one of the largest, safest and most profitable markets for investment.[51] As much as Europe is an economic competitor of the United States, it also is one of our best markets and one with which we enjoy a relatively balanced trade. Despite our infatuation with Asian markets, and Japan in particular, they have not returned the same benefits. What is even more important about Europe is that it is expanding in a very predictable way into a super trading bloc. If the EU can bring a significant part of Central and Eastern Europe together with Western Europe into one Common Market, "it can build something that no one else can," the world's largest, most self-sufficient market of 850 to 900 million people.[52] Europe's chief liability is its modest growth rate.[53]

Hence, there are two ways to assess the present state of the European economy, a narrow view and a broad view, or perhaps an inward as opposed to an outward view. I think the narrow view of Europe's economic future is shortsighted. Presently, there is too much government control, and this distorts the market and slows economic growth. These forces appear to be easing. The European Union's quest for monetary union required that government privatize more services and reduce deficits. This made financial markets more influential and grew the economy. Thus, a stop-action photograph of leading macroeconomic indicators today may find Europe lagging. But a closer look at recent progress toward market liberalization may suggest a different outcome. It is just possible that the EU could dominate foreign trade markets in the twenty-first century.

Europe's current "bunker mentality" could protect its market for a while, but not forever. Europe must learn to compete in markets where fluid capital movements and flexibility are paramount to success. It has already been noticed that Europe has run a distant third to the U.S. and Japan in these high-value markets. European companies are delaying investment at home and expansion abroad. On the other hand, product differenteration in the single market has shrunk, and the cost of goods was dropped. In this sense, at least, the single market is working.[54]

Therefore, the question naturally arises: can Europe compete with the U.S. in established markets and emerging markets worldwide? In its present circumstances, obviously not. Business virtually competes with government. Moreover, the EU states have put themselves in something of a straitjacket by choosing this time to establish a single currency. However, the result may prove to be worth the effort. It is likely to become a global reserve currency like the U.S. dollar and Japanese yen. Only one European currency, the German mark, approached this status.

The EU has other problems as well. A plan to invite other Central and Eastern European states into the union around the turn of the century won't be easy. This may be worth the effort because it would enlarge the European market with capitalist-leaning, well-educated, energetic workers with large consumption potential. The EU's expansionist tendencies don't stop here, however. To balance its proposed expansion into Central and Eastern Europe and to appease its southern members, the EU also has plans to extend its influence into the Mediterranean basin.

The last global trade initiatives of the EU are its attempts expand trade relations with Latin American and Asian nations. In times past, certain European nations had very close trading relationships in both regions. After the colonial period, these trade relationships atrophied. Now that Britain has withdrawn from Hong Kong (June 1997), the EU has only modest trading relationships with emerging economies. This doesn't bode well if the EU means to be a global trading force. To close the gap, the EU has recently undertaken initiatives to ensure that it will not be excluded from new markets. In late 1998, the EU began negotiations with the so-called Mercosur trading bloc in South America.[55] A more ambitious and wide-ranging relationship was proposed at a first-ever "summit" meeting between European and Asian leaders in Bangkok in early 1996. By being too divided at home and too slow abroad, the EU may have weakened its position in both sectors, although it is undoubted that the EU continues to grow in meaningful ways every day.[56] But corporate investment, which had been fleeing Western Europe in search of higher returns in emerging markets, may return now that those opportunities have proved risky.

By competing with the United States and its NAFTA partners for opportunities in Asia and Latin America, instead of collaborating with them to open these markets, the EU has created an opportunity for Asian and Latin American nations to pit Europe and America against one another in trade talks and get the best trading terms from each while giving the fewest concessions to either. Thus, through competition as opposed to collaboration, the two most democratic, capitalist trading blocs in the world might have unwittingly slowed the pace and altered the terms of market opening in important developing markets. That is too bad, for the EU and U.S. are natural allies for market opening. Their cooperation creates a better chance that the evolved system of global trade will be capitalistic.

The last major sectors of the world economic map to consider are India, the Mediterranean basin and Africa. Each has very different prospects in our globalization scheme, but since their impact is likely to be difficult to gauge and muted in comparison with the other regions discussed, I have treated them as a group here.

India is a very large, poor nation. Its population is around 985 million and expected to exceed that of China by the year 2050. However, its GDP is only $326 billion annually (about one twenty-fourth that of the United States), or about $348 per capita (1.2% that of the United States).

More to the point, India has a relatively closed, state-managed economy, with large subsidy programs for energy and farming, and a tiny tax base. It has a great need for foreign direct investment. Fortunately for India, it has attracted that of late. About five years ago, a severe financial crisis in India forced the government to "deregulate industry, liberalize financial markets, cut and rationalize taxes and tariffs, and open up sectors such as power and telecoms to foreign investments." Foreign money rushed in: $1.5 billion in

1994–95, $2.1 billion in 1995–96, and an estimated $2.3 in 1996–97. However, the growth rate is flattening, and it remains well below the $10 billion that the Indian government says is needed annually. (China received $38 billion in FDI in 1996.)

Part of the reason for the slowdown is that the Indian governments' coalition partners oppose any large-scale privatization. What openings there have been (in insurance and telecommunications) have been too slow or too small to sustain Western investors' interests. Some early investors (Siemens) have grown disillusioned with the pace of growth and the small size of the Indian consumer market and are downsizing or selling out. Although annual output growth is a solid 7 percent, so is inflation. And a limited and deteriorating Indian infrastructure threatens even this level of growth.[57] Hence, the prospects for a rapid and robust emergence of the Indian economy seems doubtful, but bears watching.

The missing factor seems to be the political will to abandon protectionist measures and subsidies. If it does develop rapidly, then the Indian economy will become a larger factor in the world economic picture. It might join the APEC or ASEAN trading groups, which might increase its liberalization. Or it might try to set up a regional trading block of its own, gathering some neighboring states around it. The former would be more potent than the latter, but either would improve India's position on the economic map. At present, it would appear to have more potential than clout.

The same might be said of the states of the eastern and southern Mediterranean basin. These eleven countries have a population exceeding one-half the EU (207 million). Yet only three of them (Cyprus, Israel and Malta) with a mere 6.3 million inhabitants boast per capita GDP exceeding $2,340 annually. This about one-third of what the average Greek earns. Obviously, this is a very poor region. But southern members of the European Union have insisted that it be included in its developmental plan, and so some 4.4 billion Ecu ($5.15 billion) have been earmarked for aid to the region from 1995 to 1999. This amount is roughly equal to the EU's assistance to Eastern and Central Europe (former Soviet states). But, whereas several of the latter may soon achieve membership in the EU, that seems a remote prospect for Mediterranean-basin countries, excepting Cyprus and Malta. They are not a major factor in our trade map at present.[58]

The rest of Africa, save Egypt and the Union of South Africa, is an equally impoverished region. The later undoubtedly will be the first African nation to participate significantly in the global economy. The globetrotting of President Mandela and the 1998 visit of President Clinton virtually assure that FDI will be attracted to South Africa. But the rest of the continent may be slow to follow. Most of the continent is not a factor in globalization. Dependent upon the largesse of developed nations and sporadic aid to deal with its manifold skirmishes and famines, it may be the last area of the world to be developed.[59]

I previously mentioned the potential of Latin and South America (below Mexico) as a trade zone. These countries appear to have the capacity and the will to enter the global economy. For these reasons, their fate seems brighter than that of Africa, but it is principally tied to the NAFTA states, although the EU has courted them as well.

Chapter 4

Four Economic "Models"

In describing this economic map to you, I have identified essentially four different national or regional economic models that are likely to compete for adoption as the "global" model. The first is a generally "capitalistic," free-market system, typified by the United States (and perhaps Canada). The American economy does have its share of social programs and protects certain products (e.g., sugar), but it is essentially liberal, capitalistic and free.

The second system, best typified by the current European Union, also is capitalistic, but with a much larger dose of socialism. I call it macro-managed. The people are taxed heavily and governments provide extensive benefits for heath, education, unemployment, and the like. EU governments also operate a range of businesses (air, ship and rail travel, telephone, energy) that generally are privatized in the United States. There also seems to be an antipathy towards very large business enterprises that might threaten government control or laborers' rights. The EU's common market works reasonably well as an internal customs union, but a high price is paid for its large bureaucracies, numerous regulations and large social programs. Businesses may not be able to grow to truly efficient sizes or be stifled by inflexible labor agreements. Weaker companies, particularly if they are "national heroes," may be propped up by government subsidies. In other words, the market is not competitive enough to maximize efficiency and must pay a high social tax. Yes, there is a "Fortress Europe."

Japan, once called the only communist society that works, is typical of the third model. Other examples might be Indonesia or Singapore. In this system, government and business collaborate to produce maximum economic outcomes. This may be at the expense of the consumer, however. (In a capitalist system, government more frequently regulates business to protect individuals.) Hence, the efficiency of the Japanese-type system is bought at the price of government collaboration with business "keiretsu" (business combines), to the best advantage of both. Naturally, such a system depends on being somewhat closed to imports. Obviously, the system presents numerous opportunities for corruption and may implode if external competition is allowed. This is what Japan has faced in recent years. I call this system micro-managed capitalism.

The last system is commonly called communism. Now that its primary model—the former Soviet Union—has collapsed, the only remaining examples are mainland China and Cuba. Neither has made a great success of its economy, and China now seems disposed to open itself to capitalism at a manageable pace. The principal feature of communism is that the central government owns or regulates most business and industry. It collects and distributes production, ostensibly according to need. It is the ultimate social system, *if* it works fairly and there is enough product to go around. The problem with this system is that it requires an enormous government bureaucracy. However, bureaucrats are not rewarded for their effectiveness (they may turn corrupt), and neither are the workers (they may turn desultory). In short, the system may not offer enough *personal* incentive to keep pace with changing markets. But at least it does not produce the extremes of wealth and poverty that a capitalist system can.

Of course, each of these market models is influenced and reinforced by law (as, for example, anti-competition laws, tax laws, securities regulation, tariffs, and so forth). But each also is influenced by the culture and social goals of the sovereigns involved and by political forces. Thus, the choice made in adopting one system or the other—and in moving between them— is influenced by three interdependent factors: economics, politics and law. I list them in what I believe to be their descending order. None is completely free of the others. Law is principally the normative result of the other two.

Chapter 5

Global Trade and
Global "Government"

GLOBAL TRADE

Do nations compete with one another in the world marketplace? Actually, distinguished economists disagree.[1] Whether they do or not, national economies are seriously affected by world trade. When those effects are not what the general public expects, government and businesses are expected to "do something." (What they ought to do is less clear.)

In the late 1980s and early 1990s, a number of books about Japan's recipe for success in the global marketplace appeared. They were followed by books about improving business strategies. Among these was one that anticipated, if it did not influence, the American response to global competition: MADE IN AMERICA: REGAINING THE PRODUCTIVE EDGE.[2] Whatever prompted the change, American businesses, workers and government behaved as if an external enemy threatened our standard of living. Our competitiveness began to improve.[3] But our enhanced success in world trade is not enough. We need allies.

As said previously, the EU is our most obvious partner. But these two giants don't necessarily agree about how to achieve a better world trade environment.[4] Put aside the fact that the two signed a "Declaration on U.S.–EC Relations" in November 1993 and more-ambitious and detailed agreements in 1995 and 1998. All are couched in constitutional language. Since the U.S. departed in a number of ways from the former, there is scant reason to expect the later agendas will be more binding. However, the U.S. and the EU have a great deal in common and can be expected to collaborate, at least when it is to their mutual advantage. One recent example of this is an agreement to cooperate more closely on customs procedures. If they could simplify and harmonize procedures, time and expense would be saved and bilateral trade facilitated. Furthermore, the exchange of customs information is a first step to fighting commercial fraud, which is international today. Finally, these two large trading blocs—when they collaborate—form the nucleus for future international agreements.[5]

But U.S./EU relations aren't always so cordial. The high-sounding pledges of the new Transatlantic Agenda (1995) lost inertia. The Helms-Burton Act, passed by Congress to punish those who trade with Cuba, and another concerning Iran and Libya (so-called "rogue governments") have rankled our EU partners. Some of the market openings proposed are in sectors (silicone chips) or proceed at a pace (financial services) that one or the other doesn't favor. In such cases, the U.S. or EU might proceed alone. This was the case when the U.S. walked away from the WTO financial services negotiations, and the EU steered through an agreement without us. The U.S. and Japan took the lead in information technology negotiations, and the EU had little choice but to join at the last minute—on terms it didn't favor.[6] What we are beginning to see then, in both international politics and trade, is a series of temporary and shifting alliances. Each one represents the next step in trying to cement the peace and to secure and extend prosperity.

President Clinton's early infatuation with Asia (the 1993 APEC summit in Seattle) has since been balanced by two transatlantic agreements and American leadership in Bosnia, the Middle East and NATO enlargement. But the U.S. and the EU don't always see the policy options the same way, and they tend to demur if the issue can be construed as a local one (Bosnia and Mexico).[7] Although a Transatlantic Free Trade Agreement (TAFTA) has been suggested, it probably won't happen because it would violate Article XXIV of the GATT agreement.[8] Indeed, it *shouldn't* happen, because such a arrangement would seriously destabilize other trade relationships.

On the private side, business integration accross the Atlantic and within Europe continues at a very brisk pace, although it is increasingly balanced by investment elsewhere. But the European market is integrating too. European cross-border mergers and acquisitions set new records almost every year and exceed $80 billion in 1996. Ireland and Portugal have also been the beneficiaries of foreign and European investment. German firms are establishing themselves in other European states to avoid high production costs at home, creating an investment deficit in Germany.[9] All of this consolidation and integration ought to be healthy. Since the U.S. has lost its position of hegemony and is unlikely to regain it, it needs *partners*. By this calculus, co-venturing by nations and companies ought to be encouraged and the interdependence of peoples and economies ought to be emphasized. But that is not always how it works.

If light bulbs are standardized worldwide, then the nation and producers whose standard is adopted is given a huge advantage. All others will have to retool to conform. Moreover, lighting fixture manufactures, electricians, and future electrical installations will be affected too. Since the benefits and burdens of globalization are not equal for everyone, both governments and the private sector compete to make certain that either their standard is adopted or that the standard adopted does the least damage to their commerce. In times past, tariffs, quotas and prohibitions were used to buffer the shock of foreign competition. Much of this was phased out by a series of GATT agreements that gradually embraced more trade sectors and signatory nations.[10] So other "non-tariff trade barriers" (NTBs) are imposed to protect consumers and domestic businesses.

Among these initiatives might be product specifications (already mentioned), purity standards, inspection requirements, anti-competition rules, labor standards, pollution standards and anti-dumping regulations (the practice of selling goods in foreign markets at less than their production cost or price in the domestic market), to name just a few. Often a case might be made that these measures are necessary to preserve safety and "fairness" in the marketplace. But they also can be anti-competitive and surely distort trade. They will continue to exist so long as the market isn't homonogized. However, national interests and political pressures make this process difficult.[11] Harmonization is far easier in cutting-edge industries (like computers and telecommunications), where standards evolve quite rapidly. It is much more contentious in slower-growth industries, where national standards have evolved slowly and a lot of retooling would be required. Still, the processes must begin sometime, somewhere.

The alternative to protectionism is to expand trading alliances around the world. The GATT agreement is a classic example of this. So is NAFTA. With this in mind, the European Union recently signed bilateral trading agreements with four South American countries (Mercosur) and with Canada and has sought to create closer trading links with Southeast Asian nations. The EU is behind the U.S. in each of these sectors. The frustration that this causes might make the EU a more contentious partner were it not for the many similarities in our systems and the fact that there are numerous areas of agreement.

So it was that an information technology agreement (ITA) was signed by 28 countries, representing 85 percent of the market, in December, 1996. This included the U.S., the EU and Japan. In mid-February, 1997 a telecom agreement was finally signed by 68 countries, comprising more than 90 percent of world telecom revenues. (Among large states only China and Russia are not signatories.) The terms of opening vary somewhat from country to country, with Japan retaining rather strict control over its two largest carriers, but considerable liberalization was due to begin on January 1, 1998, including privatization and foreign ownership and competition. The market, estimated to be about $788 billion in 1995 and growing at a rate of 7 percent a year, is expected to exceed a thousand billion dollars annually very soon.[12]

The ITA was an obvious first step in the further, rapid globalization of other large business sectors. Moreover, it was the first large sectorial agreement negotiated on its own, outside the GATT. Although another GATT round may begin as early as the year 2000, the Uruguay Round took eight years to complete. So it is quite likely that other sectorial agreements covering financial services, maritime transport, and so on will be completed before that round starts, and surely before it finishes.

Meanwhile, the ITA and telecom agreements provide a model for other sectorial agreements. They have established that workable agreements can be arrived at outside a GATT round. This was the untested assumption when certain sectors were left out at the end of the Uruguay Round. To have tried to include them would have further prolonged the negotiations. However, to negotiate a single-sector agreement means that all concessions have to come from within that sector. There are no other trade areas (as with a comprehensive GATT round) in which to make concessions. The sectorial agreements prove that this can be done, and so reduce the load on the GATT round, while allowing the expansion of world trade in the most difficult sectors. So they not only extended globalization, they probably hastened it as well. Just as significant, business leaders helped to break impasses and reach consensus. We can expect them to be more involved in the future, for it is to their advantage to help negotiators reach consensus.[13]

What are the principal issues confronting the world trade community in the years ahead? Some first principles are so basic to any concept of "globalizaton" that all trading nations are likely to agree on them.

The first is market access. There cannot be free and open trade when market access is artificially restricted. When one nation restricts trade, for whatever reason, its trading partners will usually retaliate. If this behavior escalates, world trade descends into trade war, protectionism and recession. Everyone loses. Yet it is politically difficult for any nation to open its market first, without agreed reciprocity.

A second principle is balanced trade; each trading country wants to be on a rough par with the others. Of course, this won't always be the case. But trade imbalances (e.g., between the U.S. and Japan or China) are most likely to exist where market access is restricted. In this situation, there will be political pressure to redress the imbalance.

A third goal has to be monetary stability. High inflation or sharp deflation undermine confidence in governments, markets and cross-border trade. Yet variations in the price of goods and services are the very essence of a free market. Competitive pricing and even currency devaluation can produce advantages in an open market and therefore cannot be prohibited entirely. On the other hand, the independence of every sovereign state to manage its currency as it sees fit is perhaps too much to claim. The Mexican peso crisis in 1995 and the Asian "meltdown" in 1997–1998 have proved that world trade is too interdependent to leave monetary policy uncoordinated. Germany's strict money policy in the early 1990s threw all of Europe into recession.

To date, the Quad 4 and G-7 nations haven't coordinated their efforts well enough to produce the kind of monetary stability that might be welcome to some. The introduction of a single currency in Europe has reduced major trading currencies to three (the dollar, the euro and the yen). But that would not effect minor currencies; and with money speculators exchanging in excess of 1 billion every day, there is little reason to expect a high level of monetary stability without some type of controls. Private trading is likely to overwhelm government intervention, no matter how concerted.

Another area of concern is foreign direct investment (FDI), or the amount of capital expanding markets can attract from foreign investors. Of course, if the savings practices of the domestic population are suitably good, the domestic economy may not need foreign investment. (China and India have high rates of saving, but their need for capital is so great that FDI is needed as well. The U.S. has a low rate of savings, but is an attractive site for FDI.)

Without capital, business cannot grow. But capital isn't always attracted to those states that need it most. The World Bank and International Monetary Fund were created to deal with shortages, but they don't control enough capital—nor do governments—to meet the needs of all expanding economies. Hence, *private* capital is needed as well. But private investors are notoriously flighty. They need incentive to invest in the countries that need their capital and to *leave* it there long enough to do some good.

In addition to capital protection, world trade needs other types of property protection, particularly intellectual property protection (since it is so easily stolen). In many developing nations there is no tradition of protecting property. Since intellectual property can easily be brought there and copied, it is to everyone's advantage (except the owner's) to traffic in the purloined property. However, as emerging economies develop their own intellectual property, they are likely to respect and protect it more. This was the experience in Japan and Taiwan and soon should be in South Korea, China and India.

The last of these first principles is the international scourge of crime, drugs and terrorism. As business and travel have become more and more international, persons and syndicates that prey on persons and enterprises have become international too. Persons who follow these trends believe that some international criminals are as sophisticated as the international operations meant to thwart them. If international crime is to be contained, it will require cooperation across national borders—operations currently limited by laws, policies and court systems.

By and large, tariffs are a thing of the past. They may raise some revenue for the importing state, but generally that is small compared to other sources of income (taxes). Tariffs are transparent attempts to burden foreign goods and services by making them less competitive than domestic goods, thereby protecting the latter from competition. Although most every economy in the world—including ours—retains tariffs in some sectors, the whole thrust of trade treaties is to reduce tariffs to zero. This effort has been ongoing for the past fifty years and has been quite successful. But tariffs have been supplanted by a series of non-tariff barriers (NTBs) that are more subtle. Among these we might list quantitative standards (quotas, such as on Japanese cars) or qualitative standards (such as health, safety or consumer protection legislation). The latter surely may be justified. However, many of these standards have simply excluded foreign products. A better alternative may be to establish a uniform standard to be followed by all or a mutual recognition of one another's standards.

Environmental and labor standards also can impose types of non-tariff barriers. Environmental and resource protection has never been a purely local matter, for water, fish stocks and so forth move freely around the globe. Deforestation in Brazil affects people half the world away. Although labor policy generally has been viewed as a more localized matter, there is an emerging consensus that safe and civilized labor conditions are a legitimate human rights concern of international trade. On the other hand, many a developing economy has exploited people (slaves on cotton plantations) and resources (oil, coal, lumber) in its quest for higher economic status. Now that world sensitivity has been raised about such matters, developed nations want to prevent exploitation. But the ability to profit from cheap labor and ready resources has transported many a developing economy into a developed one. Some of the former consider it hypocrisy for industrialized states to insist on a high level of environmental protection and labor standards. They consider such standards to be non-tariff barriers that take away their principal market advantages.

The same might be said of competition (antitrust) rules and policies. Most developed economies have such rules, to protect against the market distortion that results from monopoly positions and cartels. However, trading nations disagree about what the standard should be and how it should be enforced. Because behavior in one market can affect competition in another, a consensus about what constitutes anti-competitive behavior seems necessary.

Finally, there is the issue of foreign aid. In truth, the quantity of foreign aid in the world is steadily shrinking. Moreover, the emphasis is being shifted to developmental aid (except in humanitarian situations). In days past, there was little coordination of the grant of aid. For strategic reasons, several nations might compete to aid some underdeveloped territory, while ignoring another. This situation has changed somewhat. Today, highly industrialized nations, have cooperated to share responsibility so that gaps and overlaps are reduced. The process is neither finite nor exact. But it indicates that not every industrialized nation can be benefactor or policeman to the world. Sharing out the responsibilities in some orderly way is the only sensible approach to the future.

TOWARD A "WORLD" GOVERNMENT?

The WTO clearly has stepped to the center of the stage as the principal mechanism for trade globalization. It has as its task to produce an enforceable consensus on a broad range of trade issues, and its first ministerial meeting in Singapore (December 1996) produced a "well-defined road map for further trade liberalization" giving a "vital boost" to the WTO's stature. Against the odds, core labor standards probably will be added to the WTO agenda, as well as "new" issues like investment and competition policy (although both were deferred for two years of study). Already on the agenda were proposals for global agreements on financial services, maritime transport and trade-related aspects of intellectual property rights (TRIPs). The goal of all this activity and the goal of the WTO is pretty obvious. It is to establish "a fair, equitable and more open rule-based trading system; progressive liberalization [of markets]"; and "rejection of all forms of protectionism."[14] There once was concern that worldwide agreements might be held to ransom by large, powerful regional trading blocks. To date that has not happened. For one thing GATT rules prohibit it. More pragmatically, it would be counterproductive. Regional trading groups have proved more synergistic than obstructionist.[15]

But a multilateral approach to problem-solving means that concessions must be made with regard to *national* policies. The U.S. policy regarding global trade opening could not succeed if it resulted in injuring other traders. We have to make concessions to get concessions. In the process, national interests frequently take a back seat to global realities, and an embryonic form of "world government" emerges.[16]

That observation is not intended literally, but what else can we call the multiplicity of representative organizations in which governments pool their energies in their struggle to achieve growth with security? What else can one consider collaborative enterprises like the Quad 4 (in which the EU has a seat), the Group of Seven (G-7) industrialized nations (in which the four largest EU nations have seats), the G-10 (three more European seats), NATO, the United Nations, the International Monetary Fund (IMF), the World Bank and the Organisation for Economic Co-operation and Development (OECD), to name just the most obvious? All have decision-taking mechanisms and some enforcement capability as well. Chief among them is the WTO. In the absence of hot war, economic forces drive decision-making (public *and* private). Economic interests blend imperceptibly into social, political and legal outcomes. That which has been *de facto* long enough is often made *de jure*.

The list of issues facing world traders is extensive. Many of the issues are bound up in political and economic interests. As I have said, present alliances are fluid and shifting. Alliances of the past are breaking up, and new ones are impermanent. We are going to have to learn to get along in the brave new trading world that is carrying us along. We can resist it or try to shape it, but probably not both. Believing that the former is ultimately impossible and that the latter is our best (indeed *only*) option, let me suggest how that might proceed.

EUROPE: ALLY OR ADVERSARY?

What do we have then? A world with about 6 billion inhabitants and a net GDP just short of $40 trillion. Of that, the U.S. and the EU account for about $8.1 trillion each, or about 40 percent. But, whereas the most developed nations double their populations every 550 years, less developed nations do so every 40 years. By the year 2025, it is estimated that developed nations will have only 15 percent of world population (but a disproportionate share of world wealth), while poor nations have the rest.

World trade is the context in which nations evolve from the developing to the developed. It has increased sixteen times since 1950. This is much faster than the growth of domestic consumption. In this process, the U.S. and EU—as the largest, democratic, capitalistic traders in the world—have the chance to lead. That the U.S. and EU compete in world trade circles cannot be doubted. It is documented in this book. But the fact they can (and do) cooperate is my essential thrust. In the near term, what they do collectively almost certainly will set the world standard. But, what they do differently or separately or antagonistically will set a double standard; a situation in which other players with different agendas can pick and choose.

The EU not only has consolidated internally but is poised to add new members in Central and Eastern Europe. It also is extending its influence in the Mediterranean basin, Latin America and Asia. Outward foreign direct investment (FDI) by EU member states rose 46 percent in 1997, while inward FDI (to Europe) grew 38 percent. It is easily one of the most attractive markets in the world.

With respect to the U.S., the EU is the number one investor in 42 states and the number two investor in the other eight. The interdependence is evident. Yet consolidation can mean job and market losses, and that prospect can be a powerful incentive to protectionism. And yet the cost of job protection has been estimated to be as high as $600 thousand for even *one* job, much more than it is worth.

Another oft-cited reservation to trade expansion is a loss of national sovereignty, particularly in the EU. But economic interdependence is producing that result anyway. Trade regulations are increasingly "global," adopted in the multilateral organizations of which I spoke. But the U.S., the world's most open market and largest trader, is hardly threatened by a serious loss of sovereignty. Moreover, the natural transition from agriculture to manufacturing to service is a natural (and somewhat irresistible) process. It is not all painless, for jobs are lost and industries migrate. But adapting to change costs less than any futile to stem the tide.[17]

There are plenty of trade areas in which the U.S. and EU cooperate. The ITA agreement and telecoms are just two. They also have agreed to the mutual recognition of standards in the areas of drugs and medical devices and some agricultural products. But there also are many areas in which the U.S. and EU positions are far apart: banana imports, hormone-fed beef, Helms-Burton, and dumping, to mention just a few. Do I think that these differences will gradually be reconciled? Yes, I do. But I cannot say what standard will prevail.

Part III

Three Trading Giants?
(and Their Spheres of Influence)

Chapter 6

The United States

"The business of America is business." So said Calvin Coolidge in 1925,[1] and it is just as true today. Generally speaking, Americans like to work. They are especially motivated when their hard work results in a higher standard of living. But direct cause-and-effect relationships are seldom clear in today's trading world. The way forward is not always what it appears to be. Besides, we can't achieve our objectives alone. The interdependencies are too great.

Before World War I, world trade grew at a rapid rate. This precipitated regional jealousies that ended in war. Afterwards, the United States sought to grow its economy somewhat in seclusion. It erected the Smoot-Hawley tariff and others against foreign goods. Other nations adopted reciprocal tariffs, and the world was plunged into a global recession. Some nations sought to recover through aggression, resulting in World War II. Made wiser by their predecessors' mistakes, the victorious allies tried to construct a peacetime economic system that was collaborative. Among their initiatives were the Marshall Plan to rebuild Europe, the United Nations, and particularly the Bretton Woods conference. The latter set the groundwork for the International Monetary Fund (IMF), the World Bank, and the GATT. There is no need to discuss them in detail here (some are addressed later), except to suggest that an interdependent world economic trading system can be traced to this source.

Of course the United States dominated the process, because it was the one major trading nation not seriously crippled by war. The rebuilding was spurred by American capital and know-how. But America has lost its position of hegemony.[2]

On the other hand, the U.S. wields more influence than its single vote in the UN, the GATT, or the WTO might suggest. Indeed, by being one of the final bargainers at the table in the Uruguay Round of GATT negotiations (the other being the EU) and a prime mover in negotiating sectorial agreements in the wake of the GATT (with the EU and Japan), the U.S. has a large hand in setting trade standards that other countries must follow. Today, however, the U.S. can no longer dictate the pace. Collaborative solutions—those with a broad base of support—usually are more enduring than those that are imposed by a dominant (but generally temporal) authority.

As illustrated above, nations and businesses do not have the same interests or philosophies. Resources and know-how are not uniformly distributed. The surplus goods that one country wishes to export may threaten an industry in the importing state. Capitalists are eager to invest in developing economies, but they flee just as quickly at the first sign of instability. In the U.S. there are powerful lobbies that seek to protect U.S. industries, laborers, and goods from foreign competition. Sometimes this is legitimate, as for example when a good is "dumped" (subsidized and sold below cost) in the U.S. But cheaper goods also may result from better resources or inexpensive labor or improved technology. There are cases in which job and market protection is appropriate, but not many. More frequently it is an instinctual return to the failed tactics of the 1930s.

Preserving the status quo is simply not an option. The world is not static and cannot be made so. Workers will migrate, and so will jobs and businesses (although less often than is suggested, for there is more to trade calculus than cheap labor and lower regulation). To survive, the U.S. has to be proactive. So the question is better phrased: How can the U.S. preserve most of its advantages while helping to secure similar advantages for its trading partners? After all, global trade is not necessarily a zero-sum game, or at least it doesn't have to be.

In the economic boom of the 1980s, many American businesses fared quite well. But late in that decade they were confronted with the rapid growth and competitiveness of traders elsewhere in the world, particularly in Europe and Japan. These economies were more managed than ours and were studied closely. So was U.S. business, which seemed to be falling behind.[3] These reassessments provoked many U.S. corporations into painful process of "downsizing" or "rightsizing." Companies were restructured to concentrate more on core business and jettisoned non-performing enterprises. Many jobs were eliminated in the restructuring (although not as many as banner headlines might have led one to believe). The process resulted in smaller, more nimble and focused companies. Some jobs disappeared permanently, and others moved offshore. But by and large, smaller businesses absorbed the workers shed by larger corporations and began to supply the needs of the latter in a more flexible and efficient way. Netted out, employment rose, and U.S. global trade did too.

These changes in business practice had their corollary in government as well. President Regan's administration lacked a coherent foreign policy. However, he was a dedicated free trader and fought off many attempts to buffer the effects of free competition, both at home and abroad. In addition, the strong alliances he reinvigorated, particularly with Europe, and his insistence on a strong military eventually overtaxed the U.S.S.R., and it collapsed. To some extent, the end of the Cold War vindicated the capitalistic model, and it allowed multinational businesses to concentrate more on consumer products in an enlarged market.[4]

By virtue of his long service in political and international positions, President Bush came to office with a better developed worldview than most of his predecessors. The energy he invested in the GATT and NAFTA, and his willingness to persevere to open markets in Asia were a testimony not just to that vision but to the new realities of the post–Cold War trading world. Finally, the multinational coalition he speedily assembled to throw back the aggression of Iraq in the Persian Gulf was a master stroke of statesmanship. But it also suggested that regional peace and stability was a platform for growth and trade and a shared responsibility. In important ways, policy initiatives were shifting from the State Department to the Department of Commerce.

President Clinton came into office having campaigned chiefly on domestic issues. He quickly learned that foreign policy was the unique province of the U.S. president, whereas there are many federal officials who can (and do) oversee domestic policy. Moreover, his one major foray into a domestic area (health care) turned out to be a disaster. President Clinton's learning curve was very sharp. By the middle of his first term, President Clinton's foreign policy—particularly its commercial aspects—was moving along smartly. He was the beneficiary, of course, of the structural changes in government and business that had occurred under his predecessors. This included long-running negotiations involving NAFTA and GATT, including its improved enforcement mechanism, the WTO. To his credit, President Clinton worked hard to secure the ratification of these treaties by a cautious Senate and continued to push for "fast track" authority to negotiate other international agreements that would expand U.S. and global trade. As host of the Asian-Pacific Economic Cooperation (APEC) summit in Seattle in 1993, President Clinton's involved APEC heads of state and government in its deliberations, thereby giving its trade-expanding initiatives new impetus.

President Clinton was aided in these initiatives by an able and energetic group of negotiators, including the late Ron Brown, Secretary of Commerce; the former U.S. Trade Representative (USTR), Mickey Kantor (who succeeded Mr. Brown at Commerce); and Charlene Barshefsky, who succeeded Mr. Kantor as USTR. They worked tirelessly to promote market opening in many countries and business sectors, sometimes against fierce resistance. If their tactics sometimes seemed contentious and bullying, at least they produced results.[5] Trade globalization increased more during their tenure than it did under President Bush's USTR, Carla Hills, who was more of a consensus builder. But, of course, the pace of international trade was growing the whole time. On the public international law side, secretaries of state from James Baker to Madeleine Albright worked just as hard to promote peace and security around the world. International trade flourishes best in an environment that is stable and predictable.

The largest part of the U.S. economy is domestic, of course. Some economists have argued that it is so vast that our standard of living could be perpetuated merely by increased efficiencies at home.[6] However, Americans' consumption is already so high that it is near saturation. There is but limited room for growth. Although the export sector is, admittedly, a much smaller percentage of U.S. GDP, its growth is much more rapid. According to FOR-TUNE magazine, in 1995 the world's 500 largest corporations grew a robust 15 percent, relative to world (and U.S.) GDP growth of just 2.4 percent. Moreover, the 15 percent growth was realized on revenue growth of just 11 percent. In the case of U.S. chipmaker Intel, its expanded international sales boosted return on assets over 20 percent.[7] Revenue growth on this scale in domestic markets is virtually unknown.

Is it any wonder then that foreign markets are so intriguing to U.S. multinationals? According to the FORTUNE report, "[o]verreliance on home markets is one of the surest routes to the bottom of the pack." It cites Japan's Fuji Bank, a largely domestic enterprise, which lost 10 percent of its $31.7 billion in assets in 1995. Contrast this with the world's largest company, Mitsubishi, which saw 58 percent growth in profits since 1994, or the largest U.S. company, General Motors, which realized 40 percent growth in the same period.[8] Parenthetically, it might be observed that globalization has a significant impact on the U.S. domestic economy. As much as U.S. companies are investing and establishing themselves abroad, foreign multinationals are doing the same in the U.S., creating jobs and satisfying consumers' demands. If this were not so, we would have little basis for insisting that we be allowed to enter their markets. Among the largest twenty-five U.S. subsidiaries of foreign companies, Honda, Citgo, Food Lion, Seagram and Bridgestone earn over one-third of their revenues in the U.S.[9]

There is no question that the U.S. market is the most open in the world. It sets the standard in terms of standard of living, foreign investment (both ways), security of investment and job creation. And yet we have only begun the "globalization" process. While foreign securities account for only 1.2 percent of U.S. investors' portfolios, that amount has doubled since 1990. The flow of American capital favors foreign investment, since the returns (despite the risks) are much greater. Since 1989, worldwide foreign direct investment (FDI) has nearly tripled, to more than $80 billion in 1994. Among U.S. multinational companies, nearly 20 percent of total pre-tax profit comes from the sales of foreign affiliates. Moreover, their profit margins are twice those earned in North America, Europe or Japan. Investments in foreign infrastructure projects lock the investor into the success of the enterprise in the longer term. It is not so much speculation as collaboration. So the recent telecoms accord creates a huge market for U.S. products and know-how. According to an AT&T executive, "[t]he multiplier effects are absolutely staggering."[10] Hence, the question of U.S. companies "going global" is really not in issue. We already are part of the global marketplace, and we *want* to be.

Global business also is increasingly dependent on smaller enterprises. Large U.S. multinationals have realized that decision-making systems that are too slow are a disadvantage in the global marketplace. Even if the company is large, the operating units must be small and nimble. It is a paradox that, to the extent that global standards harmonize, the urge for individuality increases. Of course many small and medium-sized businesses often serve large multinational corporations. This increases interdependency as well as the number of participants in the global economy. The U.S. Commerce Department has been very aggressive about getting smaller companies to participate in foreign markets. Improved technology has made it easier for niche players to participate. What we do not want are some of the pains that go along with globalization, such as a failure to honor trade agreements (China, regarding intellectual property protection) or the need to secure the peace (Bosnia, the Middle East). We cannot have it both ways, however. Where there are attractive rewards, there almost certainly are risks as well. The entire world does not view the expansion of commercial enterprise through the same lens we Americans do. We cannot disengage ourselves from the process that we have tried so hard to create and which benefits us so.

Today, every American business and employee is affected by overseas competition, whether we recognize it or not. It should shock no one to learn that one-half of Xerox's employees work on foreign soil or that a number of U.S. companies already have moved the majority of their assets abroad, for example, Gillette (66%), Mobil (63%), DEC (61%), Exxon (56%) and Bankers Trust (52%). They manufacture in Europe and elsewhere to better serve their foreign customers and to expand their market. "Sales by firms with foreign activities grow at twice the rate of those with no foreign operations," and their profits are higher as well.[11]

In addition, cross-border alliances—whether through acquisitions, mergers, licensing or joint ventures—have become common. As a result, no one country suffers from a large business failure, but many countries do. Put differently, the globalization of trade increases collaboration to make markets work, because the interest in business success is spread more broadly around the world. It is less and less a case of "us" versus "them," but rather one of two or more nations or companies working together, win *or* lose. In a global economy, multilateral cooperation is a win-win or lose-lose proposition, not a win/lose proposition, as it has been considered to be in the past.

Our hope is that America's vision will dominate the policy debate, of course, but that seems unlikely. We may exercise influence disproportionate to our single vote, but our numerous foreign partners, with increasingly robust economies and different trade perspectives, are bound to contest our approach. Increasingly, there is not an "American" or "European" or "Asian" answer to problems in the global marketplace. We are moving toward a harmonized set of standards and policies that reflect the American perspective but do not ape it.

Moreover, we have learned that absolutely free trade isn't always best. Sometimes, managed systems produce better results, if they buffer rather than stifle market forces. Unilateral positions taken without regard to one's trading partners generally fail in the long haul. We cannot be surprised if our trading partners—particularly developing countries—adopt selfish, exclusionary policies, especially if the U.S. does so as well. We lead by example, so the best way to encourage trade liberalization is to practice it. This will not happen overnight, of course. Pushing too hard for unaccustomed changes almost surely will be counterproductive. There is still ample fear of the American leviathan.

Moreover, there will be losers in the process of trade globalization. Some may be American industries and jobs, but is that a justification for protecting them? A failing industry only siphons resources away from one that is emerging and has the potential to grow. The weaker enterprises fail, and the stronger ones succeed them anyway. It is simple economic Darwinism. Is it any wonder that, of the top 100 FORTUNE companies at the turn of last century, only one (General Electric) was on FORTUNE's list as we approach the turn of this century? Should we bemoan the decline of our steel or agriculture industries if U.S. firms rank number one in thirteen major contemporary industries including aerospace, apparel, beverages, chemicals, computers, motor vehicles, pharmaceuticals and photographic and scientific equipment? High-status, high-value jobs and industries are being created even as low-value, low-status jobs and industries disappear. Company-sponsored research and development investment has exceeded government-financed R & D for the first time in over 50 years.[12] That is to say that business, not government, is increasingly the engine that drives the U.S. economy. Businesses in today's trade world can be synergistic, whereas governments (reacting to political pressure) can be insular. Governments should give business as much freedom as possible to innovate and expand.

Of course, these platitudes don't take sufficient account of the measures used by laborers and voters to judge whether they are doing well or poorly in this global competition. There are expansion-killers out there. One is the persistent imbalance in U.S. foreign trade. It reached a record $211 billion in 1987 and was brought down to about $43 billion in the last year of the

Bush administration, but by mid 1998 it was rising to new heights, due to the Asian economic crisis. The Asian economies in crisis were able to import fewer American goods, but substantially increased their exports to us. Foreign investment in Asia also plummeted. Naturally the widening deficit produced calls for protectionist measures in America, but this would be exactly the wrong reaction. Moreover, the health of the American economy was somewhat immune to the deficit, because it is primarily a service economy, and demand for U.S. services continued to rise.[13] With a strong dollar and restored self-confidence, Americans simply are importing far more than they are exporting. Japan's still-protectionist market is one culprit, but not the only one. The imbalance with China is growing faster. Even our deficit with Western Europe, long relatively small, has begun to grow larger, as has has our deficit with Mexico, our NAFTA partner. To some extent, this reflects the state of the economy in each market, but it also is the result of remaining barriers to U.S. goods. Such restrictive trade practices always result in a protectionist pressure that could undercut the progress of globalization.[14]

Two other factors worth noting are labor conditions—from the inexpensive, but unhealthy conditions in developing economies to the expensive social programs of Europe—and interest rates. Neither are uniform around the world, and perhaps they should not be. For these are the economic differentials that promote competitiveness. However, if the variations are too great and result from unilateral policy decisions, they can be more distorting than competitive.

Yet another paradox of the new global economy is that it mixes competition with cooperation. MEGATRENDS author John Naisbitt calls it "the yin and yang of the global marketplace." Thus, competitor firms may license their products or co-venture in markets in which they don't wish to establish themselves independently. Cooperation is especially evident in research and development projects that have grown too expensive for single companies to afford. Cooperation also is increasing in product lines involving numerous components, which may be produced and assembled in a variety of states. These new approaches simply confound old, state-based notions of trade policy and practice.[15]

Thus, opening foreign markets for domestic goods inevitably opens domestic markets to foreign goods. As large multinational companies expand their markets, they draw more small and medium-sized businesses (SMEs, defined as those with fewer than 500 employees) into world trade. According to Naisbitt, only "7 percent of U.S. exports are created by [large companies]. The Fortune 500 now account for only 10 percent of the American economy, down from 20 percent in 1970."[16] This accelerates the speed of change, and interdependencies become greater. Since SMEs are entering the global game in large numbers, and many succeed and expand, they tend to create jobs that compensate for those being lost in multinational companies and more. According to a recent survey, midsize manufacturers that make more than 20 percent of their total sales abroad are the most likely to hire new workers, while the 30 percent of such firms that don't export are losing out.[17] U.S. trade (and domestic) policy needs to be adjusted to accommodate their needs and business styles.

Generally speaking, the U.S. occupies a pretty healthy position in the global trade sweepstakes. According to a recent report by the U.S. Trade Representative, both domestic and foreign investors are investing more in the United States. In 1995, U.S. assets abroad totalled $3.35 trillion. Foreign assets in the U.S. grew to $4.13 trillion in market value, for a net international investment position of about a negative $780 billion, which is growing wider. This is due to both large capital inflows and the greater price appreciation of U.S. than foreign securities.[18] Foreign investment weds external interests to the success of the U.S. economy.

Capital market activity also is growing rapidly, becoming more global and better integrated. In 1995, "[b]orrowing on . . . international capital markets set a new record . . . with overall financing activity growing by 30 percent to [$1.26 trillion]" according to an OECD report. Eurobond and foreign bond markets began to grow again in 1995 (to $461 billion) after hitting a high ($481 billion) in Europe's boom year of 1993. International competition among banks also is producing favorable terms, but industrialized nations' banks still account for almost 90 percent of syndicated lending.[19]

Trade surplus or deficit is another statistic used to measure the health of an economy. In this area America doesn't do as well. U.S. businesses and the government are working hard to open the protected markets of the Pacific Rim, which are responsible for nearly 75 percent of Americas' $1.25 trillion in cumulative trade deficits from 1980 to 1994. In contrast, two-way investment between the U.S. and Europe amounts to about $776 billion and supports "the world's largest commercial relationship." European investment in the U.S. represents 64 percent of all foreign direct investment. The trade relationship between the U.S. and its NAFTA partners (Canada and Mexico) may be more comprehensive, but the U.S/EU partnership means more in terms of world trade. According to the pragmatic EU trade negotiator, Sir Leon Brittan, the U.S. and EU will not stay together out of "nostalgia." There has to be a reason, and there is. Given the size of U.S./ EU trade, even modest growth in the 2.5 percent range can be equivalent to capturing a market the size of Venezuela every year. As one General Electric executive put it, "Asia makes the headlines, Europe makes the money."[20]

Europe is an inviting market for U.S. expansion not just because of its proximity, capitalist tradition and stability. As U.S. businesses went through their "rightsizing" in the early 1990s, European political and business leaders recognized that they must do so too. Many publicly owned European businesses will be privatized by the year 2000—railroads, airlines, telecommunications and energy, to name but a few. It is a good bet that U.S. firms will participate fully, either by buying sections of enterprises or by arranging new partnerships with European firms.[21] The old national markets are disintegrating, altered from within by common markets and bested from without by foreign competition. European laborers, businesses, voters and politicians have long resisted the change, but it now is upon them, and a single currency ought to accerate the pace.

The other source of change is coming from Europe's young entrepreneurs. They have learned from America's turnaround and want to try some of the same techniques in Europe. Losing enterprises, like Fokker, have been jettisoned when they cannot be sold. Concentrating on core business made Finland's Nokia the world's second-largest manufacturer of mobile telephones. And Richard Branson, of Virgin Airways, seems to launch a new business venture every day.[22]

Despite the "potential" of Asia, and the apparent reawakening of Europe, it has been America that has led the way out of the global economic slowdown of the early 1990s. It could be the sparkplug for global trade expansion for years to come. There really is nothing Americans like better than a challenge. That is why discussions of the global marketplace are frequently couched in terms of economic "warfare." Export/import and trade balance figures mobilize Americans to compete, as if the U.S. was under threat from abroad. In some ways we are, because we have grown more dependent on foreign goods and capital. But, foreign businesses have grown more dependent on the U.S. also. That is why the pain of industrial downsizing a few years back was borne so well. We Americans were at "war" with foreign competitors. We wanted to best them and regain our premier position in world trade, and we did.

Perish the thought that we should "win" this war, however. For very good reasons, we don't want to vanquish our competitors in the global marketplace. We need to coexist with them. Broadly speaking, Americans are a very "can do" lot. Generally, they are optimistic about the future, because there is much in their past to be optimistic about. They know how to play the game, and they play it well. By any standard then, the U.S. has taken the lead in global trade expansion and is experimenting with new business structures and approaches to get the most from the process.

Not surprisingly, the U.S. had eclipsed Japan at the head of the "competitiveness" table. The assessment is based on hard data, but also subjective assessments, including that of international executives. Japan stood in fourth place, and, while the EU member states were not treated as a unit, ten of its fifteen states ranked in the top 20. Each nation had liabilities, to be sure. On balance, however, the U.S. was seen as first among equals, with the capacity to boost the world economy.[23]

There are other advantages in the American marketplace as well. By and large, it has enjoyed a stable business and political environment for the past

20 years. Relative prosperity means that business has been able to tolerate increasing regulation, without being crippled by it. Business has become more proactive in areas such as workplace safety, environmental concerns, and employee education. By collaborating with government, business has achieved many of its economic goals while adjusting to political/social pressures. While a government-business alliance is not the American model, public concern about the threat of big business seems to have diminished over the past 40 years, and a collaborative approach to social and economic problems is more productive. The same is true of American political parties. There is less distance between the policies of Republicans and Democrats than previously. Each has discovered virtue in the core interests of American voters and businesspersons, and the public has grown impatient with petty party bickering. There has been more focus on global concerns.

The American economy also benefits from a uniform market, including a single currency. These common traits contribute to the tendency to think big and to act big. As the United States is the single largest exporting and importing market in the world, it should be a place where the concepts needed to create higher standards of growth, productivity and quality should be tried. The success of the American market, now stretching to embrace our NAFTA partners, is the start of a global marketplace.

In past years, many nations have been concerned chiefly with their domestic market. The source of authority was clear and the market largely homogeneous. But, in a global economy, there is a huge diversity of institutions, policies and practices. If governments don't learn to collaborate—even while competing with one another—globalized trade will continue to be uneven and contentious. There is the inevitable temptation to exploit your partner's weakness, forgetting that, in a globalized market, the position of advantage and disadvantage can be, and often are, quickly reversed.

AMERICAN DREAM—OR NIGHTMARE?

The so-called American Dream has enjoyed a certain hardiness over the years. Some of it is real, but it has a dark side. What foreigners really want is America's material wealth and freedom, without the crude excesses which the two can foster. The argument might be made that Americans have enjoyed too much wealth and freedom and that we have not always exercised it well. For this reason, ours may not be the preferred model for a global economy. It is not proved to be the predominant model in the world, no matter how much we are envied. Most nations and people in the world have opted for a more regulated and socialistic model. No society is ever completely free of either system, right down to the black markets operating in today's China. As usual, the issue is one of *balance*. How does one reap the riches of an open and competitive market and yet avoid its harshest results: disparities of wealth, social irresponsibility and crime? How does one provide for the less well-to-do (people or nations) without creating a permanent underclass?

If we are to have a well-integrated world trading system, this balance between capitalism and socialism—between openness and protection—has to be struck.[24] The temptation is very great for each model to pull back and to solve its problems internally. This is the counsel of persons like Ross Perot. Why not protect our jobs, businesses and borders and let the rest of the world fend for itself? The rationale is very tempting. But it misperceives the interdependencies described above. It is a prescription for failure. We must be more imaginative than that.

THE YIN AND YANG OF AMERICAN TRADE POLICY

There are U.S. interests to protect abroad, of course, both business and military interests. International commerce creates both opportunities and threats. There is no fence or police force that can stem the interaction. Most of these problems are not uniquely American. Pollution of the air and water is not contained by political borders. The same is true of criminal syndicates and drug dealers, who have been globalizing for years. The lessons we learned (if we did learn them) from racial integration or our struggle with diseases such as AIDS have international applicability. Without a healthy, prosperous and reasonably stable world, our own health, prosperity and security are put at risk.

That is not necessarily how the U.S. has been proceeding, however. Lately we seem to have adopted whatever technique would carry the day, be it unilateral, bilateral or multilateral. I have to admit that the technique has often been successful. It has opened markets—often more speedily than otherwise possible. Too much unilateral action could transform irritation about U.S. behavior into alliances against us, however. The U.S. may be entirely correct is protesting certain international trade practices such as bribes. But our hostility to trade practices that are commonplace or at least tolerated elsewhere in the world does not make them wrong. If there is consensus that such practices violate world trade norms, then a number of nations (not the U.S. alone) will have to condemn them.[25] Our unilateral attempt to enforce our law and moral view on others, particularly where that law is imposed extraterritorially, provokes retaliatory legislation.[26] Yet U.S. authorities keep and publish an exhaustive list of foreign trade practices that are thought to harm U.S. businesses.[27] The USTR is given the power under U.S. law to identify and sanction foreign trade practices that violate U.S. norms. The authority is more often used as a threat than employed as a punitive device, however.[28]

The best (or worst) recent example of American unilateralism is the so-called Helms-Burton Act.[29] It was passed by Congress shortly after the Cuban military shot down two small U.S.-based civilian aircraft. The bill codifies some 35 years of U.S. sanctions against Fidel Castro's Cuba and is meant to expedite his ouster by punishing foreign investors who knowingly "traffic" in Cuban-expropriated properties (formerly owned by U.S. nationals). Simply put, it is meant to increase Cuba's economic isolation.

The most contentious part of the act is Title III. It allows U.S. citizens to sue, in American courts, anyone who knowingly traffics in property confiscated by Castro's regime. The object of the legislation is Cuba, but the vehicle is a secondary boycott against foreign nationals and companies who deal with Cuba. They have not violated international norms in any way. President Clinton has taken the sting out of Title III by waiving the private right-to-sue provision. But the unilateral nature of the initiative has provoked a firestorm of protest from our closest and most valuable trading partners, the EU, Canada and Mexico. Each has passed countervailing legislation against its enforcement. The EU even asked the WTO to appoint a panel to determine whether the act violates the GATT. The U.S. responded that the WTO panel lacked competence to adjudicate the matter because it involved a "national security" issue. The latter is a basis for a nation to derogate from its GATT commitments, under Article 21.[30] Fortunately, the dispute was resolved between the U.S. and EU, for any decision the panel reached could have been destructive to the WTO and world trade. That might please some persons who feel that the U.S. should never have signed NAFTA or the GATT or subjected Americans to the judgments of some foreign tribunal like the WTO. But our refusal to obey an adverse WTO decision on Helms-Burton would have done little to advance U.S. leadership or the prospects of global trade. After all, it is America that likes to insist that trade treaties are binding.[31]

The truth of the matter is that most multilateral trade agreements have been good for the U.S. economy. The fact that about twice as many Americans believe that more jobs are lost than are gained in free trade agreements and that they stimulate imports more than exports simply reflects their poor appreciation of the facts. In 1995, the NAFTA partnership enjoyed a *favorable* balance of trade with the European Union, particularly in high-tech sectors, America's strongest suit. Moreover, studies have shown that the NAFTA has had a far more insignificant effect on American jobs than is generally thought.[32] It may be difficult for Americans to conceive of our government being held liable in any forum other than an American court. But that is what globalization is all about.

The U.S. is not alone in keeping track of its trading partners' alleged misbehavior, however. For many years the EU has published an annual *Report on U.S. Barriers to Trade and Investment.*[33] The *Report* documents those U.S. trade practices that the EU considers "extraterritorial and unilateral" or which allegedly violate GATT. Perhaps this is all political posturing—the need for national leaders to prove to their constituents that they have gained more from free-trade negotiations than they have given up. But such comparisons are a throw back to the win/lose thinking that is passe in a globalized world.

I have elected to deal elsewhere in this book with American attempts to expand its influence in Southeast Asia and the Pacific Rim and other regional and international trade initiatives (for example, the WTO). I raise the subject here only to illustrate the full scope of American trading interests and the fact that our needlessly unilateral initiatives can easily provoke a "me too" response where a cooperative approach might have been more productive. But the American approach to trade globalization (a potpourri) often tends to justify the means by the end.

The NAFTA already has drawn the majority of the wealth of the Americas into a coordinated trading system, although it is not a customs union. The remainder of the Americas has struggled for years with poverty, backwardness and political and economic uncertainty. This is beginning to change. By one account, Latin American market integration advanced more since 1990 than it had in the previous 100 years after colonialism ended.[34] Latin American population, south of Mexico, is approximately 360 million, but the region's net GNP ($1.5 trillion in 1997) represents only about 18 percent of the total GNP of the Americas. Nonetheless, the potential of this market is enormous, because it is nearby and has huge infrastructure needs that NAFTA nations can readily supply.

Quite understandably, these nations are ambivalent about associations with the U.S. and want to proceed at their own pace. Chile, with 14.2 million population and $67.3 billion in GDP ($4,739 per capita) in 1996, had long wanted to be the next NAFTA partner. When that process stalled, however, Chile associated itself with the Common Market of the South (Mercosur). That the South American market is likely to continue to grow and expand seems without doubt. But the rate of growth, its sustainability and the availability of investment capital is less certain. Although high rates of growth and return are inviting, Latin American financial systems are still shaky and domestic savings rates are low, save in Chile. The region remains heavily supported by World Bank and IMF programs. Private international investment tends to flow to the areas of maximum stability and return. Latin America has yet to prove it is that. U.S. investors and businessmen have to look in all directions—not just in this hemisphere—when plotting future growth and expansion. At this point, Europe (including Central and Eastern Europe) and certain spots in Asia and the Pacific Rim look like better prospects. However, if the FTAA develops on schedule, Latin America should boom.

Another region that has attracted America's interest is South Africa. It has an enormous head start over any other African country and may be the best place for the U.S. to begin serious trade development with that continent. The EU has long had a trade relationship with former African, Caribbean and Pacific (ACP) colonies (the Lomé Convention). That relationship is now being reworked (and reduced), and the U.S. interest is recent, so it is difficult to know how either will develop. But it is desirable to make African nations more economically independent and self-sufficient. A U.S.–Africa free trade area seems far-fetched at present. There is little political will and just as little economic impact. But there is potential. Sooner or later, business has to get involved if any serious improvement in Africa's economic condition is to occur.[35] The question is: what should developed countries do, individually or collectively, to see that capital markets and expanding business *get* involved and *stay* involved in developing economies?[36] Should this be done on a regional basis, carving up the globe and risking a new colonialism and provincialism? Or should it be done in multinational councils—and if so, which ones?

THE U.S. AND THE WORLD TRADE ORGANIZATION (WTO)

The last major arena of U.S. trade policy development is the ultimate multilateral forum, the GATT and the WTO. The Uruguay Round of the GATT was by far the most extensive market-liberalization agreement ever. Together with sectorial agreements that have been and are being negotiated, enforceable multinational trade agreements are steadily expanding their scope and influence.[37] This is due to the advent of the WTO's binding dispute-resolution process. It allows the U.S. (frequently at the urging of disgruntled American businesses) to ask the trade group to create a panel to investigate whether agreed trading rules are being violated and, if so, to require the offending trading state to change its practices.

Of course, if the U.S. insists that other GATT signatories live up to their commitments, then we have to expect that our GATT agreements can be enforced against us as well. Thus, it was probably fitting that the first WTO panel to rule against a trade practice held that the U.S. treatment of reformulated Venezuelan gasoline violated the GATT. Another panel has ruled against us in a matter involving import duties on Costa Rican–manufactured underwear,[38] and a third has rejected as too rigid a U.S. environmental law protecting sea turtles. The subjects sound almost bizarre, but it is in such obscure ways that global trading rules are tested and strengthened. Of course, the U.S. has had its victories too, among them a decision against Japan's liquor tax regime and the banana import scheme of the European Union.[39] Other complaints against the EU and Japan are pending. In fact, in the first few years after the WTO began operation in January 1995, the U.S. has filed over 20 cases, while only seven cases have been brought by other countries against our trade practices. Many other states have preferred to settle their trade disputes with us rather than have them brought before the WTO. According to the U.S. Trade Representative, "[t]he WTO dispute settlement mechanism is proving to be a very effective tool to open other nations' markets. The process is . . . working to our benefit." [40] The U.S. was given high marks for its willingness to conform in the Venezuelan gas ruling, a material test of WTO authority. The U.S. proved as good as its bargain, and world trade was strengthened.

Under these circumstances, one may wonder why the U.S. does not pursue market opening strictly through multinational agreements and their enforcement. The answer appears to be twofold. First, the U.S. does not have the same trading problems with every GATT nation. Sometimes it is simpler and more expedient to negotiate one-on-one than to take the longer, slower and possibly more uncertain WTO route. Besides, if a bilateral settlement is reached, it could be a template for a new multinational agreement. The second reason seems to be that, without "fast track" negotiating authority from Congress, it is more difficult to get our trading partners to enter trade negotiations. Fast track authority almost always is needed for complex, multilateral treaties.[41] However, the U.S. Trade Representative has congressional authority to proceed with certain bilateral initiatives. Besides, if one has a number of weapons in the trade arsenal, why not use them? To be certain, we are often considered bullies, but our trade policy has been extremely successful.

However, with new coalitions of partners emerging every day, the U.S. may find it more and more difficult to freelance when defining and enforcing world trading standards. We will need coalitions too.

Chapter 7

Afta' NAFTA: The Free Trade Area of the Americas (FTAA)

THE NORTH AMERICAN FREE TRADE AGREEMENT (NAFTA)

Depending upon whom you believe, the North American Free Trade Agreement (NAFTA) is either a great success or a failure. At the time it was approved by Congress in late 1993 and ever since, there has been a polarizing debate in America about the virtues and vices of our new trade relationships, particularly those with Mexico.[1] Independent presidential candidate Ross Perot predicted that U.S. jobs would flee to Mexico's cheaper labor markets "with a giant sucking sound." None of the euphoric or dire prediction about NAFTA have come to pass, however. All objective assessments of NAFTA agree that it will take years for the three national economies involved to harmonize and for the positive effects of the agreement to be widely felt.[2] To date, the results have been checkered, but the direction of trade relationships is generally positive for all three partners. The gains have been significant enough that they have entered negotiations to expand NAFTA membership to South American countries and/or to broaden the program to cover the entirety of the Americas, a plan variously dubbed the American Free Trade Association (AFTA), the Western Hemispheric Free Trade Association (WHAFTA), or now, by consensus, the Free Trade Association of the Americas (FTAA).

NAFTA then is merely another step in global trade liberalization and does not compete with the GATT and the WTO as much as it complements them in this region. Meanwhile, our NAFTA partners, Canada and Mexico, not wanting to become "captives" of American trade policy, have expanded their trade relations with other hemispheric traders and worldwide.[3] NAFTA really is two bilateral treaties, one with Canada and one with Mexico. They provide for further liberalization of North American trade relationships and for oversight and enforcement mechanisms. (After President Bush negotiated the basic treaties, President Clinton added side agreements regarding labor and environmental standards.)

Chiefly, the agreement drew Mexico into a coordinated trading relationship, for we already had a bilateral trade treaty with Canada,[4] albeit one weaker than NAFTA. In one sense, NAFTA only makes *de jure* what already was *de facto*. For many years, Canada has been this nation's largest single-nation trading partner; and Mexico recently replaced Japan as our second largest.[5] However, expansion into the rest of the hemisphere, selectively or collectively, will not be an easy undertaking. Nonetheless, there is considerable growth potential in the remaining countries, particularly Chile, Argentina and Brazil. Hence, a political commitment has been made to form a FTAA by the year 2005.[6]

Canada

Canada is the forgotten partner in NAFTA because it has enjoyed a long and fruitful (but not always amicable) trading relationship with the U.S. In fact, few trade partners have interests as aligned as ours with Canada. But that does not mean that Canada's politicians are not under pressure to assure that Canada does not become a "captive" of U.S. trade policy. Happily, such situations are not numerous. The U.S. enjoys a strong, stable and generally positive trade relationship with its northern neighbor. This is particularly true in Asian-Pacific and G-7 circles.[7] But, rapid changes in global trade have left Canada at somewhat at a disadvantage. Its economy lags technologically and depends a good deal on agriculture and fisheries.[8]

There are good economic and political reasons to expand the Canadian economy and make it more independent of America, but this involves significant risks. Moreover, it does not appear that Canada can expand its domestic market without increasing trade with the U.S. and the EU. As competition among them is bound to remain stiff, in the near term Canada is wise to cast its lot with the North American group, while maintaining a degree of independence. Unfortunately, Canada's global trading impact—never very robust—is in eclipse, both at the negotiating table and in market access.[9]

Mexico

Ah, but Mexico is a different story entirely. This new NAFTA partner was sold to the U.S. Congress, the U.S. public and labor and business groups as an opportunity to penetrate a proximate, emerging market and to significantly grow U.S. export trade. There is modest evidence of this.[10] But the real reasons for including Mexico in NAFTA go well beyond this. For years there has been a substantial migration—both legal and illegal—of Mexican nationals into the U.S. Many take low-paying jobs, unattractive to most Americans, and contribute their fair share to the economy. Others, particularly the undocumented ones, are believed by many to constitute a burden on local welfare and education systems, although these facts are disputed.[11] California has denied them basic public services under Proposition 187. Either way, it is pretty well agreed that they flee Mexico because of the lack of jobs and low wages. Then there are the labor, living and environmental conditions they are fleeing. These cannot be neatly confined by national borders but have an impact on the U.S. as well. The polluted environment, the ill-treated worker or uneducated child can easily become an American problem.

Finally there is the drug trade. It is a pursuit that can bring a good income for producers and traffickers. Hence, it is common for poorer countries— including Mexico and other Central and South American countries—to be involved. The government does not have the money or manpower to combat the trade and may actually condone it, for it can be a source of badly needed assets. Until and unless the standard of living in these countries reaches a level that can compete with drug-related income and/or their governments grow strong and wealthy enough to combat it, the drug trade in the Americas will continue. That will cost our government billions of dollars.[12]

For all of these reasons and because the U.S. was looking for a consolation prize should the Uruguay Round of GATT negotiations fail, it simply made economic and political sense for the United States to ally with its southern neighbor, the world's sixteenth largest economy in 1997. That is exactly what NAFTA membership was designed to do. Whatever losses American businesses and workers might suffer as a consequence are likely to be offset eventually by an improved Mexican economy. Indeed, there is already evidence that the regional arrangement is bearing economic fruit for American companies. Hence, Mexico in NAFTA should not be thought of so much as foreign aid as a "pump priming" effort to stabilize Latin America and expand American trade in this hemisphere.

At least that was the position taken before the Mexican peso collapsed in 1994–1995. President Salinas had constructed such an elaborate Ponzi scheme of the Mexican economy that it looked like it was booming even while he was cutting deeply into capital reserves. Toward the end of his term in office, the facade began to crumble, and President Salinas fled Mexico. Economic expansion stopped abruptly; confidence in the Mexican economy and its currency, the peso, was undermined; and the economy imploded almost overnight.[13] Having bet heavily on NAFTA and the Mexican partnership, President Clinton had little choice but to spearhead a massive bailout. But the World Bank and International Monetary Fund were similarly surprised by Mexico's economic collapse. Collectively they fashioned a $40 billion package of credit that allowed Mexico to weather the storm. In the process, mavens of world trade growth were sensitized to both the dangers and the potential of emerging economies.[14] Under the leadership of President Zedillo, Silinas' successor, Mexico already has paid off a large portion of its American loan and seems on the road to full recovery, although its economy remains below expectations.[15] Far from retreating after the Mexican downturn, the U.S. has redoubled its efforts to bring Mexico back and to add other promising economies in Central and South America to the NAFTA mix as well. This proactivity probably is well advised, despite its risks, for it is undoubtedly the speediest way to bring security and prosperity to these countries and to increase their demand for U.S. products and services. Besides, our competitors are interested in their trade as well.

Hence, the debate about NAFTA is a fairly academic one. If the U.S. abandons its effort to rebuild and reform Mexico's economy, the resulting migration and environmental degradation will probably cost us more than NAFTA would. Further, if the Mexican economy recovers and grows (as seems probable) then Mexico is a good long-term investment, and our experience there serves as a prototype for the rest of the hemisphere. It seems shortsighted to give up on the prospect of bringing democracy and market capitalism to our southern neighbors when it is as close as it ever has been. Even if the road is a long one, peppered with surprises yet to come, the Mexicans have proved their mettle and resilience. In just two years, Mexico has bounced back from a "traumatic devaluation" of the peso and its worst recession in 60 years and repaid $12.5 billion on its bailout loan. There is optimism about a rapid recovery even though inflation is near 25 percent and growth has slowed to about 4.5 percent.[16] The recovery will be slow unless America lends its full and continued support. The economies are that intertwined.[17] Any slowdown in the pace of the Mexican recovery would hurt not just their economy but ours as well.

Just a year after the worst point in the crisis, Mexican exports had grown 19 percent compared to the earlier year (to $7.1 billion), while imports recovered 16 percent (to $6.6 billion). Mexican exports in the first quarter of 1996 ($21.8 billion) were the highest in Mexico's history. Exports continued to grow at about a 20 percent rate, predominantly in the areas of petroleum, manufactured goods and agricultural products, to a surplus of near $800 million by mid-1996. Then the surplus position plateaued and began to shrink as Mexican consumption began to rise. Eventually, concerns were raised about the net trade deficit (due primarily to past borrowing).[18] Overall, Mexico's economy seems to be on the mend, meaning that it can gradually repay its debt, improve exports and infrastructure, and—most important to the U.S.—increase consumption of our goods.[19]

That is not to suggest that relations between Mexico and the U.S. are always cordial. Each has its own industries that it wants to protect. NAFTA simply puts their disputes into a treaty context and provides a mechanism to resolve them short of a trade war. Such seemingly innocent initiatives as labeling standards or the accusation that one country has allowed excess goods to be "dumped" in the other contribute to traders' complaints and hence to international frictions.[20] But it is not in either nation's interest to back away from the agreement. Both want to expand their bilateral trade. Obviously, this is more easily achieved within the structure of a joint treaty than outside it.

The truth is that the Mexican economy (and its politics) was changing even before NAFTA was signed. "American jobs" and businesses were migrating, not just to Canada and Mexico but elsewhere in the world as well. There is no *legal* way to prevent such things from happening. The proper response is not to attempt to corral those opportunities that putatively are "ours" but to stay at the cutting edge of trade and innovation, replacing inevitable job and industry loses with better and more productive ones. America succeeds best by opening its markets and insisting that its trading partners do likewise. Trying to protect jobs and industries is not only futile, it is belligerent. Besides, the documented loss of American jobs due to NAFTA (about three-tenths of 1 percent) paled by comparison to industrial job creation (about 2 percent). That study estimated that about 7 percent of the 5.9 million jobs created in the American economy in the two years after NAFTA began could be ascribed to the growth in U.S. exports to Mexico and Canada. (U.S. businesses also are generally positive about NAFTA's job creation.) Maybe the arrangement isn't all some people hoped, but it surely isn't the disaster that others predicted. Besides, there doesn't seem to be any broad-based will to retreat. Indeed, there is every indication that trade in the Western Hemisphere will keep integrating.[21] So, although NAFTA's net impact on U.S.–Mexican trade may be small and largely in the future, our economic and political relationship with Mexico surely has changed. American investment in Mexico now is more secure. Labor and environmental standards are bound to improve. The effort seems well worth it, by any cost-benefit assessment.[22]

Undoubtedly, some of the conflict over NAFTA is generated by different expectations on both sides of the United States' southern border. To some businessmen in the United States, NAFTA was a quick fix that guaranteed them access to a potentially large and expanding market. And, to Salinas' credit, he did "privatize large swatches of the Mexican economy, including its banks." But "[m]any of these divestitures . . . merely transformed former state monopolies into private monopolies or . . . oligarch[ies]." When a rapid return for the U.S. didn't develop immediately—and, indeed, was set back by the collapse of the Mexican economy—impatient Americans soured somewhat on the enterprise.[23]

The posture is somewhat different in Mexico. The trade liberalization that began in 1986 with Salinas' predecessor, President Madrid, has run an uneven course. At its best, it has attracted "huge amounts" of foreign capital and robust economic growth. But it also forced Mexican businesses to compete in a more open economy where the state could not protect weak industries against foreign competition. This has exposed the fragility of Salinas' reforms. If it could, Mexico would have it both ways: access American markets while protecting its own. But NAFTA won't allow that. The interrelationship of the two economies is now so great (an estimated 3,500 U.S. companies were doing business in Mexico in 1994) that not even political unrest, peso devaluation and a trade downturn have shaken the relationship off its foundations. After all, NAFTA provides a prompt and uniform method to resolve disputes.

As trade modernizes and upgrades Mexico's markets, it gives outlets for American goods and technology. Nothing has proved this better than the maquiladora program (south-of-the-border manufacturing plants that import components duty-free, assemble and then export them). The American investment in these enterprises is considerable, but they also are among the most efficient and socially responsible Mexican operations. NAFTA also has had a significant effect on agricultural trade, opening the U.S. market to Mexican exports, but forcing its exporters to improve their efficiency to compete. While the impact of NAFTA may be slow to be felt in many sectors, it has been a boon to Mexican farmers and North American consumers. Nearly 90 percent of the value of Mexican agriculture exports now goes to its NAFTA partners.[24] Hence, it seems that U.S.-Mexican cooperation is here to stay and will grow, contributing to the prosperity of both countries, stabilizing the relationship and helping to address concerns about labor standards, the environment and drugs. For—as said before—the NAFTA program is about equal parts economics and foreign policy.[25]

Of course, Mexico is not as stable and predictable as one might hope. In the recent past it has experienced guerrilla warfare, political assassinations and high-level corruption, in addition to the economic instability noted. But these problems are not unusual for developing economies in Latin America and elsewhere in the world. If America and its capitalists and businesses mean to guide the process and profit from it, then the risks involved are part of the bargain. Just recently (July 1997), the dominant Institutional Revolutionary Party (PRI) lost control of the Mexican Congress for the first time in its 70-year history. But the power-sharing arrangement that President Zedillo now faces gives him and his party more political legitimacy and absorbs his opponents into Mexico's recovery program. After all, the return to a healthy economy shouldn't be thwarted within Mexico itself and, whatever form it takes it, is more likely to succeed if it is broad-based. The only serious concern is that the new Congress will abandon Zedillo's outward-looking macroeconomic growth policies in favor of budget-busting, populist programs. Only time will tell, but Mexico has newly sought a $3.5 billion standby loan commitment to see them through this period. With American help, they almost certainly will make it. As soon as the Mexican economy stabilizes and begins to grow, the way will be clear for further trade alliances with the rest of Latin America, many of them already underway.[26]

Has NAFTA succeeded? An excellent study done for the U.S. Congress in 1992 stated that the treaty would have "little impact" in the first five years and may not have a measurable impact for fifteen years (the term of the treaty). Furthermore, that impact would vary considerably by trade sector. Among the sectors most affected are the automotive, agricultural goods, electronics and apparel/textiles sectors. But these are industries that have been downsizing in the U.S. and migrating elsewhere for years. Besides, the goods produced, from apparel to computers, often incorporate American-made components and are sold at competitive prices on both sides of the border. For example, the Mexican and Caribbean apparel industry is credited with creating 50,000 textile jobs in the United States. And Mexican farmers supply a rising percentage of fresh produce to the U.S., while Mexican demand for U.S. beef rises at the same time. Essentially, NAFTA links Mexico's future to our own. In the long term, that seems to be best for all concerned.[27]

One U.S. government study of job losses attributable to NAFTA in its first two years estimated that about 52,500 jobs would be lost at about 400 plants in eighteen industries due to the treaty. The apparel and electronics industries alone accounted for 30 percent of the losses. But this must be contrasted with an estimated 414,400 gross jobs that were supported by the growth in U.S. exports to Canada and Mexico in those two years (about $26 billion to Canada and $4 billion to Mexico, despite its downturn). Since every billion dollars in U.S. exports to our NAFTA partners or elsewhere supports about 14,000 U.S. jobs, any growth in exports would appear to counterbalance any loss of U.S. jobs due to NAFTA. It is a blow to the job losers, of course, but U.S. jobs are lost and gained and migrate constantly. NAFTA might be one reason, but so might any trade treaty. Despite the current wave of provincialism, the U.S. surely isn't going to stop negotiating them. Indeed, business cycles probably produce and terminate more jobs than all trade treaties combined. Furthermore, those workers who are certified by the Department of Labor to have lost their jobs due to NAFTA (some 133,000 of them in the agreement's first three and one-half years), are eligible to receive training, extended unemployment compensation and/ or money for job search or moving to soften the blow. Besides, according to MIT's Professor Krugman, the "whole idea of counting jobs gained and lost [in trade deals] . . . [is] a misunderstanding of the way the U.S. economy works."[28]

Hence, it can hardly be argued that NAFTA is a failure. The negative consequences highlighted in the general-circulation media is more specific than generic. Every objective study of NAFTA has pronounced it to be a positive benefit in the aggregate—improving trade among NAFTA partners, increasing economic integration and improving labor and environmental standards. Evidence shows that Mexican tariffs are continuing to shrink, that trade in liberalized sectors is growing more rapidly than trade in protected sectors and that NAFTA-prompted job displacements have been "grossly overestimat[ed]."

Indeed, there has been an "explosion" of export/import trade with Mexico (beginning before NAFTA). "In 1996, nearly one-third of U.S. two-way trade in goods with the world was with Canada and Mexico ($421 billion)." It has grown at a 44 percent rate since NAFTA was signed, compared to a 33 percent growth rate for the rest of the world. In the first quarter of 1997, our NAFTA partners accounted for 53 percent of the growth in U.S. exports. U.S. exports to Mexico grew by more than 36 percent ($15.2 billion) from 1993 to a record high in 1996, despite a 3.3 percent contraction in Mexican consumption. Moreover, NAFTA brought average tariffs in Mexico down from 10 percent in 1993 to 2.9 percent in 1996.[29] In time, economic growth should bring a range of infrastructure, political and social improvements. The first step is to improve wages and working conditions, leading to improvements on the social and political fronts. Businesses must not be allowed to exploit workers or the environment, but neither should populist programs discourage business expansion. Finally, revenues from business expansion must be channeled into social improvement, not private wealth.[30]

It cannot be denied that NAFTA has created one of the largest and richest markets in the world, with something like 360 million consumers and almost $9 trillion in annual output (about 23 percent of the world total). Mexico is one of our fastest growing export opportunities, double those in Korea and Taiwan and three times those in Hong Kong in 1991. Mexico spends 70 cents of every trade dollar on U.S. goods. It only makes sense to include it in our trading plans and sphere of influence. If not today, then in due course, the wisdom of this initiative—as well as its economic benefits—is bound to become evident.[31] Far from proving a failure, NAFTA has improved trade relations and is serving as a prototype.[32] The America's trade issue, then, is not NAFTA at all. That seems quite settled. The question is: what will come *afta* NAFTA. Shall we make the same kind of project of the rest of the Latin America?

THE FREE TRADE AREA OF THE AMERICAS (FTAA)

If linking the Canadian, Mexican and U.S. economies together in 1994 through NAFTA was such a difficult and potentially divisive exercise, with only modest returns to date, why would President Clinton want to expand the enterprise to the rest of the Americas? After all, the Canadian economy ($584 billion in GDP in 1997) and the Mexican economy ($349 billion) add very little to our huge domestic economy (about $8 trillion). The rest of the Americas would add only $1.6 trillion more. Wouldn't the cost in time and money (and political capital) far outweigh the gains?

Perhaps, but only if the global economy was static. It is not, of course. Rather, U.S. businesses and capitalists are constantly looking for new markets into which to expand. And Western hemispheric markets are as attractive as any, if they provide a decent rate of return. Besides the U.S. has always had a possessory attitude toward the Americas. Moreover, aware of their potential and attractiveness to other global traders, emerging economies in the Americas are organizing themselves and entering bilateral relationships with other trading groups, including our NAFTA partners. The potential is decidedly there, but the pace and goal are uncertain. Other global trading events may eventually subsume the project, or it may go through a period of north, south, central polarization. But, it is clear for the moment that the United States, in order to preserve its own preeminence, will have to share some of its benefits with nations that would otherwise cause us serious problems and oppose us in international tribunals. It is far wiser to include them, and NAFTA/FTAA purports to do so.[33]

Until recently, Latin American countries didn't seem worth the bother, what with their steady round of revolutions, failed attempts at democracy and unstable economies. Many persons had written off Latin America as a growth market, especially when compared with Asia or Central and Eastern Europe. They may be right. The latter are quite large, and a number of countries in those regions have undertaken market reforms in recent years. By comparison, the Latin America market (beyond Mexico) is relatively smaller and needs considerable infrastructure and political reform to compete in today's marketplace. On the other hand, several South American countries have as much potential as other emerging economies and are closer to the U.S. Lately these countries (especially Argentina, Brazil and Chile) have moved significantly toward democracy and a free market model. They have become attractive and active in world trade circles. Although Mexico is America's second largest trading partner, U.S. FDI in Brazil has been greater than in Mexico in the 1990s.[34]

So China, Japan and the EU—as well as the U.S. and its NAFTA partners—have all expressed interest in an alliance with these southern nations. In addition, some have banded together in loose trading groups to bolster their own internal trade and improve their negotiating position. Two of these groups are the Andean group (Columbia, Venezuela, Peru, Ecuador and Bolivia) and Mercosur (Argentina, Brazil, Paraguay and Uruguay), the latter group being the most active and dominant of the two.

The Mexican peso crisis could have caused South American economies to question their direction and fuel a return to populism. Instead, the crisis was a wake-up call for the region. Most Latin American political leaders realized that the reform process must intensify in order to build truly robust economies. The only question is whether the people, who initially supported and/or tolerated reform, will continue to do so. In most cases, inflation has been brought under control, but growth in trade and employment has been sluggish. What is needed is a change from low to high value-added exports, an increase in savings and FDI and improved infrastructure and education. It is not likely to happen without American involvement. Meanwhile, there are many other countries competing with the U.S. for Latin America's attention.

That is why, in the fall of 1997, President Clinton visited three emerging economies in South America (Argentina, Brazil and Venezuela), which, along with Chile, represent some of the most promising prospects in the region. He did not want to lose trade opportunities in his own backyard. Because of the unpopularity of NAFTA, however, he will have to invest considerable political capital if he wants a Free Trade Association of the Americas by the agreed target date of 2005. He also must attract outside capital and know-how. There is no doubt that there are intriguing opportunities in Latin America and a potentially large market to be serviced. But there are equal opportunities elsewhere, and U.S. capital may be more "risk adverse" to Latin America (given its history) than in, say, Europe or Asia. The FTAA is far from a done deal. The key seems to be to hold on to the NAFTA market while expanding into others. Mr. Clinton realizes, as do U.S. businesses that have invested in Latin America, that if he is to sustain the "quiet but impressive revolution" there, involving energy (oil), intellectual property protection, the environment, and narcotics, then he must make Latin America and the FTAA a top agenda item.[35]

During his South American trip, President Clinton exhorted key South American countries to persevere in and even to accelerate their effort to establish competitive, free-market economies. He also hoped that highlighting their progress would prod Congress to renew his fast-track authority. Without that he has little hope of breathing new life into the lagging FTAA initiative. Congress was reluctant to give that authority because NAFTA has been so controversial.[36] This "new American provincialism," particularly strong among labor and environmental groups, may prove unwise. The leading economies of Latin America appear to have turned a very significant corner. Democratic government is more stable. Crime and corruption are down. Economic stability and regulation is increasing, and they are growing at two or three times the rate of highly industrialized countries. Recent fiscal reversals in Southeast Asia have cooled interest in that region. And, while some of that insecurity has translated to South America, it may be unwarranted.[37]

Western Hemispheric nations consume more U.S. exports than any other region (38 percent versus 31 percent for the Pacific Rim, including Japan, and 21 percent to the European Union). Three-quarters of this trade is with our NAFTA partners, Canada and Mexico. Only 22 percent is with the rest of the Americas. However, the latter trade is growing rapidly. In 1996, the

U.S. exported more to Costa Rica than it did to all of Eastern Europe, and Brazil bought more from us than China. Moreover, this hemisphere is increasingly a target for investment, attracting 30 percent of U.S. foreign direct investment in 1994 ($188 billion of $612 billion) versus 49 percent in Europe and 18 percent in the Pacific Rim. This has resulted in a large manufacturing trade surplus in this hemisphere ($24 billion in 1994), whereas there was a $147 billion deficit with Asia in that year.

Of 26 countries in the region, 23 have made "far-reaching" trade reforms, 24 have "appreciably" decontrolled their financial sectors and half have carried out significant privatization. The U.S. Trade and Development Agency has called South America a "golden opportunity for U.S. exporters" but warned them not to delay entering that market because "international competition is intensifying." Many have not delayed. U.S. citizens invested more than $5.1 billion in Argentina alone in the first six months of 1996 (41 percent of its FDI for that period). In Brazil, it was estimated that mergers and joint ventures would involve at least 600 domestic firms in 1996, more than double the prior year, for a value of $7 billion. During his South American junket, President Clinton estimated that every 1 percent rise in the Latin American economy equated to $5 billion in exported U.S. goods and services and supported 100,000 jobs at home.[38] Not all Latin American economies have profited equally from this phenomenon, however, and there is no guarantee that it will continue unabated. Indeed, considering the multitude of problems remaining to be addressed, setbacks are almost certain, not to mention frictions over the pace and terms of market opening. Protectionism dies hard, and suspicion of the "Yanqui colossus" to the north continues.[39]

President Clinton's trip favored the two largest economies in the region, Brazil and Argentina (the ninth and seventeenth largest economies in the world, respectively), and Venezuela, a large oil producer (and the world's 42nd leading economy). He bypassed one of South America's most efficient economies, Chile (45th in rank). But recent negotiations with Chile concerning accession to NAFTA should have left no doubt about its importance to the U.S.

Brazil's economy, at $580 billion (just behind Russia), is the largest in the four-nation Southern Common Market trading bloc (Mercosur). Brazil and the U.S. have not always seen eye-to-eye on important trade issues. This includes the establishment of an FTAA by 2005.[40] That has not chilled U.S. business and investor interest in Brazil, however. U.S. investors were the first to buy a portion of Brazil's national rail lines when it began to be privatized in early 1996. A state electric company, bank and mining firm are also scheduled to go on the block, and plans to open Brazil's telecommunications market have been accelerated.[41] Despite its leadership role among South American countries, Brazil is not out of the woods. The government is burdened by heavy debt and debt-service costs. As it modernizes, its trade surplus has declined into deficit, and the fallout from the Asian contagion has pushed it into recession. This naturally encourages protectionism. Nonetheless, Brazil seems to be developing into a full market economy. Only the political will flags from time to time.[42]

Brazil's problems are symptomatic of the whole of South America and of developing economies generally. What makes Brazil special is that American financial exposure there is enormous. More than 2,000 U.S. companies operate in Brazil, including 405 of the Fortune 500. The Federal Reserve estimates U.S. bank exposure at $27.2 billion (more than that in Switzerland, Italy or Canada). Brazil accounts for 45 percent of the region's output and, while it absorbs only 3 percent of U.S. exports, the region as a whole absorbs 18 percent. A loss of confidence in Brazil would produce a sharp downtown in all Latin American economies, with a corresponding impact on the U.S.

Investor confidence, shaken by the meltdown in Asia and the political chaos and ruble devaluation in Russia, was bound to start flagging in other emerging markets as well. Latin American economies were especially vulnerable, including its two largest: Mexico and Brazil. Having had a similar experience in 1994 and as a NAFTA member, Mexico seemed better able to cope. But Brazil, the world's eighth largest economy, needed a $41.5 billion recovery package from the IMF and other nations and allowed its currency (the real) to float (and devalue) in order to weather the storm. U.S. financial markets reacted immediately and negatively, but then they promptly recovered.

It is too soon to tell whether Brazil's (and Latin America's) economic problems are temporary or chronic. In the short term, their shakiness and slow growth has put in doubt the ambitious plan for an FTAA. But the speed of the recovery of international financial markets after Brazil allowed its currency to float suggests that even sharp downturns in emerging economies are being assimilated as part of the risk of globalization and that a collaborative international response buffer their consequences.[43] If Brazil disappoints, that could mean capital flight from weaker Latin American economies as well.

Venezuela probably is the most fragile of the countries President Clinton visited. But, as the main supplier of oil to the United States and the seventh largest investor in our economy, it is likely to get the support it needs to keep its "quiet revolution" on track. Economic expansion was back up to 4 percent in the first half of 1997. Among other believers, Chrysler is producing Neons and Jeeps at a $50 million plant near Caracas. But Venezuela's continued progress depends heavily on steady earnings from oil sales, its ability to fully participate in the regional economy and political will. An unknown reformer was elected president in 1998, but he seems to support economic reform. In short, things look generally positive, but it is too early to tell.[44]

The third country on President Clinton's itinerary was Argentina. Like Brazil, Argentina is a member of Mercosur. But, unlike Brazil, Argentina enjoys warm relations with the U.S. Both nations seem fully invested in improving bilateral trade and planning for a hemispheric free trade zone by the year 2005. The U.S. is the largest single foreign investor in Argentina, at an average of some $2 billion a year. Bilateral trade between the two nations has grown from around $2 billion in 1990 to just short of $7 billion in 1996. But Argentina's robust market growth ($18.1 billion in foreign direct investment in 1994 and 1995) does not reflect just investments by Ford, TCI Communications and General Motors. Other companies in South America, Canada and the EU also contribute to its startling growth. Argentina also has pushed for relationships with the Association of Southeast Asian Nations (ASEAN). These relationships broaden Latin America's economic base and increase its bargaining power in trade negotiations. Stronger interregional trading blocs will make an FTAA more difficult to achieve or its terms less favorable to the United States.[45]

There are casualties in the move towards capitalism, of course, and they are bound to make themselves felt from time to time. The shift in economic policy has meant job cuts in the public and private sectors and reduced social benefits. Although hyperinflation has been brought under control in most large South American economies, more economic reform, spending cuts and tax increases will be needed to balance budgets after years of deficit spending. This is particularly hard on unskilled labor, which is being marginalized by the push to greater efficiency and trade competitiveness. They perceive disparities in wealth to reflect a corrupt system, and to a degree it does. But it is equally the result of a failure to adjust to globalization.[46]

A country not visited by President Clinton, but one with close trading ties with the United States, is Chile. At one point in time, it was thought that Chile might become the fourth member of NAFTA. It still may. But the Mexican peso crisis put a "chill" on NAFTA expansion for the time being. That has not slowed Chile's market renaissance, however. In the 1980s, it began to promote exports, regulate its economy and encourage foreign direct investment. As a result, Chile is today "Latin America's most successful economy," according to an OECD report. Chile is the tenth largest recipient of foreign direct investment outside the 29-member OECD for the 1985–1995 period and ranked 28th worldwide. Over 85 percent of its $17.5 billion in foreign investment comes from OECD countries, a tribute to Chile's economic and political stability and also to its relatively open market.[47] Because of its preferred position, Chile has not been overly concerned about its temporary exclusion from NAFTA. Unlike Mexico, Chile has not seen NAFTA membership as "a life or death matter." Instead, it has cemented its trading ties with Mercosur; its South American neighbors, Columbia, Ecuador and Venezuela; and our NAFTA partners, Canada and Mexico. Other countries in Latin America are not making the transition nearly as speedily as those mentioned, because of both economic and political forces. Market opening has been cautious, and the prospect of a return to populism is ever present.

The leading Latin American trade groups aren't standing still either. Mercosur has a population in excess of 212 million (about 80 percent that of the U.S.) and a combined real GDP of over one trillion dollars (about one-sixth that of the U.S.). But it is a long way from being a common market of the EU variety. Most trade within Mercosur is tariff-free, with free trade in all products scheduled for the year 2000. A common external tariff applies to most products. Trade among the Mercosur countries grew at an average of 27 percent annually from 1990 to 1995, while its trade with the rest of the world expanded at a 7.5 percent annual pace. Nevertheless, Mercosur needs to integrate further to protect its gains, and this will cut more deeply into each nation's sovereignty. It needs a better and more uniform infrastructure, more coordination of fiscal and tax policy and a competition and anti-dumping code. Its members still compete with one another for foreign capital, and Brazil—with about 70 percent of the group's population and production—sometimes strikes off on its own. Despite its weaknesses, however, Mercosur is a force to be reckoned with. It may assert itself in negotiations concerning the Free Trade Association of the Americas. Since it clearly is the dominant trading group in South America, other nations in the region, including Bolivia and Venezuela, are lining up to associate with or to join the customs union.

The mutual courtship of the EU and Mercosur has led to the first-ever cooperation agreement between two customs unions (signed December 15, 1995, in Madrid). It helped each gain leverage in their relation with the United States. The agreement calls for regular, high-level political dialogue; economic cooperation; reciprocal investment; and trade cooperation leading to trade liberalization. The EU has been among Mercosur's leading trade partners, accounting for 26 percent of its total trade between 1985 and 1992. Since 1990, EU exports to the region have risen sharply. The EU also is one of the largest investors in the region. Mercosur members attract about 70 percent of EU investment in Latin America. The EU did not want to concede the Western Hemispheric market to the U.S. and hasn't. Mercosur members wanted alternatives to the American market, both to grow their economies and to increase its leverage in trade negotiations with the U.S. After NAFTA, the EU and Japan, Mercosur is the fourth largest trading bloc in the world, but that is by some margin.[48]

But Mercosur was not content with the EU deal alone. It also is working on formal trade relations with our NAFTA partners, Canada and Mexico, and Andean Pact countries. Canada and Mexico make no bones about the fact that they would prefer a broadening of the NAFTA into an FTAA, rather than sign a series of bilateral treaties with Mercosur and other Latin American blocs. Mercosur nations, on the other hand, are not as excited by the FTAA initiative, for they know they would be overshadowed by their larger North American partners.[49]

Compared to Mercosur, the Andean Pact group is much smaller and more loosely organized. Nonetheless, its five members have a combined GDP exceeding $190 billion and a population of over 100 million. Currently, it is the third largest trading bloc in the Hemisphere; after NAFTA and Mercosur. Two other subregional trading groups currently exist in the Americas. They are the Central American Common Market (CACM), consisting of Costa Rica, El Salvador, Guatemala, Honduras and Nicaragua (with Belize and Panama as associates); and the Caribbean Community Common Market (CARICOM), consisting of thirteen independent countries in the Caribbean basin, many of them islands. Both are small and more customs unions than common markets. Yet, they have begun to grow rapidly and afford their members a better consultative and negotiating platform than if they were to proceed into FTAA negotiations alone. In August 1995, an Association of Caribbean States (ACS) was created, which cuts across some of these blocs and includes Mexico and other Central and South American countries.[50]

With so many trade groupings in the Americas, it takes more than a little chutzpah to suggest that they are simply "building blocks" toward an FTAA. Some blocs quite demonstrably want to hold on to domestic or regional preferences for a while longer. How long they can do so is questionable.[51] Neither the U.S. nor its NAFTA partners have been shy about criticizing Latin American nations for violating their WTO obligations. Trade might grow faster in an FTAA if it had concrete rules and an enforcement mechanism. That is exactly what some countries fear. But the facts clearly show that the countries that have liberalized fastest and with the greatest discipline have the strongest economies and the sharpest growth curves. Protectionism only perpetuates non-competitiveness.

As trade agreements and subregional groupings continue to evolve in South America, they may put President Clinton's plan for a Free Trade Association of the Americas out of reach. At least Chile's director of external policy planning has warned that it is "dangerous" to assume that new Latin American trading arrangements will lead inevitably to an FTAA. The blocs are advancing at different rates and have different trading priorities.[52] Maybe an FTAA *is* in the cards, however—if not in the year 2005, then soon thereafter. That is what 34 nations committed to at the 1994 Summit of the Americas in Miami. And regular summits and working group meetings continue to be held.[53] Progress is likely to be slow, however, unless President Clinton gets "fast track" negotiating authority.

THE FTAA AND "FAST TRACK" AUTHORITY

"Fast track" negotiating authority means that Congress gives the president the authority to negotiate trade deals that Congress can later only approve or reject but cannot alter. Few of our trading partners, including those in Latin America, want to negotiate trade agreements with the U.S. in the absence of such authority. The reason is that, in the absence of fast track, it is almost certain that some feature of the deal would displease enough legislators that it would be amended. That would ruin the whole deal. In complex trade agreements each party sacrifices something to get something else. Veto one element, and it's back to the negotiating table. Rejection is less likely if the treaty is negotiated under fast track authority. Then it is an all-or-nothing vote. Usually there is enough in the treaty package to get legislative approval. This puts the U.S. on a parallel with its negotiating partners. Their negotiators represent governments that are in power because they (or a coalition they head) have a majority of seats in the national legislature. Hence, it rarely is a problem for the government in power to get the legislature to ratify a treaty it negotiates. Because a number of Americans are upset that NAFTA didn't produce the boom in U.S. export trade that some prophesied or that it has cost U.S. jobs or compromised our labor and environmental standards, Congress was reluctant to give the president fast track authority after it expired in April 1994. As a result, FTAA negotiations have gone slowly.

Our Latin American neighbors also have selfish reasons for delaying the start of serious FTAA negotiations. In general, their economies improve every day. So, the longer that serious FTAA negotiations are delayed, the stronger their bargaining position. This is especially true if they can resolve some of their own differences and present a united front. Also, the delay allows Latin American traders to dilute U.S. influence.[54]

The other reason that FTAA negotiations have been on the slow track is that there is a serious difference of opinion between South American countries (particularly Brazil) and the U.S. concerning the pace and priority of the trade negotiations. Thus far the 34 American nations that launched FTAA negotiations have agreed that it should be in place by the year 2005 and that it should be a single agreement. However, the U.S. and Canada wanted to begin talks about reducing tariffs immediately after the FTAA summit in Santiago in April 1997. Brazil, speaking on behalf of its Mercosur partners, wanted the talks to proceed in three stages. They would address business deregulation first, then move on to trade-related rules and deal with tariff reduction last, possibly in 2003. This would give Latin American countries more time to prepare their economies for free-trade competition, meanwhile protecting them and avoiding the political backlash likely to follow market opening. Meantime, a number of initiatives—both public and private—were being taken to advance the FTAA negotiations and keep them on track. The most important are ongoing meetings at ministerial level. They have worked out a legal framework for the FTAA negotiations and "standstill" (no new trade barriers) provisions to apply while they are going on. Twelve FTAA "working groups" also continue their work on trade issues, ranging from rules of origin to competition and dispute settlement.[55]

Business leaders also have advised on individual sector agreements and promoted fast track authority to complete the deal as soon as possible. A number of state governors have pressed for fast track authority as well. All know that a formal and prompt opening of the Latin American market is advantageous to them or their constituents.[56] Mexico is less enthusiastic, for it enjoys special trade advantages through NAFTA and hoped to "broker" trading relationships between North and South America.[57]

Of course, this assumes that the emerging Latin American economies are based on better fundamentals than Asia's "little tigers." Latin America's leading economies were not immune from Asia's economic meltdown, after all. But they seem to be "less vulnerable to capital flight," and their banks are not as overextended as Asia's were. Nonetheless, there are "troubling signs" in Latin America's economies.[58]

Whether an FTAA can be accomplished by the agreed-upon date of 2005 is unlikely. Smaller Latin American countries will have to be cut some slack, and even the large traders may need help. But the U.S. remains insistent that the proposed FTAA be no weaker than NAFTA or the WTO. That is, the United States wants the FTAA to contribute to world trade harmonization. Given the number and diversity of the nations involved (over twice those in the EU), it is a delicate balancing act. But, with perseverance and a bit of luck, this bold initiative may yet succeed.[59] The FTAA, however, is just another piece of the global trade puzzle.

Chapter 8

The European Union: Can It Compete?

The largest trading bloc in the world today is the EU, with 374 million inhabitants (versus 268 million in the U.S.) and a gross domestic product (GDP) of $8.5 trillion in 1997 (versus $7.7 trillion in the U.S.)[1]

The EU is a true customs union, with supranational ("federalizing") institutions engaged in the massive undertaking of harmonizing European commercial law. The question is whether the EU will *act* like the trading bloc it is and have an equivalent influence on world trade. For the Union has continued to be rather enigmatic, pulling apart along national lines politically while integrating quite steadily commercially. Which of these two inapposite forces will win out? Is Europe on the verge of further integration (a single market, single currency and more)? Or is it on the verge of a meltdown (an à la carte program, with various members moving at variable speeds)? Most important, can Europe compete in the world marketplace, or will it turn protectionist and decline to cooperate with the U.S. in the process of trade globalization?

A BIT OF BACKGROUND

The modern conception of a unified Europe was hatched following World War II. It was meant to heal the age-old enmity between France and Germany and to rebuild the continent. Among its advocates were Jean Monet, Robert Schuman and even Winston Churchill (although he didn't include Britain).[2] The U.S. offered economic aid through the Marshall Plan, but only if the European states cooperated in the rebuilding process.[3] The offer was more than *noblesse oblige*, however. The U.S. wanted a strong buffer between itself and Stalin's emerging Soviet state and a rapid restoration of our most important export market in order to convert our economy to a postwar footing. Hence, in 1952, the European Coal and Steel Community (ECSC) was founded to oversee trade in the two most important components of war but also those most central to industrial rebuilding. The ECSC was comprised of six member states: Belgium, France, Germany, Italy, Luxembourg and the Netherlands.

It was so successful that in 1958 the same six states formed the European Economic Community (EEC) (First Treaty of Rome) and the European Atomic Energy Community (Euratom) to regulate the use of atomic power (Second Treaty of Rome). Subsequently, a series of treaties and new member states were added to produce the European Union of today. The most notable of the treaties were the Merger Treaty, which brought all three communities under one set of institutions; the Single European Act, to complete the single market; and the Treaty of European Union (or "Maastricht" treaty), meant to improve legislation, add competencies, and particularly to launch a single currency. The Maastricht Treaty also added two new "pillars" to the EU.

THREE PILLARS

I think it is correct to say that the European *Community* today is the original pillar (the common market); while the European *Union* consists of Pillars II and III, where greater European unity will cut more deeply into national sovereignty. However, in this book I shall use the terms "Community" and "Union" interchangeably to mean the whole of the enterprise.

Pillars II (the Common Foreign and Security Policy, or CFSP) and III (Justice and Home Affairs) might be thought of as the "union" features of the EU. These are new with the Maasatricht Treaty of 1992. These "deepening" (unifying) features of the amended treaty are much more embryonic. Whereas much of the decision-making in the economic community (Pillar I) is consigned to the supranational institutions of the EU in Brussels, Strasbourg and Luxembourg, Pillars II and III are based on intergovernmental cooperation. This means that each state has a veto, and that their broad agreements to collaborate are not legally binding.

In the meantime, the EU was expanding. Denmark, Ireland and the United Kingdom joined in 1972. (Norway was offered accession too, but a domestic referendum defeated it.) In 1981, Greece joined. Portugal and Spain joined in 1986, and Austria, Finland and Sweden became members in 1995. (Again Norway was offered the chance, but refused). So we have today an EU of fifteen member states, fresh from another intergovernmental conference (IGC) to revise the treaties yet again. The latest treaty was signed in Amsterdam in June 1997 and came into force in mid-1999. The original purpose of the Amsterdam Treaty was to streamline the Community's institutions and decision-making process to prepare it for further cohesion and enlargement. But, with the stresses of a sluggish market and the imminent launch of a single currency, it fell far short of its goals.[4]

Thus, if the EU at times seems to have lost its way, still it somehow manages to struggle along from goal to goal. It is evident that it has integrated faster in good economic times than bad, and the late 1990s have not been good to Europe.[5] Yet the process continues, and goals that seem improbable are nonetheless reached; despite numerous differences in history, economic priorities, culture and language among its members.

The U.S. too is somewhat ambivalent about the future of Europe. In the beginning, its reconstruction was a necessity. But, as the EU grew larger, stronger and more independent of U.S. influence, it became as much of a competitor as a collaborator. Although the EU and the U.S. are the world's two largest capitalist trading systems, they do not always agree about how world trade and security should be managed or on the balance of responsibility therefor. Moreover, the U.S. often is engaged in adventures or misadventures its own (Vietnam, Pacific Rim trade).[6] Thus, despite the similarities between the U.S. and the EU, there are many differences as well. They deserve our attention.

Not long ago, the EU was referred as "Fortress Europe." Some people suggested that it would become a "United States of Europe." The first is true to some extent, for the EU is a legitimate customs union, with minimal internal barriers and a common external tariff. It is not uncommon for it to use standards or subsidies to protect or aid its own products and to exclude foreign products.[7] Moreover, it has established preferential trading relationships with other European states through a European Economic Area (EEA) and with African, Caribbean and Pacific (ACP) countries—most former colonies—through the Lomé convention.

Nevertheless, the EU is not a nation-state writ large. It has no land, no completely common currency or language, no citizens (save that they are first nationals of constituent member states), no independent taxing power, and no government save the supranational institutions previously mentioned. Despite the difficulty in defining the EU as a political or economic entity, as a trader it is the closest thing to the U.S. that exists in the world today. It is our largest trading partner and invests more in the U.S. than all other nations combined. Some American companies, for example, Gillette and Caterpillar, earn substantial profits in Europe. Indeed, the European Court has referred to the EU as "a new legal order," which other trading blocs such as NAFTA certainly are not. Moreover, it was established for an "unlimited duration."

Illustrative of its growing influence and cohesion, the EU continued WTO negotiations in the financial services sector after the Americans had walked away from the table. It also has made concerted efforts to establish a closer trading relationship with Asia.[8] Americans may well wonder how this multistate customs union will work out. The EU is not without its problems, however.

The EU has faced some difficult decisions in its 40-year history—institutional reform, expansion and a single currency—but the EU seems to be divided today as seldom before. Part of the reason is structural: different economic and monetary policies. But some problems are chiefly political: should more sovereignty be sacrificed to the central institutions? Can problems (such as unemployment, security, and monetary policy) be better addressed at the national or Community level? If the people and governments of Europe don't favor more cohesion, can they compete in a world economy?[9]

Among the reasons cited for its problems are Europe's rigid labor markets and expensive social programs. But they don't tell the whole story. The pace and nature of world trade has changed and Europe has not.[10] It is not enough to protect European markets; there are world markets to be pursued. Many of the jobs lost in the EU will not be restored—any more than they will in the U.S. European businesses and laborers have to be more proactive.

Then there is the whole notion that *government* (rather than business or individuals) ought to end unemployment, supply services and social support. The expectations are too high, the scope of the vision is too narrow and the timing couldn't be worse.[11]

In June 1996, at Milan, the EU commenced yet another intergovernmental conference. Its goal was to assess the effectiveness of the Maastricht Treaty and to prepare the EU for further integration. These goals were not without contention. A number of political leaders were being criticized for conceding too much power to "Brussels" (the seat of the EU's key institutions). But national policies can't begin to address the multistate problems confronting Europe. If the EU is to play a role in world affairs equal to its economic status, it will have to speak with a single voice. It sometimes seems incapable of doing so, despite the fact that its future may well hang in the balance. However, the EU's history has been a series of ups and downs, and it has rebounded from every lull stronger and more united than before.[12] If it meant to converge further, the 1996–97 IGC would have been a perfect time for it. It had three main goals:

1. to streamline the EU's institutions;
2. to reduce Community decision-making complexity. This means an extension of qualified majority voting (versus unanimity);
3. to revise common policies (such as agriculture), and to introduce an element of "flexibility," so that willing members would not be held back by reluctant ones.[13]

Happily, the single currency was excluded from this summit agenda, but that initiative was unfolding in parallel.

The Commission presents its "work program" to the European Parliament annually, near the turn of each calendar year. The 1997 program, presented by Commission President Jacques Santer in October 1996, held no surprises. The Commission hoped to overhaul Community institutions and expand qualified majority voting, in order to bring new member states into the Community early next century; to reform structural programs that make the EU less competitive and contribute to high unemployment (about twice that of the U.S.); to increase its international influence; and to introduce a single currency on schedule in January 1999. Mr. Santer's mantra was "not more [EU] legislation but better legislation," suggesting that the EU integrate by solid steps, not by gallops as it sometimes did under his predecessor, Jacques Delors. Apart from personality differences between Santer and Delors, the times were different as well.

The "Franco-German bargain" had broken down. It was formed with the European Coal and Steel Community to rebuild Europe. But, over time, the Germans became dedicated Europhiles while the French grew increasingly cautious of Germany's growing influence in Europe and worldwide. For a while, the Germans pretended not to have returned to their prior position of dominance in Europe and the French pretended not to notice that the Germans had. But, with the prospect of a single currency patterned after the Deutsche mark and the EU's expansion into central and eastern Europe (and not the Mediterranean), that relation was stretched to the breaking point. Previously, the Germans shrank from promoting European policies without French involvement, a self-restraint possibly based on the lingering stigma of Nazism. But around the time of the reunification of East and West, Germany stepped out on its own. Britain, which was welcomed into the Union as a counterbalance to the bargain, has split Europe by choosing between Germany and France. And so, when Europe needs unity most, it seems most elusive.[14]

This is not the first time that this has happened. In its short history, the EU has experienced a number economic downturns. At these times, EU member states tend to become introverted and hostile to one another, as if one could succeed without the others. Briefly they may do so, but generally their economies are too integrated for this. Hence, they are obliged by economic circumstances to work together. Otherwise, the single market will never succeed.

On the other hand, Europe has come together in the past just when it seemed to be falling apart. Community law is gradually infusing national law in all of the member states. More cohesion seems inevitable, and probably desirable, if businesses are to be efficient and competitive. Closer economic union will almost certainly lead to closer political union.

However, nation governments are under intense pressure to put national interests above Community interests (as if they were somehow different in the long run). Sooner or later it must occur to those willing to think about it that the only way for the EU member states to become competitive glob-ally is to collaborate at a supranational level. That is, the pressure to unify Europe need not come from within, for it surely will from without. In order to compete with the United States in foreign markets, the EU will have to become more streamlined, unified and decisive. It seems paradoxical to sug-gest this, but today's ambivalence about closer "union" may just be the last gasps of national pride before the launch of a new round of intense growth and integration. It has happened before, in 1987 and 1993, and may again.[15]

While the political debate about further European integration rages su-perficially, legal and economic cohesion proceeds steadily below. It can hard-ly be doubted that trade rules have to be uniform in every EU country. Each nation must be governed by common policies regarding agriculture, fisheries, company formation and their ability to "trade" across national borders. There may be complaints about "laws from Brussels," but there is no disagreement that the EU is good for business. In a 1995 survey, nine of ten British businesses believed that the UK's future lay within Europe. Over half felt that EU membership increased business opportunities in Eu-rope, and 50 percent thought a single currency would be good for business. Moreover, the Community's institutions—particularly the Commission and the European Court—are making certain that Community law is enacted, communicated and enforced.[16] One recent European Court decision even held that a member state was liable in damages to its own citizens for its failure to transpose Community law into national law in a timely fashion.[17]

One way that integration is taking place is *inward* direct investment across EU national borders. In 1994, the fifteen European states had invested $47.7 billion in one another's businesses. This was around 80 percent greater than their extra-EU foreign direct investment of $26.5 billion. This is both good and bad. The EU needs to invest in the rest of the world as well as itself. Some EU nations do, of course (notably Germany, the Neth-erlands and the U.K.). But intra-EU investment (notably France and Spain) helps integration too.

Moreover, despite attractive opportunities elsewhere, in 1995 the lion's share of U.S. foreign direct investment (52 percent of $97 billion) went to the EU. This not only stimulates the European economy but also builds stronger bridges between the world's leading capitalist economies. America won't succeed unless the EU does as well, and vice versa. The reason for the large U.S. investment in Europe is the number of established American ventures there, the EU's relative stability and access to expanding markets in Central and Eastern Europe. The primary mode of investment is through acquisitions and mergers, now nearing historic highs. It is but one more index of global growth and consolidation.[18]

But U.S. firms seem to be capturing the majority of this business. As much as the EU has converged, the Community is not yet as uniform or aggressive as U.S. players.[19] So the EU, despite its size, has not wielded the influence in international arenas that it could or wishes to.[20] Whether the EU's anticipated "deepening" (greater convergence) and "widening" (adding new members) will be achieved is an open question. Can Europe compete? Well, let's look at its institutions and program.

THE COMMUNITY INSTITUTIONS

There are so many good surveys of the European Union's institutional structure and of how those institutions conduct their business[21] that there is no reason to treat the subject exhaustively here. Anyone who is interested in greater depth or needs more guidance on the points raised is referred to these sources. Here I treat the EU institutions only as necessary to develop the thesis of this book. But it must be remembered that the EU treaties (unlike other international treaties that depend on the goodwill and oversight of the signatories for enforcement) created *supranational* institutions, with the power to legislate and enforce that legislation. Its law takes precedence over contrary national legislation.

At first blush, the supranational institutions of the European Union look very much like those of any Western democratic government. The general structure was designed for the ECSC in the early 1950s and, after a series of modifications, continues to manage the EU today. The principal institutions include a Council that makes policy and passes laws; a Commission (chiefly executive, but with important legislative functions); a European Parliament (née Assembly), a co-legislator; and two courts, the European Court of Justice and the Court of First Instance.

This might give the impression that the EU *is* a "United States of Europe." But it would be an error to think so. The countries that formed the first Community or that have joined since were all well-developed sovereign nations. They were not about to create a federal structure that competed too vigorously with their own. Hence, they built into the Community structure certain checks on central authority, making certain that its actions were subject to a high degree of national control, chiefly through the Council.

Attempts to restrain the "federalizing" effects of the EU's central institutions are manifest. The U.S. Constitution starts with the three branches of government (Articles I–III) and devotes only a small amount of space (for example, Article I, section 8) to what the federal government is meant to do. This was done in sweeping terms, aided by a "necessary and proper" clause (the last paragraph of section 8). The Community treaty[22] is quite different. The bulk of the initial treaty (Articles 1–136a and 199–240) was devoted to what the EU is to *do* and how it is to do it (often in some detail). Only a small amount of space (Articles 137–198e) is devoted to its institutions. The EU treaty also contains a "latchstring" clause (Article

235)* that allows the Council, acting unanimously, to take "appropriate measures" if Community action is "necessary . . . [but the] Treaty has not provided the necessary powers." However, this clause has been interpreted narrowly by the European Court.[23]

Further, the Maastricht Treaty introduced a "subsidiarity" principle (Article 3b), stating that the Community will act "only if and insofar as the objectives of the proposed action cannot be sufficiently achieved by the Member States [acting alone] and can therefore, by reason of the scale or effects of the proposed action, be better achieved by the community." Hence, it seems that the founding states of the EU meant to act in concert only when it was to their mutual benefit and did not mean to delegate more sovereignty than was absolutely necessary. This may have been all that the people intended in setting up the United States. Surely they could not have foreseen its present form.[24]

Of course, all of the functions of a centralized government cannot be confined in a short document. There is competition between and among the branches of government for influence (particularly the executive and legislative), and coordinate branches sometimes collaborate to achieve a just end for which there is no clear authority.[25] In such cases, U.S. courts may brush aside minor concerns. But, in the case of the Community, that option is narrow, since the constituent states have not agreed to give it greater authority than the treaties provide, and it is important that the EU always act within its "competencies."[26]

However, if the treaty is to create a single market in Europe, involving the free movement of goods, people, services and capital in the Community (the so-called "four freedoms"), then it should be evident that "welfare tourists," contraband and criminals also will move freely in a borderless Europe. Therefore, what starts as a simple common market soon touches on national concerns like social welfare, immigration, professional standards, crimes and prosecution. Put simply, it is not easy to separate national interests from Community interests; and the latter are almost certain to win out in the end, as they have in the United States.

HOW THE COMMUNITY OPERATES

The treaties make it quite clear that the institutions of the EU must "act within the limits of the powers conferred upon [each of them, respectively]."[27] In theory, this is all the authority the constituent member states have delegated. There is no elastic "necessary and proper" clause in the EU

---

*The titles, articles and sections of the consolidated treates—through Maastricht—were renumbered by the Treaty of Amsterdam. It came into force in May 1999. The treaty sections here would be Articles 1–188, Articles 268–312, Articles 189–267 and Article 308, respectively, under the new numbering system. A conversion table is provided in the Appendix at the rear of the book to help the reader convert cites to the new system.

Treaty, as there is in the U.S. Constitution. But treaty Article 235 does offer a modicum of leeway if the Council acts unanimously. Friends of mine in Europe assure me that the means are found when needed.""[28]

Additionally, the EU has been given "legal personality," in order to sue and be sued and otherwise to carry out the functions of the Community. After all, it is ultimately a legal regime. This does not mean the EU is sovereign, however. Rather the Community "[enjoys] the most extensive legal capacity accorded to legal persons under [the laws of the respective Member States]." This means the EU has corporate status, but is bounded by its charter and may act *ultra varies.*[29]

Legislative initiative lies almost solely with the Commission. This might not be so bad, for the Commission is composed of dedicated Europhiles. The Commission does not enact legislative proposals, however. It only shepherds them along until they are either rejected or passed. Since the European Parliament still plays a minor role (although many of its proposed amendments are adopted), the "keyhole" through which all primary EU legislation must pass is the Council. These are the ministers of the respective member states, acting in the national interest. The steady expansion of qualified (weighted) majority voting, especially its further extension in the Amsterdam Treaty (1997), enables the Community to move forward on most single-market legislation without the risk of an individual member state veto. But the process of Community legislation remains slow and complicated.

The process badly needs simplification, for the current system is a pot-pourri of compromises, each appropriate for its time but now monstrously complex. It can only get worse when the Community expands again, for more national interests will be represented in Council. This seems to be the unhappy consequence of a group of diverse nation-states that seek the benefits of a customs union without a proportional delegation of sovereignty. They have seen the salutary benefits of unification, but many remain phobic about the F-word (federalism). These two visions of Europe cannot permanently coexist.

Some commentators have suggested that the Council should become the upper house (like the U.S. Senate) and the European Parliament the lower house (like the U.S. House of Representatives) in a new Community legislative structure. This proposal institutionalizes the current state of affairs under the co-decision procedure, for it calls for a Conciliation Committee (very like joint committees of Congress) to iron out differences when the two bodies can't agree on legislation. But that change would diminish national influence in at least two ways. First, assuming a positive vote of both houses would be needed to pass Community legislation, the Council would lose its ability to pass legislation after mere consultation or to override the Parliament's objections (under the cooperation procedure). Second, the Council would sit in regular session with Parliament, which would call for a greater degree of power-sharing and reduce the role of Council ministers in the central government back home.

Further streamlining will not occur until the states become more comfortable with the Community dimension, which would appear to be some years in the future. Persons who seek a more detailed explanation of Community legislative practices can readily get it,[30] so I propose to discuss the equally confusing forms that Community actions might take.

Forms of Community Action

In the United States, federal actions are fairly straightforward. Congressional legislation becomes the supreme law of the land, and the Supreme Court can overrule lower courts, including state courts. It is not so simple in the European Union. Part of the reason is that the founding members did not want to create a federal colossus to reign over their national systems.

According to the treaties, Community institutions may take action in five ways: they may "make regulations and issue directives, take decisions, make recommendations or deliver opinions."[31] "A regulation shall have general application [and] shall be binding in its entirety and directly applicable in all Member States." This is the closest thing to U.S. federal legislation that the EU has. But acceptable regulations became so detailed and it took so long to satisfy all member states with their content that they often were obsolete before they were approved. Hence, regulations were largely abandoned around 1987 in favor of directives, thereby facilitating the adoption of a host of single market legislation as part of the 1992 program.

Directives are "binding, as to the result to be achieved"; however, they "leave to the national authorities the choice of form and methods [of implementation]." There are equivalents in the U.S., but not many. This legislative form was put in the treaty to give national authorities some role in the EU legislative process. Because of this leeway, a directive is easier to pass than a regulation. However, directives present some distinct problems as well. Each individual member state has the task of "transposing" the directive into national law. The state legislatures have no choice but to do so, but they may not do so accurately, completely or by the time required. To spur them on, the European Court recently has held that they can be held liable for their failure.[32]

A "decision" is binding in its entirety upon those to whom it is addressed. The most familiar form of "decision" is that of the European courts. These may be rendered against Community institutions, member states, or individuals. But, in certain circumstances, the Council and Commission can take decisions as well. Decisions are directed to specific entities, however, such as a court decision that a member state has violated its treaty obligations[33] or a Commission decision that anti-competitive behavior should be enjoined.[34] Regulations and directives more often are directed to the entire group of member states. Since regulations, directives and decisions are binding and have legal effect, they may be challenged in the European court by anyone with the requisite standing. Recommendations and opinions, not being legally "binding," do not produce "legal effects" and are not reviewable by the Court.[35]

However, the European Court has held that it does not matter what form a Community act takes; its "effect" is what matters. Each act must have a clearly stated (and legitimate) basis in the treaty; otherwise, those affected would not know the reason for it and the Court would have no basis upon which to review its legality. Without a sound treaty basis, the Community may be acting *ultra varies.*[36]

Moreover, several passages of the treaty allow individual member states to "derogate" from Community legislation on the grounds of public morality, public security or human and animal health, for example, as long as this is not done arbitrarily or as a disguised protection of national markets.[37] The signatory states were concerned about opening their borders to people and goods without the assurance that they could inspect and, if need be, expel those persons or things that might prove harmful to public order or health. Historically, European states were suspicious of their neighbors and were not likely to accept a treaty of this sort without reserving certain national prerogatives. On the other hand, national security and national health concerns have been raised more than once (not just in Europe) to selfishly protect national markets. This rationale for protectionism is contrary to the "common" market principle upon which the treaties were founded. In practice, derogations have been interpreted very strictly by the European Court.[38] In doing so, the Court held the member states to their core bargain: to create a unified market with the fewest possible restrictions on the movement of goods, workers, services or capital.

Attacks on Community Action

Article 173 of the treaty specifies that the "Court of Justice shall review the legality of acts adopted [by the Parliament, Council, Commission or European Central Bank, or combinations of them, [if] . . . intended to produce legal effects." Thus, the treaty-drafters reposed their faith in the independence and expertise of the Community judiciary to say "what the law is." They were not willing to say that the Court's judgment was supreme (took "precedence" over national law), however. The Court did that for itself in two early landmark decisions.[39] They held that "the Community constitutes a new legal order . . . for the benefit of which the [member] states have limited their sovereign rights, albeit within limited fields, and [Community law binds] not only member states, but also their nationals." Hence, Community law could impose obligations and confer rights, independent of member state law, that must be recognized in national courts.

Consequently, "the law stemming from the Treaty, an independent source of law, could . . . not be overridden by domestic legal provisions . . . without being deprived of its character as Community Law and without the legal basis of the Community itself being called into question." This surprised some Europeans, but it could not have been otherwise. If there was to be a Community, it had to bind all equally, according to the European Court.

Treaty Article 173 also specifies what attacks on Community action the Court has jurisdiction to hear. They are four in number: "lack of competence, infringement of an essential procedural requirement, infringement of [the] Treaty or of any rule of law relating to its application, or misuse of powers." Although this enumeration might seem a little odd by American standards, it is relatively straightforward and illuminated by the cases.

A "lack of competence" suggests that Community actors have been delegated limited authority, as previously suggested. If they act beyond these delegated competencies, they act *ultra varies*, and their act is void.[40] An "infringement of an essential procedural requirement" involves not the substantive authority to take an act but the failure to do it in the right way. Here the procedural *faux pas* must be material however, not minor in nature.[41] An "infringement [of Community] law" is the most frequent complaint, and is broad enough to embrace all the others. It can be applied to the duty to act under the treaty, as well as the duty not to act. Under a civil law system (which the Community chiefly is), obligations can be drawn from general principles of law, common to the member states, such as certainty, legitimate expectations and proportionality, as well as the written standards of the Community.[42] The last grounds, "misuse of power," is not often used. It implies that power was delegated to the actor under the treaties, but that it was used in the wrong manner or to the wrong ends.[43]

Standing to Attack Community Acts

Treaty Article 173 also provides that the Community's principal actors, the Council, the Commission and the member states, have the right to question a Community action before the Court (for up to two months, save in the case of the ECSC), even if they had participated in the original decision.[44] Article 219 obligates member states to submit their disputes concerning Community Law *only* to the European Court. Article 170 allows member states to bring complaints that a sister state "has failed to fulfil an obligation under [the] Treaty," but only after bringing the matter before the Commission. Hence, suits between member states are rare, for the Commission can be called upon to prosecute the case if it has merit.[45]

Conversely, many cases have been prosecuted by the Commission (the Community's principal law enforcer) against member states (often Italy, which is perennially tardy in transposing EU directives). Suits by member states against the Commission and Council are common, as are suits between the latter two. This is the best way to ensure that the parties most affected by Community legislation will have a fair chance to test its validity before a single decision-maker, which will ensure the uniformity and consistency of Community Law.

The European Parliament and European Central Bank (but not the Court of Auditors) also are given standing by Article 173 for the purpose of protecting their prerogatives.[46]

As regards natural and legal persons (individuals and companies), Article 173 gives them standing before the European Court to contest a decision addressed to them or, if a regulation or decision addressed to another, it is of "direct and individual concern" to them.[47] This is similar to the American notion of "standing" and about as strict.

There is a two-month limitation on the initiation of an individual suit, either from the time of "publication of the measure, or of its notification to the plaintiff, or [if there is no notice] of the day on which it came to [his] knowledge."[48] Finally, there is no limit (other than discretion and proportionality) on the penalties the Court can impose on natural and legal persons.[49]

Originally there was no similar provision with respect to violations of Community law by the member states. If they were thought to be in violation of the treaties, the Commission first had to conduct an investigation. If violation was probable, then the state was given a chance to correct it, and only then was the case taken before the European Court. The Court's sole sanction, however, was to find that the "Member State . . . failed to fulfil an obligation under [the] Treaty . . . [and] required [it] to take the necessary measures to comply with the judgement of the Court." The treaty signatories hoped the moral suasion of being found "in violation" would be enough. They were not prepared to accept a greater consequence for their misdeeds or to assign greater authority to Brussels. But, with the passage of time, this fear subsided and other remedies proved necessary. Accordingly, the Maastricht Treaty revised Articles 170 to 172 allow a "lump sum or penalty payment" to be imposed and give the Parliament and Council authority to adopt regulations giving the Court "unlimited jurisdiction with regard to the penalties provided for [violations of] such regulations." These changes reflect a maturing of the Community and its constituent states and the seriousness with which they regard the binding nature of EU law.

The foregoing discussion might lead to the erroneous belief that Community law must be prosecuted in the Community courts. This is true with respect to member state and institutional suits, as previously noted. And it may be the chosen venue for significant private litigation.[50] However, Community law is equally applicable, and increasingly asserted, as a basis for actions in *national* courts.[51] In these cases, we have the possible anomaly of a multitude of state courts defining Community law. To deal with this potential problem, the EU treaty provides that, where a question of Community law is raised before a state tribunal and "a decision on [that] question is necessary to enable it to give judgement," then the court *may* (if it is an inferior court) refer the matter to the European Court for a "preliminary ruling." Where the situation arises in a national tribunal from which there is no appeal, the matter *must* be referred to the European Court of Justice (ECJ).[52] These referrals are left to the discretion of the state courts and are time-consuming but necessary. There is no other way to assure that state courts will properly interpret and apply Community law. With the passage of time and the accumulation of experience and guidance, however, these referrals (at least on points of basic Community Law) are likely to become less numerous. At present, they are a wonderful source of legal analysis and constitutional principle.

The European Court cannot refuse a request for a preliminary ruling, but it only expounds on the law. It does not settle the facts or decide the case. The guidance it provides the national court should allow the latter to do so, consistent with Community law. This is quite unlike U.S. practice. The U.S. Supreme Court has the power of certiorari and declines to hear most cases appealed to it. But, in the majority of the cases it takes, the Court resolves the facts and law and decides the case.

Of course, the treaty signatories were not prepared in 1952 or 1958 to let an untested European Court decide appeals of national court cases. Quite possibly, they are not prepared for it today. It may not matter, for the current system works fairly well, without raising another issue of national sovereignty. Judges at the Community and national levels are learned and disposed to follow the rule of law. Doubtless, this is why the Court was given (and exercised) such a pivotal role in the Community "experiment."

Mutual Recognition of National Judgments: The Brussels Convention of 1968

It is odd that the treaties that have bound the EU together so closely at an economic level (and legally, in some respects) should lack any article providing for the mutual recognition of public acts and judicial determinations. The U.S. thought this important enough to make it the subject of the first clause of the fourth article of the Constitution (immediately after describing the federal government).[53] The most that the EEC treaty provides is Article 220, which encourages "Member States [to] . . . enter into negotiations with each other with a view to securing . . . the simplification of formalities governing the reciprocal recognition and enforcement of judgements of courts or tribunals and of arbitration awards." It speaks volumes about the attitude of the signatory states that such a provision was left out of the original EEC treaty and remains outside the EU treaties today. However, all member states are signatories to the (1968) Convention on

Jurisdiction and the Enforcement of Judgements in Civil and Commercial Matters (Brussels Convention).[54] It excludes certain matters, like matrimonial property and descent, but otherwise lays down general rules for the exercise of court jurisdiction and provides for the recognition and enforcement (locally) of a properly rendered (foreign) judgment of another signatory state.[55] Thus, this agreement, binding all current EU members and a condition of accession for all future ones, serves the same effect as a treaty article. However, it cannot be interpreted by the ECJ, except on a preliminary ruling, which undercuts Community cohesion.

THE 1996–1997 INTERGOVERNMENTAL CONFERENCE

In EU parlance, an intergovernmental conference (IGC) is a little like a constitutional convention in America. We have had only one of these (in 1789) and produced a short, elastic document that, with a few amendments and a lot of federal legislation, has grown with the United States. One dreads to think what type of document a *second* constitutional convention would produce (given the numerous vocal interest groups that populate the country today).

But the EC was not so lucky. It dates back only to 1951 and is premised on a history of conflict in Europe. Hence, its founding treaties, the ECSC, the EEC and Euratom (as amended), constitute what might be called the "constitution" of the European Union. Because the member states were (and remain) somewhat suspicious of one another, the treaties that bind them together are perhaps overly detailed. It also is true that the EU has dramatically increased the scope of its activities over the past 50 years. Thus, the treaties that hold these diverse states together need constant revision as circumstances in Europe and the world change. The EC is still very much a "work in progress."

Not counting the IGC that was abruptly concluded in June 1997 in Amsterdam, the EC has had eight intergovernmental conferences. They bring together "representatives" of the governments of the EU member states (generally, the members of the European Council) for the express purpose of amending the treaties. Not every IGC is as dramatic as those that created the ECSC or EEC or that sought to produce a single market (the Single European Act) or economic and monetary union (the Maastricht Treaty). Some IGC are meant just to "fine-tune" existing undertakings. The 1996–1997 IGC seemed to be one of these.

Each IGC tells us something about the ambitions of the EU and the direction it may take in the ensuing years. The goals of the 1996–1997 IGC were not completely immodest, for the Community needed to do some consolidating and streamlining before it expanded membership again. Nonetheless, the timing might have been unfortunate, but there was no choice.

The Maastricht Treaty had provided that an IGC should be convened in 1996 to consider "to what extent the policies and forms of cooperation introduced by [that] Treaty may need to be revised."

Fortunately, economic and monetary union was not among the treaty areas to be revisited.[56] That ambitious undertaking posed problems enough. And yet, any time a constitution is revised, an opportunity is presented to tighten or loosen some provisions. What the Maastricht summiteers could not have foreseen when they agreed to the 1996 "review" was the slow, divisive struggle to get each individual member state to "[ratify] . . . the [TEU] . . . in accordance with their respective constitutional requirements." That process was not completed until November 1993. Meanwhile, a serious recession had befallen Europe and unemployment was rising; two speculative attacks hit the exchange rate mechanism, testing the EU's resolve to adopt a single currency; it principal engine (West Germany) was distracted by the effort and cost involved in the reunification with East Germany; and the Yugoslav civil war was threatening to destabilize Europe. Small wonder then that the Europhoria that swept Europe in the run up to 1992 had given way to Europessimism and Euroskepticism by 1996. The latter was particularly evident among British Conservative backbenchers, and an election was due during the probable term of the IGC.[57]

Hence, what the 1996–1997 IGC could accomplish depended greatly upon whom you consulted. The European Commission and European Parliament came up with the boldest plans.[58] Another ambitious model for the IGC was formulated by a panel of experts, called a "Reflection Group."[59] None was more remarkable than that of the British Conservative government under Prime Minister John Major. In it the U.K. government argued that the EU was—and ought to remain—a collection of sovereign nations pursuing common economic goals.[60]

Many European citizens objected to the fact that the Maastricht Treaty was too ambitious and negotiated in secret, offering little (except a vague provision for Eurocitizenship) for the average European. This time, the Commission and national negotiators took the hint and put citizens' concerns and interests first. Perhaps the most important issue to the common citizen is employment, or rather Europe's persistent high unemployment. Hence, national leaders inserted into the Amsterdam Treaty the commitment "to promote throughout the Community a harmonious and balanced development of economic activities [and] a high level of employment and social protection . . . [amended Article 2]." This means that Europeans are still committed to a degree of socialism that exceeds that typical of the United States. This could leave Europe in a stable—but low-growth—mode for years to come.

A number of minor changes were made with respect to the Parliament and Commission; in the case of the Council, qualified majority voting was extended to many new treaty provisions and several old ones as well. This progression is gradually eliminating the national "veto," except for the most sensitive issues like Pillars II and III and treaty revisions themselves. The treaty also strengthened the internal operations of the Council.[61] Fewer changes were made in the treaty sections dealing with the Commission and Court, but those changes that were made suggest a further "federalization" of the Community. It is understood that the Commission will streamline and improve its operations around the year 2000, an initiative referred to as both Agenda 2000 (covering the single currency and enlargement) and SEM 2000 (sound and efficient management).[62] Finally, the treaty expanded the co-decision process and renumbered prior treaty articles.

Because free movement of persons, asylum and immigration within the EU had proved to be Community-wide problems, a new title in the Amsterdam Treaty was to guarantee an EU policy at intragovernmental level within five years of the treaty's ratification. And the Court was given limited jurisdiction under Pillar III, another breakthrough.[63] There were a host of other small changes as well, and a new protocol was drafted to bring the member states' national parliaments closer to the work of the EU, chiefly by sharing information.[64]

The last Treaty provision could prove seminal and would allow some states of the Community to develop faster than others but may prove to be its ruin as well, because it has a sort of Jekyll-and-Hyde quality to it. Entitled "Closer Cooperation–'Flexibility,' " it really clears the way for a "two-speed" or "variable geometry" Europe. This was urged by Germany and France so that not all states would be held back by the U.K.'s reluctance to further integrate.

The introduction of "flexibility" may be seen as an admission that members of the Union either cannot or will not move forward together and hence must be given the freedom to "freelance." At its best, it allows the most avid integrationists to forge ahead with new initiatives, expecting that the others will follow when they are able (or convinced of the virtue of the move). At its worst, it would permit such a variety of agendas that a true union would be difficult and its influence weakened. Outsiders would be at liberty to deal with the EU or with individual states as they saw fit.

An example of the latter would be the various "open skies" agreements worked out between the U.S. and numerous European governments. By failing to act collectively, EU member states gave the better part of the deal to the U.S. But there are numerous examples of disunity, and so far they have not hurt the Union. Another would be economic and monetary union. It was never expected that all EU states would qualify for the single currency by 1997 or 1999, and specific opt-outs were given to Denmark and the U.K. Yet the initiative seems most salutary for the Community.

Hence, the new "flexibility" language seems more like a safety valve that may spur the whole Community to faster integration than the advent of its dissolution. The window that the flexibility provision creates is not wide. It surely overstates the case to assume that will lead inevitably to a "variable geometry" Europe.[65]

If the Amsterdam IGC began too soon after the Maastricht Treaty was ratified, it also ended too soon, before a consensus could be built around its principal objectives: to streamline the Community's institutions and decision-making process. Once again, the choice might have been unavoidable. A successful launch of the single currency was going to require a lot of political capital. With large state elections recently held or in the offing, their political leaders were not in a position to make concessions on institutional change, and there was not time to develop a consensus. The Amsterdam Treaty[66] may be a "sleeper," in that it achieved a number of the tasks set for it. But the conditions—economic and political—weren't right for a wholesale overhaul of EU management. So the really hard work of revising the EU institutional structure was deferred until at least 2000,[67] when imminent enlargement will require institutional changes. Nevertheless, further "federalizing" did occur.

A "FEDERAL" EUROPE?

Does the foregoing mean that the EU is becoming a "federal" state, a "United States of Europe?" I think not, although the comparison often is made.[68] Even persons in Brussels forswear the analogy; some because it draws unwanted attention to that prospect and others because it simply is not true. For one thing, the United States and the states of the United States are both considered to be founded by "the people."[69] It is quite clear that the European Community and European Union were founded by the constituent member states, in their sovereign capacities.

It must be remembered that federalism takes many forms, however.[70] And that "federalization" is a process, not an event. Viewed through this lens, the EU is well on its way to a federal type of union with some similarities to our own. Indeed, in some areas (agriculture) it may be even *more* federal than the U.S.[71] This is not remarkable in a world that itself is steadily converging. Nations give up some sovereign prerogative and surrender to rules and judgments made in part by others, in return for an increased measure of order and security. Europe is indeed federalizing. But so is the whole world.

It should be evident from just this brief overview of EU institutions and their operation that the European "experiment" is quite substantial and quite complex. The EU's program is no less ambitious.

Chapter 9

The European Union Program

It should be evident from the foregoing chapter that the EU has a large legislative program, quite like that of the U.S. federal government. Many diverse pressures are placed on the EU's central organs by the member states, business interests and others outside the Community. Apart from decisions of the European courts, which are reported in the *European Court Reports* (ECR; "C" for high court judgments and "T" for First Instance), the legislation of the Community is reported in the *Official Journal* (O.J.; "C" for Commission proceedings and "L" for law). The latter is like the U.S. *Federal Register*.

The treaties describe the principal objectives of the Community. Among them are to "[establish] a common market . . . by implementing . . . common policies . . . to promote throughout the Community a harmonious and balanced development . . . [including] the elimination, as between Members States, of customs duties and quantitative restrictions . . . ; an internal market characterized by the abolition . . . of obstacles to the free movement of goods, persons, services and capital; . . . a common policy in the sphere of agriculture and fisheries; . . . transport; a system ensuring that competition in the internal market is not distorted;" and so forth.[1] That is what the EU was meant to be—a customs union, with a single internal market and external tariff (Common Customs Tariff). This required the "approximation" (or "harmonization") of "Member States [laws] to the extent required" to establish a single market.[2]

The integration of the market proceeded at an uneven pace, however. It proved to be one thing to agree that there shall be no "customs duties on imports and exports . . . between Member States" and quite another thing to root out all national practices, inadvertent or intentional (e.g., labeling, purity standards), that have "equivalent effect."[3] While the European Coal and Steel Community was the prototype for a single Europe, it was the European Economic Community (EEC) that really began to integrate Europe. Its "Four Freedoms"—free movement of goods, workers, services and capital[4]—are the essential components of a common market. They must move freely if there is to be one. The EEC treaty also contained important sections regarding anticompetitive behavior in the common market and a common transport policy.[5]

However, not all these freedoms have succeeded equally. Whereas goods move relatively freely, workers (save at the professional and migrant levels) generally do not. Cross-border services have grown steadily, but capital lagged behind until the Maastricht Treaty laid the foundation for a common currency, now launched. A whole range of agreements were anticompetitive in their impact,[6] and services provided by national governments (of which there were many) had to be liberalized as well. In short, the idea of a European Common Market was an entirely sound one, but there was no "bright line" to distinguish market issues from a host of other political and social practices in each member state. The latter were *not* central to a common market, but they touched upon it in such a way that many had to be adjusted to make it work.

Some of the EC's founders of (e.g., Robert Schuman) felt from the very beginning that there should be a "European [political] federation." Now they were proving prophetic. In order to unify (or at least harmonize) the market at the supranational level, more sovereignty would have to be delegated. This antagonized some political leaders and many voters. They wanted the economic advantages of a unified market but felt that the social dimension should be handled at the national level.[7] Consequently, political friction has dogged the Community since its beginning. And yet, in the time since, the EU has both "widened" (added new members) and "deepened" (become more cohesive).

DEEPENING

After the initial burst of enthusiasm, national resistance to the Community began, and common market momentum came to a virtual standstill. British membership was twice rejected (1963 and 1967), and the French practiced an "empty chair" policy (refusing to attend Council meetings).[8] This foot-dragging persisted into the 1970s, although additional competencies (regional, environmental and social policy) were granted to Brussels; budget reform was adopted; the political leaders of the member states (now the European Council) began to meet; and the European Monetary System (EMS) was adopted, with a mechanism to stabilize exchange rates (the Exchange Rate Mechanism, ERM) and a European unit of monetary value (the ecu). The latter were established outside the treaties proper, however.

It was not until the European Parliament passed a draft treaty on "European Union" that serious integration began again. The Commission responded with a new treaty proposal of its own, the Single European Act (SEA). When the SEA was passed in 1987, it identified some 282-odd pieces of legislation needed to complete the single market and proposed that they all be adopted and transposed by a deadline: December 31, 1992 (hence, the "1992 Programme"). It was the Community's most successful program to date, even though not all legislation was passed or transposed by the deadline. Of equal and perhaps greater importance, the SEA provided for qualified majority (weighted) voting in the Council on a large scale and gave the European Parliament (EP) more influence in legislation (generally the EP is a pro-European institution). It also established consultative machinery to advance European political cooperation (EPC) and adopted a so-called social charter (covering workers only). The latter two initiatives were taken outside the treaty and have no binding legal force. Britain refused to join the social chapter, but inertia towards further market integration had been overcome.

It was not difficult to promote European unity at the time the SEA was adopted, for European economies were expanding and their leaders felt secure. National interests did not appear to need protection. Furthermore, the use of regulations ("federal" law) as a principal instrument of Community legislation was supplanted to a large degree by directives. This gave the member states some room for maneuver, and their national parliaments a role in the transposition process. Nonetheless, the SEA was an ambitious step toward European economic union. If the Commission's projections for its success were realized, then European consumers would not only have more choices but consumption costs would be reduced by 6 percent. Business would become more competitive, and labor, capital and manufacturing costs would decline. There was to be an estimated savings of ecu 60 billion ($72 billion) from economies of scale, 80 percent of which was to come from "restructuring." The Community would become more efficient and competitive.

The projected economic gain for the EU was around ecu 200 billion, or between 4 and 6 percent of the twelve states' GDP in 1988 dollars. Altogether, "market integration" was expected to add 4.5 percent to European GDP and create 1. 8 million new jobs (reducing the jobless rate by about 1.5 percent). In the medium term, the projection was an increase in GDP of 7 percent, unaccompanied by inflation, and the creation of five million new jobs.[9] In the end, the projections proved far too rosy.

The report had its dark side, too. It candidly conceded that "[r]ecent performance of EC firms in [competition] with their [Japanese and American rivals] for world and *European* markets [was] far from brilliant." Indeed, the report and underlying documents left one with the impression that European businesses have lost market share in many manufacturing sectors, while its two main competitors have gained. "The Japanese and American advantage [was] particularly pronounced in advanced technology sectors like electrical and electronic goods, office automation equipment and data-processing. EC companies . . . fared better [in] European markets, but even so there is a real danger that . . . the main beneficiaries of market integration could be non-Community [businesses]"[10] In other words, Community enterprises are not competing effectively for what I call "high-end" (high tech/high return) business, but are competing most effectively with less-industrialized nations for "low-end" business.

Another breakthrough of the SEA was to allow competition in the so-called "excluded sectors": water, transport, energy and telecommunications, most of them the traditional provinces of national governments.[11] This reflects the shift, in Europe and elsewhere in the world, away from state-run or managed economics to "privatization" and more competition. State subsidies ("aids") were to be withdrawn or declared illegal. Joint ventures, like the Airbus or European military fighter, were encouraged. But, greater liberalization in these sectors created greater opportunity for American companies as well. They have great expertise and, by international trading rules, they cannot be excluded.[12]

Thus, the Single European Act had both an upside and a downside in the evolution of the European Community. Its upside was that it ended the "Eurosclerosis" that had plagued the Community for over a decade. It simplified and democratized the EU legislative process. The signatories took a big gamble with the SEA, and won. The member states' economies are better integrated, more efficient, competitive and robust.

There was a downside as well. "[A]lthough [Europe had] changed, the rest of the world . . . changed even faster." When European companies became more competitive they also downsized. That exacerbated the problem of unemployment, which has dogged Europe for years. There was a threefold increase in company mergers and acquisitions and a doubling of trade in previously protected sectors, and yet Europe wasn't competitive enough. Moreover, there was "a poor relationship between growth and job creation, as compared to . . . other industrial Societies."[13] The breakup of the former Soviet Union and the reunification of Germany proved both a distraction and a burden on the eve of the completion of the Single Market (1992). "To pay for unification, the German government raised taxes. . . . At the same time, it reined in prices by tightening credit, which triggered higher interest rates across Europe, slowing growth in all EC countries."[14] Coincidentally, a world economic downturn was beginning to unfold, one from which Europe did not emerge until the late 1990s. Finally, Europe's high level of social spending has continued to be a drag on its growth. In 1994, it was 21.5 percent of GDP (up from 16.4 percent in 1989). This is 50 percent greater than U.S. levels, and 78 percent higher than Japan's.[15]

The Single European Act, then, was something of a mixed bag. Nevertheless, it was a net success, economically and politically. And so the Community took the next step; the Maastricht Treaty and monetary union.

The Treaty of European Union (TEU) is the last major treaty of the EU. Unfortunately, its ambitious objectives were overshadowed by increasing economic gloom. So its final ratification lay in doubt for some time.[16] What is important about the treaty is not its tortuous history (for it finally was ratified), but its remarkable provisions. They placed European integration on a much higher plateau. Perhaps Maastricht was just the next step to allow the Community to keep its Euromomentum.[17]

The TEU spent little time on common market issues, unlike the EEC and SEA. The exception was economic and monetary union, which was elevated from a modest monetary stabilization program to the centerpiece of the Treaty. The other three features of consequence were commitments to coordination in the fields of foreign and security policy (Pillar II), to cooperation in the field of justice and home affairs (Pillar III), and to the establishment of Community "citizenship."[18] It is difficult to say at this juncture which of these provisions will prove most important, but the most concrete to date is that providing for economic and monetary union.

The notion of monetary union was not new with Maastricht. A 1978 resolution of the European Council established a European Monetary System (EMS), the Exchange Rate Mechanism (ERM) and a Community measure of monetary value (a "basket" of member state currencies), the ecu (European currency unit).[19] However, this arrangement was outside the treaties proper and took a severe buffeting—indeed, weakening—in the ERM "crises" of 1992–1993.

The economic and monetary union (EMU) that was inserted into the Maastricht treaty was of an entirely different order.[20] The Treaty language came from a committee of member state central bank governors, chaired by then-Commission president, Jacques Delors (Delors report). A European Monetary Institute (EMI), established in 1994 and based in Frankfurt, did the planning for a single European currency (now called the "euro"). It was introduced as a system of account on January 1, 1999. At that time, economic and monetary policy planning for "euroland" was transferred to the European Central Bank (ECB), successor to the EMI.[21] Those currencies that didn't choose or didn't qualify to participate in EMU would be bound to the new system by a successor mechanism, ERM2. For a long time, it appeared that the mechanics of monetary union were sound, but the political will was lacking. Continued slow growth and high unemployment in the EU convinced key politicians that the solutions lay at the European rather than the national level. Besides, it was easier to blame "Brussels" for the financial restructuring of Europe than to take the blame at national level.

The two other features of the Maastricht Treaty that deepened the Community are cooperation on foreign and security policy (called Pillar II) and on justice and home affairs (called Pillar III). In 1970, European Political Cooperation (EPC) had been established, but it functioned like a "private club" of member states' foreign ministers. The Single European Act did not go much further.[22] Thus, the Maastricht Treaty's provision for a Common Foreign and Security Policy (CFSP), replacing EPC, was quite a change.[23] It moved the EU much closer to *political* union. It is no small wonder, for the EU was badly divided over the Gulf War, and its world influence suffered accordingly. Cooperation was starkly improved during its attempt to deal with the Bosnian crisis, although the results were not much better.

Included in CFSP is the pledge to work toward "the eventual framing of a common defense policy" and in time "a common defense."[24] This revived a dormant European defense pact, the Western European Union (WEU) and resulted in a renegotiation of relationships within the North Atlantic Treaty Organization (NATO). But the EU and the U.S. were to remain partners in the defense of Europe, consistent with their own security.[25] Hence, there will be no separate EU defense policy in the near term. But the need of European nations to share the expense and risk of defense in the future is obvious. They already have begun to attempt collaborations in the area of material procurement.

A second element of a joint European security program is Europol, a Community-wide law enforcement intelligence agency.[26] It replaced a host of smaller enterprises that were set up to deal with free movement within the Community (notably criminals and contraband). Europol operates as an information-exchange mechanism, but its supporters hope it will grow into a European version of the American FBI. After all, criminals do not respect borders in Europe or elsewhere.[27]

Since the TEU provision for cooperation in the fields of justice and home affairs is entirely new with that treaty,[28] it has no history on which to build. Like CFSP, this initiative is intergovernmental. Where it will lead is anybody's guess. But at least a structure has been constructed that allows for greater consultation among the member states in these highly sensitive areas. There is no doubt that greater consistency is needed to address such pressing problems as asylum and the treatment of non-nationals in the EU. Even if the principles are enforced at the national level, consistency would be good for the Community.

The same ambiguity attends the creation of "citizenship" of the Union by the TEU.[29] This embraces all persons who are nationals of a member state. So the states themselves have the final say. But once any state acts, the others are bound to certain consequences according to the treaties. EU citizenship involves some express rights, but not many. Some simply restate terms of prior treaties (the "right to move and reside freely within the territory of the Member States"), but some "rights" are new. These include the right to stand for election and vote in municipal and European parliamentary elections if resident in a member state, even if a national of another member state, and the right to "petition the European Parliament" or "apply to the Ombudsman."[30] The new article creates a harmonizing opportunity. One cannot know where it will lead.

The latest initiative is Agenda 2000, a Commission-proposed plan to extend the EU's budgetary regime through the year 2006, reform its institutions and programs, and enlarge the Community. As the plan does not favor all members equally, there was bound to be some horsetrading. There also were numerous threats to walk away from the negotiating table, but in the end there was a deal that left the EU somewhat stronger (and probably larger). But much remains to be done.

Among the Agenda 2000 provisions is a "freeze" on the Community's budget (currently about $100 billion annually). Meanwhile, regional programs and the common agricultural program (CAP) will have to be downsized, so that they consume less of the budget. Nonetheless there is tension among states that feel they contribute a disproportionate amount to Community coffers on a per capita basis and get too little in return. Also, a spending cap—particularly on agricultural subsidies—will hit southern states harder than northern ones, for the former are more agrarian.

Another area of reform involves downsizing Community institutions and improving their efficiency. This will be difficult because each nation state wants a full measure of influence at Community level, but that is useless if it hobbles Community decision-making. Moreover, the Commission has long been accused of mismanagement and graft. Recently, this nearly resulted in its censure by the European Parliament and then precipitated the Commission's resignation, *en masse*. This does nothing to increase the average European's opinion of the Community. But what are the options? A new Commission and European Parliament was selected in 1999. One hopes their working relationship will be better than that of their 1994–1999 predecessors.

Meanwhile the economics of Europe is pushing the Community gradually toward greater cohesion. There is nothing quite like a single currency and greater transparency to expose differences among the EU states with respect to social payments, tax inconsistencies, and labor costs. So social payments have gradually come down, and there is greater tax harmonization throughout the Community. European businesses are beginning the process of "right-sizing" that American businesses pursued in the early 1990s. These corrections are bound to improve the single markets' effectiveness and increase the strength of the central institutions. In the early 1990s, unemployment was generally considered to be a member state problem. Now it is widely appreciated to be a Community problem, and one of the most important facing Europe today.

Although the Amsterdam Treaty allowed for a degree of "flexibility" within the Union, new governments elected across Europe have found it better to cooperate than quarrel; the prospect of a pan-European stock market is just one example of this new spirit of union. Of course, if the EU can make Europe more competitive and reduce its chronic unemployment (now, suddenly, under 10 percent), its success is virtually assured. It is not just market economics, but also crime and military preparedness in a borderless (and sometimes unstable) Europe that bind its nations together more and more.[31]

One might wonder then whether European integration is reaching or has reached its outer limits. Surely the Maastricht Treaty would have been easier to negotiate and ratify in the halcyon economic environment of the late 1980s, when the European economy was doing well. And the ERM crises of 1992–93 would have been avoided if there a had been single currency and monetary policy was being set by the European System of Central Banks (ESCB) and ECB instead of the Bundesbank. Conversely, many nationalistic Europeans are deeply concerned about the degree of national sovereignty conceded to Brussels by the Maastricht Treaty.

The EU's "single market" has always been difficult to assess. Just when it appears to be flying apart, it unites instead in a single currency. Just when its prospects seem most uncertain, the Community finds new energy and commitment and rises like a phoenix. Sometimes it is due to political will, sometimes to economic common sense, and sometimes to both, but the convergence of the European Community has been steady, even if not consistent.

My reason for talking you through this is to illustrate how the Community is constantly reinventing itself and developing.[32] The U.S. had but one Constitutional convention. The EU has had many intergovernmental conferences and treaties. Each has contributed to the strengthening of the enterprise in its way. Almost every change has deepened integration and improved the enforceability of EU norms. The reality seems to defy the oddsmakers.

The shifts in public sentiment regarding the EU are captured in a Commission publication called EUROBAROMETER. According to its Spring 1996 issue, 48 percent of European citizens polled thought the EU was a "good thing" (down 6 percent from the last poll), but only 15 percent thought it was a "bad thing." However, if a referendum were to be held, 65 percent said they would vote to leave the EU. Support for the "euro" (the single currency) had finally exceeded one-half (at 53 percent), all of which increase came from those previously undecided. Only 33 percent opposed it. But a majority of Europeans (55 percent) prefer intergovernmental action to Community action.[33]

Obviously, the conviction of Eurocitizens lags behind that of large businesses when it comes to a more-united Europe. That is not to say that the people of Europe won't catch up. After all, for many European businessmen the consequences of the union are apparent every day. The EU accounts for about one-fifth of world exports and 30 percent of service exports. It absorbs some 50 percent of Eastern Europe's total exports. Combined with the U.S., Japan and Canada, the EU accounts for well over 50 percent of world trade, and that is where Europeans must expect to grow their economy.[34]

It is easy to see why the average European doesn't know what to make of the EU. When it opens opportunities for them (like equal pay for equal work for both sexes), they support it. If it means more regulations, they are opposed. They see it as a threat to the rich diversity that is Europe—the languages, the cuisine, the culture, history, art, architecture and economic differences. They view the national capitals as more reliable and "closer to the people" than "Brussels" (the seat of major EU institutions).

They consider the U.S. to be a different situation because it is "one nation," but there once were similar concerns in America. The issue wasn't fully settled until the twentieth century. The harmonization of Europe's economy need not eradicate national differences in other spheres. Even today, the politics, topography, cuisine and architecture of the American East and Southwest, of the Deep South and the Midwest, are quite different. Only a common language, English, holds across the nation, and that language is studied and spoken widely in Europe.

Should Eurocitizens be worried about a loss of national sovereignty? Of course they should! The process of "federalization" can be insidious. But a delegation that achieves nothing in time flows back to the delegator. It happens all the time in the United States. The problem is that the benefits of greater European integration are not always apparent. Some of the EU programs are so abstract that their value is obscured. On the other hand, a unanimous vote is needed to shrink the EU's competencies, and that happens rarely. The problem is that no nation, no matter how wealthy or how powerful, is immune to a gradual loss of sovereignty. The world, in its economic and political structures, has simply grown too interdependent. As a general rule, change is frightening, but unavoidable. Europe, like the world, is integrating steadily. A stronger market means more joint action, and that means more "European" law.

The whole progression of the EU is testimony to the fact that the future lies in integration. What began as a narrow, economically oriented Community, gradually broadened into one that embraced items such as foreign and monetary policy—once purely national issues. As described later, the Community's program expands constantly, despite the resistance to it. Not every program initiative benefits every country or benefits all countries equally. In order for the Community to coalesce as a unit, less able member states need to be assisted. This involves a transference of resources and a collective willingness to progress as a unit, even at the expense of national prerogative. In the former case, Germans are paying to upgrade Portuguese infrastructure. As the system is far more transparent than in the U.S.,[35] it is much easier to expose the benefits and burdens of membership in the Community than in the United States.

As a result, Community alliances are constantly shifting and vary from issue to issue. The old "German-French bargain" (the Germans would support the French agriculture policy and the French would support the Germans' industrial policy) seems to have broken down. The British, who were welcomed into the Community as a counterweight to this pairing, have not played that role. On the contrary, they have been a very unpredictable partner. It is odd that the British people seemed better disposed to Europe than their leaders. Margaret Thatcher's hostility to Europe eventually did her in, while Euroskeptic Tories cost John Major the election in 1996.

There still is a tendency in Europe for the people to look for solutions to their problems at the *national* level. The national capitol is closer and the politicians more attentive, even if not more effective. The truth is, that many of the problems facing Europe are *European* problems. National politicians are reluctant to recognize this. And, if there is a glaring failure on the part of Brussels, it is the failure to convince average Europeans that their lives are better as a result of being in the Community.

The EU's influence in world trade circles obviously is improved by a collective approach. It is difficult to imagine any single member state sitting at the table with the United States to hammer out the last details of the Uruguay Round GATT agreement, and yet EU Commissioner Leon Brittan did so on the Community's behalf—and won! New agreements now being worked out at the global level through the World Trade Organization (WTO) in sectors like information technology, telecommunications, financial services, and marine services will all pose competitive threats to European companies and their markets, threats that can best addressed in a collective way. For it is not just the European economy that is becoming more competitive and better integrated, it is the world economy as well.

These prospects are somewhat in the future, however. In the present, despite the footdragging and skepticism, the Community already has traveled a long way. Consider just a few of the programs in place, as described hereafter.

SUBSTANTIVE PROGRAMS

In the last section, I called the "four freedoms" of the Treaty of Rome the irreducible elements of a common market in Europe. Without them there could be no customs union or common external tariff.[36] The Treaty does allow member states to derogate from common policy if their security, economy, health, culture and so forth seem threatened by Community action. But these departures are rarely permitted.[37] However, the elimination of barriers to the free transit of goods and persons does not instantly create a unitary, free and open market. One must prevent producers in one state from "dumping" cheap goods in their neighbor's market or from subsidizing a local industry to make it more competitive. Both these practices, common in Europe and elsewhere, distort markets and were prohibited by the Treaty of Rome.[38] So the treaties did not just prohibit certain practices, but affirmatively required the EU member states to do such things as "privatize or open to competition state monopolies of a commercial character"[39] or to gradually eliminate national trade practices that had the effect of excluding foreign goods or favoring domestic ones ("non-tariff barriers" or NTBs).[40]

In order to achieve these objectives, the Community had to be given legal personality and capacity,[41] its own legislative, administrative and judicial institutions,[42] and a source of income (its "own resources")[43] as a way of carrying out all the Treaty mandates.

In creating such a leviathan as this, the founding states had to strike a delicate balance between the loss of national sovereignty and the capacity of the Community to do those things that would produce a larger and wealthier Europe and a more influential and competitive one abroad. This is one reason why the role of the European Council (the heads of state or government) has expanded steadily with the evolution of the treaties. But, as the mainspring of the EU, with constituencies of their own at home to please, the chemistry of this group is a critical index of the health of the "union." Consequently, political leaders in Europe must have been relieved by the election of Labor prime minister Tony Blair in England. John Major's Euroskepticism, or more properly that of his Tory backbenchers, had brought reform in the Community almost to a standstill. A similar skepticism was expressed by Germany's former chancellor Kohl and France's Chirac, in order to gain reelection or support for EU reforms. But as the deepening of the European Union has its own momentum, changes in leadership have little enduring impact on its agenda.

Of course, there continue to be divisions among the heads of state about the pace and direction of European integration. Mentioned before are the differences of political and social philosophy, of culture, history and language. The latter alone costs millions in translation costs annually, and yet it has not proved an insuperable barrier to Community integration. While the EU recognizes eleven "official" languages, it tends to operate chiefly in two: English (the bank) and French (the other institutions, including court deliberations). All official communications are available in all languages, save Gaelic. In the Community courts, the initiating party can choose the language of the proceeding in the interest of justice.[44]

The Community's programs were not insubstantial when the European Economic Community was formed, but they have expanded steadily since. By the time of the Maastricht Treaty, the objectives had broadened to include "economic and monetary union" and to "promote throughout the Community a harmonious and balanced development of economic activities, sustainable and non-inflationary growth respecting the environment, a high degree of convergence of economic performance, a high level of employ-

ment and of social protection . . . , and solidarity among Member States."[45]
This is the *integrative* side of the latest major treaty revision. But the same
document states that the "Community shall act within the limits of the
powers conferred upon it."[46] So there also is a disintegrative side to the
Community treaties, as well.[47] A rigid conformity will not be imposed where
it cannot be. Otherwise, it risks shattering the union. But what kind of a
"union" is that?

The answer is, a not an inconsiderable one, even when compared to the
U.S. federal model. The fact that the EU—unlike the U.S.—cannot easily
or quickly impose a uniform will on fifteen diverse member states should
take nothing away from the awesome scope and uniformity of its program.
There is no need to elaborately develop its details here, since there are so
many and other sources do so.[48] It will suffice merely to sketch in the main
themes and identify some of the representative programs.

Despite its painfully slow recovery from the 1989–93 world recession, the
EU enjoys a modest trade surplus with the rest of the world (Ecu 46.3
billion in 1996). That was its fourth straight year of surplus and a rise of 9
percent over 1995. Intra-EU trade is growing steadily as well. In 1996, trade
within the EU totaled Ecu 1,050 billion, or 63 percent of total trade. The
key to a stronger, more-competitive Europe depends not just on expanding
the Union market but also on controlling inflation, improving job growth,
and reducing public deficits. All this is increasingly being done at Community level for, as new passages in the treaties note, "[Member States']
. . . economic policies [are] a matter of common concern [and] shall [be
coordinated] within the Council."[49]

Common Agricultural and Fisheries Policies

Few policies of the EU have commanded so much money and attention
as its Common Agricultural Policy (CAP). Part of the reason is historic. All
of the original six member states had large and well-regulated agricultural
sectors, especially France. Since France wasn't going to open its industrial
sector to German competition without adequate protection for its agricultural sector (which France expected would dominate the Community), agricultural provisions (including fish) appear early in the Treaty, right behind
the free movement of goods. Although the Common Fisheries Policy (CFP)
developed more slowly and only recently became a matter of Community
concern (due to overfishing in the Atlantic), the CAP dominated the early
Community. Over one-half of the EC budget was devoted to it, and it
generated considerable legislation as well. Certainly, there was no larger or
more-detailed body of Community law in its early days. As late as 1993,
almost 49 percent of the EU budget was earmarked for some aspect of the
CAP, whereas less than 3 percent of Community GDP is attributable to
agriculture.[50]

Obviously, this distortion has to be corrected, particularly if the EU is to succeed with its many other initiatives. This conclusion is widely accepted in Europe, even in the face of staunch resistance by EU farmers and others.[51] For one thing, farm aid in the form of price supports no longer fits the modern notion of business competition contained in the 1994 GATT agreement. Hence, the EU was forced to abandon its support program, and a WTO panel recently held that the EU's protectionist "banana regime" violated GATT standards.[52] Thus, it can be expected that the CAP will shrink and the European market will open up to more foreign agricultural products. Indeed, if the CAP isn't adjusted prior to the expansion of the Community to Eastern and Central European states, it will be overwhelmed. Those states' economies are more agrarian than those of any current EU members. The adjustment process may proceed without fanfare, however. The first reason is that it is so politically sensitive. The other is that the program has been shrinking steadily over the years, despite its high profile and fierce resistance. However, the modest changes made in the CAP in the 2000–2006 budget package and the fact that the budget was "frozen" at current levels don't give one much confidence that the EU is addressing either its agricultural or its expansion problems.[53]

The same might happen in the fisheries sector. It too is relatively small as a percentage of EU GDP, and there will be no sector left if overfishing in Europe isn't brought under control.[54] This would be more difficult to do at member-state level. Indeed, the whole BSE ("mad cow") debacle suggests what can happen when member states act independently, without sufficient concern for Community principles or impact.[55]

Transport

Another important Community sector is transport. For this reason, it was placed just behind the four freedoms in the treaties. The value to a common market of an interconnected and interoperable "rail, road and inland waterway" system is too obvious to dwell upon, and yet a Community-wide transport system has developed slowly.

There are at least two important reasons. First, national systems were built to different standards. To adopt a single standard for the Community would reward those countries whose standard was selected (often the wealthiest and most advanced) while requiring the overhaul of the others. Hence, transport planning must now take these consequences into account. Second, many of these systems and others (air, energy, telephone) were owned and operated by the state itself. Hence, the treaty appears to call for either privatizing these systems or allowing others to compete with the state in commercial enterprises. For both reasons, this important dimension of Community policy has been neglected.[56]

To remedy this situation, the Maastricht Treaty included language concerning trans-European networks. But the Council has failed to approve the necessary funding, and suggests that most of it needs to come from private sources. Meanwhile, "privatization" of public-sector operators continues throughout Europe. International agreements could eventually eclipse any lassitude in the Community itself.[57] After a long delay, the Community may turn pro-active just in time. If it does, there will be loads of opportunities for American businesses.

Employment

The problem of employment—or rather, unemployment—in Europe is one of its most persistent concerns. The original EEC treaty provided for the free movement of workers in the Community and prohibited discrimination on the grounds of sex or nationality.[58] Nevertheless, it is evident that most people don't travel Europe looking for work. They wait for it to come to them. The problem is similar in the United States (that is, personal mobility is overstated), but Europe's immobility is greater. Culture, cuisine and language differences may be one reason, but generous social programs for those out of work is a significant factor. They promote a degree of inertness, but cost EU states dearly. As a result, the downsizing of European businesses to make them more competitive in the global marketplace (including the shift of work elsewhere in Europe or *out* of Europe) has increased the number of unemployed and the cost of supporting them. Yet the individual member states of the EU don't have a workable employment plan.[59] The energetic efforts of the last few years have begun to produce results, however. Member states are beginning to overhaul social programs. A single currency may make Europe more competitive, although more jobs may be lost. One report suggests that 900,000 extra jobs have been created in Europe in the past four years, and investment 2.6 is percent higher than it would have been without the single market program.[60]

A Commission white paper has ripened into a European Confidence Pact for Employment. Commission President Jacques Santer is the primary architect of the Pact and made it the Commission's "first priority" in 1997. In his view it must be founded upon (1) sound macroeconomic policy, (2) completing and extending the single market and (3) reforming and harmonizing the EU's employment systems.[61] This may be just the time for it. The whole world is changing rapidly and, by its own admission, Europe is falling behind. The old social systems have not been able to cope with a weak economy, joblessness and the demands that Europeans traditionally have made on those systems.

Germany has suffocating labor standards and must reabsorb East German laborers into its economy.[62] Various interest groups—from French farmers to truckers to fishermen—seem able to cripple the government at will and force concessions governments can ill afford to make. Only the British, who have been ambivalent about their role in Europe, have convinced their nationals that some flexibility in the labor market and social systems is the key to a revived economy.

What is likely to happen? According to the EU Commission itself, "EU economic growth was anemic" over the 1991–1996 period. "Total EU employment declined by 4.5 million jobs, . . . far worse than the US or Japanese experience in the same time span." This "resulted mainly from macroeconomic obstacles to growth within the EU," including "insufficient expansion of productive capacity, overly lax budgetary policies and inappropriate wage increases." This led to high interest rates, exchange rate instability and recession. "The fastest approach to a [better] growth pattern would be to emulate the US." But, for "social and political reasons," the U.S. approach may be "neither feasible nor desirable for the EU."[63]

A single currency could provide a big boost to economic harmonization, but the budgetary constraints that have accompanied it have produced backlash in Germany, France and elsewhere. The people of Europe want the benefits of a single market but seem unwilling to pay the economic price. This is a contradiction that has frequently slowed Community growth. Unless a comprehensive employment plan can be developed and Europeans accept lower social benefits, slow economic growth in the EU will be prolonged.

Europe's recovery from the latest economic downturn has begun. Significant changes can be expected in the areas of employment, social protection, taxation and monetary systems before it is complete. Until then, the state of the European and member states' economies at both national and supranational levels will be a touchy political subject. Unless some of these reforms are introduced and take hold uniformly, European ambitions cannot be realized. Making the European market more competitive by making it more uniform is the only way the EU is going to grow its way out of its current troubles.[64] Many of Europe's present problems are Communitywide and can't be successfully addressed at national level.

Small and Medium-Sized Enterprises

At several points, the treaties say that small and medium-sized enterprises (SMEs) should be given a preferred position in Community policy making. This is especially true with regard to competition policy.[65] There is nothing inherently wrong with encouraging emerging companies. Politicians are fond of saying that they are the real source of new jobs in the economy, and indeed they are. After all, they are many times more numerous than larger companies and employ more workers. But many SMEs are dependent on large corporations for the work that they outsource or as niche producers of goods and services. If the latter are not competitive in the world marketplace—and many of Europe's aren't—then doting on SMEs isn't going to solve the problem. Why then all this attention?

I think that there is an unspoken precept in the EU that every member state should have at least one auto manufacturer or airline or major bank. Consolidation within states may be tolerable, but consolidation across borders (which means that a German or British or French firm might dominate an EU market sector) is not tolerated to the same extent. However, this type of consolidation may be required to make *European* undertakings efficient and competitive on a global scale. (I am told by Europeans who follow EU competition law that the Commission grants most clearances sought to allow industry consolidation.) But the emphasis on keeping European businesses small (treaty article 86) is unmistakable. The ambivalence between a European Union policy that is geared to SMEs and one conscious of the economic realities of global competition must be resolved.

Community Structural Policies

The Community has a number of structural policies, ranging from the very concrete to the implied. I have addressed the more important ones here to illustrate the vast array of areas in which the Community is striving for greater cohesion.

The oldest and best-developed of the Community's structural programs deals with agriculture. Through two principal programs, the Agricultural Guidance and Guarantee Fund (AGGF) and the European Regional Development Fund (ERDF), the Community took substantial amounts of its "own resources" and redistributed them to the agricultural sector. Initially, the funding went to price supports. Today it goes to pay for land taken out of production, improvement of farming methods and retraining farm labor for alternative careers.[66]

As this has happened, the structural programs (chiefly ERDF) broadened to reach other lagging sectors in the EU. Among these are those that have high unemployment, or are undergoing transitions from agriculture or sunset industries or are simply backward when compared to the remainder of the Community. Another initiative of this sort was the "Cohesion Fund" (article 130d), introduced by the Single European Act in an effort to draw lagging states (notably Spain, Portugal, Ireland and Greece) to within 90 percent of the average per capita income of the EU as a whole.

Of course, the Community has not moved with equal speed in all areas. With limited funds, it is not easy to see just how fast Community policy will develop in any area. However, it is evident that a number of the problems Europe faces with respect to unemployment, transport networks or environment are not neatly confined to one member state. The Council recognized this by creating a Committee of the Regions. Coordinated cross-border programs to develop economically depressed regions or to improve the effectiveness of "natural" economic (as opposed to political) regions draws attention away from the national capital and towards Brussels, the "European" capital.[67]

The European Investment Bank and European Social Fund

The European Investment Bank (EIB) and European Social Fund (ESF) are both included in treaty article 130b. The former was given a much higher profile by the Maastricht Treaty and is expected to "contribute, by having recourse to the capital market and utilizing its own resources, to the balanced and steady development of the common market."[68] Its activities are aimed at development programs that might not be attractive to other capital sources or are of a "size or nature" that they could not be financed by any individual member state. The latter is considered one of the Community's structural funds. Neither initiative has proceeded as fast as might have been hoped when it was established. On the other hand, the fact that they exist at all is a testimony to the EU's cooperative design.

The EIB does not depend on the annual Community budget, but rather is funded by subscriptions from the fifteen member states. In general, the Bank supports loans to developmental enterprises for which "funds are not available from other sources [public or private] on reasonable terms." It has been called "the EU's main financing area and the world's largest international lending and borrowing agency." In 1996, the EIB provided a record ecu 23.2 billion ($27.8 billion) in loans to support EU economic development and cooperation with non-member countries, many of whose economies are interlocked with those of the EU.[69]

In 1989, a social charter was approved by eleven of the twelve member states (the United Kingdom declining to go along). British prime minister Tony Blair took Britain into the social chapter, and most Britons seem to favor it. At present, it hasn't amounted to much. The Community has passed just a few pieces of non-controversial labor legislation.[70] Indeed, most of the treaty provisions that describe the Community's "social policy" (Protocol No. 14) relate to labor issues: full employment, improved living and working conditions, dialogue between management and labor, inclusiveness and equal pay for equal work for the sexes. There is an allusion to "proper social protection," and it can be expected that the Community will set standards aimed at greater "economic and social cohesion" (Protocol No. 15). Social cohesion can be expected to follow on the heels of economic cohesion, however.

A Single Currency

The bulk of the Maastricht treaty revisions dealt with economic and monetary union (EMU), including a single currency. These are so complex that

I have dealt with them elsewhere. However, the structural principle involved deserves mention here. No EU initiative since the single market (SEA) has meant more to the EU's future.

Thanks to Maastricht Treaty article G(25)(new articles 102a–109m), Community "economic and monetary policy" has been elaborately detailed. "Member States [are to] conduct their economic policies [in order to achieve] the objectives of the Community." To make this possible, each member state is to "forward information to the Commission about important measures taken . . . in the field of their economic policy. . . . Where . . . the economic policies . . . are not consistent with [the Community economic and monetary] guidelines . . . [and] risk jeopardizing . . . economic and monetary union, the Council may, acting by a qualified majority . . . , make the necessary recommendations to the Member State concerned."[71]

Obviously, there is no completely independent national currency policy in the Community today. Any move by any major European currency—including the euro—reverberates throughout the entire EU fiscal system, if not the world. This is why a well-coordinated and farsighted macroeconomic policy, independent of the political pressures that voters place on politicians, is the best tonic for European growth and recovery.

Competition

Given the single market's interest in integration and its concern about the protection of national "heroes," it is no wonder that it wanted to prevent market distortions. The most obvious of these are anti-competitive agreements and monopolistic behavior (treaty articles 85 and 86). But a host of other market-distorting practices, such as "dumping" underpriced goods, state aids, and mergers, also affect competition.

Article 85 of the treaties prohibits a whole range of "agreements between undertakings . . . and concerted practices" that "have as their object or effect the prevention, restriction or distortion of competition within the common market." This prohibition is very like Section 1 of the U.S. Sherman (Antitrust) Act, which prohibits "contracts," "combinations" or "conspiracies" in restraint of trade.[72] Arguably, the European version is broader, since it does not require proof of a firm agreement. However, it also allows a "good" anti-competitive practice to continue, if it allows "consumers a fair share of the resulting benefit."[73]

In theory, the European Commission has to investigate every claim of violation of EU competition laws. In the U.S., it is more common for private litigants (rather than the government) to bring antitrust complaints. After all, the statute enlists their aid by offering treble damages if a violation is found.[74]

Hence, the European Commission is in a much better position than U.S. authorities to exempt parties from the strictures of Article 85. The first form of exemption is called a "negative clearance"; the second, a "block exemption." Something similar may be gotten from the U.S. government, in the form of a "comfort letter" (stating that the action proposed is not likely to violate the Act). But this doesn't forestall private suits, and the government is not absolutely bound by its opinion.

Thus, the Commission plays the role you would expect in promoting competition in the Community. It would hardly do for the treaties to forbid the French government to discriminate against German products (Article 30) and yet allow French companies to collude against German companies (in the absence of Article 85).

Article 86 is the other principal EU competition rule. It does not require two-party agreements, for it targets undertakings that, due to their sheer size ("dominant position"), may act in a way that is "incompatible with the common market insofar as it may affect trade between Member States." It should be evident that almost *any* act by a firm in a "dominant position" could be such an "abuse." But a "rule of reason" applies. What is the relevant market? How large a share represents "dominance"? Is the "act" in question truly anti-competitive?

A great deal of discretion is left with the Commission. Dominance may be defined in terms of turnover in a single state, or the Community, or the world. If a narrow limit is set, then every member state ought to have one or more players in each field of business. But, if this approach is taken, the largest operators in Europe may be too small to compete on a global scale. The common market vision would succeed internally, but fail externally. If, however, European firms are allowed to merge into large multinationals without fear of becoming too dominant, then it is likely that there would be just a few major players in Europe. Not every nation would have businesses in every commercial field. A narrow definition of dominance hurts U.S. multinationals, because they tend to be larger on average than their European counterparts. As the EU has become better integrated and more global, the Commission has had to recalibrate its approach to competition. A recent Commission "green paper" (discussion draft) proposes just such an adjustment.[75]

Dumping

"Dumping" is defined as the selling of a foreign good in a domestic market at a price lower than its production cost or that charged in its home market. The consequence can be (and indeed the *purpose* may be) to drive out competing local goods. Once this is done, the price is raised. This latter practice, called "predatory dumping," ought to be prohibited since it distorts trade and creates monopolies. But there are many circumstances in which a good can be produced more inexpensively by a foreign producer or sold more inexpensively in one market than another. That is, not every situation in which a foreign good is offered more cheaply than a local good is "dumping." If a "countervailing duty" is added to make the foreign and domestic goods equal in price, then the consumer loses the advantage of the lower-priced good and the local producer is *de facto* subsidized. This does not make for more efficient or competitive markets. Treating all alleged dumping as if it were anti-competitive results in market-distortion.

Nonetheless, the original signatories of the Treaty of Rome were concerned that their partners would "dump" in their markets or that foreigners would dump in the common market. Hence, treaty article 91 prohibits the former, while the dumping of foreign country goods into the Community market is governed by the EU's Common Commercial Policy. If the Commission or Council find that dumping has occurred, countervailing duties or retaliatory trade measures could be employed. Still, the calculus is very subtle, and the judgments are somewhat political.[76]

State Aids

A far greater threat to a competitive common market is the prospect that a state will give assistance ("aid") to a private or public enterprise that competes in the market, distorting competition. These enterprises often are called "national heroes," and their support may be a matter of national prestige or to preserve jobs. In Europe many enterprises are public, and state subsidies to them can distort what otherwise would be a more efficient and competitive market.

In general, treaty article 92 (1) forbids such aids, but there are exceptions, for example, aid to uplift an economically backward region or to promote an "important project of common European interest." The Commission is to be the judge of these exceptions.[77] But the Commission is often subjected to a lot of pressure from member states not to let a national hero fail. Happily, as more and more services are privatized in Europe and as agreements are struck to open various sectors to Community-wide competition (airlines, telephone, energy), the prospect of state aid diminishes.[78]

Tax Harmonization

Traditionally governments raise revenue through taxes. The member states of the EU are no different, and they did not delegate that power to Community institutions. Consequently, the EU is beholden to the Council to set the sources and quantity of its revenue.

What the common market requires, however, is that no discriminatory tax be imposed by any member state, "directly or indirectly," that is not imposed equally on domestic products. The object was to harmonize tax treatment throughout the Community, without interfering with the sovereign right of the member states. Hence, all EU products are to be treated alike for tax purposes, and a state tax scheme is not to be structured to protect domestic products.[79] This includes taxes on largely imported products (wine) that might compete with chiefly domestic ones (beer). A UK tax scheme (on wine) was seen as a protective measure.[80]

While the power to set taxes remains with the member states, the Council was given new powers by the Maastricht Treaty to "adopt provisions for the harmonization of legislation concerning turnover taxes, excise duties and other forms of indirect taxation to the extent that such harmonization is necessary to ensure the establishment and the functioning of the internal market."[81] In this spirit, the Community has made great efforts to harmonize the rate of value-added tax (VAT)—a principal source of revenue in each member state. Doing so would put all states on an equal footing without "federalizing" the VAT. The result is that all member states' VAT rates are within a few percentage points of one another. Eventually, a harmonized Community tax regime and a completely harmonized VAT seem likely.[82]

Harmonization of Laws

A new treaty article 100 commands that the Council, acting unanimously, "issue directives for the approximation of such laws, regulations or administrative provisions of the Member States as directly affect the establishment or functioning of the common market." In general, articles 100 to 102 are meant to increase the pressure on member states to harmonize their laws. The initiative is not new. The goal of "harmonizing" member states' law began with the Treaty of Rome, but the process remains essentially voluntary. Community law is far more common in some areas (agriculture) than others (taxation).

Concurrently, the EU Commissioner responsible for the single market has proposed that the Commission collect and publish information about countries that are failing to meet their single market obligations. "If member governments do not like the adverse publicity that could arise from [the publication of this "score board" of single market lassitude] . . . they just have to make sure that they respect the rules and correct violations if they arise." In short, it is destructive of the common enterprise for some states to accept the benefits of the single market while sloughing off its obligations.[83]

Justice and Home Affairs, Pillar III

The third "Pillar" of the European Union (comprising justice and home affairs) is intergovernmental in nature. Pillar III was added by the Maastricht Treaty, but without precedent agreements (unlike the Common Foreign and Security Policy). Like the latter, however, the development of a joint policy in the areas of justice and home affairs has proceeded slowly, since the field cuts deeply into the sovereignty of the member states. However, in modern-day Europe, asylum and immigration policy, external border controls, drug and customs enforcement, and judicial and police cooperation (especially in cross-border criminal matters) are not concerns of one nation only.[84] They are phenomena that concern all EU member states in a customs area without borders.

The emphasis here, however, is on *cooperation* among the nation states, not on a common policy. Initially, the "Member States [are to] inform and consult one another with a view to coordinating their action." A stronger policy initiative may be needed to address these dangerous problems in a liberalized and mobile Europe. Hence, Article K.3 also gives the Council the option to "adopt joint positions . . . [and] joint action insofar as the objectives of the Union can be attained better by joint action than by the Member States acting individually." The Council also may "draw up conventions . . . [and] stipulate that the Court of Justice shall have jurisdiction to interpret [those conventions'] provisions."[85]

To date, the single most-comprehensive action the EU has taken under Pillar III is to create a European law enforcement intelligence agency, called "Europol."[86] It replaces a weaker predecessor (Interpol), a European environmental office, a European trademark office, a European drugs agency and a European plant and vegetable office. Current emphasis is on cooperation and information exchange, making it harder for illegal activity simply to disappear at national borders. But, at present, Europol has no independent enforcement authority (beyond that of national police forces).[87]

"Federalizing" Europe

Of course there is another way to harmonize the laws of the fifteen member states, without a Brussels regulation or directive. That is a simple "mutual recognition agreement" (MRA), whereby each member state would accept as equal or equivalent to its own the standards applied by the exporting nation. International MRAs are underway in the food and drug industries.

As similar as the EU members are, it would be no large step to agree to mutual recognition of standards, bypassing Brussels. However, this approach would not produce a *uniform* standard; so economies of scale and interchangabililty would not be realized, and there may be legitimate health or safety concerns.[88] As long as national parliaments and the EU share competence, then there will be room for conflict. Fortunately, this problem was recognized. Maastricht Treaty Declaration No. 13 speaks to the "[importance of encouraging] greater involvement of national parliaments in the activities of the European Union." In time this relationship is bound to be smoothed out. National parliaments have not been reduced to transposing European legislation, as they sometimes claim.

How "federal" is the European Union? My stock answer is that it is "as federal as it needs to be at any given time to achieve its objectives." There was and is no great rush on the part of member state leaders to delegate to Brussels power that they don't have to. This was the situation with our early central government as well. And yet, over the course of our history, more and more things reached beyond state borders and therefore fell into the interstate and international mandate of the federal Constitution. The same seems true in Europe. In order to participate fully in the process of globalization, EU member states have had to act collectively, not individually. There is a predictable national resistance, but it weakens as it becomes evident that the Community can produce results that the individual states cannot.

Article 3 of the Maastricht Treat did not so much add as to amplify Community commitments in the important areas of "economic and social cohesion"; environmental protection; the "competitiveness of Community industry"; "promotion of research and technological development"; "trans-European networks"; a "high level of health protection"; "education and training" and a "flowering of the cultures of the Member States"; "development cooperation"; "consumer protection"; and "the spheres of energy, civil protection and tourism." Doesn't this sound like a collectivization of effort in areas that reach well beyond a common economic market? In December 1996, a Conciliation Committee of the European Parliament and Council agreed to new labeling requirements for food products. The legislation covers labeling, presentation and advertising and is meant to align national rules concerning ingredients.[89]

Patent protection is another area in which the lack of a single European system causes businessmen to choose between a few member states and the EU as a whole. According to the European chemical industry, the lack of a comprehensive patent system is a "highly negative factor for competitiveness." It was estimated that, to maintain a patent in eight EU member states would cost ten times more than one covering the entire United States.[90] Another sector badly in need of harmonization is the European electric supply market. Once again, it is dominated by national monopolies, yet it is not likely to become cost-efficient unless competition and privatization occurs. European ministers have wrangled for four years over an acceptable solution. It can't come too soon as far as the European market is concerned.[91]

These are but a few examples of numerous ways in which the European Union is harmonizing and integrating. The sectors vary, the pace of integration varies, and there is a lot of harmonizing still to be done. But the process *is* going forward in ways large and small.

As it does, the European market becomes more and more important to the U.S., as both an ally and an adversary. Every new opening in Europe is a potential opportunity for U.S. businessmen and capitalists. A "federalistic"

Europe is well launched and advances itself on many fronts every day. It bears close watching by American businessmen and policy makers, for it may play an increasingly large role in the globalization of world trade. Indeed, the EU may be second only to the United States in this sweepstakes.[92]

THE SINGLE MARKET ON STEROIDS: ECONOMIC AND MONETARY UNION

The process that led eleven EU states into economic and monetary union is so laden with twists and turns that it deserves a book of its own. No good one exists, because events in this field move so quickly that any book-length treatment would be quickly dated. Hence, I offer this brief overview just to make the reader aware of the broad contours of the plan and to try to estimate the impact of a common currency on the Community market and the global economy.

The experts who have expounded on the pros and cons of a single currency for Europe are about equally divided on its merits and achievability.[93] At one point this appeared to be a genuine issue. Today, that question seems settled. The only questions that remain are whether the political will that launched EMU in January 1999 can be sustained and what its influence on global trade will be. Some knowledgeable economists think that impact will be profound.[94]

One can venture, as more and more Europeans have, that the single currency will allow easy price comparisons, eliminate transaction costs, unify financial service markets and perhaps establish a new world reserve currency. In short, EMU will give the EU the monetary market clout to go along with its production and consumption.[95]

Background

The idea of monetary convergence is not a new one in the EU. As early as 1978, the French and Germans spearheaded a drive to establish a European Monetary System (EMS), including a mechanism to stabilize exchange rates among EC member states' currencies. The Germans wanted to bind their economy and currency firmly to the other Community economies. The French were happy to bring the Deutsche mark (DM) within the influence of the EU. The result was a program[96] that produced a "basket" of EC currencies, each of which was to be maintained within 2.5 percent of its reference value to the strongest currencies in the basket (the DM and the Dutch guilder). It also produced a basket value—the European currency unit, or Ecu.[97] Each member state was nominally pledged to help support the value of every currency in the basket. Beyond this, nothing much was done about monetary union until the late 1980s.[98]

By that time, the convergence of the European market in other areas was exposing currency diversity as a limitation. Businessmen didn't want to deal in national currencies, so more and more dealings were denominated in ecu. When foreign currency was used (by tourists and small businesses), it took a long time to compete transactions and there were costs associated with all conversions. Moreover, separate currencies had tended to keep financial markets separate as well. There were twelve or fifteen banking markets, stock markets, accounting markets, and so on. Finally, there was the issue of monetary policy. While most every member state had its own central bank that set monetary policy, in reality they were all were influenced by the monetary policy of the state with the strongest currency (Germany).

The Single European Act made reference to "the progressive realization of Economic and Monetary Union" in its preamble, but nothing more. However, at the Hanover summit in June 1988 the European Council asked that a committee be established to study the steps necessary to achieve EMU. Jacques Delors, an economist and then-president of the European Commission, chaired the committee. The "Delors Report" envisioned a three-step process to monetary union, together with a timetable and standards to determine when ERM would come into being and which countries would qualify.[99] Its terms were incorporated into the Maastricht Treaty.[100] It provided for new institutions: the European Monetary Institute (EMI) (Article 109f and protocol 4); its successor the European Central Bank (ECB); and a European System of Central [National] Banks (ESCB) (Article 4a and protocol 3). Thus, the TEU introduced a unifying initiative quite unknown under prior treaties and the EMS.

The first of the three EMU stages began on July 1, 1990, with the abolition of all exchange controls and the complete liberalization of all capital movements.[101] The second stage, which began on January 1, 1994, established the European Monetary Institute (EMI). The EMI did the technical planning for EMU and monitored progress toward that goal. The EMI also recommended to Community institutions the legislation needed to consummate EMU. The EMI was located in Frankfurt, and its working language was English. At the beginning of the third stage, the EMI ceased to exist, and the European Central Bank (ECB) took over.[102]

The third stage might have begun in 1997, if a majority of member states could have qualified under the convergence criteria. Since that was not the case, the Treaty provided that any number of qualified states could form a single currency in 1999.[103] The European Council was to decide which countries met the criteria in early 1998. This was not a purely economic judgment, for the heads of state and government were influenced by political as well as economic concerns. Accordingly, on January 1, 1999, the exchange rates of the eleven qualifying states were irrevocably fixed, the ECB superseded the EMI and the ESCB was set up. A new currency unit—now called the "euro"—was born.

This was an ambitious plan, and no small amount of planning went into it. The technical part (for example, redesigning vending machines, parking meters and ATMs and harmonizing banking and accounting systems) was hard enough. But, for a long time, political will seemed lacking. Local citizens trusted their own currency and didn't want to change.

Initially, the most important task was to bring the separate national monetary systems into closer harmony. To do this, the Delors report set out firm economic criteria, called "convergence criteria."[104] Only the states that met those criteria would be allowed to participate in EMU in 1999, although other states could qualify and join later. (Two states, Denmark and the U.K., were given "opt outs," meaning that they may qualify and yet "elect" not to join). One economic expert joked that these criteria were so tough that they allowed only those countries with very strong currencies to abolish them.[105] But the truth is, the criteria were a "pledge" to the German people that they would never be asked to give up the Deutsche mark for a weaker European currency.

With slow growth in Europe during the 1990s, this lofty goal seemed impossible to meet. A major interim report, "The Impact of Currency Fluctuations on the Internal Market," noted that since the ERM crisis of 1992, five European currencies had depreciated by 20 percent or more against the most stable EU currencies. This hurt growth in the internal market, and the cautious wait-and-see attitude was exacerbating Europe's slowdown. The depreciated economies had made competitive gains, but only at the expense of their stable partners. The report concluded that the "definitive solution to this turmoil lies in the in the *convergence of economies*" (emphasis in original). A reduction in public debt was necessary, and an efficient and competitive EU depended upon "reinforced monetary solidarity." The Commission considered the "single currency [to be] the *essential complement* to the single market" (emphasis in original).[106]

This was followed almost immediately by a detailed report from the EMI on "The Changeover to the Single Currency." It was the most detailed of the reports to date. Of course the EMI report incorporated many of the ideas of prior reports, but it put a fine point on the work that remained to be done.[107] Together with the Commission report that preceded it, it put the whole issue squarely before the European Council at its summit in December 1995 in Madrid. The Council did not disappoint.[108] It settled a wide range of outstanding issues and gave the Commission, EMI and Ecofin Council directions to complete preparations for 1999.[109] The political will that seemed to have been lacking earlier finally was mustered in Madrid.

With the timetable and legal niceties settled, Community concern naturally turned to questions about which states would meet the convergence criteria, whether they could do so by early 1998, and whether they would constitute a "critical mass" of qualified states, to make the 1999 launch date credible. The convergence criteria gave national politicians a greater chance to privatize and reduce government obligations and blame it on Brussels.

Besides a single currency would complete the single market, solidify the EU's trading relationship with developing countries in Europe, and perhaps give it greater clout in global monetary circles, such as the dollar enjoys. However, the quest to meet the criteria was making money tight, slowing growth and perpetrating high unemployment. High unemployment requires government to spend more, pushing it farther from its debt goals. The goal of EMU proved important enough in the long term to warrant the short-term pain. The EU surely was not swinging its weight in the global economy. Its strongest currency, the Deutsche mark, ran a weak third to the dollar and yen, whereas the euro quickly leapt into second place. Thus, if the public and labor market had a great deal of angst about EMU, the business sector (a strong political influence that often cannot be felt outside Europe) bet on it. Recent polls have shown that public opinion has gradually shifted in its favor, too.[110]

The doubt that troubled some did not bother European political leaders and central bankers. Throughout 1996, against all odds, they seemed to make progress toward greater monetary convergence. No doubt they knew that budgetary discipline could restore the European economy to good health by lowering social costs and tax burdens and increasing competitiveness. This united European leaders, the only reservations being their partners. As the Germans had pledged that the euro would be as strong as the mark, it was insistent that no "Club Med" countries (Portugal, Spain, Italy and Greece) be allowed to participate in the first wave of EMU. Yet it wanted France to make the cut.[111] It was equally clear that a critical mass of participants was needed for the first wave. Germany and a few other small countries (the Dutch, Luxembourg, Belgium, Austria) probably would not do. It would be Germany and a bunch of dwarfs. Another *large* state was needed—probably France.

To convince its citizens, Germany insisted on strict application of the convergence criteria. It also wanted a formal "stability pact" that allowed the EMU insiders to investigate, warn and even punish their partners who strayed from budgetary discipline. Finally, they wanted a well-defined legal framework for the euro and a substitute rate mechanism (dubbed ERM 2) for those Community currencies that could not qualify for or chose not to join the euro group. All of these matters were exhaustively studied and were put before the European Council at its critical Dublin summit in December 1996.[112]

ERM2

The Florence summit had recognized that the exchange rate mechanism for the member states not participating in the euro would have to be voluntary. Dublin did nothing to disturb this, but the Ecofin report recognized that "all Member States, whether adopting the euro or not, have a strong common interest in the good functioning of economic and monetary union." Hence, euro participants *and* non-participants had to be involved in the dialogue on EMU, "including monetary and exchange-rate matters." In return, "in Stage 3 of EMU, all member States must pursue disciplined and responsive monetary policies." In other words, the non-participants would retain their own currencies, but freedom in monetary policy-setting would be limited. Intervention and support "in principle [would] be automatic and unlimited" for participants and non-participants; "relatively wide" fluctuation bands would be based on the euro; and exchange-rate policy cooperation was to be strengthened between the ECB and the central banks of ERM2 participants. Thus, the euro "outs" were really considered (and called) "pre-ins," to be closely supervised (and aided) by the Euro "ins."[113]

The "Stability Pact"

The Germans, who are rightly proud of the inflation-fighting record of the Bundesbank, wanted a price-stability pact that would insure that the budgetary discipline of Maastricht be continued after EMU Stage 3 began. This was the "stability pact" (now called the "stability and growth" pact). Since countries inside euroland would have a common monetary policy and since those in ERM2 would be monitored, virtually every EU economy was bound (only the U.K. and Greece were outside the ERM, and Greece has since reentered). However, "Euro area Member States will be obligated to submit stability programmes and will be subject to [investigation warnings and] agreed sanctions for failure to act effectively on excessive deficits." Hence, EMU is a serious commitment, with teeth.[114]

The Euro's Legal Framework

The legal framework of the euro was "of the greatest importance," for it must be stable, definitive and legally enforceable if people were to have confidence in it. Hence the euro was given a rate of one-to-one with the ecu. National currencies would have a fixed ecu/euro value when the ERM went out of being and EMU started. Contracts already denominated in national currencies or ecu were to be treated as continuous in the relative euro value unless their terms provide otherwise.[115]

The reason that the Ecofin Council Report was so significant is that the member states' economic and financial ministers had spent the better part of 1996 (the period between the Madrid and Dublin summits) hammering out the details of EMU with the assistance of the Commission and EMI. When the European Council met in Dublin, they merely "welcomed the excellent Report by the Ecofin council" and adopted it. (It is ANNEX I to the Summit report). Their work was made much easier by the masterful job that Baron Lamfalussy, first head of the EMI, did in preparing all the technical aspects of EMU. He was succeeded at the EMI in June 1997 by Dr. Wim Duisenberg. According to the original plan, the EMI was succeeded by the ECB once EMU began.[116]

In the end, the Commission recommended, the EMI certified, and the European Council approved that eleven EU countries be allowed to join euroland (Austria, Belgium, Finland, France, Germany, Ireland, Italy, Luxembourg, the Netherlands, Portugal and Spain). Thus the founding group was pleasingly large. It has nearly 300 million consumers, 19.4 percent of world GDP and 18.6 percent of world trade. (The U.S. has 19.6% and 16.6%, respectively, for comparison.)[117]

Now that a common currency is established, a way will be found to bring the weaker currencies aboard. (It makes no sense to exclude economies that require Community support but lack the budget discipline a central bank could supply.) Besides the technical work has been done, political inertia has been overcome, and most of the short-term pain has been suffered. Europe is downsizing and right-sizing. The European economy is beginning to pick up. Bonds issued in euros already are being issued and traded, not that any of this was noticed much in the United States.[118]

It was unfortunate for the EMU initiative that many Europeans associated it with high unemployment. But, to some extent, they are related. A government with a tax-and-spend social policy can sustain high employment (or at least mollify the effects of unemployment) until the cost of support makes the system uncompetitive and a severe recession forces structural changes. The EMU criteria anticipated this and forced the reconstructive change earlier. Still, if EMU is to succeed, it must have public support. To get that, the EU had to be seen by the public to be addressing the unemployment problem. In the longer term, EMU ought to do exactly that.[119]

Of course, splitting EU member states into euro "ins" and "outs" contributes to a "two-speed" or "variable geometry" Europe. But this was done in the Edinburgh summit compromise that allowed some members to "opt out" of EMU anyway. Besides, holding back the states that favor closer integration doesn't advance union.

Stage III and the Euro

The European Council chose the eleven "euroland" states in early 1998, applying standards more liberal than strict. If a little "creative accounting" was used to get the project started on time and to bring the right mix of currencies into the group, that had to be expected. Europeans have gotten this far with their market because they are willing to negotiate important outcomes. EMU is as important to Europe as any initiative since the creation of the Common Market itself. It had to start on time and with the "critical mass" necessary. Those currencies that didn't choose to or could not participate in the euro (the "outs") will be given a derogation (Article 109k(1)). Their status regarding the convergence criteria will be reviewed every two years, or upon their request. If they meet the criteria, the derogation will be abrogated and they will be able to join the EMU (Articles 109 K(2) and L(5)).

Once the initial group of euro participants was chosen, the Governing Council of the European Central Bank (ECB) was appointed by common consensus of the governments of the participating states. They will constitute the European System of Central Banks (ESCB). The statute governing the ECB and ESCB is Protocol No. 3 to the Maastricht Treaty. The members of both groups are to be entirely independent of political influence at the Community and national levels.

Wim Duisenberg, a Dutchman and second head of the EMI, was selected as the first president of the ECB. His election was opposed by the French because they feared that ECB policy would be dominated by the tight money policies of the Germans. Serving with him are five national bankers/ finance ministers (from Finland, France, Germany, Italy and Spain), for staggered terms, and of course the heads of each participating nation's central bank. The French also wanted there to be political accountability for the ECB and that euro-outs should not participate. But the "outs" were included as observer/commenters. After all, EMU will influence their economies too, and all eventually may become euroland members.[120]

At the launch of EMU (January 1, 1999), the exchange rates of participating states' currencies were irrevocably set relative to the euro (and therefore one another). The euro became a currency in its own right, and all interbank transactions among euroland states were denominated exclusively in euro. However, national currency will continue to be used in retail sales, since there were to be no euro notes or coins until 2002. "Dual pricing probably will be gradually introduced, to help the average person acclimate to the conversion from national currencies to euros." The ECB began to "define and implement . . . monetary and exchange rate policy," while the ESCB "start[ed] conducting a single monetary policy for the European currency area." To coordinate dealings in euroland, an integrated domestic and cross-border transfer system, dubbed TARGET (Trans-European Automated Real-time Gross Settlement Express Transfer), will be operated by the ESCB. No later than two years after the start of stage three (probably January 1, 2002), euro coins and bills will be introduced. No more than six months later, all national tender will be withdrawn and the euro area will be complete.[121]

Of course, setting euroland monetary policy in the first several years will be no easy task. The ECB is dependent on the states for much of its economic data. That data is not entirely uniform and may be tinged with self-interest. Further, there is no past experience by which to steer; any correction could overshoot or undershoot the mark. Finally, a one-size-fits-all macroeconomic policy is bound to aid some state economies more than others. This will put political pressure on the Council, Commission, ESCB and ECB. The frenetic attempt of the eleven to meet the convergence criteria and the numerous meetings of the Ecofin Council, EMI, ECB and ESCB are exactly what was needed to build a consensus about European monetary policy. Much now depends on national leaders. They must stick to the commitments they have made, or the system won't work as intended.[122]

EMU was a *major* undertaking for the Community. What made it worth the effort? The goal of truly "completing" the common market with a common currency has been mentioned. So has the convenience to exporters, importers and travelers of increasing the speed and lowering the cost of transactions. A *single*, coordinated monetary policy in euroland all but eliminates the prospect of using monetary policy selfishly or competitively among European states. No longer will they have to follow—or risk the consequences of not following—the tight money policy of the Bundesbank. Now they can participate in planning and executing a monetary policy nominally favorable to all. Of course, this will continue to reflect a conservative monetary policy, for "price stability" (low inflation) is a hallmark of both systems. But other goals (employment, competitiveness) will be added. Some restructuring of the single market is overdue and is best done as a group. A coordinated, independent, *Community* policy is more likely to lead to *sustained* growth than a patchwork of national policies.[123]

If Europe speaks with a single voice in global economic policy-making, then it is going to wield more clout. This should not trouble Americans too much, but they will have to take EMU into account in future monetary-policy calculations. If the euro proves weak against the dollar, U.S. goods and services will become dearer in Europe (our largest market), cutting our export income. If the euro proves strong (as is likely, since the ECB is using the U.S. Federal Reserve and the Bundesbank as its models), it will cut into the dominance of the U.S. dollar. According to Deputy Treasury Secretary Lawrence Summers, the dollar has shrunk from about 76 percent of world reserves in 1973 to 65 percent today. The early returns were mixed, but the euro will have to earn its place in the marketplace and can be expected to strengthen in the longer term.[124]

Following heroic preparation, the launch of the single European currency was a huge success. By the time it occurred, Europeans had somewhat acclimated to the change, and governments and large businesses had swung overwhelmingly behind it. The key, however, may have been the Asian meltdown. Contrasted with Asian and Latin American markets, Europe looked rather stable and, since its strongest currency (the Deutsche mark) was to disappear into the euro, it was a good bet when launched. Indeed, about 80 percent of the European market switched in the first week from the City of London's reference exchange rates to that used by euro-managers. In addition, the single market initiatives (tax harmonization, labor costs, corporate restructuring) are bound to be aided by a single unit of measure.

Will the euro succeed? There is every reason to expect that it will (just as the single market has been a success). For one thing, a single currency and monetary policy will accelerate the consolidation of the European market and make it more efficient and competitive. A single currency especially will allow consolidation of European financial services markets (banking, securities, insurance), producing markets the size of those in the United States and Asia. A single currency also makes a whole range of pan-European projects more probable. The fact that the EMU project is such an immense and visible one ought to give an enormous boost to European pride, on a parallel with the 1992 program. Politicians and businesses are committed to its success. With greater confidence should come more investment, lower interest rates, increased productivity and mobility in labor markets.[125] In some ways, it was a perfect time to launch a new currency. Annual economic growth in the euro-zone rose to 3.2 percent in the first quarter of 1998, a dramatic upsurge after a long period of sluggish growth. Further, EMU brought more discipline to euroland economies than many thought possible. Low inflation and stability also aided the launch. The last element is the collapse of Asian economies and the weakness of the yen.

The Asian meltdown had market implications for Europe, as it did for trading nations worldwide. But the decline of the yen left the world looking for another reserve currency. The euro came along just in time, to replace the yen and Deutsche mark and create a bipolar world again. Naturally, euroland countries will shift more of their reserves into euros, whereas previously they would not have held many European currencies beyond their own. (Before the launch, it was estimated that 71 percent of euroland central bank reserves were in dollars). Asian banks also will shift reserves to euros. At present, the EU's share of world output is 31 percent, compared to 27 percent for the U.S., but the EU share of reserve holdings is only 20 percent, compared to the U.S. 56 percent. If the euro is at all successful, that will change. As one Deutsche Bank official put it, "The euro will be to the dollar what Airbus is to Boeing."[126] There is no question that the euro will cut into the hegemony of the U.S. dollar. For this reason, the euro is likely to consolidate the European market in ways unthinkable without a common currency. The four EMU "outs" (the U.K., Sweden, Denmark and Greece) may join as soon as feasible.[127]

Once the competitive lines between the American (dollar), European (euro) and Asian (yen) currencies have been drawn, handicapping and speculation is inevitable. Without suitable and amicable coordination, currency competition could precipitate *economic* "warfare."[128] This will require coordination between the U.S. and the EU, but it need not be a cause for contention. The fewer the currencies and the wider their scope, the easier the coordination. The U.S. and EU have the largest stake in fostering security in the world. As Deputy U.S. Treasury Secretary Lawrence Summers has said, "If EMU works for Europe it will work for the United States."[129] An enlarged European financial services markets would offer opportunities for American institutions. Presently, the U.S. and EU shares are about equal.

Exchange-rate volatility could increase substantially unless currency markets are monitored, which will require greater U.S./EU coordination on monetary policy than presently exists. For the U.S. is more of a debtor nation than the EU, and a leading economist predicts a global shift in portfolio assets out of dollars into euros, with each holding about 40 percent of the total. The U.S. and EU have dominated trade policy since the advent of the GATT. Now they are about to dominate monetary policy too. If, as expected, the eurozone soon absorbs the British pound—which the majority of U.K. business leaders favor—then the single market will be almost complete. For this reason, many of the "world's top money managers are betting billions on the success . . . [of] Europe's single currency." Some of their enthusiasm is fueled by the size of the eurozone market and the fact that it runs a healthy trade surplus, whereas U.S. trade is regularly in deficit. Since Europeans can be expected to invest in the euro, and Asian investors have expressed the same intention, almost all of its gain will be at the expense of the U.S. dollar. What Japan seems to have lost in the Asian crises, Europe has gained.[130]

There is only one thing wrong with this. The G-7, the International Monetary Fund and the World Bank all remain structured to treat major European countries individually, rather than to treat euroland (or the EU) as a single entity. EU officials have been invited to the table to be certain, but they haven't been able to speak with the single voice that EMU gives them. How many seats should eurozone nations have if they share one currency, and why shouldn't one of those seats be occupied by the one person who speaks for the euro, the head of the European Central Bank? Should three of seven G-7 members represent a single currency, and yet be seated as nations? Naturally, the four European nations don't want their prestige diluted. But to seat all of them *and* Euro-representatives would be overwhelming. Times change, and institutions must too.[131] Only the Quad 4 (the U.S., EU, Japan and Canada) reflects this fact. Hence, we have to ask ourselves what changes in global influence and policy-setting might be precipitated by EMU and the euro.[132]

THE EUROPEAN UNION'S EXTERNAL POLICY

Although the European Union is an economic giant, it is a pygmy when it comes to foreign policy. This is not surprising, for it is difficult for its members to delegate their foreign affairs prerogatives. However, it may be impossible for Europe to speak with a multiplicity of voices any longer. A good example is the Uruguay Round of the General Agreement on Tariffs and Trade (GATT). It was quite successfully negotiated by EU Commissioner Sir Leon Brittan and U.S. Trade Representative Mickey Kantor in the waning days of the latter's fast-track negotiating authority. But when the Commission's competence to negotiate on behalf of the entire Community was tested in the European Court, it held that the Commission *shared* authority with the member states in the areas of services and intellectual property. Consequently, GATT agreements in those areas had to be ratified by individual states.[133] It is no wonder, then, that the Commission has sought authority to negotiate on behalf of the entire Community on a wider range of issues. As the other GATT negotiators have this competence, withholding it weakens the EU's position at the bargaining table.[134]

European external policy derives from Article 110 of the EEC, stating that, by establishing a customs union, the EU member states meant to contribute to "the harmonious development of world trade."[135] A more substantive step was taken with Maastricht. It created a second pillar to European affairs, a "common foreign and security policy" (CFSP),[136] thus opening the door to collective action. But the Treaty signatories held back on a truly "common" policy, because pillars two and three of the European Union are chiefly intergovernmental (the policies are to be worked out among the leaders of the member states, generally acting unanimously). Hence, most actions in this sector cannot be taken by Community institutions, nor are they enforceable in Community courts. Nonetheless, the European Council is to define the "general guidelines" for the common foreign and security policy. The member states are supposed to "support the Union's external and security policy actively and unreservedly," but this can mean abstaining and/or not interfering with it. Because some member states of the EU are not members of the Western European Union (WEU) or the North Atlantic Treaty Organization (NATO), the treaty terms do not embrace these defense organizations but merely allude to them. While respecting those states' neutrality, however, it is clear that the treaties contemplate "concerted and convergent action" in this area.[137]

It would be wrong to suggest that the CFSP and WEU were well-defined Community programs. Indeed, NATO itself has been searching for a better-defined role since the end of the Cold War. For the time being, the U.S. and Canada will retain their roles as partners in the defense of Europe, consonant with their own security. Meanwhile, the EU needs a better-coordinated program in the external sectors. It has succeeded more in the economic than in the defense sector. But, with the expansion of the EU and NATO to the east, both sectors are involved, and more coordination is necessary. If the goals of CFSP are to be realized, a further delegation of authority will have to be made.[138]

Since the EU was endowed with "legal personality" and established for "an unlimited period," one can expect that it will exercise authority in international fora to the extent possible.[139] After all, the whole notion of a

CFSP is that systematic cooperation will gradually lead to joint action. And the expansion of joint competencies tacitly accepts that the union is more likely to negotiate a successful deal for Europe than is each state acting on its own.[140]

Even before Maastricht, it was recognized that the Community was better able to deal in international fora as a unit than the individual states. The Commission generally is delegated the responsibility to negotiate, based on guidance from the Council, and to maintain "appropriate relations" with a variety of international organizations. A more generic authority was granted by the Maastricht Treaty, particularly in the field of international affairs.[141] The full range of the EU's external activities is so vast that they are not likely to be covered in any single document, save the European Commission's annual report.[142]

The EU sits as a major trading bloc—perhaps *the* major trading bloc—in the largest trading enclaves. In addition to the GATT, the EU—generally represented by the Commission president—is an invited guest to meetings of the G-7 and G-10 (in which EU member states participate as well). The EU, as such, is a full member of the Quad 4 nations. The Commission president and rotating head of Council have two summits annually with the U.S. president. What other national head of state can claim that? Indeed, one might well wonder whether the EU is overrepresented in the G-7, the UN Security Council, the OECD, the IMF, the World Bank, or NATO, where several EU member states have seats, although nominally committed to the same policy.[143] In time these potential duplications will have to be addressed.

The Community has undertaken, concurrently with member states' programs, to offer economic and social assistance to developing countries, leading eventually to their "smooth and gradual integration . . . into the world economy." Of particular interest is a treaty relationship between EU member states and "Non-European countries and territories [that] have special relations with [them]." In general, the countries are former African, Caribbean and Pacific dependencies, hence the name "ACP countries."[144]

Other agreements have been inked with former EFTA (European Free Trade Area) states, in what is now called the European Economic Area (EEA), in which the four freedoms are generally practiced.[145] "European Agreements" have been signed between the EU and various Central and Eastern European countries, namely, Bulgaria, the Czech Republic, Hungary, Poland, Romania and Slovakia. All of these countries are viewed as prospective candidates for accession to membership in the EU. The agreements give a certain structure to the process and give these states-in-waiting access to economic opportunities in Europe they might not otherwise enjoy. Conversely, the agreements give EU businesses access to expanding markets in Central and Eastern Europe. Of course, U.S. businesses are equally interested in these promising markets, but the Europeans have the better prospect of exploiting them, due to proximity and the fact that they hope to join the EU.

The U.S. and the EU cooperate in the rehabilitation of Central and Eastern European countries, but in the area of market opening they compete. This may be one reason why the EU has lagged in developing Asian relations. The U.S. seems to have preferred Asia to Europe. Segmentation strategy is risky, however. Emerging economies in the newly independent states could one day become part of "Fortress Europe." For example, the European Investment Bank (EIB), with some Ecu 21.4 billion ($26.7 billion) invested in 200 major projects in EU member states in 1995, also supported projects in more than 120 foreign countries. The lion's share went to Europe, however. Only $936 million (8%) of the lending went to Asia and Latin America.[146]

Of course, the EU and its member states have relations with Russia as well, but Russia is equally concerned about its relationship with the U.S. Indeed, it will pursue advantageous alliances wherever it can find them (including China), in its unsteady progress toward capitalism and democracy. Moreover, the EU has invaded America's own backyard and signed trade deals with our NAFTA partners Canada[147] and Mexico and with a South American trading bloc, Mercosur. How quickly or fully these trade relationships will develop and what may happen to them if a Free Trade Area of the Americas (FTAA) is formed cannot be foreseen. For our purposes, it is enough to document that the EU has designs beyond Europe.

U.S.–EU Trade Relations

No trading relationship is more central to the premise of this book than that between the United States and the European Union. It is, quite demonstrably, a bittersweet relationship. Some remarkable market openings have resulted from our joint cooperation, but bitter hostility has erupted when we disagreed. The range of subjects is too vast to chronicle here and will grow larger as time passes. Here I wish to give just a snapshot of what this trading relation has accomplished and what it might accomplish.

The history of United States cooperation with European nations predates the European Union. But then, so does its history of conflict. In recent years the balance has continued, with the U.S. and EU competing in world trade circles, while trying to cooperate in their world-leading bilateral trade. At times the disputations seem like a petty family feud. But transatlantic trade is a high-stakes economic game, and the players don't always agree on the rules. At the root may lie a fundamental disconnect between U.S. and European attitudes. Europe is gaining power, particularly after the decline in Asia and Japan and the launch of its single currency. It wants respect. The U.S. is wedded to its own ways. Despite their differences, the U.S. and

EU can be expected to be at the forefront of economic change and integration, yet their competition is likely to continue.

A formal pledge of mutual cooperation in trade opening goes back at least as far as November 1990. However, this was a weak document. A much more comprehensive and forceful agreement, the "New Transatlantic Agenda" (NTA), was signed at a EU–U.S. summit in December 1995.[148] One of the bold initiatives of the NTA was to establish a Transatlantic Business Dialogue (TABD). It allowed businesspersons, meeting concurrently with political leaders and trade negotiatiors, to have some influence on the negotiation process. The TABD has not only proposed constructive solutions to difficult trade problems but also has kept constant pressure on both sides to improve trading relationships. It is doubtful whether the initiative would have been so successful without private-sector involvement. Not surprisingly, European and U.S. businesspersons had a large hand in promoting this tangible cementing of "the world's most important economic relationship." The TABD is premised on the fact that "traditional government-to-government communication is no longer enough [to open bilateral trade as quickly and as fully as possible]." Four working groups were established, and 70 recommendations were made concerning "practical ways to reduce impediments to trade." The standards group works on harmonizing various sectors, including automotive, pharmaceutical, electronics, telecommunications and information technology. In addition, the TABD had begun work on WTO issues, such as an information technology agreement, intellectual property protection, international business practices (including punishment for bribery of public officials), investment and research and development. According to Commerce Undersecretary Stuart Eizenstat, "No one would have quite imagined the degree to which the TABD has influenced government decision-making on both sides of the Atlantic. It has become deeply enmeshed and embedded into the U.S. government decision-making process on a whole range of regulatory, trade and commercial issues."[149] This is so because the U.S. president and EU leaders summit only twice a year, whereas government and business negotiators meet regularly.

Among the two largest market-opening successes are global pacts to liberalize basic telecommunications markets from January 1, 1998, and free trade in information technology. The former deal involves 69 nations (the EU fifteen negotiating as one) and over 93 percent of world revenues for telecom services and is expected to yield an economic benefit exceeding $1 trillion by the year 2010. In addition to basic telephony, the agreement covers electronic data transmission, telex and fax transmission involving cable, fiber optics, radio and satellite. In both the EU and US, 100 percent foreign ownership of domestic long-distance telecom services will be allowed, although some nations will retain some restrictions on foreign ownership, including Canada and Japan.[150]

The second large deal, spearheaded by the U.S. and the EU, involved some 20 information-technology producing countries, including several in Asia. The goal was to bind over 90 percent of world trade in these products and totally eliminate tariffs on computers, telecommunications equipment and other high-tech products by the year 2000. The U.S. and EU reached their original consensus at the WTO ministerial meeting in December 1996 and have been adding parties since. The liberalization will take place in four annual steps, beginning in July 1997. World trade in information technology products was worth about $500 billion in 1996 and is growing rapidly.[151]

A third initiative of enormous potential is the effort the U.S. and EU are making to reach an MRA involving product testing and certification. If a good, already tested and certified in the U.S. or EU, is tested again before import, a great deal of time and money is wasted. Yet to harmonize the practices on both sides of the Atlantic would take years. It is estimated that approximately one-half of the roughly $110 billion in U.S. merchandise exports to the EU every year require some form of certification. By eliminating this duplication, more than $40 billion worth of transatlantic trade will be expedited. "If it's safe enough for the United States, it [should] be safe enough for Europe and vice versa," according to Irish prime minister John Bruton.

This also is an important test of the viability of the New Transatlantic Agenda and the TABD. European and American businessmen have made MRAs in a variety of sectors central to their effort to reduce red tape and export costs. If they succeed in areas currently under discussion, other products will undoubtably be added. Indeed, if this experiment succeeds, global MRAs might not be too far off.[152]

With both sides feeling that the original pact had flagged somewhat, a new transatlantic arrangement was announced at the EU/U.S. summit in May 1998. Dubbed the Transatlantic Economic Partnership (TEP), it was to include services, tariff reduction and electronic commerce, with a broad program to be in place by the year 2000. Once again, business interests were instrumental in promoting the breakthrough, and additional areas for mutual recognition continue to be found.[153] By the fall, both the U.S. and EU had put forth "action plans" to implement the deal and had realized that it was of such a scale that more money would be needed to pursue all of its many facets. Some persons have suggested an Atlantic trading bloc, but there does not seem to be much enthusiasm for that (if, indeed, it would be legal under the GATT).[154]

This is the rosier side of U.S.–EU relations, however. Whether due to legitimate trade differences or an effort to protect their respective domestic markets, the U.S. and EU disagree dramatically about many areas of trade. Take, for example, the exportation of beef and poultry products. Transatlantic veterinary negotiations that have gone on for some years have failed to resolve substantial differences concerning the rigor of U.S. poultry in-

spections and a long-standing EU ban on U.S. beef fed with growth hormones. A WTO dispute settlement panel has ruled that the EU ban violates
global sanitary and phyosanitary rules, but the EU has been slow to capit-
ulate. Meanwhile, the EU's ban may prevent as much as $50 million in U.S.
poultry imports from entering the EU. If this happens, the U.S. has threatened to block the import of EU meat, exceeding $300 million.

The EU also had blocked for years the importation of genetically modified
corn for human or animal consumption. Recently, the European Commission relented, there being no scientific evidence to support the ban, but not
without seeking to impose labeling restrictions. Another long-running U.S.–
EU dispute involves the latter's licensing scheme for banana imports. For
years the EU granted preferential import treatment to some former dependencies (ACP nations). The U.S. and some Central American countries
challenged the scheme, and a WTO dispute settlement panel agreed. The
EU accused the U.S. of favoring its large multinationals over seven impoverished Caribbean countries. The U.S. retorted that it was attacking the
EU's trade bias, not the producers.[155] And so it goes. The U.S. and EU
enjoy a large and rewarding bilateral trade, and yet they cannot agree on
many trade principles.

The Mediterranean Basin

The EU's foregone expansion to the east strains the Community along
its north-south axis. The EU's "southern" members are most like the eastern expansion candidates as regards industrial base and per capita GDP.
Unlike the candidates, however, current EU members are in a position to
do something about expansion. Accession treaties require a unanimous vote
in both the European Council and the member states' legislatures. But the
European Commission does not want to play regional favorites. Its Work
Programme for 1997 stated its intention to "develop *relations with a number of non-member countries* in 1997" (emphasis in original). First, of course,
come the associated countries. Second is the United States, the EU's largest
trading partner. Third is peace in the former Yugoslavia (an embarrassment
to Europe). Fourth, however, came "the Mediterranean countries" (well
before Community initiatives in the rest of the world, including Russia and
Asia). *Bilateral* relations with key nations in the Mediterranean basin were
ended in 1995, and a *multilateral* plan for Maghreb and Middle Eastern
countries was substituted, doubling aid from the European Investment Bank
to about Ecu 9.4 billion ($11.3 billion) during 1995–99 and aiming for a
Euro-Med free trade zone by the year 2010. This would give these countries
preferential access to the EU's single market, already the region's largest
customer.

The policy has other dimensions as well. The EU hopes that peace in the
Middle East can be achieved through economic as well as political means.

It wants to stem the tide of fundamentalism in the region and shore up fragile economies that, should they fail, might require more EU assistance and send floods of refugees to Europe. The EU's Mediterranean members extracted this commitment from Germany as a *quid pro quo* for their support of Germany's pet project, expansion to the east. With the collapse of Communism, there apparently is much more to fear from economic weakness and political extremism in the south than in the east. Greater stability and prosperity would attract more foreign investment, relieving the EU of some of its aid and security burden. However, the hurdles are high. The Mediterranean basin is vast, and infrastructure is lacking. Only about 6 percent of its trade is intraregional.

The Barcelona Euro-Mediterranean agreement pledged these states to "settle their disputes by peaceful means" and "renounce . . . the threat or use of force," "strengthen their cooperation . . . [to combat] terrorism" and to "promote regional security." We have heard all this before. With the EU standing as a guarantor, however, a "free trade area" may yet be established in the Euro-Med area. The gradual improvement in relations with Turkey (already a NATO member) may give these desperate nations hope that they too might join in European prosperity.[156] If so, the EU will have expanded its market again.

Russia and the Newly Independent States

With a substantial footprint in both Europe and Asia, Russia is eager to recover the influence it enjoyed before the 1991 dissolution of the Soviet bloc. But, with fragile political leadership, a shrunken economy and an insufficient and inconsistent plan to convert to a market economy, Russia remains a large question mark, politically and economically. Because of the size of Russia's nuclear arsenal, the size of its economy and its former position of influence in the world, Western nations are keen to maintain cordial relations (witness Boris Yeltsin's warm reception in Western capitals). Reinforcing his leadership on the international scene is one of the smartest things the West can do, for it has no idea how pro-Western his successor will be. When Yeltsin felt snubbed by the West, he courted China. This may have led to Russia's being welcomed as a virtual full member of the Group of Seven (G-7) industrialized nations. (Its Denver summit in 1997 referred to the "Summit of the Eight"). G-7 nations want to do whatever they can to restore Russia to economic health (as a democratic, capitalist economy), and they want to curb Chinese adventurism. But they must wonder if that is possible and what it will cost.

It is foolish to suggest that Russia is a major industrialized nation when its economy is not as strong ($4,190 estimated per capita GDP in 1997) or as modernized as some Central and East European states now associated with the EU. Yeltsin was not strong enough to thwart NATO expansion plans, nor has he been able to get the quantity of monetary support needed (assuming it would be well used) to refloat his foundering economy. On the other hand, he has been adept at shifting his position and his political team, so that it appears that a restoration to political and economic health may be but a short way off. Finding a place for Russia in the new order is a geopolitical imperative, however, particularly for the European Union.

The EU is Russia's leading trading partner, consuming nearly 40 percent of Russian exports (especially oil and gas) and providing one-third of its imports. Germany alone accounts for 40 percent of the EU's Russian trade. Whereas a 1995 trade agreement sets the average EU tariff on Russian exports at below 1 percent, Russia taxes EU exports at almost 20 percent. In time, this protection must come down. Meanwhile, investors (even international lending institutions) are loathe to invest in Russia because of its instability and limitations on foreign investments. Between 1992 and 1996, Russia received only around 1 percent of total international investment; a fraction of that going to China. Instead of granting aid, which might be misused, the EU's main aid to Russia is through TACIS, a program to transfer technical, economic and institutional know-how. It is available to all former Soviet states, but Russia gets about 60 percent, or more than $200 million a year.

It seems clear by now that there will be no speedy turnaround for the Russian economy. It is too large, there is too much to learn and change and there are too many operatives eager to steal a piece of the action. On the other hand, it seems less and less likely that Russia will lapse back to totalitarianism or enter a communist relationship with China. Russia just seems to teeter on the brink, buffeted by events both external and internal, but not going over. For this it owes credit to its Western supporters and the resourcefulness and patience of its own people.[157]

It will be some time, if ever, before Russia may actually *join* the EU or NATO. But it is more important that they join the OECD, the WTO and G-7. That will bring Russia more into the Western group, but progress will be gradual. Large Russian monopolies like Gazprom (gas), VES (electricity), Lukoil and the railways are so insinuated in Moscow's ruling circles that it is politically difficult to bring them to heel. Hence, there is little room for any private, midsized industries to grow. In the words of the managing director of the IMF, "Russia risks being mired in a no-man's-land between a centrally planned system and a fully functioning economy." It is clear, however, that Russia's brief flirtation with democratic capitalism has badly miscarried. President Yeltsin was never in complete charge, and the competition to succeed him has never allowed any policy "core" to develop.

What the future holds is anyone's guess. The international economic community has no choice but to remain engaged and supportive (for one thing, they have a lot invested there). However, more promising players are emerging (China and Central and Eastern European countries). For this reason, private investors are likely to give Russia a wide berth, further complicating its problems. As for creditors and the international community, they have little choice but to work with the Russian authorities to restructure present debt and try to turn the economy around. But this assumes that there is some light at the end of the tunnel. In its present state of chaos, there is precious little of that. But Russia is a bear not easy to dismount.[158]

In this struggle between market good and evil, between a return to state control and free market liberalization, the odds seem to favor the latter. For one thing, public largesse has been made contingent on it. Russia cannot really profit from its large trove of natural and human resources unless it can get the capital to do so. The *quid pro quo* is market opening.[159]

Meanwhile, a range of Western states have reached out to other former Soviet states in a variety of ways. The European Union has signed cooperation agreements with Georgia, Azerbaijan and Armenia; the U.S. Commerce Department established a "state-of-the-art" business center in Uzbekistan (its thirteenth in the region) and the IMF and World Bank have made a variety of loans to help former Soviet states complete their reform programs and develop infrastructure.[160] There is a huge potential consumer market at stake, *if* it can be developed.

Before that can happen many reforms must be made, some of them quite foreign to the formerly Communist people, businesses and market. According to the World Bank, they include: strengthening legal institutions and the rule of law; improving the financial system, its security, openness and oversight; reform of the tax system; improving market access; better but smaller government; more privatization; more investment in people (training) and plant (modernization, innovation); and a true, sustained willingness to join the world economy.[161] This is a tall order, but "middle-Europe's capitalist renaissance" is receiving help from a variety of sectors. The EU offers the biggest spoils. The U.S., while robustly encouraging the process, has put up very little money.

Asia

As mentioned previously, the EU has not been as effectively engaged in Southeast Asia as has the U.S. Yet the EU is as economically exposed as we are, and perhaps more so, due to its continued high unemployment and the fact that EU economies were just beginning to grow when the Asian flu hit.

CONCLUSION

On both economic and political fronts, the EU's external programs are ambitious and keep it well in the globalization game.[162] Whether the European or American version of market liberalization takes hold in Central and Eastern Europe remains to be seen. It seems likely that the region will become the captive of the Europeans first, and then both will liberalize more along more capitalist lines. But that assessment might not take enough account of transitional economies like Russia and China. The macro-managed model, in which all interests are balanced, may yet prove the best.

Meanwhile, the European Union has to determine its destiny in the near term. The preceding account, which just hits the high points, suggests the immense scale and scope of the domestic and foreign programs upon which the EU has embarked. It has realized a number of successes, particularly since 1987. Progress toward the single market has made internal trade more robust; more common policies and standards are being developed; privatizations continue and the single currency should accelerate the process. Conversely, there are plenty of pressing problems that the EU needs to confront. For some time now it has been mired in a recession but has been slow to develop a common approach to end it. As a result, the member states often compete with one another for better economic success, when trade competition ought to be external, not internal. States continue to emphasize language and cultural differences that matter less and less in international trade. Continued high labor costs and unemployment limit national politicians' room for maneuver. Externally, the EU has run a poor third to Japan and the U.S. in the field of global trade. Presently, the EU has no well-articulated external policy.

For that reason, the Community institutions must be given the resources needed to carry out its many programs. Failure to supply enough could starve the Community's growth and hamper its effectiveness. But I have always been amazed by how much the Community does, and how well, with so small a budget and staff. The key is the leadership provided by the EU member states' heads of state or government. Obviously, each of them faces political pressures at home to produce results that equal or exceed those of their EU partners. This is a forlorn hope. There is more collectivity than separateness in upgrading Europe and the world economy.

Most of these things need to be done at the Community level, but there is a built-in bias against going too fast. The Community is still suffering a backlash from Maastricht. This may be quietly laid to rest by the generation now coming into full maturity, whose imagination and energy could turn Europe around quite suddenly. If that happens in a market as large and as important as Europe, we will be sorry that we weren't watching the European "experiment" more closely.

Chapter 10

Widening the European Community

If the European Union is facing so many challenges in the "deepening" process, should it be trying to "widen" (add new members) at the same time? It might be wise for the EU to husband its resources and attempt just one initiative at a time. But political and economic forces don't always allow this. The deepening of the Community, discussed earlier, is made necessary by rapidly changing world economic conditions. Widening has been thrust on the EU by the failure of communism in Europe.

One should not be too pessimistic about the EU's ability to deepen and widen concurrently, however. Since it was founded in 1957, the EU has expanded to fifteen states. It could well add several more early in the twenty-first century.[1] At the same time, the EU fifteen was deepening as well. So the two processes surely *can* proceed in tandem.

What makes the EU's expansion more difficult this time around is the condition of the governments and economies of the accession candidates. Harmonization in the EU's international market is more difficult if EU expansion creates greater diversity. To delay the accession of Central and Eastern European states (CEEs) too long is to risk creating political and economic instability in the region. That may cost the EU more than their inclusion would. On the other hand, absorbing them too soon (before they are economically and politically ready) might strain the Community's programs so much that there is neither a single market nor the international influence that the EU covets.

The "ins" and the "outs" seek integration for opposite reasons. EU members want stable eastern states as a buffer to post-Soviet political instability and ambitions. The CEEs want to align with the EU and NATO to get the security that those alliances might provide. They want EU capital and know-how to bring their economies up to Western levels. The EU wants access to the expanding CEEs markets but is shy about risking capital and technology in unpredictable markets. Of course, some CEEs will outperform others. Some already have. But this is a story with many dimensions. They reveal that the absorption of CEEs into the EU can be a gold mine and a liability all at once. (Some CEEs have annual growth rates equal to the Asian "tigers" and may be just as shaky.) For businessmen and bankers the situation bears watching, for its opportunities and its risks.

EFTA: THE EUROPEAN ECONOMIC AREA AND EUROPE AGREEMENTS

When the EEC was founded in 1957, a group of states that were not disposed (or not invited) to join formed the European Free Trade Association (EFTA). The EFTA was a looser, intergovernmental arrangement, its secretariat little more than an information clearinghouse and watchdog. Because EFTA nations had such close trading ties with the EU, they were obligated to follow many of its commercial practices, even though they had no voice in setting them. In time, many EFTA nations acceded to EU membership, increasing their obligations but giving them a vote.

When the Maastricht Treaty was being finalized, EFTA nations sought to restructure their relationship with the EU. The result was the European Economic Area (EEA), which added services, capital and people to the treaty relationship. When Switzerland refused to join the EEA and when Austria, Finland and Sweden acceded to the EU (in 1995), the EEA was reduced to three countries: Iceland, Liechtenstein and Norway.[2]

EXPANSION

It is widely conceded that the EU can't expand until it reforms its legislative processes and most expensive programs (e.g., agriculture). However, the European Council failed at the summits of Amsterdam (June 1997) and Vienna (December 1998) to make the institutional and budgetary changes necessary to do so. Nevertheless, the Council did agree to special summits in 1999 to assure that budget reforms would be made in the Community's 2000–2006 comprehensive financial package. Institutional reform should be completed by the year 2002. These reforms will tell a lot about how the member state governments expect the Community enterprise to develop in the near term. The modest budgetary and agricultural reforms taken to mid-1999 don't bode well, but the European Council often rises unexpectedly to the challenges that face it. As Europeans adjust to the Union and new trade paradigms, the political cost decreases.

The six Central and Eastern European nations engaged in membership talks (accession partners) are relatively poor and agrarian. They will add 63 million persons to the Community's population (17 percent), but only 3 percent to its GDP. Furthermore, to bring the candidates' economies into line with the EU fifteen would require that Community assistance to existing member states be reduced. Each member has a veto over enlargement. Thus, while the talks go forward and frustrations build in the candidate states and in Brussels, current EU member states are in no haste to expand except on the best terms. Eventually that will happen (perhaps around 2002–2003), or the EU would lose credibility.[3]

Nevertheless, the process is likely to be a long one, bedeviled by problems both within the candidate countries' control and beyond it, for example, the stability of their economic and political systems, the availability of foreign investment, the jealousies of weaker EU member states, the need to adjust structural policies and the concerns of the still-influential Russian state. Brussels is faced with a daunting task. If it is managed well, it will add millions of consumers to the EU together with "an educated labor force, an increasing degree of macroeconomic stability and an openness to foreign trade and inward investment." Over 50 years of state-managed economy had frozen CEEs out of the European renaissance, so there is quite a lot of catching up to do. Consider the time it has taken for East Germany to begin to close the gap with West Germany. However, the European Bank for Reconstruction and Development (EBRD) notes that "[i]ncreased financial stability has helped to trigger a sharp rise in inflows of funds [to CEEs] from abroad." Foreign direct investment (FDI) rose from $13 billion in 1993 and 1994 to $21 billion in 1995; roughly 12 percent of net private capital inflows.

At least this is the sunny side of the picture. Its dark side reveals that most of the capital and energy is expended on just three or four countries whose market-reorientation is most advanced, namely, the Czech Republic, Hungary and Poland. The other large beneficiary is Russia, but, as we have seen, its economic transition is slow and not assured.[4] However, "recovery" is relative. According to EBRD statistics (using 1989 numbers as 100), small declines in these state-managed economies appeared as early as 1990 (a 4 percent loss of GDP in Hungary and Russia and 12 percent in Poland). Poland began to show almost immediate improvement, posted a small gain in GDP as early as 1992 and returned to 1989 levels by 1995. The Czech Republic slid further, but turned around in 1994, as did Hungary. They stood at about 90 percent of their 1989 GDP levels by 1996. Russia, however, saw double-digit drops in GDP for almost four years and stood at just 56 percent of its 1988 GDP in 1996.[5]

The big question for the EU is how and when and whether to absorb these CEE nations. At the Essen Summit in 1994, the decision was taken to enlarge the EU to the east. Representatives of the candidate governments were invited to participate in at least some portion of future EU summits. It was hoped that this would boost contacts, warm relations and hasten integration. Instead, it has promoted monologues about preparedness and has yet to produce a clear direction or timetable. Meanwhile, the best-prepared CEEs are caught between the instability in Russia, their less able neighbors and the impatience of their own people.[6] The matter is particularly pressing for Germany, the predominant economy in the region. EU expansion to the east improves its security and is a potential boon to the German economy. Since 1993, German exports to Eastern Europe have risen sharply and now exceed those to the U.S. German direct investment in Eastern Europe nearly doubled (to DM 4.2 billion) from 1993 to 1995. Nearly 10 percent of German FDI is aimed at Central and Eastern Europe, and some German companies have started operations there. But Germany must appreciate the cost and effort necessary to reintegrate CEEs into Western Europe. It has spent many billions of DM on reunification with East Germany, and yet its per capita GDP is only about 40 percent of the EU average.[7]

Foreign direct investment is a fickle thing, however. It can and will go anywhere that conditions seem favorable. If steady, high levels of growth don't seem assured, the flow quickly changes. This will happen in Central and Eastern Europe if the assimilation process bogs down or if emerging economies suddenly appear too risky. There also are concerns about gaps in legal frameworks, deficient tax systems, and fraud and corruption. If there are more attractive venues and foreign capital departs, European integration will be slow. When the bloom was on Southeast Asia (1996), it was estimated that Singapore alone received about one-half as much FDI as all of Eastern Europe and the former Soviet Union combined. We know how quickly that disappeared in the Asian meltdown.[8]

However, the westernmost states in the Soviet bloc always did have a closer trading relationship with Europe. From their perspective, they want freer trade with the EU, not its aid. In fact, they probably need both. In 1989, for example, EU trade with the entire Soviet bloc comprised only 6 or 7 percent of extra-Community trade. However, for CEEs, 15 to 30 percent of their exports went to the West even in 1989. Between 1989 and 1992, the three fastest-reforming CEE economies (Poland, Hungary and the Czech Republic) grew their trade with the West by about 50 percent, effectively substituting Western markets for the ones that disappeared in the east.

While the EU's association agreements give states preferential access to EU markets, some sensitive areas have been protected. These include agriculture, iron and steel, textiles, footwear and chemicals, areas in which the eastern states are particularly competitive due to their significantly lower labor costs. Protecting prime markets from eastern competition stifles progress toward equalibrium (and potential EU membership) while artificially protecting inefficient Community industries. It is a sad commentary on the

EU that, when it feels its economic security threatened, it retreats into market protection.[9]

It is not by chance that the Essen Summit in 1994, when Germany held the presidency of the European Council, promised EU membership to Central and Eastern European states, when qualified. This encouraged Germans to invest and expand into eastern markets. By one account, German companies were outspending American companies by 4 to 1 in Poland, the premier transitional economy and the largest. Germany hoped for a rapid expansion of the Community to Poland, Hungary and the Czech Republic (and possibly Slovenia, a small but relatively wealthy and Westernized state). This would leave Slovakia (the poorer one-half of the old Czechoslovakia), Romania and Bulgaria outside the first wave of entrants. Also outside would be the Baltic States (Estonia, Latvia and Lithuania, although they are in pretty decent economic shape), because of Russia's sensibility about European border states moving into the Western block. The remaining Balkan states and possibly some former Soviet states may make it into the EU on a third wave of accessions. But that is far in the future.[10]

The reason for being selective about this expansion is that the process of market conversion and the volume of Western help varies considerably among the candidate nations. It seems important for Germany and its expansion-minded partners to prove that the Community can expand, before economic and political relations in Europe ossify once again or global trade claims the upper hand. Lost in the process, however, may be further development of "southern" EU states and the Mediterranean basin.

The states that began their reforms earliest and prosecuted them most aggressively not only realized the fastest and most-positive results, they also attracted the lion's share of foreign support. This made their transition to a market economy all the easier. According to a World Bank study, the three most successful transitional economies (Poland, Hungary and the Czech Republic) received foreign direct investment (FDI) from 1990 to 2000 (projected), as follows:

	1994	1995	1990–1995	1996–2000 (projected)
Poland	$1,875m	$2,500m	$7,148m	$21,969m
Hungary	$1,146m	$4,400m	$11,200m	$12,968m
Czech Republic	$876m	$2,500m	$5,666m	$15,466m

Other transitional CEEs did only one quarter as well. Russia, a significantly larger country, had an estimated FDI of only $4.4 billion from 1990 to 1995 and a projected $27 billion by the year 2000.[11] The remarkable success of the leading CEEs in transforming their economies from state-managed to market driven has been largely due to the growth of their trade with OECD nations (37 percent increase from 1989 to 1992), the EU (53 percent) and especially Germany (over 100 percent).[12]

Thus, the six countries selected in December 1997 to be in the first wave of EU enlargement were the obvious candidates: the Czech Republic, Hungary, Poland, Slovenia, Estonia and Cyprus—Cyprus only if the Greek–Turkish tensions there can be resolved. Once again, Turkey was snubbed. Estonia was a bit of a surprise, but it is the strongest of the Baltic economies.

The other candidates in the wave of accessions are significantly larger and poorer eastern states (although the strongest of the lot). Their accession negotiations may be protracted. The guidelines they have been given to prepare themselves for accession (the "Copenhagen criteria") are lofty goals indeed. Moreover, meeting them does not assure admission. Indeed, the ability to meet them may actually depend on admission to the EU.[13]

Quite recently, the Commission released a white paper intended to prepare associated countries for accession. Like the association agreements themselves, however, the white paper contains no deadlines and is not legally binding. Small wonder that the eastern states are restive. The EU wants them to revive as export markets and security buffers, but does not offer much concrete in return. For their part, the associated counties are eager to get on with it. Early accession, they reason, would only expedite the completion of the transformation.

The EU wants the CEEs to be fully ready for accession before granting membership. The CEEs counter that they may be able to close the GDP gap only if they are granted EU membership.[14] Take the case of Austria, for example. One year after accession to the EU, its trade with EU states grew 66 percent in terms of export and 72 percent in terms of import. Meanwhile, it enjoyed a favorable balance of trade with Eastern Europe and non-European developing countries. On the other hand, Norway (which rejected an offer of EU membership in 1995) has grown its trade with Europe nonetheless.

Not all of the problems are of the CEEs making, however. Several EU member states (notably Greece, Portugal and Ireland) are still growing into parity with their EU partners. Further, the large agricultural sectors in the candidate countries pose a competitive threat to weaker EU member states. Why then add more weak members? In short, if the EU intends to enjoy the economic and security benefits of eastern expansion, it will have to accept the consequences of doing so. So EU structural programs will have to be revised. In Slovenia, Hungary and the Czech Republic (the wealthiest of the associated countries) per capita income is only 45 percent of the EU average. In Romania, it is only 20 percent. Current member states of the Union were made beneficiaries of a "cohesion policy" to improve their economies. To extend this policy to states-in-waiting would bankrupt the Community.[15]

The EU's Economic Assistance Programme for Central and Eastern Europe (PHARE) was designed to help these countries build market economies (a European "Marshall Plan"). PHARE funding has grown from about 500 million Ecu in 1990 (when it started) to 1,040 million Ecu in 1993. That represents about one-third of the EU's budget for external action in 1994, but is a pittance compared to *intra*-community structural and cohesion funding.[16] Moreover, because of north-south tensions, equal funding goes to EU trading partners in the Mediterranean basin.[17]

The European Commission is reluctant to make EU expansion plans turn on a revision of its budget regime. For one thing, the next budget (2000–2006) did not increase the 1.27 percent of EU gross domestic product that is allocated to the Community's use. EU income would increase if the European economy improved, of course, and the agricultural and regional programs have been cut slightly to allow for expansion. But the EU will have to balance all these competing forces if it is to continue to expand to the east.[18]

The road is a long one, and anything can happen along the way. It took seven years to complete the accession agreements for Spain and Portugal, and they still are not fully assimilated into the EU. Hence the earliest possible date for eastern expansion now being discussed (2002) may be too ambitious. On the other hand, Germany badly wants this expansion and may be in a position to expedite the process.

To date, no deadline has been set, to the extreme frustration of the candidate nations. The Council will say only that "sound preparation" must be made (probably on both sides) and that more energy needs to be invested to "create the conditions for the gradual, harmonious integration of [these eastern] states." When that happens, entry will probably be phased in over several years, with limits on the amount of EU subsidization. Conversely, the EU has promised these nations that they could join the customs union when "prepared."[19]

The EU is not the only force that is spurring these economies. Some have joined NATO. And the Czech Republic became the first ex-communist nation to join the OECD, the most Western of capitalist clubs. It is a group of economic enablers, not the needy.

Everything was going smoothly in 1996. But 1997 was a different story. The flow of foreign investment slowed. Export growth was weak, but imports soared; wages rose faster than productivity gains. The EBRD remarked in early 1997 that, without better management and further modernizing and restructuring, Czech enterprises were not likely to regain their momentum or compete in a wider Europe.[20]

Hungary became the second post-communist member of the OECD in May 1996. In order to do so it had to further liberalize its foreign exchange and banking markets and secure a standby loan of $387 million from the

IMF. Hungary has been the principal beneficiary of foreign direct investment (about $8 billion since 1989), receiving over one-half of all that has been invested in eastern bloc nations through 1994. Like the Czech Republic, it is a smaller nation and not much dependent on agriculture. Nonetheless, there is a negative trade balance, so a surcharge on imports (illegal under WTO rules) was needed to hold imports down and allow exports to whittle away at the imbalance. But even at a growth rate of 4 percent annually, it will take years for Hungary to catch up to its western neighbors. Meanwhile, a robust black market denies the government the tax income it badly needs. If privatizing doesn't speed up and if subsidies and social benefits aren't reined in, Hungary's market transition also could stall.[21]

Poland is the largest and weakest of the candidate nations, but is geographically and politically well positioned. Because it enjoys the political support of Germany and France, perhaps Poland has been slower than its fellow accession candidates to liberalize and restructure markets. While belligerently pressing for rapid EU accession, Poland retained tariff duties on oil products for two years (in violation of its EU association agreement). Poland also has a large and inefficient agriculture sector (30 percent of the work force and 14 percent of GDP). On the other hand, Poland represents a huge export market and has attracted U.S. businesses like General Motors. Enlargement is not just about economics.[22]

The list of candidates does not stop here, of course. But only so many states can be admitted in the first wave.[23] The countries chosen and the terms and pace of their accession will help to set norms for further expansion. Only the smaller, more aggressive and robust CEE state economies are likely to follow. By that time, developments at the global level could be cutting deeply into the efficacy of regional trading blocs. To suggest how widely separated the candidates for EU enlargement are, a World Bank report separated them into four groups. Only those states in Group I had substantially recovered from the collapse of communism, liberalized their markets, privatized, gotten inflation under control, and overhauled government banking and legal systems to coordinate with the West. States in Group II were making good progress, but states in Group III had a long way to go, and Group IV was nearly hopeless. It is not surprising to find Poland, Slovenia, Hungary and the Czech Republic in Group I. Bulgaria, Romania and the Baltics are in Group II. Russia and Georgia were in Group III, with Belarus and the Ukraine in Group IV.[24]

The U.S. supports Europe's efforts in general, for it widens the scope of U.S./EU trade pacts and reduces America's obligations under NATO. There seems to be no great urge to commit U.S. money, however (a second Marshall plan), for the U.S. government increasingly considers the assimilation of CEEs into the EU to be a European problem. The U.S. is interested in expanded trade with Europe and the old Soviet bloc, of course, but it does not relish getting involved in its political squabbles. President Clinton's commitment that "no one will be left behind" suggests, however, that Russia may be a joint project.[25]

Chapter 11

Japan: Asia's Disintegrating Colossus

It is generally conceded that Japan is the third superpower in the late twentieth century's tripolar economic world.[1] Indeed, Japan's is the second largest national economy in the world (if one doesn't treat EU member states as a unit). But Japan hasn't looked so "super" of late. In a short ten years, the Japanese system has gone from being the envy of other nations to a global pariah.[2] What happened to "Japan, Inc.," and can it be corrected?

Japan provides the third of the four economic models explored here; a micro-managed economy. It is the prototype for the "Little Tiger" economies in Southeast Asia (Hong Kong, Singapore, South Korea and Taiwan) that hoped to achieve economic success by modeling themselves after Japan. The other dominant model in the region is China, a state-managed, communist system. It too is reflected in smaller Asian economies.

After the conclusion of World War II, a generation of Japanese committed themselves to rebuilding their war-ravaged nation and restoring its influence. This required a coordinated strategy that saw to it that the elements of production—capital, labor and know-how—were efficiently allocated. The strategy closely linked government and business (to manage the recovery), a cooperative and dedicated workforce (to drive the economy), and a willingness to sacrifice present consumption for future gains. That is how the Japanese economic "miracle" came about. Japanese businesses and workers focused their attention on making goods for export, beginning with toys and apparel and ending up with products like automobiles, cameras and consumer electronics. The domestic market was carefully regulated in order to keep export prices low. Competition, particularly from foreign goods and services, was tightly controlled. Furthermore, Japanese workers made legendary sacrifices to ensure the success of the various ventures, working long hours with great dedication, deferring leisure and cooperating with management to make certain that the Japanese economy did not just recover, but thrive.

The first postwar generation was utterly committed to rebuilding Japan, and the second generation was equally devoted to making its economy world-class. For forty years the "Asian system" worked marvelously well. The Japanese were single-mindedly devoted to producing superior products and increasing market share. They stressed education and personal savings to fuel the engine of production. It helped that Japan did not to have to invest heavily in security or foreign assistance. But the brilliant recovery was largely the result of a coalition of political and business leaders. The Asian respect for hierarchy was tailor-made for the situation.

This state of affairs couldn't last, however, and it didn't. There are at least three reasons. First, successive generations of Japanese couldn't be expected to sacrifice as the generations that fought and survived the war had done. They saw the wealth building up and wanted a share. Second, other traders (the U.S. chief among them) became less and less willing to allow Japanese products ready access to their markets while being denied equivalent access to Japan's.[3] Third, a long period of one-party rule led to excess and corruption. The core agreements between business and government that had made the Asian model so successful began to break down.

Now Japan is having to address the multiple problems that its economic model created. Without the benefit of a managed economy at home, it is harder to compete abroad. Whole sectors of the Japanese market, from banking and insurance to chips and film, need to be restructured to be more competitive. Meanwhile, the Japanese leadership has adjusted too slowly and inadequately to the crisis. Political and business leaders have taken baby steps toward reform, when something far bolder is required. The Asian model was too regulated.[4] But that doesn't make the Japanese success story any less interesting. China will doubtless pursue its version, for it is certain that China will resist giving up its state-managed economy except for advantages it might gain.

It may not be correct to treat the Japanese economic model as distinct. It is a prototype for much of Asia and the developing world. Thus, it surely is correct to treat it (and Asian variations on it) as a foil for the American and European models. If emerging Asian nations can follow it, they surely will. After all, it fits the oriental mind-set and was a huge success.

Asian nations have invested heavily in one another's success. They also have a relatively high savings rate. To the extent that Asia can supply its own capital needs, it will resist more-capitalistic economic models. Indeed, the evolution of the Japanese economy led to something of an "Asian ladder." As soon as Japan had graduated from toys to higher-tech articles, other emerging Asian nations took up toy production. This does not mean that the Japanese economy is going to fail. The Japanese are a proud and resourceful people, and their economy will recover. At present, however, it is in deep trouble, compounded by the sudden collapse of Asia's "little tiger" economies, in which Japan invested heavily. Nor can the Japanese economy recover until it is restructured. The restructuring guarantees more pain (bankruptcies; job losses) and increased competition, at home and abroad.

INTERNAL PROBLEMS

Japan was not unlike other industrialized economies that entered a mild economic downturn in the early 1990s. But, whereas the U.S. has made a robust recovery and the EU has begun to do so, Japan has not participated in the recovery. Indeed, its economy is in its worst recession since World War II, with more challenges on the horizon.

From 1992 to 1994 there was virtually no growth. Various government efforts at stimulus tended to be too little and too late. When a little momentum was building in April 1997, an increase in sales tax and a cut in public spending killed it. Hence, the high growth rates that used to characterize Japan's economy have disappeared. Japan's economic growth is at or below zero. The Asian model has run out of gas.

Moreover, this does not seem to be a downturn that Japan can export its way out of,[5] although it will try. The collapse of the Asia's over-extended "little tigers" just deepens Japan's troubles. Other Asian economies absorb about one-half of Japan's exports, so any slump in their economies slows Japan's as well. Japanese lenders are reported to hold nearly 70 percent of Thailand's overseas debt, and the Thai currency dropped 35–40 percent from July to October 1997. Bad debts, bankruptcies, foreclosures and currency depreciation in the rest of Asia can mean more hardship in Japan. But even before the "little tiger" debacle took much of the wind out of the sails of the Asian "miracle," there seemed to be little reason to be salutary about the Japanese economy. Recovery efforts, from stabilizing the yen to a record low one-half-point discount rate, did not have the desired effect. Personal and corporate consumption flagged. Industrial output, construction orders, retail sales and employment were all down. Vehicle sales fell 10 percent in the second quarter of 1997. If inventory builds and production is curtailed, a serious recession results. In the second quarter of 1997, Japanese GDP shrank almost 3 percent; and yet the government was reluctant to launch a large stimulus program, for the budget deficit already stood at 7 percent. Even if there were an upturn, Japanese consumers often choose to save rather than spend. The long-planned (but cautiously executed) deregulation could bring only gradual recovery. Why did all this happen; how could Japan—Asia's premier success story—have gone so wrong? What is wrong with a micro-managed economy in today's trading world?[6]

Well, it is clear from the Japanese and Asian experience that tightly knit cooperation between business and government, together with a low degree of oversight and transparency, can create the "illusion" of invincibility. The king hasn't any clothes, but it's difficult to be certain. Hence, the goal of every manager became that of perpetuating the illusion, insulating the economy from a correction until it was too late. The Japanese "bubble economy" of the late 1980s masked the fact that real productivity was not growing. As conditions within this highly structured economic model became adverse, Japanese companies began to break ranks. They cut overhead and downsized, putting jobs at risk. They moved operations elsewhere in Asia to take advantage of less expensive labor and tax systems, re-importing finished goods. Political and business scandals began to surface. Japan Inc. was disintegrating. There was a measurable increase in offshore capital investment. It signaled the "topping out" of Japan's economy and the pull of opportunities elsewhere in the world. Japanese companies not mired in the local economy or tainted by miscalculation and corruption may continue to be world leaders. But the Japanese economy may not.[7]

That economy, a "neo-mercantilism system, knit together by cross-shareholding among companies"—or keiretsu—proved to be too rigid, too slow to change. Fine-tuning the old model would not restore Japan to competitiveness. The longer Japan's political and business leaders cling to the old system, which is "largely ineffective and irrelevant" according to the head of Japan's most powerful business organization (Keidanren), the longer the Japanese economy will suffer. After many years of our trying to open the Japanese economy from without, Japan Inc. is collapsing from within. The keiretsu relationships had become an "unpleasant obligation [not] . . . a strategic edge." Citizens lost confidence in political leaders and bureaucrats. Respect for hierarchy declined. Indeed, Japanese companies are discovering that their future lies in creative alliances with other global traders, not obedience to a failing "Asian system."

The devolution arrives at the worst possible time, for the U.S. finally had forced significant openings in the Japanese market. Some of the openings are the subject of bilateral arrangements, but increasingly they are the subject of WTO negotiation or enforcement. Things certainly are changing in Japan. The virtual stranglehold on Japanese politics by the scandal-tainted Liberal Democratic Party has given way more to reform-minded politicians. The Japanese increased their purchases of foreign goods by 70 percent in 1995, most of it private or corporate, not government. In 1996, foreign direct investment in Japan was just $18 billion, versus $565 billion in the U.S. Japan accounts for about 15 percent of world economic output but absorbs just 1 percent of global investment.

The bureaucrats and keiretsu, though fatally weakened by Japan's economic malaise, still must be dealt with. The latter control 60 percent of the value on the Tokyo stock exchange. They still believe that Japan's "enemies" are external, not internal. So it is not an easy sell to persuade Japanese leaders that wholesale changes in Japan Inc. are required.[8] Indeed, their own hubris has contributed to serious miscalculations. The solution to Japan's problem is the very antithesis of what they have practiced. As a result, there is a tendency for officials at every level to deny what trade statistics plainly reveal. If failure is dishonor, then one *can't* fail. And if "official" statistics don't paint a picture as gloomy as it truly is, why should the country or its businesses be in a rush to adopt serious reforms? Can they be clearheaded about a recovery program? So deeply in denial were the leaders of some major Japanese firms that Hitachi, Mitsubishi Motors and Dai Nippon (one of Japan's largest chemical companies), paid bribes to corporate racketeers (sokaiya) so that they would not reveal damaging facts about their businesses. But the Japanese are not so patient with official and corporate mismanagement as they once were. In a society not known for its litigiousness, shareholders are suing directors for corporate wrongdoing.[9]

These scandals, as significant as they are, pale when compared to the spectacular collapse of Japan's banking sector. As the bubble economy grew, banks created housing lenders (jusen) to profit from the rising living standard and value of land in Japan. With increased capital flow to the banks, pressure was put on the jusen to maintain their double-digit growth rates. What began as cautious lending turned giddy. In the case of one of the largest jusen (Nippon Housing Loan), an "extraordinary web of relationships between banks, bureaucrats, politicians and big business" was developed to perpetuate the enterprise. When Nippon finally collapsed in the economic downturn, three-quarters of its loan portfolio was bad. Its share price declined from Y 2,310 in 1990 to Y 40 (37 cents) in 1996. Its once-respected heads are now considered the equivalent of "war criminals" by the Japanese people and press. Not only have seven large jusen failed, but they have threatened the entire Japanese banking sector. Japan's eleven largest banks—six of them among the world's largest—wrote off more than $47 billion in bad loans by mid-1996, but the numbers kept growing. By early 1998, the government admitted the number was nearly twice that, and more recently it was placed nearer half a trillion dollars. No one is certain the bottom has been reached because of the labyrinthine networking with other banking centers and business/government complicity that seems unwilling or unable to address the problem.[10]

PRESSURE FROM WITHOUT

Not only has Japan suffered embarrassment from within, but other global traders are banging on its door, insisting that it open its market to foreign goods. Japan's closely regulated economy has built a huge trade surplus with the rest of the world. That is one of the reasons the Japanese "system" has been so successful. Lately, pressure has built to redress this deficit. In the last two administrations, the U.S. Trade Representative has been quite aggressive about arranging market-opening deals with the Japanese. We have been joined in this by other capitalist traders, notably the EU and Canada. The WTO dispute settlement mechanism has proved a useful tool to pry Japanese markets open. This is exactly what the Japanese system fears most.

As a populous nation, with few natural resources, Japan needs a strong export balance. It worries (probably quite rightly) that its goods may not be as competitive in an open market. (They are not likely to become more competitive if protected, either). In the short term this is bad news for a Japanese economy already in recession. Foreign competition could precipitate even more business failures in Japan. On the other hand, this would purge the economy of its weak producers, both institutional and human. Moreover, as Western businesses seem willing to join Japanese firms to rebuild Japan's economy, perhaps only Japanese pride stands in the way. This may not be the time to bully Japan, but the U.S. doesn't want to go down with it.

Between 1970 and 1995, the U.S. trade balance with the world shifted from a surplus of $3.2 billion to a deficit of $159.6 billion. The deficit would be higher except for a *surplus* trade balance of $63 billion in the export of services. About two-thirds of the deficit is attributable to negative trade balances with Japan and China. In 1995, Japan accounted for a little over $59 billion of our deficit, and China for a little less than $34 billion. Canada, Mexico and Germany, in that order, all had surpluses between $15 billion and $18 billion, and the rest were negligible. The deficit is created by the fact that Americans consume more foreign goods than they export abroad, but it represents only about 2.2 percent of U.S. GDP. In 1970, imported foreign goods accounted for 3.9 percent of U.S. GDP, and U.S. exports contributed 4.2 percent. By 1993, imports had risen to 10.3 percent of our GDP, while exports had grown only to 8.1 percent.

These numbers might not tell the whole story. In 1970, manufactured goods represented 45 percent of the U.S. economy but fell to 37 percent by 1995. Meanwhile, services rose from 44 to 54 percent of the U.S. economy. Hence, the U.S. economy's shift toward services improves our positive balance of trade. Our exports in the services sector grew almost fourteen times from 1970 to 1995, whereas our imports, starting from a similar base, grew just nine times. With this shift in the U.S. economy, and progressive market opening in Japan and China, the U.S. trade deficit (as bad as it is), may be tolerable. Nonetheless, at 1995 rates, the U.S. trade deficit was expected to reach about $299 billion by the year 2006.[11]

Those market sectors in which deregulation has taken or is taking place are known to many—automobiles and auto parts, computer chips, insurance and film, to name just a few. Talks are going on about liberalizing telecommunications, shipping, liquor, music and intellectual property, construction and public procurement. There is hardly an important sector of the Japanese economy that is not under siege. I wish there were space here to detail all the market openings persistent U.S. officials have been able to pry out of

Japan during the past decade, but that is a book in itself. Unfortunately, many of the stories one gets in the media lead to the impression that little or no progress is being made. True, there is reticence. Every year the U.S. Trade Representative details all of these alleged trade abuses, not just for Japan, but for all nations.[12] However, the truth is that the Japanese market has been progressively opened, and even we Americans protect our markets against foreign competition.

Although understandably reluctant, Japan finally began to reform its economy. Considering that the initiative was not self-motivated, it is not surprising that the initial efforts were modest. It is a trait of Japanese culture to take action only after building political consensus. Moreover, no country likes to take orders from outsiders. A too-rapid opening would be extremely painful to the Japanese people (unemployment) and businesses (bankruptcies). It would be political suicide. One that is too slow, however, provokes more external complaint and prolongs the current malaise.

Unfortunately, Japanese bureaucrats and politicians reacted too slowly. Since the recession began in 1991, there have been numerous "false dawns" for Japan, each looking like a turnaround but none large enough to bring recovery. The only economic change that gave any hope, a sharp boost in consumer sales in April 1997, proved to be an attempt to beat a rise in sales tax from 3 to 5 percent. Together with a cutback in public investment, the tax rise pushed the recovering economy over the edge. Fearing hard times, domestic consumption dropped and the recession picked up. The invincibility of the Japanese system proved to be as much myth as reality. The protection that had brought them to the top was no longer working. Companies had grown uncompetitive under the closed system.

But the real problem is the Japanese economy itself. It has stubbornly resisted all government attempts to stimulate it (to the tune of nearly 14 percent of GDP). But all attempts were modest and incremental. Instead of turning Japan's economy around, the endless succession of stimulus packages seem to have convinced the rest of the world that Japan really wasn't very serious about doing so. None of the plans seriously restructured the Japanese economy, which is the real problem. Only when the pessimism within Japan and the external pressure to deregulate became acute (plus a sheer inability to continue to prop up the old system) did Japan begin restructuring.[13]

It began with a series of high-level meetings in June 1997. This was all part of a bilateral framework dubbed the "New Economic Partnership" that covered five important sectors: telecommunications, housing, medical devices/pharmaceuticals, financial services and deregulation and competition. In March 1998, the Japanese cabinet decided on a detailed three-year plan to promote deregulation in these sectors.[14] I think it is fair to say that Japanese market liberalization is picking up momentum (considering how new they are to it) in part because the financial crisis has forced them to reconsider old habits and work with foreign officials and particularly because Western companies have been given increased access to the Japanese market.[15] This has not solved Japan's problem, however.

By common consensus, Asian economies can't recover until Japan's does. To begin, Japan represents 75 percent of Asia's economy. It is the spark plug, but the Japanese economy relies heavily on exports. With the rest of Asia's economies in recession, they can't afford Japan's goods. Japan's exports to the rest of Asia dropped 18 percent in April 1998. This means lost income, surplus goods and eventually unemployment. But Asian exports to Japan also dropped in April, further weakening those economies. With no business expansion, banks can't lend assets, and so forth. It is a vicious cycle. What to do?

Partly in response to Western pressure and partly to clean up Japan's mismanaged financial services sector, Prime Minister Hashimoto announced a "big bang" (in Japanese, "Kinya bigger ban") financial deregulation package in April 1996. It was supposed to tighten control while opening that sector further to Western capitalists. No longer was the "convoy system" to prevail. Bankrupt institutions would be allowed to fail. A few large ones did, Yamaichi Securities and Sanyo Securities among them. But they took peoples' savings and jobs with them, so the reform was hardly popular. Besides, Japan's financial bureaucrats had reduced the program to a shell. Neither domestic nor international observers were impressed, and the malaise deepened.[16] From that point, Japan announced at least six "stimulus" programs (public spending and/or tax cuts) to help boost the economy. Most were too small, or too vague or discounted by the people and market. Only the last, a larger-than-expected Y16,650 billion ($128 billion) package of temporary tax cuts, public works spending and low-cost loans, seemed at all adequate. The package was the largest ever, but initially it was discounted by consumers and markets. They were suffering "package fatigue."

Nonetheless, the Japanese government had pledged a net of $600 billion to recovery (more than Germany spent on reunification), all no avail. Although Japan is a wealthy nation, it cannot continue in this way. Its public debt exceeds 7 percent of GDP, about twice that of Western nations. It will inflate further with mass unemployment (Japan's is at a postwar high of 4.1 percent) and a large aging population. Besides, Japan does not appear to need more public infrastructure (public works consume about 8 percent of GDP and 10 percent of workers, again twice that of Western nations). If not, another industry is just being propped up.[17]

Unfortunately, Japan is faced with a double-edged dilemma. If it takes aggressive steps to reform and open its economy and to deal with its failing institutions (which international markets see as the bottom line), then it could push itself and Asia and world markets into financial chaos. Japan's serious recession could turn into a world depression. If Japan's reforms are not aggressive enough, the Japanese people will discount the government's ability or sincerity about reform and will continue to save, not spend. For their part, international traders will find other venues, and the Japanese economy will continue to deflate. The old, hermetically sealed Japanese economy just couldn't adjust fast enough to modern market competition.

Some light may be visible at the end of the tunnel, however. The Japanese economy *is* reforming, if largely at its own pace. Western buyers are entering the market with capital and knowhow. It is anathema for Japan to put itself on sale, but doing so gives the rest of the industrialized world a greater stake (and say) in its recovery. Finally, a "bridge bank" scheme has been proposed to clean up bad financial assets in much the same way the savings-and-loan debacle was addressed in the United States. The scale is much larger in Japan, but a mechanism was needed.[18]

If America is smart, it will help the Japanese in any way that it can. We surely aren't out to "beat" the Japanese economy. We are all stuck in this interdependent global economy together. It is a win-win or lose-lose deal. The Japanese are a proud, resourceful and intelligent people. They will be back, but the "Asian system" might not be.

REFORM AND RECOVERY

Obviously, there will be no recovery in Japan until there is substantial structural reform. (Elsewhere in Asia, this discipline was imposed as a precondition of IMF bailout funds.) The pressure on Japan to make bolder reforms mounted as early plans proved inadequate. So the list of business areas slated for deregulation has grown steadily, from company reform to communications, transport, financial areas and land and housing policies. However, the details are lacking and the timeframe for implementation is too long.

Foreign investment in Japan—which has never been high—is dropping. In 1996, U.S. FDI in Japan was only $35.7 billion (5% of the U.S. total) versus $118.1 billion Japanese FDI in America (18.7% of foreign investment in the U.S.). That means that Japan has a far larger stake in our economic success than we have in its. In this sense, Japan's slow market opening may have helped American businesses. Because it was so closed, they invested elsewhere (chiefly Europe) and have less exposure in Asia. The yen was shrinking as a world reserve currency even before Europe's euro was introduced.[19]

Any turnaround for the Japanese economy will depend on a number of short-term "risks." The economy will have to adjust to international competition and the potential job losses that market opening entails. They will no longer be able to delay the inevitable through foot-dragging, bureaucratic red tape and outright bribes. Japan needs to restructure its very concept of international business. No longer will it be all take and no give. Globalization is premised on open trading systems.[20]

Is deregulation and restructuring of the Japanese economy anything more than the downsizing and restructuring of the U.S. economy in the early nineties? While the pain may be deeper and the recovery longer, that would be the *serious* beginning of recovery. This could be the first step on a very long road that should lead to a truly competitive Japan in time. To be certain, Japan Inc. will change forever. Foreign competitors will make inroads into the Japanese economy, but the surviving Japanese businesses should emerge stronger and more agile. With barriers to foreign ownership removed, they also will be linked into a world economy in which others are invested in the success of Japan.[21] The shakeout of uncompetitive businesses will be cathartic for Japan, Asia and the world.[22] Placing those protected, micro-managed economies on a competitive footing, although wrenching in the short term, will be the best for "globalization" in the longer term.[23]

Once the anchor and envy of Asian economies, Japan seems to have lost the magic formula for economic success, if it ever had it. Its economy was in recession for four successive economic quarters in 1997–98, domestic spending and investment contracted and deficit spending rose. Meanwhile, however, Japan has consolidated its position in Asian markets; pledging $30 billion to aid regional economies to recover and proposing pan-Asian action, such as an "Asian fund" (similar to the IMF), and even the yen as a "regional" currency.

Japan's economy is one of the most tightly regulated of any of the modern capitalist democracies. It worked fine while all participants adhered to the game plan. But there came a time when successful businesses weren't willing to prop up weaker ones (the so-called convoy system), and other industrialized countries finally became impatient with a system rigged to favor Japan. The pressure of market opening and failure to reform undid the "Asian model" and today threaten Japan's future. Since the Japanese model didn't allow for small corrections, it finally suffered a huge one.

Naturally, Western powers are cool to Japan's "go-it-alone" approach. But Japan seems determined to recover in its own time and way, and to carry all of Asia with it if it can. Thus far, U.S. entreaties and threats have achieved little. Without some mutually acceptable solution, a trade war is possible, for Japan's trade balance (most of it with the U.S.) grew by more than 50 percent from June 1997 to September 1998. Our negative balance with China is similar, but the U.S. wants to draw China into full participation in the world economy, so it is willing to cut China some slack that it won't give to Japan.[24] In the end, some sort of agreement is likely to be struck.

AREAS OF CONTENTION

Automobiles and Parts

No market sector has received more attention from U.S. trade negotiators than the opening of the Japanese automobile and auto parts market. Perhaps this is because Japanese automobiles have penetrated the U.S. market so thoroughly in the past two decades, whereas our auto exports have made virtually no dent in theirs. To remedy this imbalance, the U.S. threatened in 1995 to impose a 100 percent tariff on a variety of Japanese export cars unless their market was opened to U.S. cars and parts. In short order, a bilateral agreement was reached. This upset the EU, which suffered the same exclusion from Japan's market and felt that any opening agreement should be multilateral. Soon thereafter, the EU struck an access deal with Japan as well.

For a while, the arrangement seemed to work. The Big Three U.S. automakers (Ford, GM and Chrysler) sold over 77,000 vehicles in Japan in 1995, an increase of 38 percent over the previous year. But European makers like Volkswagen, Mercedes-Benz, BMW, Opel and Volvo sold over 134,000 units. In part this reflects a difference in the number of outlets in Japan handling their respective cars. The growth continued in 1996, albeit at a slower pace. This was due in part to a slowing of the Japanese economy and competition from both Japanese and European makers. But, as the Japanese economy worsened, its willingness to push forward with the agreement flagged. In late 1997, the U.S. dragged Japan back to the negotiating table, stating that it had "failed to honor" its 1995 agreement. In general, the U.S. proposals to deregulate the market had not been implemented. Foreign access to the Japanese car market remained "extremely limited." Meanwhile 3.4 million Japanese cars and trucks were sold in the U.S. in 1996, although nearly 70 percent were manufactured in this country.

So the auto accord—a version of bilateral "managed trade"—is a mixed bag. Japanese car makers, aware of what is likely to result if they don't accommodate the U.S. industry, have begun to incorporate American parts into their vehicles, and they are deregulating auto repair. But American producers will have to design for the Japanese market (only Jeeps and Voyagers are "hot"). Meanwhile, thanks to a weak yen, new efficiencies and brand recognition, Japan's car manufacturers are looking to dominate their market *and* ours.[25]

Computer Chips

Another high-visibility trade dispute between the U.S. and Japan concerned computer chips. Once again it culminated in a bilateral accord from which both U.S. and other foreign firms benefitted. They increased their share of Japan's chip market from about 8 percent in 1986 to nearly 30 percent in 1996—most of it going to American firms. That breakthrough having been achieved, the Japanese are not energized to renew the accord. But the U.S. is keen to continue and broaden the arrangement. The Japanese would be better disposed if the pact were worked out at industry level (as opposed to between governments). Given the rapid evolution of the chip industry, business involvement may result in better results all around. However, as always, there was concern that Japan would not live up to its deal. If it did not, the U.S. threatened unilateral Section 301 retaliation. This may be the spur necessary to open Japanese markets, but the heavy-handed U.S. approach is bound to be resented by both Japan and our trading partners.[26]

Insurance (Financial Services)

It is difficult to think what trade sector follows autos and chips in importance. But, eventually, trade in financial services is likely to eclipse both. Hence, there has been an equally vigorous push to open Japan's insurance and financial services markets. The incentive goes back to at least 1996, when an internal study by the Ministry of Finance confirmed Tokyo's lack of competitiveness in world financial markets. Japan wants to make the yen a more internationally traded currency and to attract more business to the potentially lucrative financial services sector. However, the U.S. dollar and the euro are almost certain to dominate the world currency markets. Even with liberalization, the yen is likely to fall further out of favor, as is the Tokyo market. In late 1996, a large U.S. investment bank moved its foreign exchange services from Tokyo to Singapore, to take advantage of more flexible market conditions there. To stem the exodus, Tokyo announced a "Big Bang" financial deregulation. From 1997, companies no longer were required to get government approval for foreign exchange transactions, nor were foreign dealings to be limited to government-authorized banks. This allows additional Japanese institutions to enter the market, creating new competition at home, but it also allows a host of foreign businesses to enter the Japanese market. This may improve the internationalization of the yen, but it surely will shake out weaker Japanese institutions and force the others to compete more aggressively. Although Japan has some natural allies in the emerging economies of the Pacific Rim, yen-denominated settlements have declined since 1993. This is exacerbated by Japanese manufacturers moving their sites offshore, thus reducing their dependence on the Japanese market.

Tokyo also has taken steps to liberalize its huge pension funds sector, the second largest in the world. Traditionally these funds were managed by trust banks and life assurance companies, but they produced a low rate of return. Major Japanese corporations and life assurance groups, upset with the returns, turned to foreign groups to boost them. This forced Tokyo to liberalize the market, opening it to U.S. and European fund managers, who have more experience managing money. They nearly doubled the assets under their management in the first six months of 1997 alone (to $63.7 billion). Specialist foreign investment advisers—mostly British and European— did even better. Annual growth of 50 percent or more is expected for the next few years. So joint ventures are likely to increase, such as those between Putnam, the U.S. group, and Nippon Life (Japan's largest insurer) and Barclay's with Nikko, forming the largest foreign investment advisor in Japan. This is just the beginning of Japan's deregulation.[27]

In another financial sector, the Tokyo stock exchange (TSE) has announced that it will substantially relax listing criteria for foreign companies and extend trading hours. Foreign interest and trading volume at the TSE has dropped since 1989, with the foreign companies listed down from a peak of 127 in December 1991 to just 64 in September 1997, and others planning to withdraw. The reform also will lift restrictions on electronic trading and streamline the order placement process. Finally, the TSE will abolish fixed commissions on stock transactions in two stages, beginning in 1998. Japan can't afford to lose more ground to other world trading centers in New York, London and Frankfurt. Ever since the Tokyo market went flat six years ago, it has remained moribund. This is in large part due to its resistance to structural reforms. The NIKKEI (TSE) average has never risen above 58 percent of its 1989 peak of 38, 916, and the Asian collapse could take it lower in the near term. These reforms are not optional. They are absolutely necessary if Tokyo is to be a player in the financial-services market in the next decade. In addition to the reforms already mentioned, Japan plans to reform its legal, tax and accounting systems to bring them into line with international standards. All these reforms probably are necessary to restore Japan's financial services industry to competitiveness. But they cut deeply into the "Asian system."[28]

Another financial sector to which foreign companies seek access is Japan's huge insurance market, second only to the U.S., with premium revenues worth about $374 billion in 1994. And yet foreign insurers are largely limited to the so-called "third sector" (accident, sickness and nursing care), where they enjoy about a one-third share of a market that covers just 5 percent of the insurance pie. In short, Japanese firms have the lion's share (93.7 percent) of the primary life and non-life market. A bilateral U.S./Japanese agreement in October 1994 and a follow-up accord in December 1996 were supposed to improve foreign access to Japan's insurance market, but foreign presence has increased only "slightly." It still is the lowest in any G-7 nation. Japan claims that it has "diligently implemented" the agreed measures, but its lengthy approval process is really a delaying tactic. Strong pressure to insure within corporate groupings, or keiretsu, has kept the market relatively closed. But the rate-setting power of Japan's insurance ratings organizations expired in July 1998 and keiretsu members have begun to break ranks in search of better coverage and lower premiums. Meanwhile, large Japanese insurers have been kept out of the third sector, but that is hardly a punishment because the market is so small. Gaining access to primary sectors for foreign insurers is the main goal, and it is being obtained at a grudging pace.[29]

OTHER AREAS OF DEREGULATION

There are so many other areas in which the Japanese economy is being forced to deregulate — due to bilateral pressure, international agreements or complaints before the World Trade Organization—that there is not space here to recount them all. To give some sense of the many fronts upon which the Japanese economy is under attack, I offer the following discussion.

Telecommunications

Japan's telecommunications industry is the second largest in the world, after the U.S. Its dominant player, Nippon Telegraph and Telephone (NTT), is the world's largest telecommunications operator (about twice the size of AT&T). NTT was privatized in 1985, and in theory any Japanese company that got a license could compete. Many new market entrants have, but as they all are dependent on NTT for access to consumers, the market isn't genuinely competitive. What will happen when liberalization finally occurs is anybody's guess, because Japan's telecommunications rates are extremely high by international standards. The government's delay in opening the Japanese market fully almost assures that NTT will not be as competitive as necessary when the inevitable opening occurs. Japan also may be squandering its opportunity to become the Asian hub of the telecommunications industry. Hong Kong and Singapore already are in line for that role. Although Japan agreed to a global liberalization of telecommunications under the WTO in February 1997, foreign involvement in Japanese telecom operations is limited and equipment procurement is still relatively closed.[30]

Film and More

Yet another complaint the U.S. has against Japan is the structure of its photo film marketing regime. The U.S. government, pushed by the Eastman Kodak Co., alleged that Japan's film market is restricted in such a way that Tokyo's Fuji film has an unfair advantage. The U.S. may be right, for it is typical of the Japanese model to skew the market. Although the U.S. took the matter to the WTO, Japan won. Generally speaking, however, Japan's trade practices have not fared well before the WTO. It already has found that the Japanese tax system discriminates unfairly against imported liquor in order to protect a local product, shochu. Although Japan has the duty to amend its liquor tax system, it has protracted the process. Japan is the second largest market in the world for distilled spirits, worth $100 million annually.

Japan also has been challenged for not extending intellectual property protection as far back as Western democracies (since Japanese innovations are generally more recent), and for "pirating" U.S. software. Another trade conflict involved a U.S. Federal Maritime Commission threat to ban Japanese ships from American ports unless Japan abandoned port practices that favored domestic shippers.[31]

CONCLUSION

It is naive to think that Japan will adopt a radical recovery plan any time soon. It has not needed one in the recent past, and the Japanese political process currently is fragile and historically incremental. Although the Japanese economy clearly needs a jump start, the "endless stream" of stimulus packages that Japan's governments have announced since the beginning of the crisis have all erred on the conservative side. Moreover, they have tended to focus on building infrastructure (to create jobs), when overbuilding is part of Japan's problem. Western economists estimate that Japan's banks are carrying $1 trillion in bad debt (the government admits to $555 billion), but a radical restructuring of Japan's banks seems nowhere in the cards, despite the fact that about one-half of them are too weak to qualify to do international banking.[32]

This is infuriating to Western economies, for they want Japan's economy to get healthy fast, to reduce sharply escalating trade imbalances and to help lead the rest of Asia out of its economic doldrums. It doesn't look as if this will happen anytime soon. The OECD has predicted the Japanese economy would shrink 2.6 percent in 1999 and barely expand in the year 2000. This seems much too slow, a threat not just to Japan's economy but to the world's as well. Nonetheless, the Japanese clearly have decided to address this problem in their own way. Western pressure is not likely to change that. Besides, Japan's rescue plans, collectively, represent the largest stimulus package ever to be adopted by a modern economy. Furthermore, Japan has acted to stimulate economies throughout Asia. Japan will suffer Western indignities in its own way. But this much is certain: the Japanese economy and model are going to change forever in some very fundamental ways. It may be seriously doubted whether Japan will remain the dominant economy in the region. Moody's already has lowered Japan's credit rating.[33]

Chapter 12

China: The Middle Kingdom in the Middle

China is the greatest enigma of all. Its economy is the least transparent and the most heavily managed of any we have examined. No doubt this secrecy hides some embarrassing facts about China's government and economy. With the passage of time, those facts almost certainly will be exposed. However, Chinese leadership probably believes that this information would damage China's competitive trade position if it were known today, and so they will do their best to hide it. This fear will keep China cautious and its trade liberalization slow, for the time being.

To some extent, China is correct. The world *will* use information it finds out about the Chinese government and economy, and the information *will* cause second thoughts about China. But this result need not be adverse. For China is the last, large communist state and clearly is caught between state socialism and capitalism. On the other hand, China has the third largest economy in the world (at $2.8 trillion annual GDP). So there is every reason for industrialized and emerging economies to hope that the modernization and liberalization of the Chinese economy succeeds. After all, marginalizing China only contributes to the instability of Asia and risks alienating a growing body of new consumers. It would be absolute folly for the developed world not to do everything in its power to swiftly integrate China into the world economy. Indeed, it could well be the test case for other illiberal or depressed economies entering the "global" marketplace; for example, Russia, India and Africa.[1]

That said, there are powerful forces resisting a too-rapid or too-complete market opening. In China, there really is no separation between business and the state. Many of its business are state-run. In a communist system, these businesses are used as much for social purposes as they are to compete in world trade circles. Indeed, much of China's recent economic success can be laid to the fact that they have delayed opening their own market, while rather freely penetrating foreign markets. This eventually must end in a WTO-dominated, "globalized" economy. But the process may have begun.

For one thing, the Chinese government isn't as centralized as it would appear. The military is very influential and runs some of the largest and most profitable Chinese enterprises. It manufactures armaments and heavy machinery sold throughout the world.[2] The bureaucrats that head other large Chinese industries also are powerful, because they supply China's consumption needs and employ thousands of people. Finally, wealthier and more advanced provinces and cities (e.g., Shanghai) are becoming power centers, as they compete for foreign capital and trade. Thus, the power once wielded by China's Communist leaders is waning.

It is very difficult to assess the Chinese situation. Its liberalization will be carefully managed, if that is possible. And it probably is possible, because no one wants to see the world's third largest economy run amok. On the other hand, China's is a relatively primitive economy by Western standards. Its per capita GDP was only $1,860 in 1994 (about double that of 1985), fourteen times smaller than that of the U.S. and just above that of El Salvador. Nonetheless, between 1978 and 1994, China went from being the world's 32nd largest exporter to its tenth largest. It has shrunk the four Asian tigers' share of labor-intensive exports from 55 percent in 1984 to 24 percent in 1994. But this has not stifled the growth of emerging Asian economies, because there is "more than enough demand for labor-intensive exports to go around." China's return to international markets has had the "greatest impact on global trade of any transition country." It has gone from a negative trade balance of $3.2 trillion in 1980 to a positive balance of $7.2 trillion in 1994.

However, China still is classed a low-income economy. Its considerable trade is diluted by its huge population; its infrastructure is inadequate and fragile; and its external debt exceeded $100 billion in 1994, trailing only Brazil and Mexico.[3] That is to say that China is a giant and a pygmy at one and the same time—a giant in terms of the sheer size of the economy, its population and landmass, but a pygmy in terms of the sophistication of its economy. It cannot reach its vast potential (for "potential" is the operative word) without liberalizing. And yet opening its huge economy must be frightening. When expectations outstrip the ability to meet them, anything can happen, as with Tiananmen Square or Russia's free-market debacle.

China's economy and population are so large that "it will become a major economic power if it achieves even a fraction of western productivity levels." However, China's rapid economic growth in recent years (the World Bank put it at 12.9 percent annually from 1990 to 1994) will slow down for three reasons. First, the economic meltdown in East Asia severely limits the affected economies' ability to consume Chinese exports or invest in Chinese enterprise. Both have been important to China's growth. Second, the decline in export trade will put more pressure on Chinese social programs, already unable to keep up with its expanding population. Third, foreign direct investment in East Asia, including China, has slowed abruptly. Attracting capital will require greater transparency, which China is certain to oppose. On the other hand, Japan, China and the Pacific Rim countries have been a principal focus of U.S. investment over the past few years. We cannot easily abandon them. Despite Asia's lack of transparency, its corruption, cronyism and mismanagement, the U.S. government and American businesses are deeply invested in Asia. Its success is to some degree our success. The recent scare and the IMF recovery package may finally give Western businesses and capitalists the platform needed to reform the region. The discipline produced by the meltdown may produce a brighter future.

But this gets us somewhat ahead of our story. Unlike its neighbors, China has been largely successful in resisting the Asian crisis. This may be due to good luck or a lack of transparency, but China will not be unaffected. After all, a lot of its financing comes from Hong Kong, Japan, Southeast Asia and Taiwan. Moreover, China is a major exporter to the region. If jittery or cash-strapped Asian consumers can't buy Chinese goods, inventories pile up and workers are laid off. China has many of the same problems that sank Asia's "Little Tigers": "a real estate bubble, industrial overcapacity, rampant corruption and unsound banks." Even before their collapse, China was experiencing a significant slowdown in foreign investment. And it still has to restructure (and probably privatize or close) thousands of state-owned companies, more than half of them operating at a loss. This means massive job losses, at a time when farm income is declining and many city dwellers are unemployed. (Although China claims a 4 percent jobless rate, Western economists think it could be 10 percent).

Worsening economic conditions may make reforms difficult to adopt, even if necessary. Economic growth slowed from 9.5 to 8 percent in the first half of 1997. Some analysts expected it to decline to 5 or 6 percent in 1998, and doubt China's claim to 7.8 percent growth. This is below the level needed to sustain China's economy and social system. Perhaps discipline will be imposed by the IMF, or as a precondition of WTO membership. Whether the impetus is internal or external, however, China will have to reform.[4]

Of course, the United States is not blameless in all this turmoil. Our policy toward China is hardly a model of consistency. Nonetheless, our interdependence with the region is significant. The U.S. sends about 20 percent of its exports to east Asia and 12 percent to Japan. About one-third of our imports come from the region. Asia's downturn will slow consumption of U.S. exports, while making Asian imports more competitive in our markets. This could trigger protectionism, but that would be exactly the wrong response. We can't improve our economic prospects if we can't export. To do that we need healthy markets abroad. The Mexican peso crisis should have taught us a lesson, and the "Asian contagion" surely must. Our best strategy is to support conversions to a market economy, not to try to wall out the disruption they threaten.[5]

Moreover, China no longer is the monolithic, authoritarian, communist nation it was under Chairman Mao. The Communist Party has lost support, and public support for China's current government is contingent on its economic success. Can China compete in world markets and take care of social ills at home? It seems headed in the right direction. The difficulty is to pursue the liberalization in the face of virtually assured culture shocks. Higher unemployment is almost guaranteed (a capitalist, not a communist phenomenon). Also there will be privatization and consolidation, shocks for which the Chinese (Asian-model economy) may be unprepared.

Hence, it was critical that the summit between President Clinton and China's Jiang Zemin in October 1997 went well. The mere fact that U.S. and Chinese leaders were to exchange visits (an outgrowth of APEC summits) was a good first step. A personal relationship generally is advantageous in international affairs. It was not expected that these leaders would agree on everything. Indeed, the U.S. and China are not of one mind about global trade and security. Yet they both know that more profit will derive from collaboration than confrontation. Thus, Jiang needed the prestige of a successful state visit to America. It must have been a relief to him to hear that America's goal with regard to China was cooperation, not containment. China also seemed ready to play a more constructive role in world affairs, if that could be done without destabilization or loss of face.

Hence, China agreed to discontinue a nuclear cooperation program with Iran in return for the lifting of a twelve-year ban on the export of peaceful nuclear technology. A large commercial airplane deal was a bonus. What sparks were generated by a news-conference exchange about human rights in China did not derail the positive aspects of the meeting. Later, in a speech at Harvard, President Jaing admitted "mistakes" at Tiananmen Square. This is the best that American liberals can expect for the moment. Chinese authority is still very rigid. And human rights almost always are sacrificed to economic well-being. It will be no different in China.[6]

Meanwhile, it seems inescapable that China's role in Asia will increase. Our help in encouraging China to gradually open its own market and help stabilize Asian economies promises the best result for both peace and economic prosperity in the region. We should not be naive in this regard. China is keen to gain an advantage, if one is to be gotten. But the U.S. is in a position to maintain regional balance, if any state is. And U.S. firms, as they integrate more fully into the Asian economy, are likely to promote opening.[7] In this respect, the grant to China of *permanent* most-favored-nation (MFN) status (now more-commonly called normal trade relation—NTR) might be a constructive first step. It should not be taken incautiously, since it is likely to accelerate China's admission to the World Trade Organization, and China's economy still seems too illiberal for that. But the annual debate in Congress about whether or not to renew China's MFN status (thus far, always resolved in China's favor) does not contribute to a constructive relationship.[8]

There is nothing that China wants more than accession to the WTO. That would secure its status as a major market player and allow it to exert influence on future market liberalization. Withholding WTO membership is one of the last limits on its ambitions. Grant it too easily, and China may never fully liberalize. Hold out too long, and WTO membership for China will become practically irrelevant.[9]

Of course, China doesn't want to open its economy any more than it has to in order to gain that prize. To do so would be foolhardy. It would invite more-competitive traders into Chinese markets before their producers are able to compete with them. Hence, China wants to know just how low the WTO membership bar can be set. It offers one modest trade opening at a time, probing for the entry threshold. The Western world, however, is looking for a firm commitment to genuine reform and market liberalization. While this cat-and-mouse game continues, the structural flaws that are plaguing Asia threaten to slow world economic growth. The reluctance of China and Japan to change could prolong and deepen the crises. Meanwhile, we are concerned about our burgeoning imbalance of our trade with China. We hardly want to fight all over again with it our protracted trade wars with Japan. So WTO membership has become the bargaining chip. If China reforms its economy sufficiently, then it gets to join the WTO and reform some more. But in the latter circumstance, it will be one of the decision-makers. Chinese prime minster Zhu thought that he had the Clinton administration cornered on this issue when he visited the U.S. in April 1999. The meeting needed a major trade deal to anchor it, and U.S. support for China's entry into the WTO was the obvious choice. But the deal lacked congressional and business support, so President Clinton backed away, angering Zhu but taking the right action given China's vague market-opening pledges to that date.[10]

Depending upon the course of the Asian recovery, China may become a WTO member in the year 2000, or soon thereafter. China is modernizing even as it tries to stave off recession. Furthermore, it is not as exposed as the "Little Tigers" or Japan to Asia's speculative "bubble." About 40 percent of foreign investment in mainland China ($54.8 billion) comes from or through Hong Kong. Although its stock market was battered in the autumn 1997 downturn, it is among the more resilient in the region. Moreover, Hong Kong is proof positive that China can indeed make the conversion to a market economy. It is the political will and a sound strategy that is lacking. Jiang's forays into the non-Asian world may help with both. First, they seem to improve his stature at home (the Western world needs strong leadership in China and Russia). And while abroad, Jiang sees the prosperity of relatively free economies, without oppressive government oversight. The Chinese would like to dismiss the U.S. trade imbalance as a "historic inevitability" and criticize the U.S. for "endless quibbling" about it. Both know it is a structural imbalance.[11]

China already enjoys two "windows" on the West, Hong Kong and Taiwan. Both are proximate to and were once part of China. Both have developed solid capitalist economies. But the policy accommodation that allowed China to reabsorb Hong Kong ("one China, two systems") cannot last forever. It must eventually move in one direction or the other. History heavily favors liberalization. China also would like to reabsorb its capitalistic "renegade province," Taiwan. Since separating from the mainland, the "free" Chinese have thrived. It is the world's nineteenth largest economy, with a per capita GDP of $12,400, about four times that of the Chinese. Yet it is an orphan in political and trading circles, increasingly tied to the mainland by trade and investment. Whether China will reabsorb Taiwan by force or persuasion is an imponderable. But there is good reason to believe that Hong Kong and Taiwan—and other economic forces—will influence mainland market philosophy in such a way that the "two-Chinas" approach eventually will disappear.[12]

Hong Kong and Taiwan are not the only strains on China's centralization, however. As China gets wealthier and more diverse, it is only natural that individual provinces and population centers will pursue their own goals. This may reinforce the Chinese economy, but it also threatens central control.[13] In time, China will adjust to this too. It already is evident that a suffocating central rule is a thing of the past.

To protect itself from U.S. hegemony, China has cultivated friends among Asian nations. Japan is the third largest investor in China (behind Hong Kong and Taiwan) at $10.7 billion in 1995. This is a whisker above the U.S. investment at $10.5 billion, but is likely to decrease due to Japan's own problems. However, there is no doubt that Japan will influence China's economy, as its industrial outsourcing migrates into Asia. Since Japan is a member of the G-7 and Quad 4 nations, Chinese interests will be protected in world trade negotiations, even before China joins the WTO.[14]

The European Union has lagged significantly behind the U.S. in pursuing opportunities in China. Among the reasons are the EU's own internal problems and its need to work out trade ties with emerging nations in Central and Eastern Europe, where the EU has a natural advantage. Nonetheless, Brussels made a concerted push in 1995 to stimulate trade with the Far East, and especially China. This has borne some fruit, but still leaves the EU in a Johnny-come-lately posture with respect to the region.[15] The EU is doing little of substance to close the gap, however. The Chinese seem to be using the prospect of closer trade relations with Europe simply as leverage against the U.S. in its demands with regard to market opening. Since the

U.S. and the EU haven't collaborated much on China, the ploy has worked reasonably well.

China has not limited its suitors to those the U.S. would approve, however. To bolster its prospects of WTO membership, to expand export markets, and to cultivate international influence generally, China has joined with its former communist adversary, Russia, to oppose U.S. "hegemony" in economic affairs. The new warmth in the relationship is not one-sided. Russia may need more economic help than the West is willing to commit. And both China and Russia would profit from reduced border tensions. Despite its many troubles, Russia still is more of a player in world political circles than China. To the extent they can agree, each reinforces the other. Besides, Russia has resources that China could help develop and use. For example, the contemplated development of Siberian oil and gas fields could result in a pipeline through China to an export terminal there. While both countries have more interest in cultivating the West than each other, a "strategic partnership" gives each an extra measure of clout in their dealings with the West.

Then there are less savory linkages, like those with Iran and Pakistan. President Jiang agreed at his summit with President Clinton that he would suspend China's nuclear cooperation with Iran in return for President Clinton's lifting of a ban on the sale of nuclear energy technology to China. Where this leads no one knows, for China is still one of the world's largest arms exporters, including nuclear.[16]

All one can say for certain is that China is newly energized to reach out to all major economic players—Japan, Russia, the EU and the U.S.—to establish closer economic and political ties. Under President Jiang, they seem to be succeeding; in part by reducing their communist polemic and suffering (to the extent necessary) the conditions of engagement. But the underlying thrust of China's policy does not seem to have changed. It is intent on being a major economic and political force in Asia. In the long term, the prospects of success are reasonable. But to realize this ambition, China will have to deal a staggering set of obstacles.

CHINA IN THE MIDDLE

To say that China is at a "crossroads" today is merely to state the obvious. It wants the prestige and influence that membership in the WTO would bring, but it seems unwilling or unable to make the concessions that would allow for it.[17] China is a market of enormous potential, and yet it is still an agrarian society (about 21 percent of GDP and about 55 percent of population depend on agriculture).[18] That China will suffer from the "Asian contagion" is beyond doubt. It is too deeply integrated in the economies of the region to avoid it. Indeed, China saw contractual foreign investment drop 35 percent in the first ten months of 1997, (compared to 1996). State planners had projected that foreign investment would jump 15 percent in 1997. Instead, 1997 figures did not equal those of 1996. This ends consecutive annual increases in direct overseas investment that stretch back to 1990 and averaged 12 percent annually from 1993 to 1996. Just how much China will be affected by the economic turmoil of the region is almost impossible to say, for official economic statistics are so poor or so rigged that even the Chinese leadership may not know the extent of its problems.[19]

Hence, China is another example of the failed Japanese "model" with its dependence on fresh capital, a centrally controlled economy and incautious investment. Besides, China has such grave structural problems (businesses privatization, environmental degradation and farm migration) that it seems impossible to address them all without economic dislocation. This is in dramatic contrast to China's ambitions and recent success.

The market opening that is prerequisite to meeting China's regional and global ambitions presents serious risks of destabilizing China's transitional economy. So the Chinese leadership is understandably cautious. Despite its admirable progress these past ten years, China has a good distance to go, and time is running out. Some who might help (e.g., foreign corporations and investors) have been held somewhat at bay by the uncertainty of its market liberalization.[20] And the massive restructuring needed risks political backlash of the type that paralyzed Russia. Of course, the two countries are quite different. Russia's venture into "capitalism" was abrupt; China's is much more structured. Whereas Russia has lost its industrial base, China is gaining one. And its service sector has grown dramatically. Whereas Russia's per capita GDP has shrunk nearly 30 percent, China's has grown steadily.[21]

China's long-term economic isolation and centralized economy are not easy things to shrug off, however. The process began a while ago; and the easy bits have been done. Further economic reforms promise economic hardship. That is what makes them politically "risky" and difficult to chronicle.[22]

THE STRUCTURE OF CHINESE INDUSTRY

Following a politically sensitive change of leadership from Deng to Jiang, the Asia "crisis" made it more difficult for China to initiate economic reforms. China's troubled Asian partners will not be able to absorb Chinese products and will compete with them in export markets. The best antidote for this is a creative, lean and aggressive market economy. China's is anything but that. It's public sector is bloated and inefficient. The military sector is a significant counterweight to civilian leadership. Necessary "downsizing" could threaten labor unrest. China's state sector employs about 12 million persons, or about 56 percent of the urban work force. It is estimated that 15 to 20 percent of them could be released. But unemployment would rise to an unsupportable 13 percent if capitalist efficiency were introduced.

Moreover, the Chinese economy is not likely to create many new jobs in the short term. Retraining programs have been begun, and privately owned businesses are growing rapidly. But they are not growing fast enough to pick up the slack produced by state industry restructuring. And yet this cannot be delayed, for state business inefficiencies take a toll on the Chinese economy that it can ill afford. China cannot afford labor unrest, either.

After all, political legitimacy depends upon the government's ability to sustain trade and employment.[23] Both are threatened by the Asian downturn. And so President Jiang, in an address to the People's Congress, set a three-year timetable to reform China's 300,000 state-operated enterprises (half of which lose money and borrow more from state banks than they are likely to repay). Indeed the Chinese banking sector itself is thought to be bankrupt many times over. Hence, a major restructuring of Chinese business is overdue. Domestic demand is slack and foreign investment is shrinking. The problem is made worse by the large stockpiles of Chinese goods that were allowed to accumulate rather than to cool the Chinese economy when it was expanding. Now those surpluses may be dumped into Asia markets, depressing prices further.[24]

A second hard-to-regulate feature of the Chinese economy is the portion controlled by the People's Liberation Army (PLA). No longer Mao's "personal army," the PLA has turned into "an industrial combine that trades in weapons and uses police to stamp out unions in its sweatshop factories." The PLA is estimated to control 50,000 factories, producing goods ranging from steel to cosmetics. Clearly, Chinese leadership has to take into account the influence of the military. While no one advocates a return to the repressive, Communist, slow-growth economy before 1989 (when Deng began liberalization), the process has to be managed effectively from the top unless China wants to risk the type of lawless chaos that crippled economic reform in Russia. This is not easy to achieve in a country as large, diverse and populous as China, for it is in the very nature of capitalism that it is decentralized, and stresses efficiency over social policy.

On the other hand, economic events in Asia and around the world require decisive action. President Jiang acknowledges this. In order to "rejuvenate the nation" he sought "new breakthroughs in economic restructuring." According to him, "state-owned enterprises lack vitality," although they monopolize such important sectors of the national economy as energy, transport, chemicals and financial services. China needs a system more congenial to foreign investment.[25] But a system as poor and as centralized as China's, where the economy is changing very rapidly, presents many opportunities for abuse and corruption. One has to look no further than Russia's experiment with "capitalism" to see this. Civil servants are among the corrupt. This undermines confidence in the economy, both internally and externally.[26]

PRIVATIZATION

Clearly China cannot allow itself to go bankrupt by reason of over-staffed, inefficient enterprises. One of the solutions is to downsize government and to privatize the economy. This must be terribly difficult for the largest socialist country in the world to do, and that is exactly what Jiang has proposed. In his speech to the Communist Party Congress in September 1997, he used language unthinkable in China five years ago. Terms like "merger," "bankruptcy," "laid-off workers," "downsizing," "efficiency" and "modern enterprise system." The speech was so laden with weasel-words and short on specifics that it is difficult to say exactly what steps will be taken or when. That may be the whole point: run the idea up the flagpole, see who shoots or salutes and then respond accordingly.

The time frame seems clear enough, though: "from the present to the first decade of the next century [2010] will be crucial to China." The object also is reasonably clear: to "promote [a] fundamental shift [in] the economic system and . . . mode of economic growth." Jiang acknowledged two (seemingly contradictory) problems: "a more or less ideal socialist market economy" and "[sustaining the] rapid and sound development of the national economy." Thus far, the latter as been possible through the type of capitalism practiced by Japan for many years. So the operative words here may be "more or less." It is too risky to cut China's economy loose the way Russia's was. As "a socialist country, China must keep public ownership . . . in a dominant position." This would mean that core enterprises like national resources (coal, oil and hydropower, defense, petrochemicals, telecommunications and infrastructure) may remain in state hands. Jiang called these "the life-blood of the national economy." But Jiang recognized that "China [also] needs to develop diverse forms of ownership . . . [including] any form [within reason] . . . that . . . can . . . serve socialism." These "diverse economic sectors [are to] develop side by side, gradually removing the fetter of the irrational ownership structure on the productive forces." In short, Jiang recognized that the "non-public sector is an important component . . . of [China's] socialist market economy."

The developed world can well hope Jiang is right. Otherwise, there will be a considerable economic and political backlash in China. The developed world doesn't want this any more than Jiang. Rather they want a reliable business partner, a market, and an anchor in the Asian region. But China is insecure and sometime secretive. Western pressure could be counterproductive.[27]

CHINA'S INSECURITY

China is the most populous nation in the world. It has a long history and a culture of which it is justly proud. And yet, it is insecure. China does not feel that it gets the respect it deserves. It is pressed to open its markets and adopt Western practices. But China can see the social discord attendant on capitalism. It would like to enjoy its benefits without its liabilities. So the country seems trapped between its pride, its ambition and its doubts. China knows that its period of isolation is over, but has yet to accept (far less embrace) its emergence as a world economic player.[28] The result is that the Chinese leadership is constantly vacillating between tight regulation and liberalization, trying to find the right balance. Consequently, the opening and closing of China's market seems to be an almost daily affair. The pressure from the West is unrelenting; and the retrenchment in Beijing can be sharp. Meanwhile, U.S. businesses, eager to participate in the promising Chinese market, seem to switch from pessimism to optimism, depending on current economic and political relations.[29]

CHINESE TRADE PRACTICES

This is not to suggest that everything is regular and above board with respect to Chinese trade practices. Far from it. One might understand how China, emerging from a long period of isolation in 1996 and somewhat naive in the ways of capitalism and global politics, feared that it was about to be triangulated by Japan, Australia and the U.S. Too much pressure by then Secretary of State Christopher had resulted in a two-year chill in U.S./ China relations. Some positive steps were taken at the APEC meeting at Osaka in November 1995, when China agreed to adhere to "international [trade] norms" as a precondition of WTO membership. Still China's doubts and suspicions about full economic engagement in the Pacific continued. However, President Clinton, en route to the 1996 APEC meeting in Manila, stated that the United States intended to remain engaged in the region, notwithstanding its new treaty with the EU. Moreover, he said, U.S. efforts would aim to *involve* China ("engage" it) in regional affairs, so that it would not become isolated. Personal meetings between President Clinton and Chinese President Jiang and the agreement to regular, reciprocal summits (that have begun) helped to improve U.S.–Chinese relations.[30]

A more open and productive trade dialogue between the industrialized world and China may prove salutary. But the short-term result is not rosy. China remains wary of the West. For example, China does not hesitate to close, or to impose restrictions on, markets that it considers threatened by foreign competition. Among those markets are insurance, telecommunications, heavy equipment, pharmaceuticals and foreign labor.[31] This behavior contradicts China's market-opening pledges, which seem valid only to the extent that they serve China's purposes. This makes doing business in or with China both difficult and risky.

Other breaches of China's own agreements or accepted international trading rules are almost too numerous to mention. A few have an especially high profile, for example, special duties placed in the import of capital equipment by foreign firms. (This had the negative effect of discouraging foreign investment, manufacture, or expansion in China). Another anti-competitive practice is the "dumping" of surplus Chinese goods in foreign markets.[32] Of greater culpability perhaps was a government scheme to circumvent textile export quotas (under a 1994 bilateral agreement) by transhipping cloth and apparel through Hong Kong, Mongolia and Fiji. Although China professed its innocence in the matter, the practice was not stopped until the U.S. imposed $19 million in penalties on Chinese exporters. The dispute was finally resolved only after the U.S. threatened to deny China most-favored-nation (MFN) trade status and oppose its WTO membership.[33]

Two other high-profile areas of U.S./China trade friction involve intellectual property and nuclear weapons and technology. The problem of intellectual property "piracy" is epidemic. Japan and Taiwan practiced it in their time; as has just about any nation that has little intellectual property to protect and can profit by pirating that of others. It is not evident that the Chinese government is involved, but it has been lax about enforcing property rights. And its market is so ill-regulated that it is difficult to know how much is going on. But the amount is significant. Repeated attempts to get China to address the problem have been met with earnest pledges, but mediocre results. As U.S. frustration and trade threats have mounted, China has made periodic attempts to clamp down.[34] But any real solution seems a long way off. In China's state-managed economy, there does not seem to be any notion of private rights or anti-competitive behavior, except as the *state* defines it.

Of greater concern, perhaps, is China's inability or unwillingness to closely monitor and/or account for its trade in nuclear weapons and technology. This is a sensitive matter, even within China, for the military controls these industries. It enjoys an enviable position in a world that is rapidly reducing production and trade in nuclear weapons. For this reason, so-called "dual-use" products and technology are sent to China selectively and then only with the understanding that it will be used for peaceful purposes and not reexported. Nonetheless, export agreements are being violated, with substantial risks to national security. China seems sensitive to the issue and has tried to demonstrate good faith[35] (although its cycle of negligence and contrition in this and other trade areas is far from convincing).

Surely, some of China's problems may be laid to the newness of the whole Western, capitalist trading scheme. Conversely, a degree of self-serving calculation seems to pervade China's market-opening negotiations. Virtually no opening is offered by China. Every step forward has to be coerced, and backtracking is regular. China's hope may be that it will gradually wear away the resolve of western traders and gain its objectives on the cheap. Indeed, there is evidence that, by negotiating with China independently instead of collectively, the U.S. and EU have been split, and each has made concessions in order to prevent the other from getting a preferred status.[36] A united front would have been better.

Recent events have thrust China into the forefront. The once-golden Little Tigers have lost their luster and have some painful rebuilding ahead of them. South Korea may be in even worse shape, and Japan may be losing its leadership position in the region. The industrialized world now is hoping that China will not devalue its currency or turn protectionist, and continue to grow its economy (albeit at a reduced pace). China has emerged from the Asian turmoil as one of the region's strongest prospects, but only if its leaders don't shrink from their task as markets are opened and competition bites. The time is near when the U.S. and its WTO partners will stop making exceptions for China. The same thing happened in our trade relations with Japan. At some point, "Asian model" markets have to be accessible.

The only real option left to China is to liberalize its market to the extent necessary to gain WTO membership and to attract the capital it needs to grow its economy. It is going to have to produce better-quality goods more efficiently. It also is going to have to deal with some serious infrastructure problems that can't be delayed much longer. And it may have to deal with economic and political repercussions precipitated by market reforms.[37] I already have mentioned unemployment, a weak banking system, surplus goods and uncompetitive, loss-making industries as some of China's problems. Add the problems listed below and you can appreciate just how large a challenge the Chinese leadership faces.

China has a notoriously weak agricultural sector, despite the fact that some two-thirds of China's people are farmers or rural laborers. Unsophisticated farming methods produce low yields and degrade the land. It is estimated that one-fifth of agricultural land in China has been lost to erosion or development since 1957. Since grain production depends heavily on the weather, it fluctuates enormously due to floods or drought. What is produced is often consumed locally, since transport doesn't exist to take it to distant markets.[38] There also are severe pollution problems in China's urban centers. This is due to rapid growth, concentrated populations and heavy dependence on high-sulfur coal. It is estimated that 178,000 people die each year from the pollution. The lead levels in children's blood in many cities is almost twice that considered safe for normal mental development. The pollution is of concern to China's neighbors because it produces acid rain. Water also is in short supply in China, particularly in urban areas where use threatens to outpace supply. Many sources are polluted by industrial effluents, and it is estimated that only 10 percent of sewage receives treatment.[39]

China's population has been the largest in the world for years. It also is aging and migrating. China's recent economic growth has benefitted mostly coastal and urban areas. Inland, rural populations, unable to subsist on the land and no longer adequately supported by government, migrate to the cities, where there is little work and no amenities. Additional unemployed created by China's market reforms will only exacerbate the problem and could lead to political unrest. To make matters worse, China's population control program has effectively been abandoned. Much of China's transportation, communications and energy infrastructure is so poor that the government has announced plans to spend hundreds of billions of dollars during the next five years to upgrade infrastructure. But China needs foreign capital to do this.[40] In short, its structural problems are daunting.

Are they insurmountable? Probably not, and especially not if China is willing to work with Western governments and businesses to insure that the capital and know-how are forthcoming and used effectively. But this means Western involvement in China's internal politics; something about which it is acutely sensitive. When resources are scarce and political leadership is stressed, then the prospect of retrenchment runs high.

FOREIGN BUSINESS, FOREIGN CAPITAL AND CHINA'S FINANCIAL REFORM

One of the reasons for our intense interest in trade with China is that its trade gap with the United States is so great. It is relatively easy in centrally managed economies to make it difficult for foreign businesses to compete in your market while structuring export trade to penetrate theirs. But it appears that our national leadership is not going to tolerate this situation as long as it did with Japan. The president and Congress can use MFN (or NTR) trading status and WTO membership as leverage. Private businesses can use the leverage of capital investment. China is quite dependent on foreign capital to grow its economy. It cannot avoid reforms that are a prerequisite to receiving it. The sharp decline of "little tiger" economies has led to a slowdown in China too. Perhaps that will accelerate China's market opening and fiscal reforms, but one can never be certain how a vulnerable nation will react. If China devalues its currency, a whole new wave of economic contraction may be unleashed in Asia.

The flow of foreign direct investment (FDI) into Asia has slowed significantly since 1997, when economic troubles began. China's Ministry of Foreign Trade reported that contractual foreign investment in China declined 29 percent that year. This is a serious downturn, when China needed a hefty increase to continue its reforms. Moreover, another drop was expected in 1998. Western capital is more important than ever because other Asian economies that might have invested in China and bought her exports are in recession. I am not predicting a wholesale embrace of Western capitalism, of course. If anything, the embarrassment of their collapse and the strict terms imposed on them by IMF rescue packages have left East Asian nations smarting. When they revive, they may turn protectionist again. For the moment, however, they need Western capital and the debate is chiefly about the terms.[41]

China's prospects would be much brighter if the state itself were not such a large part of the problem. Its tens of thousands "loss-making and bloated" state-owned enterprises (SOEs) represent a huge drain on the Chinese economy. It is one thing for President Jiang to pledge to reform them, but it is quite another to do so. The Chinese must be wary of unleashing market forces that will threaten the government or the stability of the economy. An evolutionary pace is undoubtedly preferable to a revolutionary one.[42] Is there time available? Will Western investors be attracted if reform is uncertain and there is too little transparency?

That depends on several things. First, what opportunities are offered? Foreigners are likely to be most interested in large, profit-making state enterprises. But this puts more strain on the weaker ones. Besides, many of the former are run by the military. Second, how large a stake can foreigners have? Presently, domestic investment is encouraged, but foreign control has been strictly limited. Finally, what other options do investors have, say, in the U.S., Europe, Latin America, India or even Africa? China knows that it has to make an offer good enough to compete with other expanding economies. But it is not keen to offer more than it has to, even though its economic future may be threatened by its failure to reform more speedily. On one hand there is the China ready to expand, reform and welcome foreigners.[43] And on the other there is the China that is wary, insecure and keen to maintain control of its own economy.[44]

Notwithstanding all this seeming uncertainty, major U.S. businesses have bet on China. They hope to be in on the ground floor when its long-anticipated market conversion takes place. Large U.S. firms like Boeing, Aetna and Motorola invested heavily in the Chinese market in the medium to long term. Whether it is a good bet remains to be seen. But change clearly is afoot in China, and that alone is progress.[45] Fortunately, investor interest in China was not crippled by the Asian crisis, so the capital is available on the right terms.[46] But these steps only presage the next step, which is to reform China's domestic capital markets. Its highly protected banking sector has a legacy of policy-driven rather than profited-oriented lending.

The four largest state-owned banks account for some 80 percent of China's banking business. Officials estimate that 5 to 6 percent of their loans are so bad that they will have to be written off. Another 20 to 25 percent would be considered "problem loans" by Western standards. Having observed the problems caused in other Asian economies by ill-run banking sectors, China's leadership appears committed to change. Weaker banks will have to be closed, producing unemployment. Banking practices will have to be brought in line with international norms, if growth is to begin again. Finally, China pledges to allow the expansion of foreign bank activity. It would appear that China is quite serious about this. But, once the pain is felt, policies can change.[47] Furthermore, natural disasters such as a poor harvest or devastating flood still can wreak havoc with China's marginal economy.[48]

LOOKING OUTWARD

Beyond the sheer economic pressures on China to make these changes, there is a political rationale. China's economy has been isolated for too long. It is clear to all that the isolation has not produced a better state, but a weaker one. The Chinese people are increasingly aware of this fact and Chinese leaders covet the prestige that its size and prominence in Asia might bring. However, China's economy is still out of step with members of the Association of Southeast Asian Nations (ASEAN) or APEC or the WTO. None wants to be dragged down by China's needs. Hence, China has to reform in order to grasp the brass ring of full partnership.

Its best alliance may be with ASEAN. China's premier, Li Ping, addressed that group in August 1997, pledging that China would try to promote a "new and fair political and economic order in the world." He said that some countries "attempt to bully the weak and poor." Li Ping was speaking to the converted because ASEAN members have long felt that they have been asked to reform their economies too much and too soon. Yet ASEAN represents Asia's smaller, weaker states. Adding China would add immensely to their clout, but wouldn't help China very much. To make good Li Ping's pledge, however, China gave $1 billion in financial assistance to Thailand as its economy faltered. Just months later, China joined in a $23 billion Indonesian rescue package arranged by the IMF and expressed interest in a special "Asia fund" (proposed by Japan) so that ["Asian nations could] all pursue [their] own economic development."

China joined APEC in late 1991 and has attended its recent summits. APEC is comprised mostly of Asian nations that have close trading ties with China. It was but a small step to bring China aboard, but it still needs to comply fully with the terms of trade harmonization in the Pacific Rim. The U.S. has used APEC to this end, and other APEC members (e.g., Canada) also have bilateral trade agreements with China. Still, it is WTO membership that China really covets, and wanted to achieve before the November 1999 WTO summit meeting in Seattle. But China must satisfy WTO members with its trade opening first.[49]

We have seen, and I think will continue to see, a gradual and carefully measured relaxation of government control in China's economy. If one closes one's ears to the political rhetoric (both ours and theirs) and instead looks at what is going on, then I think that conclusion in inescapable. The strongest force for change afoot in China today is not political or, in the context of WTO membership, legal. Rather it is economic. Let Western businesses do the heavy lifting. They operate outside the glare that politicians seek or suffer.

Just about every world trading state, *including* Taiwan, Hong Kong, Japan, the U.S. and EU, wants to see China succeed as a trading nation, if not a global power. When this happens, it will be much better for them to be perceived to have contributed to the process. It is possible that China's embrace of capitalism is a ruse and that, as soon as it becomes a powerful trading nation, it will return to isolation and repression. To some degree, the West is taking a risk. But it may not be much of a risk. If China is able to stay on course, continue market opening and avoid devaluation, it will have *earned* its place in the world economy. Its challenge is to avoid serious retrenchment, and ours is to be patient and constructive.[50]

One measure of China's new perspective is its willingness to deal multilaterally in fora like APEC and ASEAN. Previously China preferred to negotiate one-on-one. Mr. Jiang has agreed to and succeeded at summits in the U.S. and Russia, and high-level Chinese officials are engaging other states in the region in common initiatives. Certainly this builds China's constituency and status. It is more likely to deal with the West and to honor its agreements if it feels that it was treated equitably. The U.S. will be less able to dictate trade terms, but perhaps that is the price of a deal being honored. It is a rare moment of opportunity. One hopes it will not be lost because a more powerful China is seen as a threat to American workers or because of its human rights record. Human rights should improve as the economy does.[51]

Economically and politically speaking, China may be *the* success story in Asia, although its metamorphosis is still far from complete. Jiang's goal of a "socialist market economy" needs better definition. Still, his team has walked the tightrope thus far and may make the transition from a failing communist state to a form of managed capitalism without plunging into Russian-style chaos. This means gradually privatizing China's enormous public sector without creating too much economic hardship. The gradual exposure of China's systemic problems is a cause for grave concern. It suggests that the depth of China's economic problems may not be known or knowable. But the fact that China is releasing negative news (the world's largest coal-producer announced plans to close 25,800 mines in 1999) gives hope that it is prepared to join the global trading community—warts and all.[52]

CONCLUSION

China is genuinely caught in the middle. Because it has a closely managed economy, it can resist some economic problems, but China cannot stave off reform forever. At present, China is missing its own prescribed growth targets, which suggests a lack of capacity (or will) to turn its economy around. If China protects its markets, it might realize 8 percent growth in the near term, enough to keep its economy expanding. But the cost of that protection would put it behind technologically. If China opens to foreign competition, its growth would slow to about 5 percent, not enough to buffer the huge social costs of market opening. Moreover, there will be no real recovery until Asian markets in general pick up.[53] So China must not just reform, but lead.

It cannot do so without foreign capital and knowhow. To attract that, China must convincingly commit to a less-regulated economy, which it finds difficult to do. Because China's financial structure still is decidedly unsteady and because the signals the Chinese government gives to foreign investors are confusing, it does not have a strategy that builds confidence. So Western businesses and investors remain cautious. Nonetheless, FDI in China is beginning to grow again, and that is a hopeful sign. If China can stick with its reform program, it may be one of the best bets in Asia.[54]

But that only brings us to another concern for the Chinese leadership—the speed at which market reform proceeds. China's civilian government is firmly committed to separating the Communist Party and the state from their business interests as soon as possible. This will establish a capitalist market atmosphere. So far, they have been dramatically successful, particularly where the People's Liberation Army is concerned. But this changeover is going to cost millions of Chinese their jobs, so pressure will increase to buffer the hardship with some old-fashioned communism. The dependance of the Chinese people on a socially conscious government will not disappear overnight (witness Russia). This reform process, which might take just a few years under the right conditions, will be a real test of the government's political and economic acumen.[55]

It is a rude world out there, and the Chinese are about to learn that. The prize may be worth the pain, for China knows it must compete in world markets. I think that China, eclipsed and embarrassed by the West, will redouble its efforts to master the skills needed to prosper in today's trading world. It is sad that it has stayed with its micro-managed economy for so long. Its miscalculations have affected the whole world and held China back. Despite its occasional vacillation, China has contributed heavily to what stability there is in Asia, surprising even the West. It is one of the few Asian economies that is continuing to grow, and at the fastest rate. China has reached out to help its neighbors, notably Russia and Hong Kong. Occasionally, however, China's reform efforts stall, and it turns protectionist (for example, repatriating its currency and currency controls generally). These retrenchments must be balanced against the remarkable progress China has made, however. In sum, China has been a very solid player during the Asian crisis and could eventually replace Japan as the economic lynchpin of the region.[56]

Chapter 13

Asia's Emerging Economies: "Miracle," Myth or Neither?

INTRODUCTION

For nearly a quarter of a century, futurists have taken as a veritable article of faith that global influence would gradually—but irrepressibly—move west.[1] Given the rapid growth of Asian economies, it was not remarkable that President Clinton, at the first APEC leaders' summit in Seattle in 1993, declared that America's trading future lay in the Pacific Rim. The Asian "economic miracle" was to beget a "Pacific Century."[2] This prospect so unnerved our European partners that they negotiated a New Transatlantic Agenda. Now America is engaged on two fronts.

In the last fifteen years Pacific Rim economies became the darlings of investors, public and private. Early news told of the incredible economic turnaround of these nations from sleepy agrarian economies to modern, export-oriented states. Many dubbed this warp-speed transition the "Asian Miracle." To some extent it was. In 1960, East Asian economies accounted for only 4 percent of the world's gross product. By 1991, they represented 25 percent, approximately the same as the United States. By the year 2000, they were expected to represent one-third. The news was unbelievably good. Between 1965 and 1995, the per capita GDP of Asia's four "Little Tigers" (Hong Kong, Singapore, South Korea and Taiwan) had increased from 17 percent to 72 percent of that of the U.S. Recently, however, the news coming out of East Asia has told a different story, a story of excess, collapse and attempts to rebuild. Prior to that, the West lost ground to the East quite steadily. In 1950, at the apex of its industrialization, the West claimed 56 percent of world production with only 17 percent of its population. Asia, with 66 percent of world population, had a meager 19 percent of its income.[3] By 1993, however, two-way U.S. trade across the Pacific reached $361 billion (about one-half more than transatlantic trade), quadrupling since 1979. In 1992, EU trade with Asia reached $249 billion, eclipsing EU trade with America. Thus, trade between and among these three trading blocs was about equally distributed, but was growing most rapidly in Asia.[4]

SUN RISING

East Asian economic growth has taken place in waves, of which four can be identified. Japan is the traditional regional success story. Its success was followed by what may be deemed a second wave, dominated by the Little Tigers. The third wave was led by Indonesia, Malaysia and Thailand, after which a fourth wave of rapidly growing economies emerged in the region, notably China and Vietnam. All of these emerging economies achieved success by aping the Japanese model: a macro-managed economy in which emphasis is placed on exports, even at the expense of domestic considerations. Indeed, the successive waves of economic emergence can be ascribed to a ladder effect. As each Asian economy became more sophisticated, it outsourced more labor-intensive tasks and pursued more capital-and skill-intensive enterprise.[5] Real income in Japan and the Little Tigers grew four-fold, while in the third-wave countries it more than doubled. The economies of the third- and fourth-wave countries were predicted to grow between 5 and 6 percent annually over the next ten years, while industrialized countries grow at about one-third that rate.[6] In short, these emerging Pacific Rim countries were gradually "catching up" with market leaders. Hence, the belief grew that, if developed countries didn't participate in the Asian "miracle," a golden opportunity might be missed. So the Western world slowly turned its attention to Asia, and specifically to East Asia. As Western businesses became more involved, markets started to open. In some circumstances, the Western world was invited.[7]

Many predictions were made about the rate of expansion possible. In June 1996, the Pacific Economic Cooperation Council (PECC) declared that the "region will experience higher growth and steadily decreasing inflation over the next two years, with no end to the recovery . . . in sight."[8] Predictions like these increased Western interest and investment. Individual East Asian countries' statistics vary greatly, but they all reflect remarkable growth. For example, between 1970 and 1995, the per capita gross national product of South Korea rose almost elevenfold, that of Hong Kong fourfold and of Thailand 350 percent. This is unprecedented, when compared to the United States. In 1970 Korea's per capita real income was just 15 percent of that of the U.S. By 1995, it was over 40 percent of that of the US.

Much of this economic success derived from macroeconomic policies. Although each country had a different recipe for success, each followed some variant of the "Asian model." Its characteristics include, but are not limited to (1) a dramatic shift of the labor force from agriculture to industry, resulting in a sharp increase in exports; (2) state-managed capitalism; (3) a period of fixed exchange rates with a stronger currency, such as the United States dollar; (4) savings rates well above Western standards; (5) a stated commitment to gradual "liberalization" of the marketplace; and finally, (6) underdeveloped financial, telecommunications and transportation infrastructures. Some of the very characteristics that led to Asia's success also contributed to its "collapse" because the economies were over-managed and not based on sustainable growth.[9]

Emphasizing Exports

East Asian economic growth has been closely associated with a sharp rise in exports. This resulted primarily from a shift from agriculture to the production of manufactured goods. For example, Singapore, Hong Kong, the Republic of Korea and Taiwan have increased their combined share of world manufactured exports from 1.5 percent in 1970 to 8 percent today. This extraordinary rise in exports has rapidly integrated East Asian economies into the world economy. In 1990, export growth (to GDP) was approximately 150 percent for Hong Kong and Singapore and 24 percent for Indonesia. These export rates are more impressive when compared with the rates for the rest of the world, for example, 3.4 percent for the countries of Latin America and 7.3 percent for South Asia.

As each East Asian economy moved up the economic ladder it improved the lot of other emerging economies. Production facilities of labor-intensive industries such as toys, textiles, and footwear were moved to the latter countries. This speeds the industrialization of the former and allows all to profit from the cycle of growth.[10] The economic success of these nations cannot be explained merely by their shift in industries, however, or by intra-Asian cooperation. Another factor is the role played by their centralized governments.

Policy Setting

In order to keep their economies growing, many East Asian governments exercised authoritarian control over the marketplace. Some people have called them despotic capitalists. In the four Little Tiger economies, private industry always was centralized and managed. Usually centralized control consisted of large ruling families or government bureaucracies that manipulated the marketplace to keep it expanding.[11] The growth continued with the benefit of foreign capital. But it was insulated from the discipline of competitive markets.

Infrastructure

During the growth period there was a great feeling of security. Building for the future was visible everywhere. A strong infrastructure (communications, transport, financial services) was needed to proceed to the next level of growth, and these governments knew it. In June 1996, the U.S. Trade and Development Agency (TDA) released a list of 58 energy and transportation projects in Indonesia, Malaysia, Thailand and the Philippines valued at more than $90 billion. It announced that Southeast Asian nations "represent[] one of the fastest-growing markets in the world."[12] The future was bright and getting brighter.

Of these many infrastructure projects, possibly the most grandiose was Malaysia's "multimedia super corridor." This project was aimed at replicating California's silicon valley. It was a 750 square kilometer zone near Kuala Lumpur, with an administrative capital called Putrajaya. This one project had an estimated cost of $20 billion ringgit. The corridor was to have a "multimedia university" built in a planned futuristic city called Cyberjaya, at an additional $5 to 10 billion ringgit. Accompanying this futuristic city and super corridor was an international airport costing $9 billion ringgit and, to top it all off, twin office towers were to be built in Kuala Lumpur. These enormous projects could not be pursued without a great deal of foreign capital, however. To attract that, inflation had to be kept down and exchange rates needed to be steady.

Fixed Exchange Rate

Controlling inflation was not only important to the success of these projects, it was important to liquidity and stability in the marketplace. Growth cannot be sustained with high inflation. Inflation distorts prices and price volatility discourages investment. Until recently, the East Asian economies managed to control inflation rates extraordinarily well. From 1965 to 1980, inflation in the third-wave countries averaged 15.5 percent, while Japan's averaged 7.7 percent for the same period, and that of the Little Tigers was 10.5 percent. From 1980 through the early 1990s those same figures sank to 5 percent, 1.5 percent and 5.6 percent, respectively. However, rapid economic growth tests financial infrastructures. Without sufficient financial controls, inflation can rise rapidly and capital will flee. The risk of capital flight was real, but it was minimized by the fact that these East Asian nations were invested in one another and because their people have a very high savings rate. In 1980, the seven leading East Asian banks had 17 percent of global bank reserves, but in 1994 they held 41 percent. By 1993 East Asian savings rates had risen to around 30 percent of GDP, compared to the G-7 economies with an overall savings rate of only 8 percent.

SUN SETTING

A closer look at the superficial Asian "miracle" revealed weaknesses that have now come to light. All of East Asia's emerging economies had aped the Japanese model. Japan had ridden it to unprecedented heights. Why wouldn't it work for these transitional economies as well? Asian trade with both the U.S. and Europe was growing rapidly. And then there was the intra-Asian trade produced by the ladder effect. As Japan moved into semiconductors and high-tech products, it relocated its auto and consumer electronics operations to Thailand, Malaysia and other emerging Asian nations. The newly industrializing Little Tigers moved their labor-intensive industries (toys, textiles and footwear) to China and Vietnam. As Asian economies became more interdependent, they became less and less concerned about U.S. trade (Taiwan now trades more with Beijing than Washington) and capitalist market discipline. For the Japanese model was developed in the somewhat rarified air of a micro-managed system. Accordingly, it was not always allowed to make the market corrections that were necessary.[13]

There were other differences as well between the rapid growth of Japan and that of the Little Tigers. In Japan's case, much of the capitalization was internal and productivity grew as a function of both labor and efficiency gains. In the case of the Little Tigers, a lot of capital was imported, and labor was the principal component of growth. As MIT's Professor Krugman put it, this is a one-time input. It needed to be succeeded by other market gains, and was not.[14] Hence, the rapid expansion of these economies was built on a soft foundation. The weaknesses that have recently come to light are (1) government corruption and cronyism; (2) lack of basic infrastructure, despite the plans for building the same; (3) lack of regulation and transparency in financial markets; (4) an unmatchable shift in the labor force; and finally (4) the interdependency that saw the crisis spread from economy to economy. A slowdown in the growth of the Little Tiger economies was predicted, but the scale and depth of the crisis surprised everyone.[15]

Export Focus

The export boom never produced a dramatic increase in efficiency, which is what the "Asian model" was premised upon. Rather, like the former Soviet Union, the rapid growth of the Asian Tigers appears to have been the result of the mere mobilization of resources, especially cheap labor and large capital inputs. As Professor Krugman put it "Asian growth has so far been mainly a matter of perspiration rather than inspiration—working harder, not smarter."[16]

One vivid example of this was Singapore. Between 1966 and 1990, Singapore achieved an average annual growth rate of 8.5 percent. The major reason was the mass mobilization of the population. The percentage of persons serving industry grew from 27 percent in 1970 to 51 percent in 1995, a feat that cannot be repeated. However, "[m]ere increases in inputs, without an increase in the efficiency with which those inputs are used . . . must run into diminishing returns; input-driven growth is inevitably limited."[17] In other words, as the divisor increases the numerator must also, or the growth rate slows. The Tigers' inability to continue this level of workforce mobilization limits their ability to continue their expansion without shifting gears. Hence, the East Asian slowdown was only a matter of time. No matter how the marketplace was manipulated, it could not sustain prolonged growth. As the growth rate decreased and strains on the business infrastructure developed, foreign capital began to withdraw. The loss of fresh capital accelerated the slowdown and, in some cases, caused a collapse of systems that had been pushed beyond their limits.

Financial Markets

A slowing growth rate was not wholly responsible for the recent economic crisis, however. The largest factor was the weakness of East Asian financial markets. In general, free and equal access to those markets never existed. Until recently a foreign entity could not own more than a 49 percent interest in Thai banks or finance companies. In closely managed economies, there is a fuzzy line between that which is public and that which is private. Decisions are not always based on market considerations, but frequently turn on some agenda of the state or political interests or cronyism. The growth of investment and lending was not accompanied by an equivalent responsibility and transparency. Foreign investors were too eager to participate in the next "big play" without sufficient knowledge about it.[18] The economies were growing too fast and too speculatively. East Asian banks were overextended and poorly regulated. These almost-conscious errors of judgment could be papered over as long as fresh capital poured in. It was like a legal Ponzi scheme, centered on speculative stock and real estate prices. But eventually the economies had to slow, investors got cold feet, and the house of cards began to collapse. There was simply too much government interference with market forces.[19] As a result, neither local nor foreign investors had any ultimate control over domestic banking systems. Consequently, investment was short term and, when trouble starts, is the first to flee.

Centralized Policy Making

Investors who were welcomed with open arms found that they were playing a game in which there were no clear or consistent rules. One example of this was Indonesia. When Indonesia found its financial markets in trouble, its central bank governor changed the rules. Traders began dumping the rupiah and, as its value slid, domestic interest rates rose. As the currency fell to historic lows, limits were imposed on foreign trading, and speculative capital fled. When similar conditions struck Malaysia, Dr. Mahathir, its outspoken leader, also imposed controls on the marketplace. He said it was done to prevent the ravaging of financial markets. The Tigers began to close their financial markets early or place limits on the types of foreign investment allowed. Now it appears that government actions meant to stabilize the situation had just the opposite effect.[20] As more money rushed out, new controls were imposed in an attempt to avert financial disaster. But this only exacerbated the panic. It does not take much to spook an over-leveraged market. Much of the speculative borrowing had been in dollars and, to make matters worse, some Asian currencies were pegged to it. As the dollar strengthened against the yen, Asian imports became more dear and local prices could not keep up. Devaluation followed, and the whole speculative bubble burst.

In truth, the opportunities in Asia were never as rosy as they once appeared, nor are they as dismal as they have seemed recently. In their darkest hours, Asian securities markets lost up to one-half their value. But, at that point, speculators appeared willing to return again. In the meantime, however, the weaknesses of the Tigers' banking systems were exposed; and substantial reform was made a prerequisite of an IMF bailout. These desperate measures further shook confidence in Asian markets and those throughout the world. It lowered world stock prices and drove Asian currencies to new lows. This spurred fears that East Asian economies were about to abandon their free-market policies. International markets began to question whether these economies could actually compete in world trade circles.[21] In the end, Asia's authoritarian leaders were forced to devalue their currencies in order to prop up their economies and regain control. This further reduced investor confidence. When tested, the Asian market seemed to have no fixed rules.

The decline in currency values and the stock market slump made it difficult for many companies to meet their loan repayments. This precipitated further financial chaos, resulting in business and job losses as projects were put on hold or permanently suspended. For all the praise heaped on these heavily managed economies, they really weren't well managed at all. They were too politically motivated and too insulated from market forces. The downturn revealed the deep structural flaws that the boom seemed to have papered over. In the end the Asian "miracle" wasn't. The region will rebuild eventually, but on a firmer footing.[22]

Near the low point in the crisis, the Hong Kong market lost nearly a quarter of its value in just four days. Net losses in Malaysia, the Philippines and Thailand exceeded 40 percent, while they were near 30 percent in Singapore and South Korea. The Thai stock market that handled $1 billion in trades daily at its peak was processing only $20 million a day by late 1998. As is frequently the case in economic crises, the problem is as much political as economic. If the political leaders who once sought to protect their economies would now reform them, then recovery may take no more than a few years. But, if the *new* "Japanese model" of resistance to rapid and substantial structural change is to be followed, then the process could take much longer. If cronyism and excess capacity are wrung out of these economies and bankruptcies are allowed to concentrate business, then a return to a 4 percent annual growth rate is not unrealistic.[23]

Infrastructure

As one Asian economy after another experienced capital flight, numerous infrastructure projects were suspended. Malaysia's "super corridor" project was put off indefinitely. It might have been imprudent anyway, since Singapore was pursuing a similar project and Malaysia's was motivated as much by a wish to compete as by any concrete need. It was the zeal to succeed—not to be left behind in the mad dash to modernize—that made the whole process so intriguing—and dangerous.[24] With chaos in the marketplace and government contracts suspended or in doubt, this race is moot for the moment.

The shock of Asia's meltdown was magnified by the fact that it seemed incredible. The region had succeeded so miraculously for so long that it was difficult for anyone (particularly those in charge) to imagine that the region would go under, much less how *far* under. Even the World Bank had predicted that Asia's developing economies would keep racing ahead at nearly 8 percent annually. FORTUNE magazine reported that "the emergence of East Asia as a first-rate industrial power offered enormous opportunities." But it cautioned that there may be risks. No one seemed to pay attention.[25] No one—from the IMF, to Western leaders, to the East Asian government themselves—wanted to be a Cassandra. So the early warnings were timid. Given the lack of transparency, it is possible that no one knew the full extent of the problem. Hence, at first there seemed to be no great urgency about addressing it.[26]

For their part, Little Tiger national leaders and those in Japan were in denial far too long. In past downturns, they always were able to export their way out or raise more capital. Not this time. The sheer size of the problem, the interconnectedness of the economies and the leaders' refusal to take the harsh steps needed to cut losses and restore confidence undercut even relatively healthy economies like Hong Kong's. Their leaders had developed such a "belief in Asian values and [the] Asian model that [it] gave them a sense of impregnability." Instead, they blamed currency speculators and a Western capitalist conspiracy. Even as the IMF and industrialized states were assembling rescue packages, Asian leaders were resisting the discipline needed to save their economies. One reason was that they had led their people to expect progressively better times. Their own future was at stake in this crisis. The lack of trustworthy regulatory standards and independent oversight left these countries facing a financial crisis like that faced by Mexico in 1995, only far worse.[27] There was too much money and too little regulation.

At its peak in 1996, $308 billion in private capital flooded into 29 emerging economies. Fund assets alone doubled between 1995 and 1997. But, as the news turned sour, this "hot" money fled just as quickly, falling to $242 billion in 1997 and expected to drop to about $160 billion in 1998 and 1999, about one-half of its peak. Without fresh capital, the "bubble" imploded. In addition, it appears that foreign capital had been supporting a network of corruption. Because of the lack of regulation and the sheer volume of foreign investment, the money could not be properly absorbed. Until securities regulations are promulgated and payment systems set up and enforced, foreign capital will stay away.[28] South Korea, the latest East Asian nation to seek international help for its ailing economy, got the largest IMF bailout ever. The IMF share alone will be over $20 billion, with an equal amount coming from other nations. This bailout is surprising in its size, but its causes were not. That these "miracle" economies could not survive a competitive drop suggests their inherent weakness.

One example among many is the inefficiency of Vietnam's state steel industry. Vietnam has more than 6,000 state-owned enterprises. Many operate at a loss and are technically bankrupt. They were kept afloat only through massive infusions of government support. Vietnam kept producing steel, although steel imported from Russia was far less expensive. The result was huge stockpiles. But the steel mills employ tens of thousands of workers, so cutting back production would mean massive layoffs and possible social instability. That is not to say that every one of the Asian economies played the crisis the same way or delayed too long. The Asian economies are a mixed and varied bag. Some, like Hong Kong and Taiwan, are reasonably strong and should weather the storm. Others, like Malaysia, willfully and pridefully hoped to avoid a foreign rescue. There will be a lot of sorting out, with some Asian economies recovering faster and more fully than others (and probably establishing stronger relations with Western businesses and capitalists in the process). But the lack of regulation and transparency probably are gone for ever. Meanwhile, the IMF and industrialized states were trying to contain the "Asian contagion." After all, Asia is a major market for the West.[29]

Interdependent Economies

Swings in one economy typically cause reaction in another. East Asian economies are so intertwined that these effects are bound to be more dramatic. In 1994, intra-Asian trade accounted for 45 percent of the region's total. Taiwan was the largest foreign investor in Malaysia and Vietnam, and

Taiwan and Hong Kong accounted for more than two-thirds of China's foreign direct investment. Even before China took control of Hong Kong, it held over $100 billion in reserves for Hong Kong.[30] Therefore, when the Hang Seng index dropped sharply at the end of October 1997, stock values of some mainland China's companies fell as much as 80 percent. The intertwining, does not stop there, however. Twelve percent of Japan's exports go to Indonesia, Thailand, Malaysia and the Philippines. An additional 8 percent go to Singapore and South Korea. Roughly 40 percent of Japan's trade is with the rest of Asia. While it is broadly conceded that Asia can't recover unless Japan does, Japan's recovery depends to some extent on Asia. Intra-Asia connections were so tight that the failure of the Tigers led to failure right down the ladder. American exports to Asia, however, account for only 20 percent of our total.[31] America's smaller position protected it for a while, but it lost an important export market.

Most of Asia's debt was denominated in U.S. dollars, and many Southeast Asian currencies were pegged to it. As the dollar rose in value and the loans had to be repaid, new capital became harder to get and was more dear. The economic reality is that, without international bailouts, many of these countries would have very poor short-term prospects. Recovery would be protracted. Now that an international recovery plan has been developed, one hopes they will get back on their feet with sounder and more transparent economies.

The Scope of the Crisis

The question might reasonably be asked: how deep and broad is the Asian crisis? The answer is that no one knows. Surely it is the largest in recent history. Because banking regulation is lax and the Asian economies not very transparent, it may take a long time to assay the full extent of the damage. But it is considerable. When first it began to unfold in Thailand, the government was forced to close 58 finance companies that were technically bankrupt. But to fail is to lose face in the culture of the east. So the Thai central bank spent $2.6 billion a month to prop up its hemorrhaging financial system. Other bad news poured out of the region until late October 1997, when Hong Kong's Hang Seng stock index collapsed under the weight of falling capital value and soaring interest rates. This affected markets from Japan to London to Wall Street. By November it was South Korea's turn, and the rot there proved far deeper than first thought. By some estimates, the non-performing loans of East Asian banks could exceed 20 percent of their portfolios, versus a mere 1 percent in the U.S. As the crisis deepened, it appeared that it may cost Japan alone 25 percent of GDP to address its bad-debt problem, five times more than the share of U.S. GDP it took to cure the S & L scandal.[32]

The autumn 1997 Asian "meltdown" and its impact on securities markets reminds us—as if we needed reminding—just how interdependent global markets have become. It is one thing for a massive sell-off in New York or London to impact investor confidence worldwide. It is quite another thing for abrupt downturns in three or four smallish, developing East Asian economies to have the same impact. Large, diversified markets like that of the U.S. experienced drops of about 5 percent and quickly recovered. Within weeks of the crisis, the Dow Jones industrial average was back in near-record territory. But more fragile economies, such as Indonesia, Thailand, South Korea, and Mexico, experienced dips of 10 to 15 percent. And some—Hong Kong and Brazil—quickly lost 20 to 25 percent of their value. In the first eleven months of 1997, Asian stock markets as a whole lost $400 billion. Unfortunately, their economies got caught between the labor-intensive industries they were exiting and the mid-range businesses in which they were not yet competitive.

Led by the International Monetary Fund, a number of countries have arranged "bailout" loan packages that range from $23 billion for Indonesia (about the size of Mexico's "peso crisis" bailout in 1994) to $55 billion for South Korea (nearly twice Mexico's). With the guarantees come requirements for greater transparency and accountability. If anything, this is late in coming. There is no "free lunch" in international trade. Eventually, those countries and businesses that do not play by the immutable rules of economic common sense will be found out and punished. Rather than derailing "globalization," however, the Asian experience is likely to enhance it and place it on a more positive footing.[33] Nonetheless, the sheer magnitude of the debacle indicates that the unchecked flow of global capital and trade creates a untested witches' brew that no one country can contain.[34]

It isn't just an Asian crisis. On the day that Hong Kong stocks took their largest dive, so did the Dow Jones average (554 points, or 7.2 percent of its value). Admittedly, it rose to new highs in 1999, but the interdependence of the global economy during these fateful days in 1997–1998 could not have been better illustrated. U.S. businesses, capital and goods were going overseas in increasing volume. The markets there were different and the risks greater. To a remarkable extent, American businesses and investors have accommodated to this turmoil, although they are keen to bring it under control.[35] The point is that the Asian meltdown wasn't localized. It has seriously affected European and U.S. markets, with emerging South American markets (being the most like Asia's) taking the hardest hit of all.[36] Of course, the debacle had repercussions beyond the price of stock shares and the global economy. Peoples' livelihoods are at risk, which generally prompts a sharp political retorsion. It is not surprising that Indonesia's Suharto, whose family had long been at the trough, was deposed and the South Korean government replaced. In time, Malaysia's Matiher may be a victim as well.[37]

SUNRISE OR TWILIGHT?

World Bank Involvement

The World Bank arranged lending packages for individual Asian economies to pull them through the immediate crises and to help them help themselves. By early 1998, the IMF and developed economies had engineered over $100 billion in rescue aid for the ailing Asian nations. The packages come with strings attached, however. Of these, the requirement to overhaul their financial systems and to open them to foreign participation is the most important. As part of Thailand's $17.2 billion international bailout it must establish a Financial Restructuring Authority. It will take over the assets of bankrupt institutions and auction them off. In addition, East Asian governments must abandon certain practices, like giving contracts as political favors, and close financial institutions that are insolvent. Thailand was told to close 58 failed financial institutions, yet it resisted. The reason was that these institutions are owned or operated by some of its most influential citizens. Government closure would be tantamount to political suicide. Nepotism is common throughout East Asia, and it is a part of its problem. Appropriate practices and independent oversight are needed for these packages to succeed. The World Bank should provide that oversight.

A Role for the WTO?

One oft-suggested solution to the financial instability of developing nations is to bring financial services under the auspices of the WTO. The reasoning is that "[f]ree trade in financial services could generate considerable benefits, including improved access to foreign capital, deeper financial integration . . . and stronger financial infrastructure."[38] The theory is that capital liberalization, transparency and stability are mutually reinforcing and that a WTO standard could produce the necessary discipline.

The Asian market collapse indicates that many developing economies need external discipline. In theory, a WTO accord would set reliable international standards, accelerate reform of national financial systems and restore market confidence and economic growth.[39] The problem with this solution is that it is the antithesis of what these regimes traditionally have practiced. While welcoming foreign investment, they have not been willing to open their financial markets to foreigners, to make them more transparent or subject them to independent oversight. This is not just a preference on their part, but a part of their business culture. By comparison, Western practices are more structured and soulless. Asians are suspicious of them. But the Tigers have failed the test of a capitalist marketplace and are paying the price. If they want to restore their financial markets to health, they must restructure along traditional capitalist lines.

The International Monetary Fund

Although much criticized for its draconian remedies, the real hero in the Asian crisis may be the International Monetary Fund. IMF involvement in Asia is unusual because, unlike the Latin American countries that the IMF has helped so often, most Asian countries have high savings rates and borrow very little. When Thailand approached the IMF, many eyebrows were raised. Asian nations always have looked to one another for help. Borrowing in international markets mean indebtedness to foreigners. The nation loses control of its own destiny and is subject to foreign oversight. The days of inflated pride are over in East Asia, however. In this crisis, the most proud of the region's economies are suffering. They *need* outside help. Only the amount and terms are at issue.

Originally, the IMF believed it had the capacity to restore confidence in East Asia. But it set tough conditions for its involvement. Wasteful projects and trading monopolies must be eliminated, budgets must be cut, and banking reforms implemented. The "lender of last resort" was approached first by Thailand, and later by others. The Thai move brought immediate investor approval.[40] But Thailand was just the tip of the iceberg. The "string of devaluations, speculative attacks and stock market slumps" that the collapse of the Thai baht unleased spread throughout Asia. By the time the political leaders of Pacific rim nations gathered in Vancouver (late 1997) their push for closer economic relations among APEC states had been sidelined by events in Asia. Moreover, there was no consensus about a rescue plan. Thus APEC leaders limply stated that the "Asia-Pacific will continue to play a leading role in the global economy" and asserted their "strong interest in . . . a quick and enduring restoration of financial stability and healthy and sustainable [economic] growth [in the region]." They also expressed "no doubt that the fundamentals for long-term growth . . . for the region are exceptionally strong." There was little concrete that they agreed to do, however. They stuck to the capitalist notions that "[p]rudent and transparent policies particularly sound macroeconomic and structural policies" would restore financial stability and growth. They urged their finance ministers to work harder in 1998 on a financial framework, but recognized that "the role of the IMF remains central." In other words, the very organization that should have anticipated and led in addressing the crisis seemed weak and divided and deflected responsibility. The one point the leaders agreed upon was to urge a speedy completion of the WTO financial services negotiations. This did come to pass, for there is nothing like a crisis to spur healthy economies to cooperate.

In short, APEC's regional efforts to integrate and harmonize the region may have run their course. The thought of an Asia Fund (an IMF for the region) was briefly entertained so that Eastern leaders wouldn't have to go hat-in-hand to Western countries for help. The contagion was so widespread, however, that this proved impossible. Besides Asian nations didn't want to police one another. By the time the crisis is resolved, the point may be moot. The reforms required (and supervised) by the IMF in return for its loans will gradually convert Asian economies into something akin to a capitalist model. At that point, regional funds would be unnecessary, particularly if trade was not principally local.[41] Right now, however, it is uncertain when and how the "Asian contagion" will end. It is that big, that complicated, and the affected economies are not all cooperating with their would-be "saviors." Leadership within the region is needed, but Japan (with serious problems of its own) seems unwilling or unable to provide it. With leadership in Asia discredited, it has fallen to the West to bring ailing Asian economies back. That is in our best interest, because they represent export markets for Western goods. With their collapse, however, trade has become even more imbalanced.[42]

Of course, the bitter economic medicine that the IMF and its Western supporters dispensed has not gone down well in Asia. Western remedies are pretty standard: to allow bankruptcies and consolidation in order to purge markets of weak players; to improve financial infrastructure and transparency; to restore consumer confidence and to provide short-term loans that allow a struggling government to overcome its liquidity crisis. But this previously successful, "one-size-fits-all" solution may not work in this case. Asia's problem is worse than normal, and its governments have created much of the problem. (Thus, it could be said that the IMF is only bailing out the imprudent). One wonders what the alternative is, however. The region isn't able to rescue itself. The West wants financial stability and restoration of Asian markets (in part for selfish reasons), and IMF nations are not going to risk their capital without adequate protection.

As the world hoped for good news, more bad news emerged. In January 1998, one of Hong Kong's highest-flying investment banking establishments, Peregrine, failed. At about the same time, South Korea, the largest and one of the most stable Little Tiger economies, began its meltdown. Its closely owned conglomerates, or "chaebol" (similar to Japan's keiretsu), proved to be just as corrupt and as badly managed. South Korea's second largest auto manufacturer, Kia, went bankrupt, with $10 billion in debt. The country quickly agreed to the largest IMF bailout ever and was eager to get the first payment to stem the run on its currency. There was political resistance at first but, as the crisis deepened, reality set in and stunned Koreans capitulated. The "reform" was aided by the fact that there was an election that allowed the voters to turn out the offending government. In the end, the new government and Korean citizens pulled together under a new austerity plan. They took the corrective steps they knew could not be avoided. But it may be years before its economy is robust again and its dignity restored.[43]

The problem in Asia today is that the economic model that has been thrust on its economies as a precondition of the IMF-led bailout is intrusive and foreign. They would rather solve their problems themselves. Until recently, their success and wealth were the envy of emerging economies. Now the politicians and businessmen who profited most are being asked to change radically. No wonder they are ambivalent, even hostile, to the recovery process. Even the IMF admits that a different approach may be desirable. But the room for maneuver is limited. Asian political leaders are trapped too, between the pressing need to reform and the political and social (as well as economic) turmoil caused by those reforms.[44]

On the other hand, the IMF has brought some discipline, resources and transparency to Asia, which seems to have stabilized it, although a full return to normalcy may take years. As the healing process begins, entrepreneurs and investors may return as swiftly as they left. The herd instinct seems to operate in both directions.[45] If the bailout works, it will be worth its cost. The crisis has consolidated the region *and* the world's economy. But the world economy will not be normal until Asia is back on its feet.

The question is: Whose responsibility is Asia? It is one of our largest export markets (despite a negative balance of trade) and has huge upside potential. Thus, the U.S. has sought to assemble a broad constituency to reform the Asian economies and the global economy. As Deputy Treasury Secretary Lawrence Summers put it, the roots of this crisis are "not in improvidence, but in economic structures" (the Asian model). It is not macroeconomic, but microeconomic. The U.S. has put pressure on Japan in particular, to accelerate its recovery program and stimulate economic growth in the region.[46] Nonetheless, investor wariness has infected other emerging economies as well (e.g., South America, India, Eastern Europe).[47]

All exports to Asia will face harder times, but U.S. exports will be especially dear and Asian products will be especially inexpensive (Asia has a surplus, remember). As a result of lower expectations, the Dow Jones index fell; trade deficits with Asian nations exploded; and U.S. jobs were threatened. However, cheap foreign goods will keep inflation in check.[48] America's trade deficit with Asia is likely to double in the short term, although monthly numbers may be smaller as trade shrinks generally. But this is clearly not the time to put unilateral pressure on Asian traders.[49]

"Recovery"

The Asian financial crisis of 1997–1998 illustrates that many threats to global security in a post–Cold War world are economic, not military. Indeed, during the Cold War the world's great powers may have spent too much time considering warfare and not enough planning for the financial interdependence that followed. The Asian crisis has dramatically shifted the attention of developed and developing nations alike. The problems of the Little Tigers certainly are not unique. To some degree, they are symptomatic of all emerging economies. They expand too fast and don't have the regulatory systems to cope. Some are undercut by nepotism, corruption and unsustainable populism. For a while the rapid growth of these economies attracts enough foreign investment to mask the systemic problems, but when they inevitably emerge, investors leave and collapse ensues. In Asia, the problem may have been made worse by the fact that many Asian currencies were pegged to the U.S. dollar. This could have given investors a false sense of security. A thorough fiscal housecleaning is in order throughout the region, but this produces a new kind of problem, social and political instability.

Will Asia recover? Almost certainly. The question is: How long will it take and what will the new system look like? First, Asian nations need to candidly admit the size and nature of their economic problems and devise an adequate strategy to deal with them. To date, there have been differing degrees of both candor and remediation among them. So the recovery could be drawn out and not uniform. Indeed, one can expect a certain amount of competition. The successful recovery of one may retard the recovery of another. This may drive a wedge between them as each seeks to return to its pre-crash stature. Or it may cause Asian nations to cooperate more to avoid destructive competition and resist Westernization.

From the Western perspective, there is a need for both cooperation and restraint. There has been a sharp escalation in trade surpluses with Western traders. However, short of dumping, Asian economies need the capital that foreign sales will bring. Despite the predictable distortion in the balance of payments, it is not the time for Western markets to turn protectionist. Neither is it a good time for the U.S. to press its trade-opening agenda too aggressively in Asia. New pressures would be resented, rather than successful. On the other hand, the West must be vigilant that the Asian crisis not be used as an excuse to perpetuate the protectionism that created it. This will require some careful calibration, for the Asian business culture is likely to cling to the Asian model even in the face of a shift toward capitalism. To some extent, the latter has "triumphed" and major Asian economies will be changed forever. But to say that Asia has accepted Western capitalism may be a bit of an overstatement. It may have won the contest among economic models, but features of Asian political and business culture won't disappear overnight. Meanwhile, leading Asian economies might return to growth at a 3 to 5 percent annual rate and grow out of their worst difficulties in two to three years.

The Asian "ladder" may be rebuilt in time. But it is just as likely new trading relationships will be established, with Western approaches more in evidence. Surely the pace of recovery will vary from nation to nation, with those that are more flexible likely to lead the pack. Of course, one swallow does not signify spring. There is a lot of work to do before the recovery can be considered assured and the crisis past. And, like aftershocks of an earthquake, there may be a lot of surprises hidden below the surface. The longer they continue and the more serious they are, the slower the recovery.

It remains for struggling Asian businesses and politicians to meet the conditions of the bailout. This will be a tender issue as IMF recovery terms begin to chafe Asian sensibilities and foreign entrepreneurs begin to infiltrate local businesses.[50] The Asian recovery program involves risks, both domestic and foreign. Not everyone supports the rescue of markets that have flaunted world trade principles. But not to help presents more serious risks: a seriously distorted world economy, in which one of our largest export regions can't afford our goods and in which American investment and business is at risk. That doesn't make sense either. The better answer is to provide the help and make it contingent on market reform.

When the worst of the Asian crisis seemed to be over, American companies and investors began to reenter the market. Some entrants were bottom-fishing to be sure, but others were legitimately looking for fresh opportunity in a market newly receptive to American capital and involvement. The private sector was completing what the public sector had started. These forays into the recovering Asian market are not for the faint of heart, however. The turmoil in the region is not over, but the bottom seems to be near.[51]

This is only the first step in a much longer process, of course. The process seems well begun, however. There is a new sobriety about what must be done, if not how to do it. Asian governments and businesses generally are less insular and more competitive. And export growth around 5 percent is not bad. The halcyon days may be over, but more stable growth is welcome.

Just as the collapse wasn't uniform, neither will the rebuilding be. Some nations, like Taiwan and the Philippines, seem to have been only slightly affected. Others, like Indonesia (which stubbornly resisted reform) remain in dire circumstances.[52] And yet each individual country will have to deal with its diminished expectations. They also will have to deal with the displaced workers that competitive downsizing produces and with collateral problems like environmental degradation, dumping and intellectual property piracy. The road back will be long and uneven. Hong Kong has tried to do its part to stimulate recovery.[53] Japan probably has done more than it gets credit for. Admittedly, Japan has been slow to open its protected markets or to stimulate consumption demand in Asia. But its bilateral loans to the Thai, Indonesian and Korean rescue packages totaled $19 billion, compared to $8 billion from the U.S. and only $6.2 from European countries.

Change is coming, however. Japan's leadership in the region is flagging.[54] With a more constructive and centrist policy, China may be taking over, with profound implications for the Asian region, the U.S. and world trade. Thus far, China has agreed not to devalue its currency, to close or sell its state-run "corporate dinosaurs" and liberalize trade. These changes involve profound shifts in Chinese social structure and economy.[55] Meanwhile two factors threaten recovery. The first is the American reaction to sharply higher trade deficits with Asian nations. The other is the irrepressible urge of capitalists to invest somewhere.

Everyone knew that the failure of Asian economies would make their goods cheaper and U.S. goods more expensive. Hence, a slowing of the U.S. growth rate was expected. This should keep inflation low and, hopefully, employment will remain high. Although importation of goods and services into the U.S. recently passed the $1 trillion mark, it represented a smaller percentage of U.S. GDP in 1997 than it did in 1987. In one sense, we were prepared for the large increase in trade surplus that the Asia contagion precipitated.[56] Nonetheless, when the figures came in they were astounding. Japan took a hit that it can ill afford. Asian nations are among its principal clients. With their economies in turmoil, they are less able to afford Japanese goods. Although Japan appears solvent for the moment, the loss of its regional markets thwarts its recovery. As for the United States, its trade deficit is expected to double from 1997 to 1999. This is bound to shock U.S. workers and taxpayers, no matter how well prepared.[57] If their reaction produces polarization in world trade and a new protectionism, then trade tensions will increase, and there are enough between East and West already.[58] While such imbalances can't be endured forever, the short-term problem is more political than economic. The impact on Asian economies is far more serious than on the U.S. The WTO predicts a modest cooling (2 to 3 percent) in world trade growth from an almost overheated 9.5 percent increase in 1997.

Private capital flows both reward and punish markets. In order to recover, troubled Asian nations have to rebuild themselves in investors' esteem. This is more easily said than done. Downsizing and streamlining of business and government almost surely will increase unemployment. Meanwhile, private capital will seek out other markets. Foreign entrepreneurs are eager to penetrate markets as close to the bottom as possible, but serious private capital will stay out of Asia until market conditions improve. The challenge is there. Asian nations, if they are serious about recovery, must address it.[59]

The most important of these is Japan. It is the region's largest and most sophisticated economy. It has the capacity to improve conditions in the entire region. For this reason, the U.S. has put considerable pressure on the Japanese to liberalize their market and to stimulate domestic demand. Thus far, the Japanese have resisted U.S. pressure. Each of their "big bang" reform and stimulus programs has proved too modest. They have been described as a series of "pops" or a reform "striptease." But Japan has genuinely tried. In the process, the stranglehold that Japanese bureaucrats had on the economy has gradually given way to Western forms of capitalism, in which the fittest survive.[60]

China, on the other hand, seems to be replacing Japan as the principal economic player in Asia. Its new president, Jiang Zemin, and premier, Zhu Rongi, seem quite committed to reforming China's bureaucracy, banks and

numerous state industries. Normalizing relations with Hong Kong and Taiwan—its outlets to the capitalist world—was a good first step. Reform of
the entire Chinese economy is vastly more difficult, due to its enormous
size and complexity. So far, Chinese leadership is pressing ahead with reform
and liberalization. The West seems reasonably pleased. At least the Chinese
leviathan seems to be fully engaged and on a positive course by Western
standards.[61]

If Asia is no longer the darling of private capital markets, then other
investment venues must be. Europe and the U.S. seem most likely because
they are stable, but they also are low growth. Indeed, Asian nations began
to invest in American bonds as a hedge against declines in their own currencies. Among the biggest beneficiaries would appear to be Central and
Eastern European republics, where expansion is robust, but the risks somewhat lower than in Asia. Latin and South American countries also might
benefit, although Brazil seems shaky. India (also decidedly shaky) and Africa
also might benefit from a discredited Asia.[62]

But that does not diminish Asia's potential in the longer term. Some Asian
leaders believe that the crisis was influenced by Western powers' eagerness
to recover control of the global economy. Western nations have been critical
of the IMF's rosier-than-warranted picture of Asian economies before the
crash and its willingness to insulate those economies from self-inflicted
wounds. If this sounds like scapegoating, it is. But it could prove serious if
the region turns inward and the West writes it off. Both reactions would
delay the process of globalization.[63]

The ultimate question is whether or not, and to what extent, the world
economy should take responsibility for such problems. Everyone wants to
participate in a booming market. If private capital is allowed to "cherry
pick" the best opportunities and eschew the worst, there will be a lot of
economic turmoil. In other words, the industrialized nations of the world
must decide what type of world trading regime they intend to support. The
EU needs an Asian policy, and the U.S. needs "fast track."[64] Both need to
collaborate on a new vision of the world's economic architecture. What is
needed is constructive engagement, a joint and collaborative approach to
the problems that are indigenous to every emerging economy. There is no
mystery involved. In the end, distortions in trade hurt all traders, large and
small. There is no isolating the problem. It is a win-win or lose-lose, *global*
economy.[65]

Existing agencies, such as the IMF, may be equal to the task of overseeing
a global system, but only if they have access to the information they need.
Without such transparency, business confidence will be slow to return to
shaky markets. Thus, the Asian financial crisis was a practical lesson for the
globalized trading world.[66]

PREDICTIONS FOR THE FUTURE

In order to get back on track, emerging East Asian economies must increase their competitiveness and stability. Efficient capital markets must be developed, attracting institutional investment.[67] If this does not happen, capital will pursue the next best opportunity. It is important to remember, however, that the crises in Asia was not unique. In 1994, Mexico's economy fell sharply when its peso crashed. It recovered rapidly. Although the future looks dim right now, Asian countries are far from moribund.[68] It is equally important to remember that multinational corporations and large investors have been through this before. Generally speaking, they know the risk, *and* the reward. They often take the risk.

President Clinton and U.K. Prime Minister Blair have proposed an overhaul of the IMF and World Bank.[69] This may be more regulation than Asia needs. The IMF may have bungled a speedy recovery by being "tone-deaf" to Asian sensibilities and economic structure. And free capital movement seems to have failed in this instance. But overregulation caused the crisis in the first place. Perhaps increased transparency is all that is needed to correct it.

THE DEATH OF THE "ASIAN MODEL"?

It has been said that the "Asian economic model" is dead. In some respects it is. It did not adjust rapidly enough to market forces. Because micromanaged economics now are suspect, it is unlikely that free-market countries will tolerate their heavy regulation and lack of transparency. In that sense, the Asian model *is* dead.[70] But the free market is not without its problems. Speculators make millions and leave investors in ruins. In other words, a "fair" market is to some extent a regulated market. An absolutely "free" market is simply too chaotic. As long as there is general consensus about the rules, macro-management is good. The huge bailouts and financial disruption attending the collapse of Southeast Asia virtually insure it. In that respect, the "Asian model" survives.

The world economy will not fully stabilize until emerging Asian economies do. Until then, a prime export market for industrialized nations (Asia) will have dried up and the influx of Asian exports will encourage protectionist measures in Western markets. The tension will not be broken until there is a return to balanced trade. But that prospect may be on the horizon. Some Asian nations are beginning to move out of recession, notably those that were least protectionist. Some, such as South Korea, continue to struggle with the tension between economic reform and corporate recovery. As prospects improve, foreign investment will return, if more cautiously than before.[71] The key is to rebuild Asian markets. If Japan and China prove to be the prime architects of recovery, then regional groupings such as APEC and ASEAN will lose much of their influence. But it is too early to assume that they won't play a large role in rebuilding Asia. After all, collective action is probably best.[72]

It is anyone's guess just when Asian economies will start to recover, how fast their recovery will be and which countries will lead the pack. The obvious place to start was the 1998 APEC ministerial at Kuala Lumpur. It was a dismal failure. Among other things, Japan—which accounts for well over one-half of the Asian economy—refused to honor prior market-opening commitments. Oddly, it was the weaker regional group (ASEAN) that showed the most gumption.

The countries that promptly addressed their weaknesses (Thailand) and those that were strongest to begin with (Taiwan), will be first. However, Asia's structural problems (based on the Japanese model) are so deep that they may take years to correct.[73]

Part IV

"Globalizing" Trade

Chapter 14

Metamorphosing the GATT:
The World Trade Organization (WTO)

Prior to World War II, international trade was conducted primarily through trading blocs—among countries with similar economic systems and complementary needs. There was no true "global" trade. In their zeal to compete, these blocs eventually became military blocs, and World War II began.[1] After the war, international trade continued to be compartmentalized. There was no central authority and no agreed-upon or enforceable rules. The Bretton Woods/GATT conference was supposed to provide such a mechanism— the International Trade Organization (ITO). But the U.S. Congress opposed the ITO, because it didn't want America's trade practices policed by others. The U.S. wanted to do the policing and so the ITO never was created. In its place was the General Agreement on Tariffs and Trade, known as the GATT. But the GATT had no enforcement power and was never meant to be as far-reaching as it became by the end of the Uruguay Round (1993).

The trading rules of the GATT are negotiated in sessions called rounds. The first GATT round was concluded in 1947, involved 23 nations and covered about one-half of world trade in goods. The next round, in 1949, involved only thirteen nations. From then until 1964, there were periodic renegotiations of the GATT, involving anywhere from 26 to 38 nations. The latest GATT round (the Uruguay Round), the eighth overall, was concluded on December 15, 1993, and signed into force in March 1994. It involved 117 nations and took seven years to complete (1986–1993). Moreover, it did not address just tariff barriers (as past GATT agreements had) but added trade in services, intellectual property, textiles and agriculture.

The number of nations involved in this international agreement is surprising enough, but the amount of trade regulated by the GATT is truly astounding. The first GATT round dealt with goods worth approximately $10 billion, while the Uruguay Round involved almost $7 trillion. It was the most ambitious and created a new umbrella organization—the World Trade Organization (WTO).[2] The WTO was the most contentious issue of these negotiations and frequently threatened to stall the round. The reason for this was that the WTO would have a legal status and enforcement power that the GATT lacked. The "general agreement" was just that. It was not enforceable except for moral suasion. The WTO charter, however, established an international mechanism to enforce the GATT.[3] However, the GATT and WTO are threatened by regional trading groups that are constantly forming and may set different and competing standards.

THE WTO STRUCTURE

The WTO's highest authority is the Ministerial Conference. It is composed of one representative from each WTO member state. It meets at least once every two years and decides any number of issues under a growing list of multilateral trade agreements. However, the administrative work of the WTO (the bulk of its work) is performed by subsidiary bodies. Of these, the principal one is the General Council, which reports to the Ministerial Conference. The meetings of the General Council take two forms: the Dispute Settlement Body, which oversees the procedures for dispute settlement, and the Trade Policy Review Body, which conducts regular reviews of the trade policies of WTO member states.[4]

WTO DECISIONS

The WTO tried to maintain the GATT tradition of consensus decision-making. If a consensus cannot be reached, a vote is taken, but only in limited circumstances. Each country has one vote, but different decisions require varying majorities of the votes cast. The adoption of an interpretation of any of the multilateral trade agreements or a waiver of an obligation imposed on a member by a multilateral agreement requires a three-quarters majority. Amendments to the provisions of the multilateral agreements and the admission of a new member require a two-thirds majority.[5]

In order to understand the importance of the WTO, the weakness of the GATT must be recalled. Under the GATT, a complaint by one member that another had engaged in unfair trade practices went through a process called "dispute resolution" or "dispute settlement." Their dispute was heard by a "panel" of three independent legal experts. The panel considered arguments from both sides and then issued a ruling. That ruling then had to be ratified by the GATT membership in order to become effective. Therein lay the problem. The offending nation could vote against implementation and block the panel's ruling. Although compliance often was achieved through political pressure, it was never consistent or assured. Many countries, including the U.S., simply ignored GATT rulings. The WTO charter avoided this problem by requiring only a consensus. In the WTO, however, the consensus must be to *reject* the decision of the panel (called a "negative consensus"). This is a drastic change from the GATT. The "negative consensus" effectively eliminates a veto by the offending nation.

By the time of the Uruguay Round, the weakness of the dispute resolution process had become evident. Something had to be done to expedite the process and put some teeth into it. Since the U.S. was no longer able to dictate the terms of world trade, it was in its best interest to have the agreed-upon terms of world trade enforced. The new dispute settlement procedure was the sort of policing system that the U.S. had vetoed during the first round of the GATT. Now, however, the U.S. needed an international enforcer.

One of the first complaints brought under the WTO was brought by the U.S., together with Ecuador, Guatemala, Honduras and Mexico. It involved the European Union's "banana import regime." The regime granted privileged access to the EU for bananas from African, Caribbean and Pacific (ACP) countries under the Lomé Convention. ACP states had historic trade ties with EU states by virtue of being former colonies or dependencies. The complaint argued that the banana regime violated fair trading rules by unfairly discriminating against non-Lomé producers. This case is a perfect example of the difference between the GATT system and the WTO. A complaint previously had been filed under the old GATT regarding the same regime. The GATT also had found that the EU's program violated GATT trading rules. But the GATT's weaker dispute settlement procedures allowed the EU to block any remedial action.

In June 1997, a WTO panel found against the EU with respect to part of the complaint and for it on another part. The ACP countries were covered by a waiver granted by the WTO in 1994 that allowed special conditions of trade with developing nations. The quota and licensing system developed under Lomé was aimed at helping their economies. That was not a problem.[6] But the panel condemned the licensing procedure insofar as it established import quotas. Under the GATT, the EU was able to block enforcement. Under the WTO's negative consensus, standard blockage was not possible.

One way to avoid a panel decision, or perhaps to mitigate its effect, is to appeal. And appeal the EU did.[7] In September 1997, however, an appellate body affirmed the panel's finding that the banana regime violated WTO fair trade practices and would have to be dismantled. On October 16, 1997, the EU announced that it would abide by the decision, but set no date to comply. This brought immediate reaction from the U.S. and the other parties to the suit.[8]

Under the WTO's dispute settlement procedures, the losing party has a "reasonable period of time" to implement a panel decision. The reasonable period is determined by one of three methods: mutual agreement, arbitration or the dispute settlement body. When the parties to the banana litigation could not reach a mutual agreement, they requested that the time frame be fixed by binding arbitration. An arbitrator was appointed and the EU requested fifteen months to comply, arguing that dismantling its regime would be extremely difficult and time consuming since it involved treaties with many ACP nations. The U.S. and the other complainants argued that the EU should not be allowed so much time. After all, it had been apparent for some time that the EU practice violated GATT rules. The WTO-appointed arbitrator disagreed, concluding that the difficulty of implementing the decision would require at least fifteen months. He therefore gave the EU until January 1, 1999, to comply with the decision. But the EU gave no evidence that it intended to meet that deadline, and the U.S., upset by the delay, threatened retaliation. It seems like a small matter, but the banana case has proved to be a real test of the dispute settlement process, including the right of the injured state to retaliate under Article 22. So far, the WTO has been equal to the task. But the EU, having accepted its defeat, still did not meet its GATT obligation, and the U.S. has claimed the right to retaliate, possibly setting off a tit-for-tat trade war.[9]

DISPUTE SETTLEMENT PROCESS

The Uruguay Round dispute settlement process just described has 27 articles. The new procedure allows any member government to submit a WTO complaint against another, often at the request of a national business that feels that GATT terms have been violated. The first step in the process is to request consultations with the government whose trade practices allegedly violate GATT rules. The offending party often will seek to delay adjudication through the process of consultation, but the complaining government can insist that a dispute panel be appointed if the consultation does not resolve the situation within 60 days.[10] Once that request is made, another series of time limits begin. The panel must be created within two months of the request and panel members must be appointed within 20 days thereafter. The panel then has six to nine months to investigate the case and make a decision. Meanwhile, the nations can and usually do continue their settlement negotiations. It often is in their best interests to reach a mutually acceptable resolution before the panel decides the case. At any time prior to the implementation of the panel's decision, the two parties can suspend or abandon their dispute or resolve it. About one-fourth of the complaints brought to the WTO have been settled without ever reaching a panel. Panel reports are called "interim" reports and must be finalized and made legally binding within 60 days of the date of decision, unless either the losing party files a notice of appeal or the WTO membership decides (by consensus) not to finalize the report panel decision.

APPEALS PROCESS

Article 17 allows the losing party to appeal to an "Appellate Body." Of the panel reports circulated between 1995 and 1997 all were appealed.[11] The reason for this is that the loser at the panel level almost always improves its position on appeal. Whereas the panel reaches a largely legal decision, the Appeal Body mixes in some policy as well. Besides, an appeal delays the enforcement of an adverse decision.

The Appellate Body has 60 days to rule on any claim of legal error. Its decision will become legally binding within 30 days, unless (again) the WTO membership decides by consensus not to finalize the decision. Overall, the WTO dispute settlement procedure has proven to be very effective, especially for the U.S. It has been the complainant in 39 of the first 114 complaints filled with the WTO. The EU also has been very active, having filed 25 complaints. The U.S. and the EU also have been named as defendants in more cases than any other WTO members, with the U.S. appearing as defendant in 26 and the European Union in 29. It appears from the number of cases brought by the U.S. compared to complaints brought against it that we benefit from the WTO mechanism, because enforcement would be quite difficult outside the WTO.

THE ENFORCEMENT OF DECISIONS

Enforcement is possibly the most complex reform of the GATT system resulting from the Uruguay Round. Articles 21 and 22 establish a sequence of enforcement steps. The first is to decide how much time an offending nation has to comply with an adverse ruling. The standard period is fifteen months, but its length can vary with the situation. If compliance does not occur within the time allowed, the offending nation is given an additional 20 days to negotiate a reduction of the trade barriers in question or to set a reasonable compensation for the damage done. If these negotiations aren't successful, then the complaining nation is free to retaliate by setting trade barriers of its own against the offending nation. Should the offending nation feel that the retaliatory measures are excessive, then the two nations enter a binding arbitration procedure. Article 22:3 of the Uruguay Round agreement prohibits "cross retaliation." That occurs when the complaining nation imposes trade barriers against exports not the subject of the original suit. The new dispute settlement procedure established under the WTO applies to all the trading agreements contained in the final acts of the Uruguay Round.

As the number of nations and trade sectors covered by GATT increase, more and more complaints arise. Presently 134 nations and customs territories are members of the WTO. From its inception in 1994 to the end of 1997, 114 dispute settlement complaints were filed. The U.S. has used the dispute settlement procedure liberally. The ability to prosecute its trade grievances, even at the expense of being prosecuted, is the reason the U.S. finally favored the creation of the WTO.[12]

The fact that the United States has used the WTO to resolve trade issues rather than resorting to unilateral means is not surprising, insofar as the WTO charter specifically states that WTO mechanisms shall be the only means of settling disputes between its members, under the covered agreements. The WTO proscribes unilateral responses to alleged trade violations. As a result, unilateral imposition of economic sanctions by one country against its trading partner should be ended. However, the dispute resolution mechanism permits the imposition of sanctions for continued violation of the agreements.

One example of such unilateral procedures is the Special 301 provisions under the U.S. Omnibus Trade and Competition Act of 1988. Special 301 is meant to deal exclusively with intellectual property. Within 30 days after the issuance of the National Trade Estimate Report, Special 301 directs the U.S. Trade Representative (USTR) to identify foreign nations whose trade practices are found to violate intellectual property rights. Those nations whose practices are particularly egregious are placed on a "priority watch list." Thirty days after that, the USTR must begin investigating the alleged illegal practices. If those practices do not abate within six months, the USTR is authorized (but not required) to retaliate by imposing import restrictions.[13] However, Special 301 sanctions could violate the GATT by using unilateral measures. Using multilateral dispute settlement procedures is a better course of action.

U.S. EXPERIENCE WITH THE WTO

One of the first cases brought under the WTO's new procedures was against the U.S. In December 1994, Brazil and Venezuela complained that U.S. Environmental Protection Agency (EPA) rules for reformulated gasoline violated the GATT. Under the EPA's Clean Air Act, domestic refiners were allowed to set a baseline using the average quality of gasoline sold in 1990. The rule required foreign refiners to meet a different baseline. The EPA reasoned that this was necessary because foreign companies did not have complete data sets allowing them to set an accurate 1990 baseline. In January 1996, the first WTO dispute resolution panel decision found that the EPA provisions violated the GATT, and the U.S. could no longer set different baselines for foreign refiners.[14] The U.S. appealed the panel's finding, but the decision was upheld. Having lost its appeal, the U.S. agreed to abide by the decision, setting June 1997 as the date. By January 1997 the

U.S. still had not implemented changes, and Venezuela and Brazil complained that the U.S. delay "impose[d] costs on Brazilian gas exports on a daily basis."[15] In February the U.S. announced it was on track to comply with the WTO ruling, and a mid-August 1997 deadline was set. On August 19, 1997, the U.S. finally adopted a rule granting foreign oil refineries the option to request fuel quality standards similar to those used at U.S. refineries.[16]

Even though the first decision under the WTO regime went against the U.S., we continued our support. In order to assure enforcement of GATT rules we needed an international enforcement mechanism. The U.S. expected that it would profit more from the ability to enforce trading rules against our trading partners than they would in applying them to us. The U.S. has used the WTO dispute resolution process frequently, and it has been used almost as often against us. But the U.S. has won more cases than it has lost. Excepting the Venezuelan oil and Fuji film cases, the first few years of U.S. experience with the WTO has been reasonably positive.

One of those first winning cases involved hormone-fed U.S. beef. Since 1989, the EU has banned the import of U.S. beef produced by using synthetic growth hormones. The U.S. viewed this as a discriminatory practice, outlawed by the GATT, and accused the EU of using it to protect its own beef industry. The U.S. estimated that the ban prevented $250 million worth of beef exports to the EU annually.[17] A WTO panel sided with the U.S., saying that the EU exclusion was "inconsistent with the requirements of the WTO's agreement on the Application of Sanitary Phytosanitary Measures (SPS) because it was not based on a risk assessment . . . of the potential adverse impact . . . on human health." The EU appealed, and the appellate body reversed or modified several of the panel's conclusions. This is not an uncommon phenomenon, but the appeal decision only allowed the EU a second opportunity to prove that there was a health reason to exclude hormone-fed U.S. beef from the EU. It was in the EU's best interest to challenge the finding of the panel, and the appellate body did find that WTO members are entitled to a level of protection higher than current international standards. However, the appellate body agreed with the panel's finding that the EU had not scientifically justified its ban.

The appellate decision caused a stir because the standard for health protection previously had been an international standard. Now a WTO standard may be in the offing. The appellate body also overturned the panel with regard to the scope of risk assessments used to exclude on imported food for health reasons. Prior to the appellate body's decision, the standard was limited to laboratory methods commonly associated with the physical sciences. The appellate body allowed, however, that risk assessment could involve "risk in human societies as they actually exist, in other words, the actual potential for adverse effects to human health in the real world where people live and work and die." This makes the analytical process more subjective and places a shadow of uncertainty over other health-based import exclusions, such as the Canadian-Australian dispute about salmon imports or the U.S.–Japanese dispute regarding quarantine rules.[18]

The EU used a "zero-risk" standard for imported beef. The irony is that the U.S. used that same "zero-risk" standard against the importation of EU beef. So the U.S. victory over the EU may cause it to reduce its own protections. Meanwhile, the WTO upheld the panel's decision, and the EU expressed its determination to keep the ban in place while it searched for further evidence of the dangers of hormone-fed beef. Eventually, a WTO appellate panel (in an unrelated case) declared that the risk assessment needed to check the spread of pests and disease is more stringent than that applied to threats to human and animal health posed by additives, but the latter must be ascertainable, not theoretical.[19]

The debate over hormone-treated beef is not an isolated matter. It is closely intertwined with the importation of all foreign food. The EU wants a special labeling requirement for genetically modified food. Its labeling campaign is vigorously opposed by the U.S. as a protectionist measure. The U.S. estimates that the EU's labeling requirements would add approximately $5 billion in overhead to our agricultural exports.[20] A number of disputes, such as the U.S. complaint about Japan's quarantine rules for imported fruits and vegetables, could be affected by the WTO's resolution of the beef conflict.

One dispute that seemed to end in a draw involved photographic film. The complaint was promoted by the Eastman Kodak Co. It alleged that the Japanese government used a retail system that burdened foreign film in order to buffer Japanese market openings.[21] Although, the case was technically between the U.S. and Japan, it began as a Section 301 trade case brought by Kodak, alleging violations of GATT rules. The complaint evolved into a WTO dispute between the U.S. and Japan, as each country took up the cause of its national "hero." The petition alleged that the Japanese government systematically created barriers to the sale of imported consumer photographic paper and film by allowing domestic film makers to control wholesale film distribution. Fuji was the alleged beneficiary of these government actions.[22] In September 1995, a WTO panel was formed to decide whether Japan had violated GATT rules, using non-tariff barriers. One year later, the dispute settlement panel rejected the U.S. claim. This was not the end of the dispute, however. In February 1998, the USTR announced that she would form an "interagency monitoring and enforcement committee" to test the validity of Japan's claim that it had an open film market.[23] So the WTO process is not always the end of the matter.

It is less the content than the context of these disputes that matters to the WTO members. Just about every nation that has commented on the WTO's dispute settlement body (DSB) procedures (currently under review) agrees they are too slow. Moreover, they are legal only at that trial level and are influenced by political considerations on appeal. American representatives are frustrated when they lose what they consider strong cases (Fuji film) or wait seemingly forever for enforcement when vindicated (bananas; beef hormones). Nonetheless, the U.S. and the EU have been pushing the envelope to its limits in the banana dispute. The condemned practice was not a simple piece of national legislation, but a multiparty agreement. Negotiations were delicate. Moreover, the U.S. was pushing for a prompt dispute panel review of the EU's substituted program and threatened unilateral sanctions if the dispute dragged on. It was all very new (and politically charged) terrain for the WTO and its members.

The U.S. behavior might be justified if the U.S. had not done very well in the dispute settlement process. But why put so much pressure on the system that it might collapse? The U.S. has not made any friends among those WTO members (including its litigation partners and the EU) who know that the process is partly political and that trade agreements must be given time to mature and strengthen. In due course the banana dispute is likely to be resolved. Moreover, the EU already has agreed to allow the import of U.S. hormone-fed beef (another case they lost to the U.S. in the WTO). And the EU suspended (but did not drop) its complaint in the WTO that the Helms-Burton law (probably an illegal secondary boycott) violated the GATT. If other members can be sensitive to the pressures on the neophyle WTO, why cannot the U.S.? Perhaps the answer lies in a little-discussed provision of the U.S. legislation implementing the Uruguay Round that allows us to revoke U.S. membership in the WTO if it rules against the U.S. three times in five years. With two clear losses before the year 2000, perhaps U.S. litigators are playing to Congress, showing that the WTO works to our benefit. Indeed, it does. And it would be insane to walk away from so useful a vehicle when there is not an equal one in sight.[24]

A full review of the WTO's dispute settlement system was well underway before these latest strains were placed up on it. Among common complaints are that it is slow, too secretive, and that outside parties—particularly non-governmental organizations (NGOs)—are not allowed to make input into or to observe the proceedings. Revisions are likely to speed up and strengthen the system and are likely to be adopted before the next round of trade negotiations.[25]

Meanwhile, sectoral talks are continuing in a variety of areas. Some could bear fruit early in the new century. The financial services agreement reached in December 1997 was ratified by fewer than one-third of its 70 signatories by the agreed-upon deadline in early 1999, but ratifications continue. The agreement covers 95 percent of global financial services (bank lending, securities and insurance) worth $58 trillion. Fast action also is urged in the fields of agriculture and other services (although U.S./EU bickering about the former has slowed progress in that area). Both topics were on the "built in" agenda for the GATT ministerial meeting held in November 1999 in the United States.[26]

That meeting, among the last before a full GATT round begins again, served as a preview of what has been dubbed the "Millennium Round." The U.S. was lukewarm to the idea for the longest time, but support from other WTO members grew steadily. Eventually, in his 1999 State of the Union address, President Clinton endorsed the idea, calling for an "ambitious" round that would produce "concrete early results." He urged that intellectual property protection and government procurement be emphasized. Developing countries are accepting of the new round but want it to be limited. They fear that they will be forced by industrialized nations into tariff concessions that will threaten their economies. They also want to keep labor and environmental standards off the agenda.[27]

The WTO also is under some pressure to expand its membership. Latvia's admission in February 1999 (only the second ex-Soviet member) brought membership to 134. But there are some 30 states on the waiting list, including China, Russia and Taiwan. The former two are particularly anxious to join, but their accession presents a classic dilemma in "globalization." The WTO should be as inclusive as possible, but it should set a single, high standard. It may be easier to work with countries that are members, but once they achieve that goal the greatest reason to liberalize their economies disappears. So accession negotiations are typically difficult. China was dedicated to becoming a member by the year 2000, in time for the "Millennium Round." That put immense pressure on its government to make trade concessions. But there also is pressure on the WTO to compromise, and let the world's most populous nation in. Russia's prospects are not nearly so good.[28]

SIDE AGREEMENTS AND SECTORAL AGREEMENTS

Core Agreements

Side agreements are sub-agreements to the GATT, to which not all members of the Uruguay Round are party. However, they were negotiated during a full GATT round. These appear in Annex 4 to the Treaty, which lists all side agreements. They deal with such diverse subjects as civilian aircraft, government procurement, dairy products and bovine meat. They bind only those GATT members that are signatories.

Like side agreements, sectoral agreements are binding only on those individual WTO members that voluntarily subscribe. But, unlike the side agreements, sectoral agreements are not concluded under a full GATT round. The sectoral agreements often deal with issues that could not be concluded during a regular round, for fear of stalling the process. As a result, these agreements are negotiated separately, outside the GATT. Because it takes so long to negotiate a full GATT round, sectoral agreements became the preferred form of multilateral trade agreement in the late 1990s. The reason is that they permitted focused negotiation on a single area of trade, whereas a full round forces members to get involved in a much broader area of negotiation. Among the sectoral agreements currently being pursued are financial services, telecommunications and many more.

It seems foregone that there will be another GATT round, the Millennium Round, beginning in the year 2000. Even if a full round does begin, it may take years to complete. Meanwhile, sectoral agreements may be negotiated. Much has been accomplished through them, and while it is likely that a full round might eventually absorb them, they remain an important negotiating tool. For example, consider the information technology case, in the following section.

Information Technology

The sectoral agreement that has been the greatest success so far is the agreement on information technology (ITA). It was worked out at the WTO ministerial meeting in Singapore in 1996. The ITA committed signatories to the elimination of customs tariffs on computers, semiconductors and other products of information technology in July 1997. The agreement covers over 180 products, which are estimated to account for over $600 billion in sales annually. The agreement has been signed by some 45 countries, representing 93 percent of world trade in information technology, both goods and services.[29] Talks continue about expanding the agreement to cover more products. These talks, dubbed ITA-II, involve the U.S., Australia, Canada, the EU, Hong Kong, Japan, New Zealand, Norway, Switzerland and Taiwan. What products will be covered by ITA-II is not clear, but it may add as many as 250 new products. The date set for reaching agreement was September 1998, but that date has slipped. Any further ITA opening is likely to be modest, because Asian economies in decline do not feel they can make trade concessions.[30]

Telecommunications

Another sectoral agreement was concluded in the field of telecommunications. It contains commitments to open trade in the international supply of telecommunications equipment and services and allows foreign firms to establish a domestic presence and operate an independent telecommunication network as a competitor to local providers. The agreement opens up not only voice communications, but electronic data transmission as well. Sixty-nine countries signed the agreement. They account for more than 90 percent of telecommunication business, with annual revenue of $600 billion. Most signatory countries agreed that implementation should start in early 1998. However, the U.S. and Morocco were unwilling to do so. The U.S. did not want to be bound before knowing how things would work under the agreement in countries that had not yet ratified it. The Council agreed to extend the deadline until July 1998. The delay concerned some signatories, however, because the Fourth Protocol to the General Agreement on Trade in Services (GATS) states that, if not all members have signed by the deadline, those that have ratified may set a new date for the agreement to enter into force.[31]

The European Commission has threatened to sue the U.S. for violations of the fourth protocol, which could be a harbinger of things to come. With telecommunications networks opening up worldwide, issues of interconnection and the fees to be charged foreign entrants will increase. There also are issues of the availability of radio frequencies (to accommodate mobile communications) and the use of differing satellite systems. Many problems remain to be worked out, but the belief is that the benefits of an agreement outweigh our present segmented system of telephony. It is believed that liberalization could be worth over $1 trillion in revenues by the year 2010.

Financial Services

Following closely on the heels of the telecommunications agreement came another sectoral agreement, this time dealing with financial services. The agreement is meant to open banking, insurance and securities markets to foreign competition in 95 percent of the global financial services market. It would cover financial services in 70 countries and commit another 50 to binding WTO rules, subject to dispute settlement procedures. The agreement encompasses $17.8 trillion in global securities assets, $38 trillion in global (domestic) bank lending and $2.2 trillion in worldwide insurance premiums. The final pact was agreed in December 1997 and was supposed to take effect in March 1999. Due to financial instability in Asia and worldwide, ratification has been slow.[32]

Maritime

When the Uruguay Round of GATT was concluded in December 1994, three service areas upon which the negotiators could not agree (financial services, telecommunications and maritime transport) were taken off the table. Meanwhile, substantial sectorial progress has been made in the former two areas. But the shipping sector remains stuck in neutral. Up until mid-1996, negotiations were ongoing in the WTO's Maritime Committee. Of 37 participating nations, 24 had tabled offers to liberalize maritime trades. However, the U.S. refused to make any offer until its partners agreed to "approximate the current openness of the U.S. market." As the arbitrary deadline for agreement approached and other nations had not satisfied the U.S., its representatives walked away from the negotiations, saying that existing offers "merely [sought to] lock in place restrictive, and anticompetitive measures" in each country. Japan and the EU were eager to reopen the talks again in 1997 or 1998, but the U.S. was content to leave them "on hold" until the year 2000, when a new round of trade talks is likely to be launched.[33]

Multilateral Agreement on Investment

A Multilateral Agreement on Investment (MAI) was negotiated by representatives of the 29 member countries of the OECD and a representative from the EU. The process, begun in 1995, is intended to commit nations to a policy of non-discrimination in the field of investments.[34]

The OECD conducted the negotiations because many emerging nations were hesitant to liberalize their investment markets. Now the economic problems in Asia and the need of those nations for foreign investment means they will have to liberalize their financial markets and make them more transparent. So there is a push to move the MAI under the WTO umbrella. But before that, it had run into numerous snags.[35] A group of 50 nongovernmental organizations (NGOs) vowed to campaign against the MAI unless it refocused negotiations to account for labor and the environment. Their concern is that the agreement would eventually "elevate the rights of investors far above those of . . . workers, and [concern for] the environment."[36] Then France walked out of the OECD talks, effectively shifting momentum to the WTO.[37] It is unclear whether or not an MAI will ever be reached, but it is an important enough objective that negotiations are expected to continue. Indeed, the financial turmoil recently experienced makes an agreement more necessary.

State Aid

The Uruguay Round agreement required WTO members to substantially reduce state aid, particularly for agriculture.[38] State aid is a government subsidy to a particular industry. This subsidizing usually is justified by the need to stabilize or preserve an industry, but in fact it distorts competition. The practice has been the topic of numerous WTO disputes; arising when an exporting country feels that it is put at a disadvantage when a national subsidy is given to domestic enterprises.

A typical form of state aid is that seen in Canada's dairy industry. Canada maintains a system of special milk classes through which it maintains high domestic prices. It also provides export subsidies for dairy products going into world markets.[39] These subsidies are restricted by the GATT, but there are exceptions. New Zealand has complained that Canada is providing export subsidies for dairy products without regard to its WTO commitment. The U.S., Argentina and the EU have also joined in the informal consultations.[40]

Procurement

During the Tokyo GATT Round, parties agreed that federal government purchasing would be governed by a procurement code, intended to open up government contracts to competitive bids and eliminate favoritism for national providers. However, the agreement was not signed by many countries, and those that did sign insisted upon sizable exceptions. Furthermore, subordinate governmental units (states, provinces and cities) are not covered. The U.S. wanted a better agreement. It especially wanted to compete for public procurement contracts of European sub-governmental units. Conversely, the EU wanted access to the public procurement market in the U.S. The result of this mutual interest was the Government Procurement Agreement (GPA) that became effective in January 1996. It provides for nondiscrimination and transparency with respect to government purchasing. Procurement decisions under the agreement are to be taken on the basis of economic considerations only. The GPA is a voluntary agreement and binds only those sub-units that agree. Thirty-seven of our 50 states have signed the agreement.

These cases demonstrate the difficulty of establishing simple, uniform and enforceable rules for international trade. Not only must divergent national interests and practices be harmonized, but semiautonomous governmental units must be brought aboard as well.

Origin

In July 1996, the U.S. implemented rules placing duties on textiles depending upon their country of origin. The EU then filed a complaint arguing that the new rules were obstacles to trade. U.S. rules of origin state that, for custom purposes, a textile product originates wherever the cloth was manufactured, not where it was cut or fabricated.[41] Historically, rules of origin have been important because different tariffs or quotas apply depending on where a product "originates." Harmonization of rules of origin under the WTO has been slow and sketchy. Although it is progressing now, the original deadline for completing an agreement (July 1998) was not met. Nonetheless, the WTO Rules of Origin Committee was able to endorse over 1,000 rules covering non-agricultural products. They have not been able to agree on more controversial issues concerning the origin of textiles and agricultural products, however. The textile conflict between the U.S. and the EU is especially sharp.[42]

In general, WTO rules provide that a product originates at the place of "substantial transformation." Textiles have been a problem since that sector was added to the GATT agenda in the Uruguay Round. The reason is that textiles (and agricultural products) often are the chief industries in emerging countries. It is natural for them to try to protect their domestic market from foreign competition and to penetrate foreign markets with inexpensive exports. The U.S. has been on both sides of the dispute regarding textiles. As complainant the U.S. filed a claim against Argentina and won, since Argentina's specific duties on textiles and apparel were excessive and violated WTO rules. The U.S. also has objected to the transshipment of Chinese textiles through Hong Kong to gain a lower tariff valuation.[43]

Dumping

Harmonized rules also prohibit the dumping of products. In July 1997, South Korea filed a complaint against the U.S. in the WTO, alleging that it had levied unfair anti-dumping duties on Korean color television sets.[44] The Antidumping Act of 1916 provides a remedy for dumping even in cases where predatory pricing is not alleged. The statute provides that importers are barred from selling articles in the U.S. at prices below actual market value in the country of production, if the importer intends to destroy, injure or prevent the establishment of a U.S. industry or to restrain or monopolize trade and commerce in the subject market. The act has been tested numerous times, but it has always survived. Although South Korea dropped its complaint regarding televisions, it continued to prosecute a suit objecting to dumping duties on dynamic random access memory semiconductors (DRAMs).[45]

In January 1998, the WTO agreed to establish a panel to settle the dispute between the U.S. and South Korea over DRAMs. The panel will examine Korea's complaint that the U.S. anti-dumping duties are in violation of the WTO agreements, including the 1994 Anti-Dumping Agreement. Dumping complaints have increased with Asia's expansion, especially now that the region is trying to export its way out of its economic problems. But often such complaints are just another form of market protection.[46]

Mutual Recognition

Mutual recognition is another GATT trade goal. The focus of mutual recognition treaties is to eliminate the cost of complying with different technical regulations and the certification process of different countries. Multiple inspections can slow trade and add to costs. Mutual recognition (where countries agree to recognize one another's testing and certification processes) eliminates these barriers. This does not mean a single standard for the whole world. Rather, it accepts that rigorous testing systems should produce results that need not be replicated. Obviously, this is a very lofty goal. But it is being realized, particularly in cutting-edge industries where standards evolve quite rapidly. WTO members are encouraged to enter into MRA negotiations with other members. The ISO 9000 standard series is an example of an international agreement leading to the establishment of an international standard. Mutual Recognition Agreements (MRAs) are increasingly made part of many technology agreements in both bilateral and multilateral settings.

Harmonization

Harmonization has been a goal of technical experts for many decades. The work of the International Standardization Organization (ISO) is instrumental in achieving that goal. Harmonization under the WTO also took a giant leap forward with the Technical Barriers to Trade agreement (TBT).

The agreement encourages WTO members to use existing international standards when formulating national ones. If this happens, over a period of time national (versus international) standards will gradually harmonize.

Sometimes there is a good reason for differing national standards, however, as when national security is involved. However, the TBT agreement encourages members to join international bodies that will gradually harmonize national standards or set international ones.

The TBT recognizes the difficulties that developing nations face in meeting international technical standards. Therefore, it temporarily relaxes provisions that would require too rapid a change in standards. The TBT even allows for the preservation of indigenous technologies. The unique thing about harmonization, and a point often missed, is that it does not mean "the same" standards for all countries. Rather harmonization is the development of similar standards that do not pose obstacles to international trade.[47]

Peripheral Agreements

Insurance

Many sectoral agreements have sub-agreements, which may or may not have been fully negotiated when the sectoral agreements were concluded. One of these was the agreement on insurance, a part of the financial services agreement. This sub-agreement is aimed at opening up insurance markets to foreign companies. It covers the entire range of insurance products, including life, non-life, reinsurance, brokerage and auxiliary services. For U.S. companies in the insurance industry the agreement could expose a market worth more than $200 billion in foreign premiums. Fifty-two countries have joined the pact, guaranteeing broad market access, while another fourteen nations have committed to partially open their markets.

The U.S. put considerable pressure on India, Malaysia and Indonesia to open their health insurance markets. Enormous numbers of people who live in these countries have been unreachable by foreign insurance companies, because their national markets are completely closed. For a time it looked as if the negotiations would not be completed by the December 1997 deadline. In the end, the U.S. excluded Malaysia from the U.S. commitment. But many exemptions were granted at the last minute in order to get an agreement.[48]

Labor

Once in a while GATT disputes arise that deal with human rights issues. Labor and human rights standards vary widely from developed to developing nations and yet they affect trade, for example, through the difference in the cost of goods produced by high-wage nations versus those produced by prison labor. Yet there are no well-defined GATT standards in the labor sector. Like the environment, the WTO finds itself in a very uncomfortable position. However, labor issues are starting to appear in WTO complaints and are testing the limits of the dispute resolution procedures. Like environmental issues, human rights issues are subjective and politically sensitive. The WTO cannot adjudicate them without adequate standards. Eventually, some international understanding must evolve. Thus far, the WTO has allowed the International Labor Organization (ILO) to take the lead.

Environmental

The WTO's promotion of global trade also takes into account that increased trade can have a negative impact on the environment. However, former WTO Director General Ruggiero argued that trade liberalization can play an "important role" in protecting the environment by "reducing market inefficiencies." An agreement in the agricultural sector, for example, would help to reduce state subsidies to farmers and remove barriers to food imports. This is important because "study after study shows how market access restrictions, domestic support policies, and export subsidies have been the cause of direct and significant harm to the environment in many developed countries."

Despite this rhetoric, the WTO has been harshly criticized by environmentalists. They are concerned that the body, focused as it is on trade, will override national policies dealing with environmental protection. Several WTO decisions have done just this, finding that national environmental legislation violated the terms of the GATT. One WTO panel upheld Mexico's complaint that the U.S. dolphin-safe-tuna requirement was a violation of the international trade rules.

WTO rules provide that "[g]overnments can use any type of trade restriction, including import and export quotas . . . [and] . . . taxes for the purpose of environmental protection or resource protection . . . as long as basic requirements relating to non-discrimination and least trade-restrictiveness are met." Hence environmental-protection legislation is permissible as long as it is legitimate (not a subterfuge to protect domestic products) and does not materially interfere with the "process and production methods" of other traders.[49] During the Uruguay Round, future WTO members agreed to examine ways to transfer environmental technology and services to developing countries, thereby improving their production processes environmentally. For the latter, the cost of this technology often is prohibitive.

However, environmental rules have been slow to develop in the WTO. This is partly because of their politically sensitive nature and partly because the issues are so complex. But the failure to lead has produced other concerns. Developed nations are concerned that the WTO will take the power to protect the environment out of the hands of individual nations, while developing nations are concerned that their economic growth will be slowed by the environmental legislation of developed nations.

One example of this tension is the so-called "shrimp/turtle" case. It involved the application of GATT rules to a trade dispute over the production and process methods (ppms) used when trawling for shrimp. Certain trawling methods allegedly kill sea turtles, a species that the U.S. considers endangered. The case involved competing trade and environment issues, each of which had merit. The WTO panel chose to seek advice from a group of environmental experts. This is the first time in WTO (or for that matter GATT) history that a dispute panel has formally sought outside expert advice.

The case turned on the panel's interpretation of Article XX of the GATT, which sets forth "General Exceptions" to GATT rules. In June 1987, the National Marine Fisheries Service enacted regulations requiring shrimp trawlers of a certain size operating in the Gulf of Mexico to use either turtle excluder devices (TEDs) or limit the time they tow shrimp nets without boarding a catch. A group of Louisiana shrimpers filed suit in federal court trying to block the regulation, but it was upheld. Of course, this put U.S. shrimpers at a disadvantage compared to non-Gulf fishermen, because it raised the cost of the catch (TED nets) or reduced their volume (shorter time). In November 1989, Congress passed legislation instructing the president to initiate negotiations to develop bilateral and multilateral agreements consistent with the national standard. The president delegated this duty to the State Department, which interpreted it as applying only to "the wider Caribbean and Western Atlantic region." This interpretation was challenged in the U.S. Court of International Trade, which found the regulation applied to "the importation of shrimp or products of shrimp wherever harvested." Thereafter, Thailand, Malaysia, India and Pakistan filed claims against the U.S. in the WTO.

Such cases are not new to the WTO. In fact, the shrimp-turtle case resembles the tuna-dolphin case decided under the GATT. The U.S. tried to prohibit the importation of tuna from countries whose fishing fleets were not certified to be "dolphin safe." The dispute resolution panel found that the prohibition violated GATT rules, but the panel's ruling was never adopted because of the GATT's policy of consensus voting. One major difference between the tuna-dolphin case and the shrimp-turtle case, however, is that turtles have been recognized as being endangered by an international agreement.[50]

In March 1998, the dispute settlement panel issued a preliminary ruling condemning the U.S. ban. The U.S. appealed the decision, believing that the ban was necessary to protect sea turtles from extinction and because Article XX allows exceptions to protect animal and plant life. The appellate body agreed, stating that the U.S. could, under WTO rules, adopt restrictions in order to protect the environment, but said that it had failed to impose its ban in a nondiscriminatory manner.[51] Because the issue is so difficult and pits developed against developing nations, Director-General Ruggiero called for the establishment of an international framework to define the relationship between environmental agreements and the WTO objective of promoting trade. In his opinion, "[a]sking the WTO to solve issues which are not central to its work, especially when these are issues which governments have failed to address satisfactorily in other contexts, is not just a recipe for failure, it could do untold harm to the trading system itself."[52] Mr. Ruggiero's frustration is understandable, but it is misplaced. Environmental problems are as international as trade itself. If international standards are not developed by the WTO, then national standards can be used to protect not just the environment, but local markets as well.

Computer

Another case that irritated the U.S. involved the lucrative computer industry. This dispute was between the U.S. and the EU and involved trade worth $2.5 billion. In 1994, the EU decided to reduce tariffs on data processing equipment, including computer equipment. Later in the year, however, Ireland and the United Kingdom decided to reclassify Local Area Network (LAN) equipment as telecommunications equipment. In 1995, the EU followed suit. A LAN interconnects a number of computers and computer peripherals using a cabling system. These cables allow for the flow of data from one device to the other. The effect of the reclassification was to double the applicable import tariff on LANs. The U.S. filed a complaint arguing that this was a violation of Article II.1 of the GATT. In February 1998, the WTO dispute settlement panel upheld the U.S. complaint. However, the EU decided to appeal the decision, and the WTO appellate body favored the EU position. Meanwhile, EU trade in LANs had doubled.[53]

THE FUTURE

Few international organizations have as much potential to harmonize world trade as the WTO. Its membership is broad-based, and is steadily increasing the trade sectors under negotiation. But the WTO is facing a series of "choice points" that could influence its long-term success. Among these are the replacement of its first director-general, institutional reform, the accession of new members, and the prospect of more sectorial agreements or a new "round" of trade negotiations or both. Any one of these changes, and far more the lot of them, could have a profound impact on the future of world trade. For, if progress falters at the multinational level, regional trading groups are almost certain to develop their own standards, competing with the WTO.

Leadership Succession

The selection of the first WTO Director General took three months because each of the three major trading blocs (the EU, Japan and the Americas) put forward a different candidate. When the U.S. candidate (former Mexican president Salinas) was discredited, consensus formed around Renato Ruggiero, a former Italian minister and businessman. The U.S. reluctantly agreed to his appointment, but only if he would step down after one four-year term (April 1999), not to be succeeded by a European.[54] Whomever succeed him (there were four nominees, again by region; Hassan Abouyoub of Morocco, Roy MacLaren of Canada, Mike Moore of New Zealand, and Supachai Panitchpakid of Thailand) had his work cut out for him. For Mr. Ruggiero proved to be an extraordinarily effective leader, insisting that the terms of the GATT be adhered to and pushing sectorial negotiations, but shrewd enough to know that the GATT is a political as well as legal document, requiring some forgiveness when the trade liberalization pace set by some nations, or the treaty itself, cannot be met by others. His deft balancing of the competing pressures of international trade has given the WTO tremendous credibility and produced about as much trade harmony as could be expected in four short years. At the same time, he broadened the reach of the WTO, insisting that leading traders make concessions for the world's poorest countries and that the concerns of nongovernmental organizations (NGOs) be taken into consideration in setting trade policy. From a global trade standpoint, Ruggiero was a brilliant first choice to head the WTO. The selection of his successor was to be something of a referendum on his strong, practical leadership. Will developing nations support another director general who so transparently favors a Western, capitalist approach? Will the world's industrialized nations trust a second-tier trading nation (which hold over one-half of WTO seats) to lead so important an institution? Should the WTO directorate be highly legalistic, or more conciliatory?[55]

Institutional Reform

A second challenge to the WTO is to reform its dispute resolution process. Its critics claim that it needs to be made more participatory (at present, only WTO members can initiate and prosecute complaints), transparent (the proceedings are private) and speedier (the average proceeding takes about 34 months to complete). Reform suggestions have been submitted by a number of WTO members, including Japan, the EU and the U.S. "Substantive talks" began in October 1998 but are not expected to conclude until sometime in 1999. If that schedule is adhered to, then improvements in the process might be adopted at the next ministerial meeting or round of negotiations. Meanwhile, those parties that feel that they did not get "justice" in the WTO process (for example, Kodak in the Fuji film case) or that won their case but had difficulty enforcing the decision (the U.S. in the hormone and banana disputes) may resort to unilateral retaliation (allowed under GATT rules).

This will put even greater pressure on the WTO to reform, but it may also polarize its membership. A number of WTO members, particularly those with weak economies, say they are threatened—not aided—by strong enforcement mechanisms and rapid market openings. These nations are more numerous than industrialized WTO states and may react negatively to persistent pressure from the latter to strengthen enforcement devices. Any change is likely to strengthen, not weaken, the WTO enforcement mechanism legally. But one has to remember that there was no true enforcement mechanism prior to the WTO. It is almost certain to be improved soon, for experience has shown that reform is needed. But it would be a shame if a multilateral system with great potential was abandoned for unilateral methods that would be divisive and probably no more successful.[56]

Expanding WTO Membership

There is a long queue to join the WTO, for membership gives a nation status and a voice in today's trading world. Membership also gives nations the right to enforce GATT terms against other members, although it carries the reciprocal duty to obey them. In global trade terms, the more inclusive the WTO, the better.

Two of the world's largest trading nations—China and Russia—remain outside. Until they can be absorbed into a global trading system, the WTO will not have the scope or the influence it needs to be a complete success. And yet the economic problems in China and Russia may be so large and fundamental that there is no way of finessing their WTO membership. Until the Russian leadership is stable enough and the Chinese leadership cooperative enough to allow them to join the WTO, perhaps it is better that they be excluded. This is destabilizing in itself. But, as the 1990s ended, Russia seemed to be drifting farther away from rather than closer to WTO membership and China was making only modest progress.[57]

The Millennium Round

The last major challenge facing the WTO is whether to begin a new "round" of trade negotiations around the year 2000. That seems likely. Although the Uruguay Round was long (eight years), difficult and exhausting, it was undoubtedly the best round ever. Perhaps the negotiators learned something from it or forgot what an ordeal it was. Most probably, the agreement on a new round reflects the fact that the sectoral agreements negotiated since the end of the Uruguay Round did not allow most WTO members much influence. If the U.S. and EU can agree to terms, the other nations pretty well have to go along. They would have more influence in a full round. Besides, a long agenda is building up in the WTO, from agriculture to foreign investment to competition policy. Not all of these can be addressed speedily in sectorial negations. But neither does a new round exclude sectorial talks.[58]

In such economically and politically sensitive areas as environmental protection, human rights and state aid, WTO member countries differ considerably in their traditions and abilities to conform to a global standard. While human rights may be of great concern to the U.S. and other developed nations, the subject is of less concern to developing countries that are eager to improve their economies by any means possible and depend heavily on human labor. The WTO can move forward only with the consensus of a majority of its members. To assume that there is an American answer for every situation is a non-starter. While saving sea turtles may be of utmost importance to us, it is less concern to third-world fishermen struggling to make a living. Because such differences are somewhat subjective and not central to trade as such, they may lend themselves to more voluntary agreements than to WTO negotiations.

WTO Director General Ruggiero recently argued that involving the WTO in environmental issues is "[a]sking [it] to solve issues which are not central to its work." On the other hand, the WTO is emerging as the last, best resort for an enormous range of trade and social concerns that eventually must be handled at the multinational level.[59]

Chapter 15

A New Era in World Trade

I have written so much about various economic models and their prospects that my central thesis may have become obscured. It is that trade globalization is a powerful and complicated force in today's world, beyond the ability of any single nation to control. For that reason, attempting a conclusion to this book would be folly. There are too many themes to collect them all into a nice little bundle. Besides, the subjects addressed here are very fluid. The future changes even as I write. While many events are foreseeable, some are not. Consider for example that Latin American economies from Mexico to Brazil have largely deflected economic shocks that would have sunk them a decade ago, the "no fail" Japanese economy has failed, and Asia's Little Tigers have been declawed.

As I suggested earlier, world trade advances in "spurts." This latest one may be the greatest of all in terms of size and inclusiveness, but it won't be the last. Global commerce, social and political trends all move at different paces. So long as there are *national* interests to protect, they will act as a brake on globalization. And I don't perceive any rush toward *international* government at present. On the other hand, I think further trade harmonization is inevitable. It is simple economic Darwinism. Some form of managed, enforceable, participatory capitalism lies in the future. To some extent, developed nations will have to sacrifice in order to assist those less developed. This is not altruism, but enlightened self-interest. Unchecked competition can be very destabilizing. Developed and emerging economies alike crave an orderly, upward process. Eventually, they are likely to get it. In the meantime, the best I can offer here is some "benchmarks" that might allow one to handicap the process as it unfolds.[1]

COMMUNISM VERSUS CAPITALISM VERSUS SOCIALISM

Recent events have exposed the shortcomings of micromanaged (Russia and China) and macromananged economies (Japan and the EU). They either are too costly or they do not allow enough incentive/reward (or punishment) to properly calibrate market behavior. The result can be a major shock of "crisis" proportions (the Asian meltdown), rather than a series of smaller, tolerable corrections. On the other hand, the type of "cowboy capitalism" that has bedeviled Russia and East Asia can't be allowed either. It is likely to produce extremes of wealth and poverty, without regard for the underclasses, the environment and non-renewable resources. Obviously, some type of managed capitalism is likely to emerge, capitalistic enough to encourage and reward enterprise and innovation, yet socialistic enough to cushion capitalism's extreme consequences. The fact that our European, Russian and Chinese partners all seem to have opted for a type of socially conscious capitalism suggests it that might be the wave of the future.[2]

GLOBALIZATION

I believe that business has outpaced government in integrating the world's economies. Increased contact has made it easier to co-venture. More consensus about business practices (financial services, accountancy) and product interchangeability (the Information Technology Agreement, or ITA, and mutual recognition agreements) increase cooperation, reduce polarization, promote accessibility, widen markets and improve economies of scale. Admittedly, these processes start first at the national level, then move to the regional and finally to the global level. But it isn't always so. Because global enterprise can exceed the ability to control it, the need for nations to collaborate multilaterally will increase.[3] One nation could set the pace, as could a regional bloc, or a standard could be set from the top down, (such as GATT rounds). However, more homogenized and transparent markets generally produce greater wealth and so the process of globalization is likely to continue.

Nonetheless, globalization is frightening. It seems to be beyond anyone's control, and its advantages have not been well publicized. The best study I have read on the subject, OPEN MARKETS MATTER, reports that world trade in merchandise is sixteen times greater today than in 1950. Outflows of foreign direct investment (FDI) have grown 25-fold in the past 25 years (from $14 billion to $350 billion *a year*). Although the process is not painless, liberalized economies grow at twice the rate of protected ones. Furthermore, the cost of saving jobs through market protection is estimated to vastly exceed the value of the jobs saved.[4]

There always will be a need to redistribute wealth, for there will always be a maldistribution of skills and resources. Peoples and nations whose needs are greatest may be least able to help themselves. Aiding them is important. However, a steadily improving and expanding market creates more wealth. The strongest traders need to encourage the less strong, without waste or warfare. The constant tension between liberty and equality (the essential differences between capitalism and socialism) will be more carefully calibrated in the future.[5]

Is There a World Government?

If taken literally, this question is foolish. Of course there isn't! There are no directly elected world leaders, or parliament or courts with global jurisdiction. But, if one shifts the prism from the *de jure* to the *de facto*, the answer is less clear. There are a number of international organizations, ranging from those with broad membership and modest influence (like the United Nations) to those with more limited membership but more concrete rules (NAFTA and the WTO). Through them the world's sovereign nations are gradually subordinating national prerogatives to multinational authority in return for more-or-less enforceable agreements. That is to say that economic globalization has diminished the capacity of any individual state to take action. International trade has grown too complex and interdependent for this. Even the largest economic player in the world (the U.S.) is becoming too small to act independently.

A large number of international organizations have grown up with various memberships and objectives. Collectively, they comprise a system of world *governance*, if not a world government. The range is enormous; from the UN to the GATT/WTO. Ranged between them are organizations with varying memberships and influence, such as the IMF, World Bank, the OECD, NATO, the Group of Seven industrialized nations (G-7), and the Quad 4 (the U.S., EU, Japan and Canada). None are governments in the traditional sense, but all have some degree of influence on global policy. Depending upon the nature and enforceability of the agreements, these organizations can have a more or less profound impact on global trade and security. But virtually every agreement favors regional or global norms over national norms. The benefit is that global traders play on a larger stage with more standardization. But the disadvantage is that there is less scope for national action. So, individual state sovereignty shrinks, *de facto*.[6] Naturally, this has an impact on each state, since not all will benefit equally or as soon from each agreement. Thus, there is a legitimate concern that the agenda of industrialized nations might dominate world trade at the expense of emerging economies.

The concern is real enough, but perhaps misplaced. We are learning that there are few truly marginal players and that even relatively small players can produce considerable destablization. In particular, developing countries fear the prospect that developed countries will advance world trade at their expense. This is unlikely, for global traders count on emerging markets for growth.[7] But neither do developed countries want their investment squandered in corrupt, non-transparent, unregulated markets. Consequently, one mission of these international organizations is to bring less-developed nations into the world trade system. Lately, they have been "more active participants" in world trade. So there is less likelihood that their concerns about labor, environmental, competition and agricultural standards will be ignored by developed nations. Conversely, existing international arrangements may prove too weak to manage the global economy, and we may need more collectivity to make the system work. There is a lot of sorting out still to be done.[8]

There can be no true world economy unless weaker nations are brought along with the strong and the concerns of both addressed. But in order for this to happen there must be leadership and a degree of consensus. Hence, there must be continued strong leadership in the WTO now that its initial head has stepped down. This choice alone has implications for the future. Most international organizations—like the G-7 and APEC—aren't tightly organized. So regional trading blocs could operate to obstruct global trade as much as to reinforce it. The right leadership and increased consensus is needed to develop a well-honed global trading system.[9] The problem is, of course, that however well-integrated various multilateral organizations may be, they are not like national governments. Their agreements suggest a direction, but not necessarily a pace. It is easy to criticize them for not being more open and forceful. But they are, after all, political talking-shops. And at least some participants (and critics) don't want them to be more.[10] On the other hand, all economies benefit from stability, and the latest G-7 effort to achieve it is a more-inclusive, so-called GX.[11]

Is the U.S. Still the Leader?

There probably is nothing Americans enjoy so much as a good challenge. In the early 1980s, the prophesy of an "Ascendent Asia" seemed to be correct. An MIT study, MADE IN AMERICA, challenged American businesses and workers to change, and change they did. When other international competitors seemed to be beating out U.S. products at home and abroad, Americans mobilized for a fight. In a series of related but largely independent moves, American industry improved its products and increased efficiency; labor accepted new conditions of work, necessary to restore competitiveness; and government asserted itself to assure that American goods and services had fair access to world markets. The program was aggressive and by-and-large successful. It continues today. By the late 1990s, ours had proved a very resilient economy, perhaps the strongest large economy in the world. Despite the fact that ours is a steadily shrinking share of world trade and consumption, America still may be the trader with the most clout in the world.[12]

But we are not out of the woods. Nor will we ever be. We can't reform the global trading system on our own. We need allies. We are not likely to get them or keep them if we do not collaborate with other world traders, however, the EU first among them. All the world does not view the "globalization" process as we do. We can expect to lose allies and influence if we always insist on doing things our way. Eventually, a critical mass of traders will coalesce around different principles and different leaders.

One advantage America does seem to have is that it is the only trading nation or group fully engaged in every major trading region. The U.S. is a member of APEC, the core of NAFTA (which it hopes to expand), and has signed a new Transatlantic Economic Partnership with the EU. However, this new approach to world trade—"open regionalism"—could just as easily turn into a "new provincialism," in which members of regional trading blocs agree with one another but not about a world standard. We see evidence of that here in the U.S. and also in groups like Mercosur, ASEAN and the EU itself. Consensus about trade liberalization often is easier to achieve in smaller, more-cohesive regional trading blocs. If those agreements are well-crafted and advantageous, they could serve as a prototype for an international agreement. Some have done so in the past.[13] But the U.S. undercuts its influence when we criticize and threaten our trading partners and yet won't give our executive "fast track" negotiating authority.[14]

Every year in recent times, the U.S. Trade Representative (USTR) has set out a trade agenda for the year and published a report detailing our trading grievances with around 50 trading partners. The 1998 version of the report is over 400 pages long and devotes one-third of its length to some of our best partners—50 pages to Japan, 30 to the EU, 22 to South Korea and 18 to China. Pointing out violations of trading rules and chiding partners to obey them surely has merit, but it is not the way Europeans or Asians prefer to resolve differences. Our approach to trade liberalization can produce results (and often has), but it also can cause resentment.[15]

The turmoil in Asia, and its own inability to stave off recession, has hurt Japan's pride. Even if it objectively violates some agreed-upon trading rules, this may not be the best time for moralizing. That can promote polarization. We have to expect that an economy in great turmoil will have little political room for maneuver. Meanwhile, the status quo has produced large trade imbalances. Both economies must coexist in the same trading environment.[16] Besides, the high dudgeon of the USTR's report gives ammunition to those neo-isolationists in America who feel that we concede more than we get in world trade circles (contrary to statistics). This would be exactly the wrong time to turn isolationist.

The process of opening must begin somewhere. American leadership in the past has been crucial to trade liberalization. Are we going to forsake that leadership at this critical juncture? If we do, won't some other trader pick it up (perhaps the EU), so that U.S. influence will be further reduced?[17] In order to exercise in the future the influence that America enjoyed in the past, we must foreswear isolationism and protectionism. Unilateral and extraterritorial measures such as Helms-Burton, the Iran-Libya Sanctions Act (ILSA) and Super 301 have not particularly helped our trade position, have been condemned by our trading partners and may violate the GATT.[18] This weakens our alliances. Besides, our sanctions (or threatened sanctions) don't seem to work, either because other nations ignore them or because they are toothless. If we are going to collect a working majority around our position, then we must use a more "European" approach, one that is less confrontational and more directed at consensus building. It is increasingly clear that our more-confrontational style encourages other bilateral arrangements that leave us out of the loop. U.S. leadership could be on the wane.[19]

A substantial corps of conservatives in Congress, influenced by public reaction to our escalating trade deficit, seem prepared to deny the executive "fast-track" negotiating authority. There is much to fear from that. In recent years, the U.S. has been the most competitive nation in the world, and global trade has honed that competitiveness. Sitting on the sidelines will not improve our position, nor protect our interests. In the financial service talks, the EU showed its willingness to take the laboring oar when the U.S. walked out. That should be a lesson to us. Although a great deal of public anxiety is unleashed as our trade balance worsens, the response isn't to cut access, but to find allies that will help us to restore stability to troubled economies. The bottom line is that the U.S. be part of a global economy. We cannot succeed if the rest of the world is failing. To its credit, the Clinton administration has rebuffed appeals for protectionism as foreign goods flooded the U.S. market. To have done otherwise would have set trade liberalization and recovery back.[20] Quitting the race or becoming protectionist will not preserve our economic health.[21] Full engagement across a huge range of issues, from non-tariff barriers, to state aids, to monetary stability, to competition standards, to weapons proliferation, confront us and the rest of the world. The solution lies in going forward, not back. We need allies and should start with the EU.[22]

The U.S. and the EU: Conflict or Cooperation?

Will the U.S. and the EU collaborate to advance the globalization process, or will they compete? The answer is that they will do both. The political and economic pressures on each is different, as is their market philosophy. Where the U.S. and EU agree (telecommunications, financial services liberalization) we can expect rapid, multilateral progress. Where they disagree (agricultural policy, business concentration and Helms-Burton), we can expect stalemate, conflict and the development of other alliances.

Two of the issues about which the U.S. and EU currently disagree are whether or not to initiate an Atlantic trading bloc and to launch a new extended GATT round. Both ideas are the brainchild of former EU Commissioner and principal trade negotiator Sir Leon Brittan. He was keen to keep up the momentum of trade integration and to thrust the EU into the forefront. The former idea builds on the current bilateral arrangement (the Transatlantic Economic Partnership), but would eliminate more technical barriers through MRAs and harmonization, eliminate all industrial tariffs by 2010, create a free trade area in services, and further liberalize investment, public procurement and intellectual property. A new GATT round would doubtless expand the number of trading sectors covered, including the possible absorption of existing sectoral agreements.

The U.S. was lukewarm to both ideas. First, it already enjoys an enormous bilateral trade with the EU. No new treaty is required to expand it, and we don't want to be perceived to favor trade with Europe over that with other regions (Latin America and Asia). Second, the EU has indicated that the agricultural sector is not to be involved in this negotiation. Our access to their agricultural markets is one of the sharpest disputes between us. Finally, a stronger U.S.-EU partnership may violate WTO rules, because it might exclude traders from a huge proportion of the global market.[23]

The proposed Millennium Round of GATT negotiations may come too soon after the exhausting Uruguay Round. Since then, the U.S. has done quite well in negotiating sectoral agreements, without the EU playing an equal role (except in the area of financial services). This approach—where negotiations are narrowly focused in one trade sector, and the U.S. can exert unilateral pressure by offering improved access to its markets in return for equal access to its partners'—favor the U.S. with the E.U. as a consenting junior partner. A full GATT round puts many more trade sectors on the table. In this environment, the EU is more likely to collect allies and to negotiate bargains more favorable to it. Thus, the U.S. is willing to go forward only if the round produces quick results ("early harvest").

The U.S. and the EU are the largest democratic, capitalistic traders in the world. But their interests are not identical. Therefore, while the prospect of bilateral trade improvements seems perpetually in the offing, the devil is in the details. Both American and European businessmen wish that the integration process would go more swiftly. But as long as there are politicians to take the credit and blame for economic decisions and as long as politics influences economic policy, the frictions continue. On balance, cooperative arrangements exceed conflicts. Bilateral negotiations are ongoing, and the areas of general agreement many.[24] Take for example MRAs. Among the earliest was a mid-1996 agreement that the U.S. and EU would recognize each other's testing and certification procedures for electronic products, including telecommunications equipment. Somewhat later, agreements were negotiated in the pharmaceutical sector and one covering medical devices. It was estimated that the elimination of duplicate testing in these sectors would cut the cost of transatlantic trade by some $40 billion annually. More recent negotiations have resulted in a Science and Technology Agreement, allowing for joint and shared research in a variety of fields. The agreements should cover about $3 billion in transatlantic trade and could gradually be expanded. Private linkages, such as an alliance between the Chicago Board of Trade and Eurex (an all-electronic European exchange) have the result of standardizing practices and increasing volume, while reducing cost.[25]

Not all negotiations are so successful. It is not always clear whether differences are legitimate or protectionist. A good example would be the exclusion of U.S. hormone-fed beef from the veterinary agreement. The U.S. said that the product posed no danger to human health, while the EU insisted that it did. Neither side would retreat, and finally a WTO panel agreed with the U.S.[26] The whole agricultural sector has long been a source of friction between the U.S. and EU. This is not because it is particularly important to either economy. However, there is a great deal of political pressure to protect farmers and a disappearing agrarian lifestyle. Americans are constantly urging the EU to stop subsidizing farm products and to open its agricultural market. Eventually it will happen, for agricultural policy is more of a liability than an asset. However, repeated efforts to reform the Community's Common Agricultural Policy (CAP) have met with stiff resistance.[27]

Equally serious disputes have developed between the U.S. and the EU over unilateral legislation like Helms-Burton, the protection of "personal" information in the transmission of electronic data, Internet regulation, economic assistance to Asia and even "open skies" agreements reached with individual EU member states rather than the Community itself.[28]

If this sounds a bit like a trade "turf war," it is. For the U.S. and the EU disagree somewhat about how global trade ought to be managed. The European culture is much more acclimated to state ownership or state aids, whereas the American business culture is more capitalistic. Consequently, the U.S. exerts steady pressure on European governments to privatize their key businesses and to eliminate state assistance to keep weaker ones afloat. The culture of state involvement is common in Europe and, of course, distorts trade. So the pressure from the U.S. to fully privatize Europe's competing industries is understandable. The same protective instincts carry over into labor and social programs. Theirs are more protective than those here in the States, and no doubt they burden competitiveness. However, European socialism will not go quietly; it is a highly politicized issue. Recently, three major EU states (France, Britain and Germany) have made a shift to the political left. This is closer to the world norm, but quite opposite American capitalism.[29] EU economies are under pressure to be more competitive, while ours is under pressure to be more socially sensitive. In time, there should be some meeting of the minds.

Conversely, there are strong integrative trends in Europe. The common currency (the euro) is just one of these. It will unite EU economies a great deal more by reducing transaction costs and developing a central monetary policy. While the euro was launched into unsteady financial conditions, it certainly won't have to compete with the yen to become the world's second reserve currency. Indeed, both Japan and China have indicated that they will shift reserves from dollars to euros.[30] The euro also may help the EU address its chronic unemployment and productivity problems. Recent data suggest that unemployment is dropping in Europe, and the single currency ought to increase labor and business mobility, reduce costs and increase integration.[31]

Then there is the prospect of enlarging the Union early next century. As explained previously, the "bridesmaid" countries will have difficulty reaching the EU average without significant help. This makes them a liability of sorts for EU members, but it also captures a trained workforce, various resources and a competitive edge in developing markets. Despite the risks, EU enlargement would appear to offer at least as many benefits as the expansion of NAFTA to all the Americas (FTAA), and probably more. While the European share of world trade may continue to grow, the U.S. share just might shrink, even with a FTAA.[32] The U.S. will not stand idly by while the EU cherry-picks the best opportunities, of course. We will be competitive, as we always are, but the continued convergence of our two economies and the world economy will increasingly bind us to a single fate.

The fact that EU member states gave it intergovernmental competence (under Pillar II of the Maastricht Treaty) to pursue a common foreign policy suggests that the EU is now willing (and able) to play a larger role in world affairs. Using these new powers, the EU is fully capable of dealing directly with our trading partners and in so doing cause the U.S. to alter its own economic strategy. The EU simply is taking a stronger role in world affairs. That promises to reshape our thinking on matters that range from the NATO to the G-7 to the IMF and beyond. When the U.S. and EU are allies the world almost certainly will have its standard. When we are adversaries, other nations can pick and choose. Those choices might not always benefit the U.S.[33]

THE FUTURE OF WORLD TRADE: IS "FREE" TRADE "FAIR" TRADE?

The answer to the question is "no," of course. A completely *laissez-faire* economic system would allow extreme maldistributions of wealth, provoke jealousies and probably end in warfare. That doesn't seem "fair." On the other hand, what is "fair" often depends on one's point of view. Each nation tries to promote its strengths and protect against its weaknesses. It would be difficult to develop a consensus about what is "fair." But it may not be as difficult to develop a consensus about what is "abusive," or "unreasonable" or "distorts trade." Even the offending party might be able to calculate that objectively.

Progress toward a globalized trading system is neither steady nor efficient. Participants cannot assume that all adverse by-products of trade globalization (job losses, environmental degradation) are avoidable. Some are not. So the question is: How do we achieve a free *and* fair global trading system as swiftly as possible and with the *least* disadvantage to the largest number? And how do we ease the pain of those who suffer the changes most? Looking for a system in which there are no losers is not to start at all. We must start.

A New World Order

To call this a "New World order" sounds pompous. Besides, the term is overused. Yet the globalized trading system that is emerging today is like nothing we have experienced before. It calls for new approaches in a variety of areas.[34]

Flexibility

The first step is to embrace a system that is flexible and comprehensive. Recent history has proved that no single system among those I have discussed is entirely free of defects. Some will succeed in various ways at various times. But none is perfect. Constant adjustment is necessary. This means that the negotiations that lead to corrections must be inclusive and continuing. For *any* system, unconstrained and uncorrected, will eventually run off the rails. If a problem can be foreseen and corrected, it must be. To begin, the traditional approach of national programs with fixed ideologies has to be abandoned.[35] The world economy is too interdependent.

A new group of economists believe that global competitiveness will eventually lead to worldwide overcapacity, market glut, underemployment and deflation.[36] If their estimates prove true, then there has to be an equitable way to share the pain, or a whole new round of trade restrictions will be spawned. Hopefully, the world economy will have grown so integrated by that time that coordinated adjustments can be made. But it is in the nature of people to break ranks in times of difficulty.[37] A group that aims to succeed together must be prepared to fail together as well.

Leadership

The second element is leadership, and preferably broad-based leadership. There can be no doubt that the U.S. (possibly NAFTA) and the EU are the dominant trading blocs in the world today. They are relatively close to one another in strength and vision, so that, if they can agree, things usually get done. The U.S. is deeply engaged in every major trade area. Its temporal flirtation with APEC, NAFTA/FTAA and the EU may be nothing more than hedges until the World Trade Organization consolidates regional blocs. However, regional trade agreements can be halfway houses to global norms. Moreover, the EU seems to have made a massive commitment to centralization (the Single European Act, the Maastricht Treaty and a single currency). One might say that the 1990s have produced a fundamental (and overdue) shift in Europeans' thinking about their own and the global economy. Japan has fallen from its position of influence, but one expects Japan's economy will recover. Either way, all of Asia will have a large impact on the global economy and must be included.[38]

That still leaves a sizable number of the world's economies outside the principal trading groups. Non-members' interests and concerns have to be considered. The U.S., the EU and others will want to extract some firm trading commitments from them as the price of entry. But to exclude these nations from core deliberations doesn't make sense. It probably will not improve their trade commitments beyond a certain point, but their economies, their market behavior and their human rights records may improve more rapidly through inclusion than exclusion. A country is more likely to be protectionist and cavalier about international norms if it is poor *and* isolated. These countries include Russia, China, North Korea, India and Africa, but all are developing at uneven rates. Nonetheless, they are eager to share in the riches, if possible.[39]

THE WORLD TRADE ORGANIZATION

In the previous chapter, I discussed the operation, strengths and weaknesses of the WTO and U.S. experience with it. Whatever its limitations, the WTO is by far the most salutary vehicle to harmonize global trade that has existed. Indeed, its very success has put it under strain. The number of disputes being submitted for resolution escalates steadily, and more items are being added to its crowded negotiation agenda. Many important trade concerns (like labor, the environment, and competition standards) have not yet been added. Disparity of approach in these areas will have a heavy impact on trade until a workable global standard is agreed. Hence, the resources of the WTO need to be increased, its jurisdiction expanded and its processes streamlined. At present, appeals from panel decisions almost always are taken. It can take years from the time a request for a dispute settlement panel is made until the judgment is complied with. In the meantime, trade-distorting behavior can go unmodified. Expanding the WTO's authority means a further delegation of national sovereignty, and that is never easy. Meanwhile, multinational corporations press on with their business ventures, raising new problems for trading nations and therefore the WTO. If the WTO and other public sector organizations can't keep up with the pace of global business, then the private sector surely will strike off on its own.[40]

Some insight into the WTO's future was revealed in 1999. Its first director general (a European) was replaced. But the succession was anything but smooth. A second European was unlikely, as was a North American at this stage in the WTO's development. So an Asian was the likely choice. But the protracted struggle between a Thai and a New Zealander polarized industrialized and developing members of the WTO, split the EU, and left the WTO rudderless for a period. Jockeying among the U.S., the EU and Asian states continued throughout the summer of 1999. Some WTO member states wanted to put the issue to a vote, but that would have damaged the consensus approach that characterizes GATT negotiations. Finally, an agreement was reached to split the director's six-year term between Moore and Supachai, in that order. The solution serves as a perfect metaphor for the progression of world trade outlined in this book. First, the influence of Asia is steadily increasing in world trade circles, but "Western" influence (Moore) remains strong. Second, the interests and positions of emerging Asian economies (Supachai) are likely to be taken more into account in future trade negotiations and not just at the GATT level. However, the compromise victors will have to play catch up to restore relations within the WTO and recover its momentum. Will they be as successful as their predecessor? Are they likely to pursue a trade policy that is less capitalistic than that of the U.S. and Europe? (The U.S. and the EU could virtually have assured their choice of candidate, had they agreed. But they couldn't do so the last time or this time. As a result, smaller states in the WTO are gaining influence.)

Shortly after this process was complete, changes in the WTO's dispute resolution mechanism were addressed. Will it be streamlined? Made more transparent? Will non-parties be allowed access to deliberations? Will decisions be expedited and less political? The answers to these questions bear on the pace and direction of trade globalization. If the WTO matures too slowly, alternatives surely will be found.[41]

Among the many problems facing global traders is the sheer speed at which new technologies are hatched and grow. This creates inevitable bottlenecks that may inhibit trade, as may any national or regional standard adopted to deal with an emerging issue. The latter can be protectionist, however, so it is important for market regulators to agree on harmonized standards even if that means deferring national action until a consensus is reached.[42] Selecting common standards or agreeing on the mutual recognition of national standards is the best way forward. Any domestic standard impacts world trade, just as any world standard will impact domestic trade. The product or practice that is closest to the harmonized standard has an advantage. For these reasons, developing countries may need relief. But for how long?

GLOBAL FINANCE

If businesses and markets are to thrive, they must have financing. Yet financial resources are concentrated in a handful of highly industrialized countries. The flight of capital to and from developing markets can have a destabilizing effect on local economies *and* on the world economy. Even before the Asian meltdown, it was evident that economic conditions in larger trading nations and the stability of emerging countries were affected by the global flow of capital. It is difficult to think of another area of world affairs in which the U.S. and EU have a greater role or so much at stake. And yet the Mexican peso crisis in 1994 was treated as an "American" problem. Not so the Asian crisis, which was much larger and reached around the world. It concentrated interest on the availability and use of capital as never before.

Monetary policy continues to be dominantly a matter of local concern. (The new European Central Bank may be a slight exception.) But the loose coordination of monetary policy attempted through the G-7 or Quad 4 nations or the OECD no longer seems adequate. And so, under the auspices of the OECD, serious talks about a Multilateral Agreement on Investment (MAI) have begun. This is not an easy task, for flexibility and national interest lie at the core of monetary policy. Yet "cowboy capitalism" can be ruinous to world trade. Fiscal policy talks continue not because the traders are enthusiastic, but because the Asian problem made it necessary.[43]

We are learning that the free movement of capital works well only if there is an adequate infrastructure to deal with it. It took many years for Western democracies to develop their infrastructures. It should be no surprise that those in the emerging world are inadequate. More to the point, a multinational structure may now be needed.[44] By late 1998, the Asian crisis—or reactions to it—had spread widely enough that the U.S. and EU economies were seriously threatened. So the G-7 heads of state responded. In a speech to the New York Stock Exchange, Tony Blair, England's prime minister, set "five key priorities [for the] international financial system." They were greater openness and transparency, improved financial supervision and regulation, the ability to respond to short-term liquidity crises and enable reforming economies to get the capital they need to sustain growth, handling massive capital flows, and greater openness and accountability on the part of international financial institutions (the IMF in particular). According to Mr. Blair, "recent . . . global capital flows have provided stark demonstration that while open capital markets do bring substantial benefits, they also pose serious challenges." Within days, President Clinton threw his support behind the issue and offered a more concrete proposal (G-7 finance ministers already were discussing what might be done to stabilize the global finance system).

By late October 1998, G-7 officials had reached an agreement to create a new $90 billion fund that the IMF could "[use] to ensure the stability of the international financial system." This fund would "provide a contingent short-term line of credit for countries pursuing strong IMF approved policies." The agreement also called upon "international regulatory and supervisory organizations" (especially the IMF, World Bank and OECD) to "work more closely together." G-7 leaders called for "the establishment of a process for strengthened financial sector surveillance," reform of the IMF, and for "appropriate private sector involvement" (debt rollover). "[B]eyond these short-term steps," the G-7 heads of state called for "further reforms . . . required to create a strengthened financial architecture for the global market-place of the next millennium."[45]

As usual, the G-7 statements were long on principle, but short on detail. Nonetheless, there was an unmistakable political commitment to a more-managed global economy. This is in stark contrast to the "liberalization of capital markets" and "free flow of capital" mantra that was gospel just a short while ago. Moreover, the Western world was taking some responsibility for allowing (even promoting) the free flow of speculative capital to emerging economies that were ill-equipped to deal with it. Suddenly "capital controls" are not an unthinkable concept. Once the G-7 has set off on a regulatory tack, it is not impossible that a multilateral agreement to regulate capital flows and harmonize financial sector practices will emerge.[46] After all, from 1990 to 1997 FDI grew at three times the rate of international trade in goods. It can no longer be thought that unregulated capital flows will not destabilize the world economy. Greater security in financial markets encourages multinationals to invest—and to *stay* invested—in emerging economies. That said, however, it is entirely possible that—with enough transparency and oversight—regulation could be unnecessary or short lived. After all, it was a lack of knowledge, as well as a lack of regulation, that caused the Asian crisis.[47]

REMAINING BARRIERS TO FAIR TRADE

Bribery and States Aids

Other national practices that distort markets and skew competition are bribery and state aids (subsidies). A positive step on the bribery front was taken when OECD ministers agreed to disallow the tax deductibility of bribes as a business expense. The U.S. wanted the agreement to stretch further, to make bribery a criminal offense. That has been the case in the U.S. since the Foreign Corrupt Practices Act was passed in 1977. That act puts American businesses at a disadvantage when they compete abroad. Legalized bribery distorts competition. In the end, the treaty provided only that signatories would "take all necessary steps to outlaw bribery in international business transactions." This has the anomalous result of only disallowing the tax deductibility of criminal payments.[48] Nonetheless, some progress is better than none.

State aids (government subsidies to commercial enterprises, public and private) are more difficult, because every nation is under a great deal of political pressure to support local "heroes." They provide jobs, contribute to national pride, and so forth. But to prop them up through tax breaks, direct cash subsidies or preferred contracts (especially when they are uncompetitive) often does not save the company but does distort competition. However, such national heroes as Credit Lyonnais or Olympic Airways are not likely to be sacrificed to foreign competition. Even though Article 92 of the Treaty of Rome forbids state aids, Article 93 allows the European Commission to make exceptions, and they are fairly easily gotten. This type of incestuousness between government and business is even greater in Asia.

The practice has the effect of perpetuating non-competitive businesses that cost everyone in the long run. One reason for the subsidies is that, in much of the world, it is common for governments to provide a range of goods and services that are provided by private companies in competitive markets like ours. Hence it was a breakthrough merely to get a GATT agreement on subsidies. Their prohibition makes for a far more level playing field. But enforcing the principle, in the face of national interests, is not easy.[49]

Global Competition Standards

Speaking of free and open markets, there probably is no remaining issue as important as determining what behaviors are anti-competitive in international trade. We have our Sherman Antitrust Act, which declares, in effect, that there is no such thing as a "good" monopoly. Yet we more or less tolerate oligopolistic industries and some "natural" monopolies, like Intel and Microsoft. The EU dislikes "dominant" undertakings and agreements between undertakings that restrict trade (Articles 85 and 86 of the Treaty of Rome). Yet it allows for "good" monopolies and agreements that "[improve] . . . production or distribution . . . or [promote] technical or economic progress, while allowing consumers a fair share of the resulting benefit." In much of the rest of the world, either there are no competition rules at all or they are laxly enforced. The assumption is: If the market can be divided and managed for the good of the people, what is the point of competition rules? In a state-managed economy, competition is simply not a factor.

· The result is that many of the world's economies are playing by vastly different sets of competition rules (or none at all). How big is too big? Should a company be able to sell at a premium in one market (where competition is restricted) so that it can undercut its competitors in a market where it must compete? Are preferential contracts, tying arrangements or market subdivision anti-competitive? What if a business takes an action at its home office (where it is legal) that has an anti-competitive "effect" in another state? Is it best to keep all enterprises in an industrial sector small so that none will dominate, even at the expense of greater efficiency and economies of scale? Well, you can see where this leads. It is increasingly hard for multinational firms to compete on a global scale if they don't know what the rules of competition are. However, there is no consensus answer to these questions. The WTO has a working group considering the subject, as does the U.S. Department of Justice. And the U.S. and EU have agreed in their new Transatlantic Economic Partnership (TEP) action plan to exchange views on "means of enhancing international cooperation among competition authorities." But a consensus is elusive because of the differences among the various economic models.[50]

Rules of Origin and Dumping

Among many other non-tariff barriers, there are rules of origin and dumping. Rules of origin contemplate that goods that "originate" (are substantially fabricated) within a country may be treated differently from those that originate elsewhere. Since more-complex and more-valuable products often contain components from several sources, the true origin of such goods can become a metaphysical exercise in "bean-counting." The whole idea is somewhat arcane in a world in which pure "American" or "British" products hardly exist anymore. When the label on even a simple product tells you that it was "made in one or more of the following [six] countries," notions of origin lose all of their importance. They become what they are, backward-looking protections of domestic markets against "foreign" goods. In time the exercise won't be worth the effort, because product commingling will become so great.[51]

"Dumping" (at least *predatory* dumping) is more of a problem. It is the practice of selling imported goods in a domestic market at less than their cost where produced. But the yardstick used to judge "cost" can ape the cost of the competing domestic product. That is, if the imported product is less expensive than the local one, it *must* be dumped (and a countervailing duty should be charged to make their costs more alike). This denies a price savings to the consumer and reduces the incentive to improve the local product. Perhaps the foreign manufacturer overproduced and is happy to get whatever he can for his surplus. He can't afford to sell at a loss too often, so selling below cost occasionally can hardly be considered serious dumping. A healthy economy should be able to shrug off such surpluses. Generally, dumping claims are just another way to protect local industries against competitive imports.[52]

Nominal differences in pricing can be distinguished from predatory dumping; the practice of lowering prices—perhaps taking a huge short-term loss—in order to drive domestic competitors out of business, after which prices can be raised. This practice clearly violates principles of fair marketing and needs to be outlawed. Most alleged dumping probably masks protection. Some material injury to the local economy should be a prerequisite for any dumping duty.[53]

Labor Standards

Another huge issue in international trade is labor conditions. It includes child and forced labor, working conditions, wages and health and safety. Emerging countries often have surplus labor and not enough work, so labor-intensive industries (agriculture, textiles, shoes) migrate there. High-skill, high-value work migrates to industrialized nations, where technical skills and labor costs are higher. But some components of high-tech work (assembly) might be done in lower-wage areas, so we see some work (and jobs) migrating from the U.S. to Mexican border industries, from Japan to China and from Germany to Ireland, Portugal and Spain. Developed economies often are sorely distressed by this, and their politicians are pressured to stem the migration. However, every nation has at some time exploited its natural advantages. So it is unrealistic to think that this process can be stopped. Indeed, we see it right here in the U.S., with furniture and apparel manufacturers migrating to the Southeast and agriculture to the Midwest. Besides, much more fuss is made of labor (or business) migration than objectively measured behavior justifies.[54] As developing nations become more prosperous, wages and working conditions will improve and disparities will shrink. It is naive to think that there can ever be a uniform labor standard or to insist that developing nations adopt those of developed nations. Emerging country laborers want the work, even at reduced wages. To deny it will simply mean that we have to send aid to them (assuming this is a humane world), because they will not have the work to support themselves.

What needs to be guarded against is not differential labor standards, but exploitation of children, prisoners, the environment, and so forth. In other words, the best consensus on labor standards in a competitive world market would be to set minimum (or core) standards that address issues of danger and exploitation and leave it to governments and/or businesses to set higher standards if conditions allow. In today's increasingly transparent world, there is a penalty to be paid for exploitation, as Nike has learned. But, short of that, businesses will seek to hold down labor costs if they can.

At the WTO ministerial meeting in Singapore (1996), it was decided to defer the consideration of labor standards for at least two years and to allow a working group of the International Labor Organization (ILO) to work on them. The WTO had enough conflicts between developing and developed countries (agriculture, fishing, the environment) to deal with. Besides, the private sector was represented in the ILO. Further, the globalization of trade and business was producing a consensus about forced and child labor. It is estimated that 250 million children between the ages of five and fourteen are working full or part time. But the ILO, working with individual countries, is reducing resistance to "core" labor standards and deflecting more children into school. As resistance decreases, prospects increase that the WTO may reenter the picture sometime during the Millennium Round.[55]

The key to achieving an international agreement on core labor standards is to convince developing countries that those standards are not a subterfuge by the developed world to neutralize their cheap-labor advantage. Rather, a minimum standard would reduce the political bickering that now clouds the issue and distinguish developing economies that want social reform from those few that truly are exploitative.[56]

Environment

Protecting the environment is another sticking point in international trade. Obviously, emerging economies may abuse the environment in ways that developed nations forbid. This is not to say that developed countries do not subordinate environmental concerns in the interest of economic advancement. They have, and it would be generous to say that they always did it unwittingly. However, most developed nations now are disposed to protect the environment. For this reason, developing nations often view environmental protection standards as another way in which developed nations retain competitive advantage. The environment is of growing concern to developed nations, whereas simple survival often is a greater concern for developing ones. So developing nations are naturally suspicious that the cost of "environmental protection" may rest most heavily on them.

Although this issue is highly sensitive, a common solution is needed. Unilateral initiatives, however well-meaning, are bound to be viewed as non-tariff barriers, while regional initiatives are criticized by environmentalists as inadequate. Thus, some sort of core standard is needed. But, in order for this to happen, the WTO or some other international body has to be given clear authority. The timid resolves of the Kyoto conference (1997) indicate that all nations are a long way from consensus in this sector.[57]

Agriculture Policy

Another sector of great sensitivity is agriculture. This is not because it forms such a large part of industrialized nations' economies, but because of the political influence the farm sector enjoys. The hearty, self-sufficient farmer is an image that plays well, and politicians worldwide respect it. Eventually, agricultural protection will shrink, if only because the cost of protecting the sector in industrialized economies doesn't make sense. They guarantee an adequate food supply and its safety, of course. But most agricultural limitations go well beyond that. Abundant and wholesome food is produced by emerging countries. They should not have to compete with their developed neighbors for agricultural markets. But the farm lobby is strong, and every health scare (Mexican strawberries) arrests market liberalization, at least briefly. The OECD reports that total worldwide government support for agriculture (about $166 billion in 1996) was down by 7 percent from 1995 levels. More important, this support is gradually shifting from price supports (state aid) to direct payments to farmers (welfare or retraining grants). In due course, developing countries will supply a larger percentage of our agricultural products. But we must insure that they don't destroy the environment in the process.[58]

Global Security

I cannot conclude this discussion of global problems without mentioning national and world security, albeit briefly. The globalization of trade in goods and services includes weapons, military know-how, and crime. Trade liberalization and the disappearance of political borders allows antisocial elements to move as freely as any other. Hence, it is beyond the capacity of any state to protect itself and its population adequately without the cooperation of others. Yet it is difficult to think of any area of human affairs so intensely national as public security. In theory, it is for each nation to decide what behavior is criminal and how to punish it. No nation wants to be dependent on another for guns or aircraft. At least, that is how security architecture grew up. But it is no longer equal to the task. A new architecture is needed.

To some extent, the process already has begun. Many nations share information about criminal behavior through such organizations such as Interpol or Europol (the EU's network). Pillar III of the Maastricht Treaty provides for intergovernmental cooperation among the fifteen EU states in the fields of justice and home affairs. The growth of extradition treaties is further evidence of this cooperative trend. But progress is rather slow when compared to the growth of international crime.[59]

One of the more notable examples of multinational cooperation is the reconfiguration of NATO and its expansion after the fall of Communism. NATO was formed after World War II to guarantee security in Europe and to contain Communism. When the Soviet Union imploded in the early 1990s, NATO needed to reassess (and reconfigure) its objective. NATO has begun to welcome former Communist states as members. There are some EU member states that would like to see the Western European Union—a long-dormant military pact among many EU states, but not part of the EU treaty structure—take over more of the responsibility for security in Europe. The WEU is not up to the task presently, but the U.S. would like to reduce its presence (and expense) there, without losing its voice in European security matters. The U.S. wants a secure world but does not want to be the world's policeman. Other nations want autonomy, but they welcome our monetary contribution and leadership. Will the responsibility for ensuring national and global security eventually be shared out on a worldwide basis? Possibly. Meanwhile, there is growing cooperation and collaboration so that security functions also are becoming "globalized." One just wonders if the process is moving as rapidly as the threat it is meant to contain.[60]

ONE TALE ENDS, ANOTHER BEGINS

And so this latest "great leap forward" in global trade relations has been both like and unlike past changes. The globalization of trade, as I have defined it, is quite unlike most past trade integration. Yet some of the tensions and problems it has spawned are as old as foreign trade itself. Some of the trade arenas in which we are engaged have evolved over hundreds of years; others were unknown until quite recently. But the pace of trade, its enormous volume and value and the growth of interdependence at the public and private level grow exponentially. Just think of what the microchip, the computer and the Internet have meant to global trade in the past decade.[61] We now know that this is just the tip of the iceberg.

Greater trade liberalization should mean more economic growth, more security and a better life for all. The U.S. and the European models seem to have triumphed. And yet, there is a cautious footnote to this conclusion. It's called "sustainability." Sustainability is the notion that economies ought not to grow so fast that they cannibalize the environment, or that they outstrip the capacity of modern technology to solve the myriad problems that progress can create or that they allow overpopulation, overproduction or rogue nations to sidetrack the process.

What kind of global trading system will result? I will venture a guess that it will not be as free as the one we Americans are used to. Many nations in the world are not blessed with the institutions, heritage and resources that we are. Besides, some regulatory oversight is necessary to assure a "fair" sharing out of opportunities and resources. If this is done on a world scale, then those nations furthest in the lead may be slowed a bit. This brand of socially regulated capitalism is far closer to the economic models pursued by the majority of the countries of the world than it is to ours. A balance must be struck between capitalistic and socialistic systems. Competition will be restrained to some extent in the interest of the whole. The hope is that continued experience with globalization, harmonization and multilateral regulation will supplant the tendency to handicap national economies as if they were horses in a race that only a few can win. That type of national competitiveness is contrary to globalization. If political pressure is brought on national leaders whenever their economy is "below average"[62] the process of globalization will be retarded. "League tables" aren't very relevant in a global society, and they shouldn't be.

One hopes that we can count on the two trading systems I have especially featured in this book to provide the vision and leadership needed in the years ahead. Competition surely has its place in world trade. But so does collaboration. Our increasingly interdependent *economic* world has been *politically* divided too long.

Appendix

Table Comparing Numbers in the EU and EC Treaties—Through the Treaty on European Union (Maastricht)—with Renumbered Sections (Treaty of Amsterdam, Article 12, May 1999)

Treaty on European Union

Previous Numbering		New Numbering	
	Title I		Title I
Article B		Article 2	
	Title II		Title II
Article G		Article 8	
	Title V*		Title V
Article J.1		Article 11	
Article J.2		Article 12	
Article J.3		Article 13	
Article J.4		Article 14	
Article J.5		Article 15	
Article J.7		Article 17	
Article J.8		Article 18	
Article J.9		Article 19	
	Title VI*		Title VI
Article K.1		Article 29	
Article K.2		Article 30	

*Title restructured by the Treaty of Amsterdam.

Previous Numbering	New Numbering
Article K.3	Article 31
Article K.4	Article 32
Article K.5	Article 33
Article K.6	Article 34
Article K.7	Article 35
Article K.8	Article 36
Article K.9	Article 37

	Title VII		Title VIII
Article L		Article 46	
Article N		Article 48	

Treaties of the European Community

	Part One		Part One
Article 1		Article 1	
Article 2		Article 2	
Article 3		Article 3	
Article 3a		Article 4	
Article 3b		Article 5	
Article 3c*		Article 6	
Article 4		Article 7	
Article 4a		Article 8	
Article 4b		Article 9	
Article 5		Article 10	
Article 5a*		Article 11	
Article 6		Article 12	
Article 6a*		Article 13	
Article 7a		Article 14	
Article 7c		Article 15	
Article 7d*		Article 16	

	Part Two		Part Two
Article 8		Article 17	
Article 8a		Article 18	
Article 8b		Article 19	
Article 8c		Article 20	
Article 8d		Article 21	
Article 8e		Article 22	

	Part Three Title I		Part Three Title I
Article 9		Article 23	
Article 10		Article 24	

* New Article introduced by the Treaty of Amsterdam.

Previous Numbering	New Numbering
Chapter 1	Chapter 1
Section 1 (deleted)	
Article 12	Article 25
Section 2 (deleted)	
Article 28	Article 26
Article 29	Article 27
Chapter 2	Chapter 2
Article 30	Article 28
Article 34	Article 29
Article 36	Article 30
Article 37	Article 31
Title II	Title II
Article 38	Article 32
Article 39	Article 33
Article 40	Article 34
Article 41	Article 35
Article 42	Article 36
Article 43	Article 37
Article 46	Article 38
Title III	Title III
Chapter 1	Chapter 1
Article 48	Article 39
Article 49	Article 40
Article 50	Article 41
Article 51	Article 42
Chapter 2	Chapter 2
Article 52	Article 43
Article 54	Article 44
Article 55	Article 45
Article 56	Article 46
Article 57	Article 47
Article 58	Article 48
Chapter 3	Chapter 3
Article 59	Article 49
Article 60	Article 50
Article 61	Article 51
Article 63	Article 52
Article 64	Article 53
Article 65	Article 54
Article 66	Article 55

Previous Numbering	New Numbering
Chapter 4	Chapter 4
Article 73b	Article 56
Article 73c	Article 57
Article 73d	Article 58
Article 73f	Article 59
Article 73g	Article 60
Title IIIa**	Title IV
Article 73i*	Article 61
Article 73j*	Article 62
Article 73k*	Article 63
Article 73l*	Article 64
Article 73m*	Article 65
Article 73n*	Article 66
Article 73o*	Article 67
Article 73p*	Article 68
Article 73q*	Article 69
Title IV	Title V
Article 74	Article 70
Article 75	Article 71
Article 76	Article 72
Article 77	Article 73
Article 78	Article 74
Article 79	Article 75
Article 80	Article 76
Article 81	Article 77
Article 82	Article 78
Article 83	Article 79
Article 84	Article 80
Title V Chapter 1 Section 1	Title VI Chapter 1 Section 1
Article 85	Article 81
Article 86	Article 82
Article 87	Article 83
Article 88	Article 84
Article 89	Article 85
Article 90	Article 86

Section 2 (deleted)

* New Article introduced by the Treaty of Amsterdam.
** New Title introduced by the Treaty of Amsterdam.

Previous Numbering		New Numbering	
	Section 3		Section 2
Article 92		Article 87	
Article 93		Article 88	
Article 94		Article 89	
Article 95		Article 90	
Article 96		Article 91	
Article 98		Article 92	
Article 99		Article 93	
Article 100		Article 94	
Article 100a		Article 95	
Article 101		Article 96	
Article 102		Article 97	
	Title VI		Title VII
	Chapter 1		Chapter 1
Article 102a		Article 98	
Article 103		Article 99	
Article 103a		Article 100	
Article 104		Article 101	
Article 104a		Article 102	
Article 104b		Article 103	
Article 104c		Article 104	
	Chapter 2		Chapter 2
Article 105		Article 105	
Article 105a		Article 106	
Article 106		Article 107	
Article 107		Article 108	
Article 108		Article 109	
Article 108a		Article 110	
Article 109		Article 111	
	Chapter 3		Chapter 3
Article 109a		Article 112	
Article 109b		Article 113	
Article 109c		Article 114	
Article 109d		Article 115	
	Chapter 4		Chapter 4
Article 109e		Article 116	
Article 109f		Article 117	
Article 109g		Article 118	
Article 109h		Article 119	
Article 109i		Article 120	
Article 109j		Article 121	
Article 109k		Article 122	
Article 109l		Article 123	
Article 109m		Article 124	

Previous Numbering	New Numbering
Title VIa**	Title VIII
Article 109n*	Article 125
Article 109o*	Article 126
Article 109p*	Article 127
Article 109q*	Article 128
Article 109r*	Article 129
Article 109s*	Article 130
Title VII	Title IX
Article 110	Article 131
Article 112	Article 132
Article 113	Article 133
Article 115	Article 134
Title VIIa**	Title X
Article 116*	Article 135
Title VIII	Title XI
Chapter 1***	Chapter 1
Article 117	Article 136
Article 118	Article 137
Article 118a	Article 138
Article 118b	Article 139
Article 118c	Article 140
Article 119	Article 141
Chapter 2	Chapter 2
Article 123	Article 146
Article 124	Article 147
Article 125	Article 148
Title XII	Title XV
Article 129b	Article 154
Article 129c	Article 155
Article 129d	Article 156
Title XIV	Title XVII
Article 130a	Article 158
Article 130b	Article 159
Article 130c	Article 160
Article 130d	Article 161
Article 130e	Article 162

* New Article introduced by the Treaty of Amsterdam.
** New Title introduced by the Treaty of Amsterdam.
*** Chapter 1 restructured by the Treaty of Amsterdam.

Previous Numbering	New Numbering
Title XV	Title XVIII
Article 130f	Article 163
Title XVII	Title XX
Article 130u	Article 177
Article 130v	Article 178
Article 130w	Article 179
Article 130x	Article 180
Article 130y	Article 181
Part Four	Part Four
Article 131	Article 182
Article 132	Article 183
Article 133	Article 184
Article 134	Article 185
Article 135	Article 186
Article 136	Article 187
Article 136a	Article 188
Part Five	Part Five
Title I	Title I
Chapter 1	Chapter 1
Section 1	Section 1
Article 137	Article 189
Article 138	Article 190
Article 138a	Article 191
Article 138b	Article 192
Article 138c	Article 193
Article 138d	Article 194
Article 138e	Article 195
Article 139	Article 196
Article 140	Article 197
Article 141	Article 198
Article 142	Article 199
Article 143	Article 200
Article 144	Article 201
Section 2	Section 2
Article 145	Article 202
Article 146	Article 203
Article 147	Article 204
Article 148	Article 205
Article 150	Article 206
Article 151	Article 207
Article 152	Article 208
Article 153	Article 209
Article 154	Article 210

Previous Numbering	New Numbering
Section 3	Section 3
Article 155	Article 211
Article 156	Article 212
Article 157	Article 213
Article 158	Article 214
Article 159	Article 215
Article 160	Article 216
Article 161	Article 217
Article 162	Article 218
Article 163	Article 219
Section 4	Section 4
Article 164	Article 220
Article 165	Article 221
Article 166	Article 222
Article 167	Article 223
Article 168	Article 224
Article 168a	Article 225
Article 169	Article 226
Article 170	Article 227
Article 171	Article 228
Article 172	Article 229
Article 173	Article 230
Article 174	Article 231
Article 175	Article 232
Article 176	Article 233
Article 177	Article 234
Article 178	Article 235
Article 179	Article 236
Article 180	Article 237
Article 181	Article 238
Article 182	Article 239
Article 183	Article 240
Article 184	Article 241
Article 185	Article 242
Article 186	Article 243
Article 187	Article 244
Article 188	Article 245
Section 5	Section 5
Article 188a	Article 246
Article 188b	Article 247
Article 188c	Article 248
Chapter 2	Chapter 2
Article 189	Article 249
Article 189a	Article 250

Previous Numbering	New Numbering
Article 189b	Article 251
Article 189c	Article 252
Article 190	Article 253
Article 191	Article 254
Article 191a*	Article 255
Article 192	Article 256

	Chapter 4		Chapter 4
Article 198a		Article 263	
Article 198b		Article 264	
Article 198c		Article 265	

	Chapter 5		Chapter 5
Article 198d		Article 266	
Article 198e		Article 267	

	Title II		Title II
Article 201		Article 269	

	Part Six		Part Six
Article 210		Article 281	
Article 211		Article 282	
Article 217		Article 290	
Article 219		Article 292	
Article 220		Article 293	
Article 228		Article 300	
Article 228a		Article 301	
Article 229		Article 302	
Article 235		Article 308	
Article 240		Article 312	

* New Article introduced by the Treaty of Amsterdam.

Notes

CHAPTER 1. THE "GLOBALIZATION" PROCESS

1. LESTER THUROW, HEAD TO HEAD: THE COMING ECONOMIC BATTLE AMONG JAPAN, EUROPE AND AMERICA (Morrow & Co., 1992), pp. 55–66.

2. *See e.g.*, Peter Norman, "Dollar 'has risen enough'," FINANCIAL TIMES, February 10, 1997, p. 4; Gerard Baker, "Dollar could be buoyed in spite of G-7," FINANCIAL TIMES, February 11, 1997, p. 7.

3. For a brief, but complete, discussion of this point in the context of financial markets, see Gordon R. Walker & Mark A. Fox, "Globalization: An Analytical Framework," 3 INDIANA JOURNAL OF GLOBAL LEGAL STUDIES 375, pp. 379–381, citing Jost Delbrück, "Globalization of Law, Politics and Markets—Implications for Domestic Law—A European Perspective," 1 INDIANA JOURNAL OF GLOBAL LEGAL STUDIES 9, p. 10, n.3.

CHAPTER 2. REGULATING GLOBAL TRADE

1. LEA BRILMAYER, AMERICAN HEGEMONY: POLITICAL MORALITY IN A ONE-SUPERPOWER WORLD (Yale University Press, 1995).

2. Its "Action Plan . . . identifies over 150 specific actions where the EU and the US have agreed to *work together*" (emphasis mine), but its four general goals: "Promoting peace and stability, democracy and development around the world. . . . Responding to global challenges. . . . Contributing to the expansion of world trade and closer economic relations . . . [and] Building bridges across the Atlantic . . ."are too vague to be considered a trade-regulation "plan." European Commission, *Progress Report on EU/US Relations*, No. 7, December 1995, pp. 4–5.

3. Guy de Jonquières, "WTO urged to act on regional pacts," FINANCIAL TIMES, February 6, 1997, p. 6.

4. "Nowadays economic and social analysts debate whether, or to what extent,

financial globalization poses risks to Western economic and political stability. . . . [There is] growing middle-class and working-class [insecurity] caused by decline in manufacturing industries, intractable unemployment, widening gaps between rich and poor, and ruthlessness among talented elites who prosper in the global economy." Geoffrey Barker, "Malign or Benign? Global Market Mania," THE AUSTRALIAN FINANCIAL REVIEW, November 25, 1996, p. 14.

5. *Id.*; *see generally*, WILL HUTTON, THE STATE WE'RE IN (Vintage, 1996) concerning the prospects and problems of the international economic market, with particular attention given to the United Kingdom and Europe.

6. Peter Norman and Richard Waters, "G-7 resolves to put brakes on strong dollar," FINANCIAL TIMES, February 10, 1997, p. 1; Peter Norman, "Dollar 'has risen enough'," FINANCIAL TIMES, February 10, 1997, p. 4; *cf.*, Gerard Barber, "Dollar could be buoyed in spite of G-7," FINANCIAL TIMES, February 11, 1997, p. 7.

7. Simon Kuper, "Yen at 3½-year low against $," FINANCIAL TIMES, December 28–29, 1996, p. 1; William Dawkins, "Japan's surplus shows 31% drop," FINANCIAL TIMES, February 11, 1997, p. 6.

8. Donna Rosato, "Asia becoming top market," USA TODAY, June 28, 1995, p. 2B (citing a study by Deloitte & Touche); *cf.*, Edward Luce, "Latin America steps up pace," FINANCIAL TIMES, February 3, 1997, p. 31 (stating that "Latin American stocks rose by 15 percent in 1996, compared with 3.5 percent in Asia" and that "the first signs of Asia-sclerosis" will produce a "strong shift of [money] flows to Latin America"); Stephen Fidler, "[Latin America] Toughened by experience," FINANCIAL TIMES, February 10, 1997, p. 19.

9. Michael Elliott, "Taking the Cake: Dollar Diplomacy," NEWSWEEK, July 11, 1994, p. 32; Martin Wolf, "A lesson for the Chinese," FINANCIAL TIMES, March 26, 1996, p. 12.

10. Speech of U.S. Federal Reserve Chairman Alan Greenspan at the University of Leuven (Belgium), January 14, 1997. *See generally*, Dominic McGoldrick, "Sustainable Development and Human Rights: An Integrated Conception," 45 INTERNATIONAL AND COMPARATIVE LAW QUARTERLY 796, October 1996.

11. The Group of Seven (G-7) industrialized trading nations is composed of Canada, France, Germany, Italy, Japan, the United Kingdom and the United States. The so-called G-10 is made up of these seven plus Belgium, the Netherlands, Sweden and Switzerland (actually eleven).

12. David Marsh, "Can Europe compete? Balance of economic power begins to shift," FINANCIAL TIMES, March 9, 1994, p. 8 (*citing* OECD, World Bank, Union Bank of Switzerland and Coopers & Lybrand reports); Martin Wolf, *op cit.*; Robert J. Samuelson, "Why America Creates Jobs," NEWSWEEK, July 29, 1996, p. 49. *See generally*, Organization for Economic Cooperation and Development, OECD ECONOMIC OUTLOOK No. 60, December 1996; MASSACHUSETTS INSTITUTE OF TECHNOLOGY, MADE IN AMERICA (MIT Press, 1987).

13. David Marsh, *op cit.*; Conner Middelmann, "State sell-offs may raise $58 bn," FINANCIAL TIMES, January 31, 1997, p. xiii; John Case, "Small business and jobs— The issues," BOSTON GLOBE, June 16, 1993, p. 84; "In Brief," EURECOM, January 1994, p. 4. The last article states that 99 percent of EU businesses employ 50 or fewer persons and account for half the jobs and nearly one-half of turnover. Service jobs account for only 55 percent, and manufacturing accounts for 29 percent of jobs.

14. MILES KAHLER, REGIONAL FUTURES AND TRANSATLANTIC ECONOMIC RE-
LATIONS (Council on Foreign Relations Press, 1995), pp. 10–12.

15. *Id.*

16. Examples would be the U.S. complaint to the WTO about Japan's overregulation of its auto parts or film market, the U.S./EU Transatlantic agenda, and
the 1995 GATT, respectively.

17. "Fast track" authority, granted by Congress to the executive department (usually for a specified period of time), means that a treaty concluded in that time by the
negotiators and presented to Congress must be approved in its entirety (without
amendment) or not at all. This seems to improve the prospect of the treaty being
approved as negotiated, and thus improve the confidence of our treaty partners when
they invest their effort in negotiating the fine points of an agreement.

18. See *e.g.*, Hartford Fire Insurance Co. v. California, 113 S.Ct. 2891 (1993);
"Clinton (Again) Suspends Title III of Helms-Burton," EURECOM, January 1997,
p. 2.

19. "WTO proposes panel to handle Helms-Burton complaint against U.S.,"
BNA INTERNATIONAL TRADE DAILY, February 5, 1997 [2/5/97 BTD d5]. *See
generally*, MILES KAHLER, *op cit*, p. 45.

20. Commission of the European Communities, "Report on Convergence in the
EU in 1996," COM (96) 560 Final (November 6, 1996), pp. 61–64.

21. *See generally*, THE EUROPEAN CHALLENGE/1992: THE BENEFITS OF A SIN-
GLE MARKET (Gower Publishing Co., 1988), sometimes called the "Cecchini Report," for its chairman.

22. At the multinational level, the EU negotiated on behalf of its constituent
member states on most of the Uruguay Round sectors, leading to the latest GATT
and the WTO. For many years the EU has had a convention (now Lomé IV) with
so-called African, Caribbean and Pacific (ACP) countries (most in great need of aid,
and former or current possessions or colonies of EU member states). The EU also
has individually negotiated trade treaties (called Europe agreements, and creating a
European Economic Area beyond the EU) with Norway, Switzerland, Lichtenstein
and a number of former Russian bloc countries.

23. *See generally*, LESTER THUROW, HEAD TO HEAD: THE COMING ECONOMIC
BATTLE AMONG JAPAN, EUROPE AND AMERICA (Morrow & Co., 1992). Many more
examples of this analogy can be found, but even Professor Thurow backs away from
it somewhat in his more-recent book, THE FUTURE OF CAPITALISM (Morrow & Co.,
1996).

24. In the collision of ideas between Professors Thurow and Krugman, discussed
in the text, I side more with the former; although I think both overstate their case.

25. ARTHUR OKUN, EQUALITY AND EFFICIENCY (The Brookings Institution,
1975).

26. *See generally*, LESTER THUROW, THE FUTURE OF CAPITALISM, *op cit.*

27. MILES KAHLER, *op cit.*, p. 50.

28. World Trade Organization, Ministerial Conference, "Singapore Ministerial
Declaration," December 13, 1996, points 4, 16, 19–20.

29. MILES KAHLER, *op cit.*, p. 43.

CHAPTER 3. AN ECONOMIC MAP OF THE WORLD

1. It is hardly necessary to expound at length on a geopolitical map of the world. The political boundaries of most important countries, are well known. Sometimes countries dissolve (for example, the former Yugoslavia), are freed (India/Pakistan) or change their name (Rhodesia). But by and large the political map changes far less swiftly than its economic counterpart.

In this chapter, I have not attempted to address each nation, but rather the leading trading nations/groups, and have grouped them (crudely, I admit) into four generalized categories: "capitalist," macro-managed, micro-managed, and autocratic or communist. This is not exact, but used for the basis of comparison. Since extreme political positions tend to shift in the opposite direction, I think we can expect gradual movement in each model; particularly in the U.S., Europe and Asia.

2. All statistics are taken from U.S. BUREAU OF THE CENSUS, STATISTICAL ABSTRACT OF THE UNITED STATES: 1995, 115TH ED. (U.S. GPO, 1995), at the following charts and pages, respectively: Chart No. 2 (pp. 8–9), Chart No. 520 (p 335), Chart No. 1319 (p. 802), Chart No. 2 (p. 8), Chart No. 1319 (p. 802) and Chart No. 702 (p. 453).

3. *Id.*, Chart No. 1341 (pp. 819–822). In 1994, the U.S. exported $9,290 million in goods to China but imported some $38,780 million in goods from the Chinese, a negative balance of $29,490 million or 315 percent. Our negative balance with Japan, while large, is only 123 percent, on two-way trade valued at $172 billion. *Id.* Our negative trade balance with all of Asia, excepting Japan, was $73,050 million in 1994. *Id.*, Chart No. 1320 (p. 804), Chart No. 1340 (pp. 817–818) and Chart No. 1341 (pp. 819–822).

4. *Id.*, Chart No. 1319 (p. 802) and Chart No. 1321 (p. 804); Canada: $7,767 million; Mexico: $95 million; EU: $13,065 million; and Japan: $14,016 million. *Id.*

5. *Id.*, Charts Nos. 1324 and 1325 (p. 806).

6. U.S. BUREAU OF THE CENSUS, STATISTICAL ABSTRACT OF THE UNITED STATES: 1996, 116TH ED. (U.S. GPO, 1996), Chart No. 1283 (p. 784).

7. Nancy Dunne, "Trade deficit in US surges to $114 bn," FINANCIAL TIMES, February 20, 1997, p. 4. According to the chief economist at the Economic Strategy Institute, "[e]verything is going in the wrong direction."

8. Public Law 103–182, § 2, December 8, 1993, 107 Stat. 2060. 19 U.S.C. § 3301 *et seq. See generally*, Thomas J. Schoenbaum, "The North American Free Trade Agreement (NAFTA): Good for Jobs, for the Environment, and for America," 23 GA. J. INT'L & COMP. L. 461 (1993); JEFFREY J. SCHOTT, NAFTA: AN ASSESSMENT, REV. ED. (Institute for International Economics, 1993); U.S. CONGRESS, OFFICE OF TECHNOLOGY ASSESSMENT, U.S.–MEXICO TRADE: PULLING TOGETHER OR PULLING APART? (U.S. GPO, 1992).

9. (AP) "Mexico completes repayment of $13.5 billion US loan," SUN JOURNAL, January 16, 1997, p. B5.

10. EUROPEAN COMMISSION, THE EUROPEAN UNION AND WORLD TRADE 1994, chapter 2.

11. LESTER THUROW, THE FUTURE OF CAPITALISM (Morrow & Co., 1996), p. 143, citing Charles Wold, Jr., "The fine art of the false alarm," WALL STREET

JOURNAL, November 1, 1994, p. A20; WORLD BANK, WORLD TABLES 1994 (Johns Hopkins University Press, 1994).

12. LESTER THUROW, *op cit.*, p. 147.

13. WTO, REGIONALISM AND THE WORLD TRADING SYSTEM (Geneva, 1995).

14. Michael J. Mandel, "The Triumph of the New Economy," BUSINESS WEEK, December 30, 1996–January 7, 1997, p. 68.

15. Since 1980, the U.S. has fallen from a high of 9.7 percent in 1982 to 5.6 percent in 1995, and a projected 5.4 percent for 1996 and 1997. OECD ECONOMIC OUTLOOK, December 1996.

16. Michael J. Mandel, *op cit.*

17. *Id.*

18. *Id.*

19. C. FRED BERGSTEN & MARCUS NOLAND, RECONCILABLE DIFFERENCES? UNITED STATES–JAPAN ECONOMIC CONFLICT (Institute for International Economics, 1993), p. 24.

20. *Id.*, p. 29.

21. OECD ECONOMIC OUTLOOK, December 1996.

22. *Id.*

23. BERGSTEN & NOLAND, *op cit.*, pp. 26–27. "The U.S. deficit was clearly the major international imbalance of that period, indicating that the dollar had become substantially overvalued against all other major currencies." *Id.* at 27.

24. LESTER THUROW, *op cit.*, p. 148.

25. Michael J. Mandel, *op cit.*

26. "The Japanese economy has yet to show signs of recovery from the downturn which began in 1991. . . . The sharp appreciation of the yen during the first half of 1995 threatened to set back further the prospects for recovery." WORLD ECONOMIC OUTLOOK, October 1995 (International Monetary Fund, 1995), p. 15; OECD ECONOMIC OUTLOOK, December 1996.

27. *Id.*

28. BERGSTEN & NOLAND, *op cit.*, p. 24.

29. International Monetary Fund, International Financial Statistics 1995.

30. European Commission, EUROPEAN ECONOMY, No. 12, December 1995, p. 24.

31. OECD ECONOMIC OUTLOOK, December 1996.

32. Japan over the years has not been the same force in current account figures as in merchandise trade. Noland and Bergsten note that this can be attributed to a sizable services deficit because of its huge foreign expenditures for tourism and transportation, even though its foreign investment portfolio is now producing enough income to convert that deficit into a surplus in the future. BERGSTEN & NOLAND, *op cit.*, p. 29.

33. European Commission, EUROPEAN ECONOMY, *op cit.*, p. 25, Table 33.

34. BERGSTEN & NOLAND, *op cit.*, p. 79, *citing* J. DENNIS, RIVALS BEYOND TRADE (Cornell University Press, 1992).

35. Julius and Thomsen, "Foreign-owned Firms, Trade, and Economic Integration," Tokyo Club Papers 2 (Royal Institute of International Affairs, 1988).

36. BERGSTEN & NOLAND, *op cit.*, p. 67, *citing* JAMES C. MORGAN and J. JEFFREY MORGAN, CRACKING THE JAPANESE MARKET (Free Press, 1991).

37. In a 1992 OECD Economic Survey of Japanese manufacturing firms investing

overseas, 25 percent of firms noted lower labor costs as a motivation for investing in ASEAN countries. A similar pattern has recently taken place in Germany where FDI flows to Central and Eastern Europe have increased in response to the mark's appreciation in 1995. BERGSTEN & NOLAND, *op cit.*, p. 67, at note 6. Nonetheless, Eurostat notes that trade relations between the EU and the ASEAN countries and China, Japan and South Korea have improved vastly in 1996. From 1989 to 1994, the share of the ten Asian countries in total EU external trade went up by more than 3 percent, reaching 20.6 percent of EU imports and 14.4 percent of exports. "This trend was mainly due to the strong performance of EU trade with the seven ASEAN countries and China, while the Japanese share went down." EUROSTAT, "Statistics in Focus, External Trade," 2nd quarter 1996, p. 1.

38. OECD, *op cit.*, p. 26, Table 16. "According to an August [1996] survey of 373 major Japanese manufacturing firms, their fixed investment abroad during FY 1996 was planned to increase by 11.6 percent, compared with 8.9 percent in Japan. Moreover, as of August, the purchase of material from abroad by these firms was planned to rise by 13.8 percent, compared with a planned increase of 2.7 percent of their purchases of material from domestic sources." *Id.*, *citing* THE NIHON KEIZAI SHIMBUN, August 19, 1996.

39. *Id.*

40. *Id.*

41. *Id.*

42. EUROSTAT, Europe IN FIGURES, 4th ED. (Brussels, 1995), pp. 140, 351.

43. While it is true that the U.S. can boast a low rate today (in October 1996, the unemployment rate was 5.2 percent), in many years our rate of unemployment was higher than Europe's. From 1964 to 1967, the U.S. had an average of 4.6 percent of the civilian labor force unemployed, compared to 2.4 percent in the EU and 1.2 percent in Japan. "The Community Economic Outlook: 1995–1997," EUROPEAN ECONOMY, Supplement A, Economic Trends, No. 12—December 1995 (European Commission, Directorate-General for Economic and Financial Affairs, Table 18).

44. LESTER THUROW, HEAD TO HEAD: THE COMING ECONOMIC BATTLE AMONG JAPAN, EUROPE AND AMERICA (Morrow & Co., 1992), p. 87, *citing* Ferdinand Protzman, "East Germany's economy far Sicker than expected," New York Times, September 20, 1990, p. D6.

45. *Id.*, *citing* Guentin Peel, "Two sides of a coin to German monetary union," FINANCIAL TIMES, July 26, 1991, p. 2, and Deutsche Bank Economics Department, "Unification Issues: Growth Forecast for 1991 Revised Downward" (Deutsche Bank, 1991), p. 1.

46. LESTER THUROW, *op cit.*, p. 87.

47. "Credit Crunch," THE ECONOMIST, August 17–23, 1996, p. 14. "The affair is also noteworthy because it is the first time that the Commission, which has already dealt with hundreds of cases involving industrial firms such as steel makers or airlines, has to apply its state-aid rules to a bank."

48. Greg Steinmetz, "UPS confronts german postal monopoly," WALL STREET JOURNAL, March 25, 1996, p. 10. Nonetheless, UPS's German business has grown steadily from nearly 75 million deliveries in 1991 to almost 125 million deliveries in 1995.

49. The Community Economic Outlook, "Europeans Are Moving to Overhaul Welfare," *op. cit.*

50. Terrence Petty, "Protesters in Germany decry cuts in sick pay," BOSTON GLOBE, October 2, 1996, p. A2.

51. Joan Warner, "Where on earth can you turn?" BUSINESS WEEK, December 30, 1996–January 7, 1997, p. 100.

52. LESTER THUROW, *op cit.*, p. 192.

53. "IMF Warns over Fed's reluctance to raise rates," NEW YORK TIMES, September 26, 1996, *citing* FINANCIAL TIMES. The Commission agrees, as it expects output growth to be 2.6 percent in 1996 and 3 percent in 1997. "The Community Economic Outlook: 1995–1997," EUROPEAN ECONOMY, *op cit.*

54. EUROPEAN COMMISSION, THE EUROPEAN CHALLENGE 1992: THE BENEFITS OF A SINGLE MARKET (Gower Publishers, 1988), p. 89. *See also* Andrew Fisher, "Bundesbank urges structural reforms," FINANCIAL TIMES, February 20, 1997, p. 26; Commission of the European Communities, "Report on Convergence in the EU in 1996," COM (96) 560 Final (November 6, 1996), pp. 62–64.

55. Mercosur includes Argentina, Brazil, Paraguay and Uruguay.

56. Ted Baracke and Peter Montagnon, "Europe and Asia in accord to increase volume of exchange," and "Asia and the EU," FINANCIAL TIMES, March 4, 1996, pp. 4 and 17, respectively; Alicia Wylie, "Europe offers safe haven for nervous investors," LONDON TIMES, June 21, 1998, p. 43.

57. *See e.g.*, Tony Tassell, "Foreigners cool plans to invest in India," FINANCIAL TIMES, February 25, 1997, p. 4.

58. EUROSTAT, EUROPE IN FIGURES, *op cit.*, pp. 404–405. The EU created a Euromed economic zone at the Essen Summit in 1994.

59. *Id.*, p. 406.

CHAPTER 5. GLOBAL TRADE AND GLOBAL "GOVERNMENT"

1. *See e.g.*, LESTER THUROW, HEAD TO HEAD: THE COMING ECONOMIC BATTLE AMONG JAPAN, EUROPE AND AMERICA (Morrow & Co., 1992); Paul Krugman, "Competitiveness: Does It Matter?" FORTUNE, March 7, 1994, p. 109; "The Fight over Competitiveness: A Zero-Sum Debate?" FOREIGN AFFAIRS, July/August 1994, p. 186.

2. This is the report of the MIT Commission on Industrial Productivity (MIT Press, 1989). It is heavy reading, and many of its recommendations have come to pass.

3. Peter Wilson, "Clinton puts free trade at top of agenda," THE AUSTRALIAN, November 28, 1996, p. 1.

4. MILES KAHLER, REGIONAL FUTURES AND TRANSATLANTIC ECONOMIC RELATIONS (Council on Foreign Relations Press, 1995), p. 44.

5. EC Delegation (Washington), EUROPEAN UNION NEWS, No. 66196 (November 7, 1996).

6. "EU Properly Labeled LAN Equipment as Telecom Apparatus, WTO Body Rules," 15 ITR 1013 (June 10, 1998).

7. Martin Walker, "Clinton's Foreign Policy and Europe," EUROPE, October 1996, p. 12; Lionel Barber, "EU-US Relations," EUROPE, November 1996, p. ESR2.

8. GATT (Uruguay Round), article XXIV: 5(b) recognizes and permits regional trading blocks if they involve "substantially all of the trade" between the constituent countries. This is true of NAFTA, but wouldn't be of the proposed TAFTA.

9. Bruce Barnard, "Where the Action Is: Investing in Europe," EUROPE, November 1996, p. 26.

10. "45 years of doing the rounds," FINANCIAL TIMES, December 16, 1993, pp. 4–5.

11. Caroline Southey, "EU struggle for deal on pollution," FINANCIAL TIMES, March 3, 1997, p. 2.

12. Alan Cane, "Getting through: Why these talks matter," FINANCIAL TIMES, February 14, 1997, p. 6; Frances Williams and Alan Cane, "World telecoms pact set to slash phone call costs," FINANCIAL TIMES, February 17, 1997, p. 1; Alan Cane, "A ringing endorsement," FINANCIAL TIMES, February 18, 1997, p. 21.

13. Guy de Jonquières, "Template for trade talks," FINANCIAL TIMES, February 18, 1997, p. 21; Paul Taylor, "Top-tier software companies 'must be global'," FINANCIAL TIMES, February 5, 1997, p. 2 FT-IT.

14. "Singapore Meeting Boosts WTO, Trade Liberalization," EURECOM, January 1997, p. 1. *See generally*, World Trade Organization, "Singapore Ministerial Declaration," 13 December 1996.

15. Guy de Jonquières, "WTO urged to act on regional pacts," FINANCIAL TIMES, February 6, 1997, p. 6. *See generally*, MILES KAHLER, *op cit.*, pp. 41–58.

16. See generally, LESTER THUROW, THE FUTURE OF CAPITALISM (Morrow & Co., 1996), pp. 134–140.

17. "1998 World Population Data Sheet," http://www.prb.org/prb/info/98wpds.htm; "Where next?" THE ECONOMIST (A Survey of World Trade), October 3, 1998, p. 1; "In Brief," EURECOM, October 1997, p. 3; Emma Tucker, "Europe outpaced by US on competition," FINANCIAL TIMES, November 16, 1998, p. 18. See generally, OPEN MARKETS MATTER: THE BENEFITS OF TRADE AND INVESTMENT LIBERALIZATION (Organisation for Economic Co-operation and Development, 1998).

CHAPTER 6. THE UNITED STATES

1. U.S. President Calvin Coolidge, Speech to the Society of American Newspaper Editors, January 17, 1925.

2. LESTER THUROW, HEAD TO HEAD: THE COMING ECONOMIC BATTLE AMONG JAPAN, EUROPE AND AMERICA (Morrow & Co., 1992), pp. 56–66.

3. MIT, MADE IN AMERICA (MIT Press, 1987).

4. Murray Weidenbaum, "American Isolationism versus the Global Economy," EXECUTIVE SPEECHES, February/March 1996, pp. 18–22.

5. MILES KAHLER, REGIONAL FUTURES AND TRANSATLANIC ECONOMIC RELATIONS (Council on Foreign Relations Press, 1995), pp. 6–10, 17–19, 45–48.

6. See generally, PAUL KRUGMAN, PEDDLING PROSPERITY: ECONOMIC SENSE AND NONSENSE IN THE AGE OF DIMINISHED EXPECTATIONS (W.W. Norton, 1994), especially pp. 109–129, 229–280. *See also*, Alan Farnham, "Global—or Just Globaloney?" FORTUNE, June 27, 1994, p. 97.

7. Kim Clark, "FORTUNE's Global 500: A Bigger, Richer World," FORTUNE, August 5, 1996, p. 102.

8. *Id.*, pp. 104, F 1–2.

9. *Id.*, pp. 104, 108.

10. Louis Richman, "Global Growth Is on a Tear," FORTUNE, March 20, 1995, pp. 108–114.

11. *Id.*

12. Murray Weidenbaum, *op cit.*

13. Gerard Barber, "US trade deficit hits record," FINANCIAL TIMES, May 21, 1998, p. 1; "U.S. Trade Deficit Widened in March, Reflecting Fallout from Asian Turmoil," 15 ITR 924 (May 27, 1998); "Japan's April Trade Surplus with U.S. Rose 29.2 Percent," 15 ITR 918 (May 27, 1998); "Jasinowski Sees Mounting Protectionism," 15 ITR 970 (May 27, 1998); Gerard Baker, "Service jobs boost counters Asia crisis," FINANCIAL TIMES, June 6–7, 1998, p. 1.

14. Irwin Stelzer, "Growing trade gap stirs protectionists," The LONDON TIMES, March 23, 1997, p. 3.8; Nancy Dunne, "Record US trade gap as imports surge," FINANCIAL TIMES, March 21, 1997, p. 3.

15. John Naisbitt, "Global Paradox" ABI/INFORM, Vol. 13, No. 5, pp. 3–4.

16. *Id.*

17. "General Developments; Survey of Mid-size Manufactures," 13 ITR 1565 (October 9, 1996).

18. "General Developments, Foreign Investment; U.S. Net Global Investment Position in 1995," 13 ITR 28 d33 (July 10, 1996). See generally, EDWARD M. GRAHAM & PAUL R. KRUGMAN, FOREIGN DIRECT INVESTMENT IN THE UNITED STATES, 3RD ED. (Institute of International Economics, 1994).

19. Samer Iskandar & Conner Middelmann, "Capital markets borrowing reaches record level," FINANCIAL TIMES, March 5, 1996, p. 7.

20. "1996 Trade Figures," 14 ITR 325 (February 26, 1997); "U.S.–Europe Economic Relationship Called Strong, Major Source of Jobs," 13 ITR 1425 (September 11, 1996); Peter Koenig, "If Europe's Dead, Why Is GE Investing Billions There?" FORTUNE, September 9, 1996, p. 114.

21. Stewart Toy & others, "Europe for sale," BUSINESS WEEK, July 19, 1993, pp. 38–39.

22. Larry Reynolds, "US Firms Create Jobs in Europe," EUROPE, September 1996, pp. 26–27; Bruce Barnard, "Europe's Entrepreneurs: Creating Jobs Globally," EUROPE, September 1996, pp. 18–21.

23. Vivian Brownstein, "The U.S. Is Set to Be the Winner from Worldwide Expansion," FORTUNE, November 28, 1994, pp. 22–23; Guy de Jonquières, "U.S. ranked as 'most competitive' nation," FINANCIAL TIMES, September 6, 1995, p. 5, *citing* WORLD ECONOMIC FORUM, THE WORLD COMPETITIVENESS REPORT (Geneva, n.d.).

24. For an enlightening essay about how business might contribute to solving social problems, *see* Laurie Morse, "International youth: Global companies' most pressing case," FINANCIAL TIMES, February 2, 1996, p. I.

25. "Sir Leon Brittan, Europe's trade commissioner, yesterday warned the US that its attempts to solve trade disputes through unilateral action were no longer effective and called for a new co-operative approach based on multilateral principles. . . . 'An increasing number of countries are now prepared to resist unilateral pressure.' . . . He said the EU and the US had worked hard [in the Uruguay Round of GATT] to establish an effective multilateral trade system and now must make it work." Guy de

Jonquières, "Brittan urges US to stop use of unilateral trade pressure," FINANCIAL TIMES, March 20, 1996, p. 6. See also, "Sanctions: U.S. Trend Toward Unilateral Action 'Disturbing,' Canadian Official Says," 13 ITR 15 d34 (April 10, 1996).

26. So-called clawback or blocking laws make it punishable in a foreign country to release records or otherwise cooperate with a U.S. investigation or suit that is thought to intrude on the sovereignty or prerogative of the legislating country. If there is recovery in a U.S. court, the defendant is allowed to sue in foreign courts to "clawback" damages.

27. "U.S. to Unveil Broad Strategy to Fight Foreign Practices That Hurt U.S. Firms," 13 ITR 21 d12 (May 22, 1996).

28. Trade Act of 1974, 19 U.S.C § 2411, particularly as amended by Pub. L. No. 100–418 (1988) and Pub. L. No. 103–465 (1994). *See*, for example: "USTR Fact Sheet on Special 301 Findings," 13 ITR 17 d82 (May 1, 1996); Nancy Dunne, "Not so super 301 after all," FINANCIAL TIMES, October 6, 1994, p. 6.

29. Cuban Liberty and Democratic Solidarity (Libertad) Act of 1996, Pub. L. No. 102–484, codified as 22 U.S.C. § 6001 *et seq.*, amending the Cuban Democracy Act of 1992, Pub. L. No. 102–484.

30. The following articles drawn from the International Trade Reporter (ITR) and BNA International Trade Daily (BTD), respectively, give a quick sketch of the progress of this matter. Many other sources are available. "EU Protests Helms-Burton Law," 13 ITR 17 d35 (April 24, 1996); "EU Approves Response to Helms-Burton," 13 ITR 1684 (October 30, 1996); BTD, "Clinton Extends Suspension of Right to Sue Under Helms-Burton," 1/6/97 BTD d2; BTD, "U.S. says WTO Panel Not Competent to Judge Cuba Dispute," 2/21/97 BTD d3.

31. Guy de Jonquières and David Bucham, "Clinton yields to pressure over US trade initiatives," FINANCIAL TIMES, June 29–30, 1996, p. 1.

32. "Labor: Poll Shows Public Believes Agreements on Free Trade Lead to Fewer U.S. Jobs," 13 ITR 13 d21 (March 27, 1996); "In Brief," EURECOM, February 1997, p. 3; NAFTA Jobs Impact Termed Overstated," 14 ITR 25 (January 1, 1997).

33. The twelfth such report was published in July 1996. It is available from the European Commission. It is also available from the Bureau of National Affairs (BNA) in the U.S.

34. Stephen Fidler, "Mercosur: Trade pact sets the pace for integration," FINANCIAL TIMES, February 4, 1997, p. 16.

35. "Trade Policy: House Aides Draft Paper Calling for U.S.–Africa Free Trade Area by 2010," 13 ITR 23 d62 (June 5, 1996); "Foreign Investment: Vice President [Gore] Urges U.S. Companies to Continue to Invest in South Africa," 13 ITR 1211 (July 24, 1996). The latter reports that "U.S. companies with direct investments in South Africa have doubled their sales and assets in the country over the past three years." However, the number of companies involved is just 251, and the total investment just $2 billion.

36. Graham Bowley, "G10 recipe for bond defaulters," FINANCIAL TIMES, May 16, 1996, p. 5.

37. *See*, for example, "WTO Agenda Focuses on Technology, Telecommunications," 1/24/97 BTD d8.

38. "U.S. Promises WTO It Will Change Reformulated Gas Rules," 3/12/97 BTD d6.

39. "USTR Barshefsky Praises Ruling by WTO on Japan Liquor Tax Revision,"

2/19/97 BTD d9; "European Commission to Appeal WTO Panel's Banana Import Ruling," 3/12/97 BTD d9.

40. "WTO Agenda Focuses on Technology, Telecommunications," *op cit.*

41. This means that Congress gives the executive branch the authority—usually for a set period of time—to negotiate a treaty, the terms of which cannot be amended when the Senate is asked to ratify it. It must be approved in its entirety or not at all, such as the GATT and NAFTA. In the absence of such authority, our negotiating partners are less certain that the terms negotiated will be approved, since our president (unlike most heads of state) does not hold his office by virtue of controlling the largest number of seats in the legislature.

CHAPTER 7. AFTA' NAFTA: THE FREE TRADE AREA OF THE AMERICAS (FTAA)

1. Among innumerable commentaries, the following are illustrative: Martin & Kathleen Feldstein, "Who loses if NAFTA fails?" BOSTON GLOBE, October 19, 1993, p. 44; Thomas Schoenbaum, "The North American Free Trade Agreement (NAFTA): Good for Jobs, for the Environment, and for America," 23 GA.J. INT'L & COMP. L. 461 (1993); Russell Watson, "Everyone Has Got His Own Spin," NEWSWEEK, August 30, 1993, p. 42; Charles Stein, "Blue-Collar Woe Either Way," BOSTON GLOBE, November 17, 1993, p. 1. The NAFTA agreement provides for the phase-out of tariffs between Canada, Mexico and the U.S. over a fifteen-year period.

2. The most thorough and objective assessment of NAFTA's prospects that I have read is: U.S.–MEXICO TRADE: PULLING TOGETHER OR PULLING APART?, U.S. Congress, Office of Technology Assessment, U.S. G.P.O. (1992). *See also*, Patti Waldmeir, "Jobs aren't being sucked down Mexico way," FINANCIAL TIMES, February 27, 1996, p. 7.

3. "Canada-Japan Cooperation," 13 ITR 19 at 51 (May 8, 1996); "Canada, EU Sign Bilateral Customs Agreement," 14 ITR 2142 (December 10, 1997); "EU, Mexico Sign Trade Accord Calling for Free-Trade Talks in 1998," 14 ITR 2142 (December 10, 1997). Canada also is a member of the G-7 and APEC. Mexico also is an APEC member.

4. The full text of the NAFTA agreements is found at 32 I.L.M. 289 (December, 1992). Our 1988 free-trade agreement with Canada is at 27 I.L.M. 281 (January, 1988). A good interpretation of NAFTA's "side agreements" regarding labor and the environment are at 32 I.L.M. 1499 and 32 I.L.M. 1480, respectively (September, 1993).

5. "Mexico Is Second-Largest Buyer of U.S. Goods," 14 ITR 1121 (June 25, 1997).

6. "The Summit of the Americas, Second Ministerial Trade Meeting, Joint Declaration Adopted March 21, 1996," 12 ITR 13 at 94 (March 27, 1996).

7. "Canada's Export Performance Closely Linked to U.S. Economy, Study Shows," 13 ITR 17 at 34 (May 1, 1996). In 1994, 30.1 percent of Canada's GDP was attributable to exports (up from 21.6 percent in 1991), with 81.6 percent of those exports going to the United States. Since NAFTA began, Canada and Mexico "significantly increased their shares of the U.S. market," but Canada's share of that market for manufactured goods was only about 3 percent in 1994, with Mexico's

similarily low. Over one-half of Canada's goods trade with the U.S. is due to intra-firm trading.

8. "Canadian Trade," 13 ITR 1577 (October 9, 1996); "Canadian Export Strength to Weaken," 13 ITR 1907 (December 11, 1996); Caroline Southey, "Deal close over fishing rights," FINANCIAL TIMES, April 3, 1995, p. 1.

9. "Canada's Current Account Deficit Hit $2.28 Billion in Second Quarter" (its third consecutive quarterly deficit), 14 ITR 1476 (September 3, 1997); "Balance of Trade: Trade Among Canada's 10 Provinces [almost] As Important as Exports, Stats-can Says," 13 ITR 1352 (August 21, 1996); "NAFTA—EU Deal Is Canada's Best Hope to Revive Trade with Europe, Study Says," 14 ITR 1475 (September 3, 1997); "Marchi and Barshefsky discuss U.S.–Canada Trade Portfolio" (including wheat, salmon, Helms-Burton, and wool products), 14 ITR 1243 (July 16, 1997).

10. Initial results seemed very positive; a 17 percent rise in U.S. exports to Mexico (to record levels) in the first six months of 1994 (versus a year earlier) to $24.5 billion, and a 21 percent increase in imports from Mexico to $23.4 billion. "NAFTA succeeding," BOSTON GLOBE, August 19, 1994, p. 71. Even following the peso debacle, the assessment is modestly positive: "Administration Report says NAFTA Has Had Modest Positive Impact," 14 ITR 1241 (July 16, 1997).

11. Linda Chavez, "The myth of migrants and welfare," USA TODAY, May 3, 1994, p. 11A; Sam Verhovek, "Stop benefits for aliens? It wouldn't be that easy," New York Times, June 8, 1994, p. A1.

12. Leslie Crawford, "Mexicans lament the timing of U.S. operation on money laundering," FINANCIAL TIMES, May 22, 1998, p. 4; "Time to rock the boat," THE ECONOMIST, November 15, 1997, p. 17.

13. See generally, Harry Hurt, "It's Time to Get Real About Mexico," FORTUNE, September 4, 1995, pp. 98–108. Hurt reports that the latest "economic meltdown," in which the value of the Mexican peso plunged more than 40 percent, was the country's fourth in less than 20 years. He estimates that 20 percent of the population still lives on "roughly a dollar a day."

14. I give a reasonably full account of this episode, and the American and world response to it, in Chapter 18 of THE EUROPEANIZATION OF AMERICA: WHAT AMERICANS NEED TO KNOW ABOUT THE EUROPEAN UNION (Carolina Academic Press, 1995), pp. 305–310.

15. Leslie Crawford, "Austerity urged on Mexico [by OECD]," FINANCIAL TIMES, September 27, 1995, p. 8; "Mexico Moves to Repay Half of Remaining U.S. Bailout Debt," 13 ITR 22 at 26 (June 26, 1996); "Mexico's Market Seen Mending," 13 ITR 1282 (August 7, 1996).

16. Leslie Crawford, "Mexican economy bounces back," FINANCIAL TIMES, January 20, 1997, p. 4.

17. U.S. Congress, Office of Technology Assessment, PULLING TOGETHER, *op cit.*

18. "Proportion of U.S. FDI in Mexico Has Decreased Since Peso Crisis," 13 ITR 27 at 35 (July 3, 1996); "Mexican Trade Surplus $1.85 Billion for First Quarter of 1996, Data Say," 13 ITR 20 at 35 (May 15, 1996); "Trade Deficit Still a Concern for Mexico, Central American Nations," 13 ITR 1350 (August 21, 1996).

19. "Industrial Development Policy Announced by Mexican Official," 13 ITR 20 at 33 (May 15, 1996); "Mexican Economic Plan Calls for Growth Rate of at Least 5 Percent," 14 ITR 1047 (June 11, 1997).

20. "Mexico to Examine Options Following Latest Ruling," 4/7/97 BTD at 2;

"Dumping: Mexico Imposes Duties Against U.S.–Made Cellophane," 14 ITR 1004 (June 4, 1997); "Mexico Disputes NAFTA Challenge," 13 ITR 15 at 45 (April 10, 1996); "Florida Lawmakers Seek Enforcement of NAFTA Farm Issues in Fast-Track Debate," 14 ITR 1570 (September 17, 1997); "Mexico Faulted on Telecom Compliance . . . USTR Says," 13 ITR 15 at 28 (April 10, 1996).

21. PULLING TOGETHER, *op cit.*, pp. 108–109, 111, 98–99; Congressional Research Service (Mary Jane Bolle), "NAFTA: Estimates of Job Effects and Industry Trade Trends After Two Years" (updated April 19, 1996); Library of Congress; "New Survey [of Businesses] Shows Job Gains Under NAFTA," 15 ITR 427 (March 11, 1998). *Cf.* Jesse Rothstein & Robert Scott, "NAFTA's Casualties," Economic Policy Institute, Issue Brief #120, September 19, 1997. *See also*, PAUL KRUGMAN, "The Uncomfortable Truth About NAFTA," in POP INTERNATIONALISM (MIT Press, 1996), pp. 155–165.

22. *Id.*; PULLING TOGETHER, *op cit.*, p. 5; "Side Accord a Mechanism for Making Changes in Mexico, Unions Say," 13 ITR 1304 (August 14, 1996); "U.S., Mexico to Hold Conference on Labor Concerns," 14 ITR 1574 (September 17, 1997); "U.S.–Mexico Border Environmental Plan," 13 ITR 24 at 69 (June 12, 1996); "Evidence of NAFTA Environmental Impact Expected by End of 1996, Official Says," 13 ITR 28 at 52 (July 10, 1996); Leslie Crawford, "Clinton wins backing from Zedillo on trade," FINANCIAL TIMES, May 8, 1997, p. 6; "Mexico and U.S. explore common ground," FINANCIAL TIMES, May 6, 1997, p. 6.

23. Harry Hurt, "It's Time to Get Real About Mexico," FORTUNE, September 4, 1995, p. 102; Marc Levinson, "Oh No, Not NAFTA Again," NEWSWEEK, September 25, 1995, p. 59.

24. "NAFTA a Significant Influence on Mexican Agriculture, OECD Says," 14 ITR 2235 (December 24, 1997).

25. "New Guidelines Expected to Resolve NAFTA Contract Disputes," 13 ITR 1533 (October 2, 1996); "NAFTA Credited with Aiding Modernization of Mexico," 14 ITR 1396 (August 13, 1997); "Mexico Expands Maquiladora Program; Changes Expected to Boost Exports, Growth," 13 ITR 1670 (October 30, 1996); "NAFTA a Significant Influence on Mexican Agriculture, OECD Says," *op cit.*

26. Leslie Crawford & Daniel Dombey, "PRI loses control of Mexican congress," FINANCIAL TIMES, July 8, 1997, p. 1; Daniel Dombey, "Opposition to Mexico awakes to bigger role," FINANCIAL TIMES, September 1, 1997, p. 4; "Zedillio Urges New Congress to Stay Economic Course," 14 ITR 1472 (September 3, 1997); Leslie Crawford, "Mexico asks banks group for stand-by credit of up to $3.5 bn," FINANCIAL TIMES, September 26, 1997, p. 1.

27. PULLING TOGETHER, *op cit.*, pp. 4–6, 58–72, 115, 149, 159–172, 189 and 197–210; "Apparel Imports from Mexico, CBI Are Good for U.S. Industry, AMI," 14 ITR 1484 (September 3, 1997); "Vegetable Imports," 13 ITR 20 at 74 (May 15, 1996); "NAFTA Expands Cattle Trade with Mexico, ITC Reports," 14 ITR 1245 (July 16, 1997).

28. Mary Jane Bolle, "NAFTA: Estimates of Job Efforts and Industry Trends After Two Years," *op cit.*, pp. 2–5; "Nearly 133,000 Workers Eligible for Aid Under NAFTA Trade Assistance Program," 14 ITR 1246 (July 16, 1997); PAUL KRUGMAN, *op cit.*, p. 157.

29. Nancy Dunne & Phillip Gawith, "Washington hails NAFTA as success," FINANCIAL TIMES, August 19, 1994, p. 16; "NAFTA Spurs North American Trade,"

13 ITR 1537 (October 2, 1996); Office of the U.S. Trade Representative, STUDY ON THE OPERATION AND EFFECT OF THE NORTH AMERICAN TRADE AGREEMENT, G.P.O. Jacket #42788 (July 1997). In early 1997, two-way trade with Canada and Mexico accounted for 53 percent of the growth in U.S. firms, SUN JOURNAL, July 12, 1997, p. A9; "NAFTA Boosts Trade and Investment, but U.S. Firms Cite Non-Tariff Barriers," 14 ITR 1204 (July 9, 1997), *citing* an American Chamber of Commerce of Mexico report, based on a survey of 227 U.S. firms doing business in Mexico; RAÚL OJEDA AND OTHERS, NORTH AMERICAN INTEGRATION THREE YEARS AFTER NAFTA, UCLA (North American Integration and Development Center, December 1996). *Cf.*: "NAFTA Has Not Performed As Promised, Groups Say," 14 ITR 1149 (July 2, 1997), citing a report—THE FAILED EXPERIMENT: NAFTA AT THREE YEARS—by a number of public interest groups; but also conceding that NAFTA had "benefitted some North Americans."

30. International Trade Representative, "Agreement on Health Care Services Needed in NAFTA, Legal Opinion Says," 13 ITR 12 at 18 (March 20, 1996); "NAFTA Countries Working on Registry of Environmental Compliance by Firms," 13 ITR 1367 (September 4, 1996).

31. David K. Karnes, "International Trade at a Crossroads: The Role of International Law and International Institutions in the Post Uruguay Round Era," 71 Neb. L. Rev 438, 443–445 (1992); PAUL KRUGMAN, "Challenging Conventional Wisdom," in POP INTERNATIONALISM, *op cit.*, pp. 147–154.

32. "NAFTA Ministers Agree to New Tariff Cuts on Chemicals, Textiles, Manufactured Goods," 15 ITR 752 (April 29, 1998); "NAFTA Advisory Committee Is Exploring Alternative Dispute Settlement Mechanisms," 14 ITR 2235 (December 24, 1997).

33. LESTER THUROW, THE FUTURE OF CAPITALISM (Morrow & Co., 1996), pp. 254–261.

34. "Aaron Sees Shift in Greatest Opportunities for U.S. Business to Western Hemisphere," 15 ITR 832 (May 13, 1998); Geoff Dyer, "Washington on red alert over Brazil," FINANCIAL TIMES, September 29, 1998, p. 8.

35. Statistics from the U.S. BUREAU OF THE CENSUS, STATISTICAL ABSTRACT OF THE UNITED STATES: 1996, 116th ED. (U.S. GPO, 1996), display No. 1334, p. 835. Marc Levinson, "Let's Have No More Free-Trade Deals, Please," NEWSWEEK, August 17, 1992, p. 40; Sebastian Edwards, "Latin America's Under-performance," FOREIGN AFFAIRS, March/April 1997, p. 93; Nancy Dunne & others, "Clinton hails 'the quiet revolution'," FINANCIAL TIMES, October 10, 1997, p. 5.

36. Raymond Colitt, "Praise for region's democracy," FINANCIAL TIMES, October 14, 1997, p. 6; Mark Suzman, "Clinton set on fast-track for trade deals," FINANCIAL TIMES, October 20, 1997, p. 5; Geoff Dyer, "Lower trade barriers in Americas, says Clinton," FINANCIAL TIMES, October 16, 1997, p. 5.

37. Stephen Fidler, "Asian cloud hanging over Latin American," FINANCIAL TIMES, January 16, 1998, p. 3; "Latin America scrambles for capital," FINANCIAL TIMES, February 10, 1998, p. 3; Geoff Dyer, "Vote shows Brazil serious about tackling deficit," FINANCIAL TIMES, February 13, 1998, p. 7; "Business in Latin America: Back on the Pitch," THE ECONOMIST, December 6, 1997, p. 3; "Aaron Sees Shift in Greatest Opportunities for U.S. Business to Western Hemisphere," 15 ITR 832 (May 13, 1998).

38. Stephen Fidler, "Latin America: Chance to break the cycle of sorrow," FI-

NANCIAL TIMES, June 24, 1994, p. 5 (arguing that "economic measures" taken by many Latin American governments in the last five years have "brought budget deficits under control, ended years of protectionism and sharply reduced the role of government [in the economy]." He wonders, however, whether "the new economic order is politically sustainable" since "the benefits of reform are [not] equitably divided"; Raymond J. Ahearn, "Western Hemisphere Trade Developments," Congressional Research Service/Library of Congress, June 13, 1996 (96–54IF); "Latin American Growth Rate to Be 5 Percent," 14 ITR 1574 (September 17, 1997); "Argentine Investment," 13 ITR 1371 (September 4, 1996); "Joint Ventures, Buy-Outs Increase in Brazil as Foreign Investment Rises," 13 ITR 24 d47 (June 12, 1996).

39. "FTAA Hemispheric Trade Negotiations Strain Smaller Countries' Resources," 14 ITR 1637 (September 24, 1997); "USTR Official Signals U.S. Readiness to Help Smaller Economies in FTAA Process," 14 ITR 1077 (June 18, 1997).

40. U.S. BUREAU OF THE CENSUS, STATISTICAL ABSTRACT OF THE UNITED STATES: 1996, *op cit.*, p. 835; "Brazil Will Oppose Efforts to Accelerate Tariff Reductions Under FTAA, Official Says," 14 ITR 1147 (July 2, 1997).

41. Jonathan Wheatley, "First Brazilian rail concession sold to U.S.–led consortium," FINANCIAL TIMES, March 6, 1996, p. 1; "U.S. Investors Buy Brazilian Rail Line; Bank, Mining, Electric to Be Privatized," 13 ITR 15 d31 (April 10, 1996); "Brazil Official Announces Speedup of Plans to Open Up Telecom Market," 13 ITR 25 d22 (June 19, 1996).

42. Jonathan Wheatley, "Brazil falls out with its trading partners," FINANCIAL TIMES, July 30, 1996, p. 4; Geoff Dyer, "Optimism in short supply in Brazil," FINANCIAL TIMES, November 15, 1996, p. 6; Richard Lapper, "Latin America 'facing recession this year'," FINANCIAL TIMES, March 16, 1998, p. 8; "Mercosur Leaders Stress Unity in Face of Brazil's Economic Crisis," 16 ITR 335 (February 24, 1999).

43. Geoff Dyer, "Brazil provokes jitters in world markets," FINANCIAL TIMES, January 8, 1999, p. 1; Stephen Fidler & Geoff Dyer, "Brazil moves to limit damage," FINANCIAL TIMES, January 18, 1999, p. 1; "Storm clouds from Brazil," THE ECONOMIST, January 16, 1999, p. 17; Sara Webb, "Emerging Markets Get Fresh Look," WALL STREET JOURNAL, January 19, 1999, p. C1.

44. "Venezuela Committed to Reform, Cleaning Up Corruption," 14 ITR 1572 (September 17, 1997); Raymond Colitt, "IMF stamp of approval for Venezuela," FINANCIAL TIMES, May 9, 1997, p. 3; "Chrysler Neon Produced in Venezuela," 13 ITR 17 d51 (May 1, 1996). *Cf.* ROGER FONTAINE, VENEZUELA: FROM SHOWCASE TO BASKETCASE (Cato Institute, 1996).

45. "Direct Foreign Investment in Argentina Hit $18 Billion in 1994–95, Study Says," 13 ITR 12 d20 (March 20, 1996); "Argentine Government to Seek Approval for Privatization of Energy Facilities," 13 ITR 13 d20 (March 27, 1996).

46. David Pilling, "Argentina paralyzed by strike over economic policy," FINANCIAL TIMES, August 9, 1996, p. 12; Ken Warn, "Argentina tries to do justice to demands for legal reform," FINANCIAL TIMES, September 16, 1997, p. 4.

47. "Chile expects nod to join NAFTA," BOSTON GLOBE, December 2, 1994, p. 23; "No Chile Fast-Track Authority in '96, White House Advisor Says," 13 ITR 19 d28 (May 8, 1996); "Chile Significant Recipient of Aid in South America," 14 ITR 1732 (October 8, 1997).

48. Stephen Fidler, "Mercosur: Trade pact sets the pace for integration," FINAN-

CIAL TIMES, February 4, 1997, p. 16; "Venezuela May Will [*sic:* Join?] Mercosur by End of 1996, Sources Say," 13 ITR 1348 (August 21, 1996); "Mercosur Countries to Establish Supranational Bank and Court," 13 ITR 24 d42 (June 12, 1996); "EU Signs Accord with Mercosur," EURECOM, January 1996, p. 2.

49. "Canadian, Mercosur Officials to Discuss Association Accord," 14 ITR 1119 (June 25, 1997); "Former Mexican Official Says NAFTA Model Is WTO-Compatible, Preferable to Mercosur," 13 ITR 1869 (December 4, 1996).

50. Raymond J. Ahearn, "Western Hemisphere Trade Developments," Congressional Research Service 96–541 F (June 13, 1996), Library of Congress, pp. CRS-2–6.

51. "Mercosur, Andean Nations to Sign Framework Agreement," 15 ITR 423 (March 11, 1998); "Sub-regional Integration May Impede FTAA, Expert Says," 15 ITR 833 (May 13, 1998); Imogen Mark, "U.S. sidelined as Mercosur power grows," FINANCIAL TIMES, April 20, 1998, p. 3.

52. "Chile's Mercosur Membership Takes Effect," 13 ITR 1576 (October 9, 1996); "Columbia Implements Market-Opening Measures but Some Investment Barriers Remain, WTO Says," 13 ITR 1536 (October 2, 1996); "Administration Is Ready to Work on [Caribbean Basin Initiative] Compromise Lang Says," 14 ITR 1635 (September 24, 1997). The CBI would help a number of small economies in the Caribbean Basin by giving their products the same duty and quota treatment that Mexico receives under NAFTA.

53. "Clinton Expresses Support for Mercosur, Urges Resolution of Brazilian Disputes," 14 ITR 1769 (October 15, 1997); Stephen Fidler & Leslie Crawford, "American leaders to start Free Trade Area talks," FINANCIAL TIMES, February 27, 1998, p. 5; "Mercosur: FTAA Talks Can Advance Despite U.S. Inaction on Fast Track," 15 ITR 285 (February 18, 1998); "Summit Leaders Officially Endorse Launch of Negotiations for FTAA," 15 ITR 701 (April 22, 1998). *See also*, RICHARD FEINBERG, SUMMITRY IN THE AMERICAS: A PROGRESS REPORT (Institute for International Economics, 1997).

54. John H. Jackson, "Keeping the President on the Fast Track," LAW QUADRANGLE NOTES (University Michigan), Fall/Winter 1997, pp. 74–75; Nancy Dunne, "Clinton goes too slowly on fast-track," FINANCIAL TIMES, September 24, 1997, p. 4; Ed Brown, "It's Put Up or Shut Up Time for U.S. Trade Policy," FORTUNE, October 27, 1997, p. 34; "Clinton Urges Senate Leaders to Vote for Fast-Track Legislation This Year," 14 ITR 1804 (October 22, 1997).

55. "Next FTAA Declaration Will Provide Legal Framework for Negotiations," 14 ITR 1393 (August 13, 1997); "Chairs of 11 FTAA Working Groups Meet to Improve Coordination, Private Sector Input," 13 ITR 1305 (August 14, 1996); Geoff Dyer, "Americas' free trade talks get green light," FINANCIAL TIMES, May 19, 1997, p. 4; "Summit Leaders Officially Endorse Launch of Negotiations for FTAA," *op cit.*

56. "Services Forum Makes Recommendations on FTAA," 14 ITR 1829 (October 22, 1997); "U.S. Business Urge 'Swift' Approval of Fast Track," 14 ITR 1609 (September 24, 1997); "Governors Urge Quick Action on Fast Track," 14 ITR 1814 (October 22, 1997). The text of the initial "fast-track" legislative proposals can be found at: 14 ITR 1687 (October 1, 1997) [Senate]; 14 ITR 1788 (October 15, 1997) [House]. The president's fast-track proposal and accompanying documents are at 14 ITR 1585 (September 17, 1997).

57. "U.S., Canada Will Talk with Mercosur With or Without Mexico, Official Says," 13 ITR 26 d11 (June 26, 1996).

58. Stephen Fidler, "Is Latin America on market hit list?" FINANCIAL TIMES, September 9, 1997, p. 7; "Latin America Urged to Cooperate with Private Sector, Avoid Populism," 13 ITR 28 d53 (July 10, 1996).

59. "USTR Official Signals U.S. Readiness to Help Smaller Economies in FTAA Process," 14 ITR 1077 (June 18, 1997); "Eizenstat Says FTAA Standards Should Match the Best of NAFTA and WTO," 13 ITR 1716 (November 6, 1996).

CHAPTER 8. THE EUROPEAN UNION: CAN IT COMPETE?

1. THE WORLD BANK, WORLD DEVELOPMENT REPORT: KNOWLEDGE FOR DEVELOPMENT, 1998/99, Table 1, pp. 190–191 (1997 figures).

2. Speech at Zurich University, September 19, 1946. *See also*, Quentin Peel, "Churchill's vision of Europ[e] recalled," FINANCIAL TIMES, September 18, 1996, p. 10.

3. Proposed by then Secretary of State George C. Marshall, in a speech at Harvard University, July 5, 1997.

4. Most of this information is available from small brochures published by the European Commission. A short treatment is Lionel Barber, "Europe since the Rome Treaty" and "Forty and fatter but it's still worth celebrating," FINANCIAL TIMES, March 25, 1997, p. 3. For a long time, the various European treaties were published as free-standing documents. There was no single comprehensive, amended treaty. Now there is a single source for treaty material.

5. Commission of the European Communities, EUROBAROMETER [Public Opinion and Europe], #45, Spring 1996; Gilliam Tet and others, "Slowdown hits confidence in EU," FINANCIAL TIMES, January 16, 1996, p. 2.

6. A good, short discussion of EU–U.S. relations from 1946 to 1996 is: Reginald Dale, "Marshall to Maastricht: US–European Relations since World War II," EUROPE, June 1995, pp. 12–15.

7. For example, Michael Smith, "EU seeks 30% rise in wine subsidies to beat off competitors," FINANCIAL TIMES, June 15, 1998, p. 1.

8. Guy de Jonquières, "EU embraces the cause of free trade," FINANCIAL TIMES, August 6, 1996, p. 5; Kiernan Cooke, "An Asian embrace for Europe," FINANCIAL TIMES, September 25, 1995, p. 4.

9. Martin Walker, "The European Political Landscape '96," EUROPE, October 1996, pp. 25–31.

10. See for example, THE EUROPEAN CHALLENGE/1992: THE BENEFITS OF A SINGLE MARKET (Cecchini Report) (Gower Publishing Co., 1988); Jacques Delors, Address to the European Parliament, January 1991; Frances Williams, "Europe seen slipping behind a global competitiveness," FINANCIAL TIMES, May 30, 1996, p. 5 (*citing* a GLOBAL COMPETITIVENESS REPORT by the World Economic Forum in Geneva); "The EU's feel-bad factor," THE ECONOMIST, September 30, 1995, pp. 57–58.

11. *Id.*; Peter Norman, "Kohl calls on Germans to become risk takers," FINANCIAL TIMES, October 17, 1995, p. 1; Jay Branegan & others, "Europe: Why a Good

Job Is Hard to Find: Despite Political Promises, the Problem of Unemployment Is Only Getting Worse," TIME, February 26, 1996, p. 20.

12. Leon Brittan and John Redwood, "EU: Angel or Demon?" FINANCIAL TIMES, May 16, 1996, p. 11; Lionel Barber, "EU streamlining splits Bonn and Paris," FINANCIAL TIMES, April 8, 1993, p. 2.

13. Commission President Jacques Santer, Address to the European Parliament, "The Commission Programme for 1997," COM (96) 507 final and SEC (96) 1819 final, both October 17, 1996, Brussels; *See also*, "The Dutch presidency of the EU, 1 January to 30 June 1997," procured from the Royal Netherlands Embassy, London, January 8, 1997; Ian Davidson, "A budding agenda," FINANCIAL TIMES, April 2, 1997, p. 20.

14. *See*, Stanley Hoffmann, "Back to Euro-Pessimism?" FOREIGN AFFAIRS, January/February 1997, p. 139, at 140, reviewing TONY JUDT, A GRAND ILLUSION? AN ESSAY ON EUROPE (Hill & Wang, 1996). Lionel Barber, "EU streamlining splits Bonn and Paris," *op cit.*, p. 2; Axel Krause, "What Is France's Long-Term Strategy?" EUROPE, May 1998, p. 8; Philip Stehewus, "Demon in the wings," FINANCIAL TIMES, April 7, 1997, p. 20; Peter Norman, "Germany to seek ceiling for contributions to EU," FINANCIAL TIMES, September 9, 1996, p. 3; Neil Buckley and others, "Budget row threatens EU summit," FINANCIAL TIMES, June 15, 1998, p. 2.

15. Martin Walker, "The European Political Landscape '96," *op cit.*

16. Michael Cassell, "Implementation of EU law 'over-zealous'," FINANCIAL TIMES, November 7, 1995, p. 8; "The Laws of Canute," THE ECONOMIST, October 7, 1995, p. 62.

17. Case c-91/92 Faccini Dori v. Recreb Srl [1995] 1 CMLR 665 (July 14, 1994).

18. "EU Invests Mostly in Itself" (In Brief), EURECOM, September 1996, p. 3. *See also*, Martin Walker, "US is looking to Europe again," EUROPE, (Inside), July/August 1994.

19. Robert Rice, "A law unto themselves," FINANCIAL TIMES, April 3, 1997, p. 23; "Advisers on global completed deals," FINANCIAL TIMES, January 31, 1997, p. IV 4. According to the last source, of the top ten advisers on mergers and acquisitions (the top being Morgan Stanley), seven are U.S. firms, accounting for nearly three-quarters of the market share, nearly 1,100 deals and a value of $901,841 million.

20. According to a study by the OECD, the EU and its member states provided more than $31 billion (53.5 percent) of the world total of development aid in 1995. Most of that went to ACP (Lomé convention) countries, but that relationship is due to be reviewed (and probably altered) in the year 2000. Japan provides 24.4 percent of world development aid; the U.S., 12.4 percent. *Cited* by Dick Leonard, "Eye on the EU," EUROPE, March 1997, pp. 4–5.

21. DOMINIC LASOK & JOHN BRIDGE, LAW & INSTITUTIONS OF THE EUROPEAN COMMUNITIES, 6TH ED. (Butterworths, 1994); P.S.R.F. MATHIJSEN, A GUIDE TO EUROPEAN COMMUNITY LAW, 6TH ED. (Sweet & Maxwell, 1995); DAVID A. EDWARD & ROBERT C. LANE, EUROPEAN COMMUNITY LAW: AN INTRODUCTION, 2ND ED. (Butterworths, 1995); THOMAS C. FISCHER, THE EUROPEANIZATION OF AMERICA: WHAT AMERICANS NEED TO KNOW ABOUT THE EUROPEAN UNION (Carolina Academic Press, 1995). This book was written expressly as a primer for American businesspersons.

22. The desk reference I recommend is published in Luxembourg by the Office for Official Publications of the European Communities: EUROPEAN UNION, SELECTED INSTRUMENTS TAKEN FROM THE TREATIES, 2 vols., 1995. The treaty proper is in volume I, pp. 91–402. An amended version will undoubtedly be published now that the Treaty of Amsterdam (May 1999) has been ratified.

23. *See*, for example, Case 45/86 Commission v. Council.

24. Two oft-cited examples are: THE FEDERALIST (many publishers) and ALEXIS DE TOCQUEVILLE, DEMOCRACY IN AMERICA (Gryphon, 1988).

25. *See*, for example, Fullilove v. Klutznick, 65 L. Ed. 2d 902 (1980), involving affirmative action, or Shaw v. Reno 215 L. Ed. 2d 511(1993); Case 22/70 Commission v. Council [1985] ECR 1513, involving the respective roles of Community institutions under the treaties.

26. For example, Case 45/86 Commission v. Council (Generalized Tariff Preferences) [1987] ECR 1493; Case 68/86United Kingdom v. Council (Hormones) [1988] ECR 855. Article 3b* of the Treaty provides: "The Community shall act within the limits of the powers conferred upon it by this Treaty."

27. TEU, articles 3b and 4–4b.

28. *See, e.g.*, European Commission v. European Council (ERTA), [1971] ECR 263.

29. TEU, articles 210 and 211.

30. My own brief treatment is in THE EUROPEANIZATION OF AMERICA, pp. 65–76. Other standard treatments are in: T. C. HARTLEY, THE FOUNDATIONS OF EUROPEAN COMMUNITY LAW, 3RD ED. (Clarendon Press, 1994), pp. 38–48; P.S.R.F. MATHIJSEN, *op cit.*, pp. 29–35; LASOK & BRIDGE, *op cit.*, pp. 197–204, pp. 219–222. A good, although dated, study of the dynamics of Community decision-making is: E. J. KIRCHNER, DECISION MAKING IN THE EUROPEAN COMMUNITY (St. Martin's Press, 1992), written before the Maastricht co-decision process was adopted.

31. TEU, article 189.

32. For example, cases C-6 and 9/90 Francovich v. Italy [1991] ECR I-535; and C-91/92 Dori v. Recreb Src [1994] ECR 3325.

33. For example, case C-101/91 Commission v. Italian Republic [1993] ECR I-191.

34. For example, case 792/79R Camera Care Ltd. v. Commission [1980] ECR 119; cases C-48 and 66/90 Netherlands v. Commission 1992 ECR I-565.

35. TEU, articles 173 and 189. Case 60/81 International Business Machines v. Commission [1981] ECR 2639.

36. Cases 16–17/62 conféderation nationale de Producteurs de Fruits et Légumes v. Council [1962] ECR 471. TEU, article 190, requires that "[r]egulations, directives and decisions . . . shall state the reasons on which they are based." *See*, case 248/84 Germany v. Commission [1989] 1 CMLR 591. A rather good treatment of the forms of Community legislation is found in LASOK & Bridge, *op cit.*, pp. 112–135.

*The cites in these notes are drawn from the consolidated treaties of the EC and EU through the Treaty on European Union (Masstricht). The Treaty of Amsterdam (May 1999) renumbered most treaty titles, articles and sections. The Appendix at the back of this book will enable the reader to convert to from one numbering system to another.

37. The broadest set of these allowances is in article 36, modifying articles 30 to 34, respecting the free movement of goods, and allows "prohibitions . . . on imports, exports or goods in transit justified [by] public morality, public policy or public security; the protection of health and life of humans, animals or plants; the protection of national treasures possessing artistic, historic or archaeological value; or the protection of industrial and commercial property." Other, generally narrower, allowances are to be found in other treaty passages, modifying other legislative programs, notably: Articles 48(3), 55, 56(1), 66, 73(c)-(g), 75(3), 92, 93, 100, 103(a)(2), 198, 198(h)-(i), K, and (L), and 115.

38. *See*, for example, case 41/74 Yvonne van Duyn v. Home Office [1974] ECR 1337; case 48/75 State v. Jean Noël Royer [1976] ECR 497; case 8/74 Procureur du Roi v. Dassonville [1974] ECR 837; case 120/78 Rewe-Zentral AG v. Bundesmonopolverwaltung für Branntwein (Cassis de Dijon) [1979 ECR 649; case 286/82 and 26/83 Luisi and Carbone v. Ministero du Tesoro [1984] ECR 377.

39. Case 26/62 van Gend and Loos v. Nederlandse Administratie de Belastingen [1963] ECR 1; Case 6/64 Costa v. ENEL [1964] ECR 585. A truly excellent short article that deals broadly with EU lawmaking and enforcement is: Bernhard Grossfeld, "The Internal Dynamics of the European Community Law," 26 INT'L LAWYER 125 (1992).

40. For example, case 10/56 Meroni v. High Authority (ECSC) [1957–58] ECR 133. (Duty to "state reasons," art. 190.)

41. For example, case 138/79 Roquette Frères v. Council [1980] ECR 3333. (The European Parliament had a right to be consulted under the treaty and was not.)

42. For example, case 4/73 J. Nold KG v. Commission [1974] ECR 491; case 112/77 August Töfer and Co. v. Commission [1978] ECR 1019.

43. For example, case 105/75 Guiffrida v. Council [1976] ECR 1395. (The power to appoint Community officials was proper, but was misused to advance a particular individual.)

44. Case 166/78 Italy v. Council [1979] ECR 2575.

45. Case 141/78 France v. United Kingdom [1978] ECR 2923 is an exception.

46. Compare case 302/87 European Parliament v. Council [1988] ECR 5615 with case C-70/88 European Parliament v. Council [1991] ECR I-2041, the problem now cured by the Maastricht Treaty's revision of article 173.

47. It is possible for a regulation or a decision addressed to another to comprehend so small a group that all of them could be said to be "directly concerned." *See*, for example, cases 16–17/62 Confédération Nationale v. Council [1962] ECR 471; cases 41–44/70 NV International Fruit v. Commission [1971] ECR 411.

48. TEU, article 173.

49. EEC articles 185, 186 and 192.

50. *See*, for example, case 6/72 Europeamballage Corporation and Continental Can v. Commission [1973] ECR 215; Case C-221/89 R. v. Secretary of State for Transport, ex parte Factortame [1991] ECR I-3956.

51. *See*, for example, case 41/74 Yvonne van Duyn v. Home Office [1974] ECR 1337 (right to travel) case 71/76 Jean Thieffry v. Conseil de Paris [1977] ECR 765 (right to establish); case 6 and 9/90 Francovich v. Italy [1993] 2 CMLR 66.

52. TEU, article 177.

53. U.S. Constitution, Article IV, §1, provides, in relevant part: "Full Faith and

Credit shall be given in each State to the public Acts, Records, and judicial Proceedings of every other State."

54. For EC purposes, this is reported at OJ L-304/77 (October 30, 1978), as amended.

55. *Id.* Articles 2–24 (jurisdiction) and 25–45 (recognition and enforcement), respectively. A decent, short treatment will be found at LASOK & BRIDGE, *op cit.*, pp. 762–767.

56. TEU, article B, paragraph 5 provides for the IGC. The IGC amendment process is TEU article N(1), but revision in 1996 was limited to express articles (TEU, article N (2)).

57. After a Danish referendum initially rejected the Treaty, resistance to it increased throughout Europe. For a brief treatment of the process of ratification, *see*: THE EUROPEANIZATION OF AMERICA, *op cit.*, pp. 119–120, 139–140.

58. Secretariat General, European Commission, "Report to the 1996 IGC; Contribution of the European Commission, Commission Opinion: Reinforcing Political Union and Preparing for Enlargement" (February 28, 1996.) *See also*, Emma Tucker, "Brussels advances plans to end the national veto; EU federalist agenda set to go before conference," FINANCIAL TIMES, February 22, 1996, p. 12.

59. Reflection Group's Report (Brussels; December 5, 1995), SN 520/95 (REFLEX 21). *Cf.*: Robert Taylor & Caroline Southey, "Heavy fire aimed at EU 'wise men'," FINANCIAL TIMES, June 19, 1995, p. 2; Lionel Barber, "EU divisions surface over Reflection Group report," FINANCIAL TIMES, December 6, 1995, p. 2. *See also*: Michael Netwich & Gerda Falkner, "Intergovernmental Conference 1996: Which Constitution for the Union?" 2 EUR. L. J., pp. 83–102 (March 1996).

60. "A Partnership of Nations" (White Paper of the U.K. government concerning the 1996 IGC), March 1996.

61. Amsterdam Treaty, Chapter 15, The Council, especially Treaty article 151.

62. European Commission, "The Commission's Work Programme for 1997," COM (96) 507 final (October 17, 1996).

63. Amsterdam Treaty, Chapter 17, the Court of Justice, amending Article L of the Maastricht Treaty.

64. Amsterdam Treaty, Chapter 18, Other Institutional Issues, sections (a) to (f); Chapter 19, Role of National Parliaments (Draft Protocol on the Role of National Parliaments in the EU).

65. Amsterdam Treaty, Closer Cooperation—"Flexibility," Sections A to C; "Goodby, Federal Europe?" THE ECONOMIST, November 15, 1997, p. 51; "Euro-apartheid?" THE ECONOMIST, November 22, 1997, pp. 55.

66. Amsterdam European Council, Draft Treaty of Amsterdam (Document CONF/4001/97), June 19, 1997; hereinafter "Amsterdam Treaty" (brought into force May 1999).

67. "EU Leaders Put Off Reforming Commission, Council of Ministers," 14 ITR 1116 (June 25, 1997).

68. I addressed this question in an article comparing EU and U.S. "federalism," concluding that they are different, at present. Thomas C. Fischer, " 'Federalism' in the European Community and the U.S.: A Rose by Any Other Name," 17 FORDHAM INT'L L. J. 389 (1994).

69. *McCullock v. Maryland*, 17 U.S. (4 Wheat.) 316 (1819).

70. ALEXIS DE TOCQUEVILLE, DEMOCRACY IN AMERICA (Gryphon, 1988), p. 311.

71. Fischer, "Federalism," *op cit.*, pp. 401–403.

CHAPTER 9. THE EUROPEAN UNION PROGRAM

1. This language appears in treaty Article 3, as amended.

2. The terms "approximation" and "harmonization" are used throughout the treaties, almost interchangeably. Purists tell me there is a difference, however. This language is taken from Article 3(h).

3. TEU, article 9(l).

4. These four "freedoms" form the core (as well as the opening Articles) of the EEC Treaty. They still are the centerpiece of the amended treaties, comprising TEU Articles 9–73(h), inclusive, excepting Articles 38–47 (dealing with agriculture).

5. TEU, articles 85–90, and 74–84, respectively.

6. See, for example, case 48/75 State v. Jean Noël Royer [1976] ECR 497; cases 56 and 58/64 Consten and Grundig v. Commission [1966] CMLR 418.

7. This was the position taken by British Prime Minister John Major at the 1996–97 Intergovernmental Conference.

8. A short and readable history of the Community's development will be found in DAVID A. EDWARD & ROBERT C. LANE, EUROPEAN COMMUNITY LAW, 2ND ED. (Butterworths, 1995), pp. 3–14. A longer treatment is DOMINIC LASOK & JOHN BRIDGE, LAW & INSTITUTIONS OF THE EUROPEAN UNION, 6TH ED., (Butterworth's, 1994), pp. 13–23.

9. THE EUROPEAN CHALLENGE/1992: THE BENEFITS OF A SINGLE MARKET (Gower Publishing Co., 1988), pp. 75–102. This slim volume (127 pp.) is just a precis of the Ceechini Report (named for the deputy-director of the Internal Market Directorate General that oversaw it). It tried to objectively "prove" the advantages of the single market. The report itself was published by the Office for Official Publications of the European Community (OOPEC), L2985, Luxembourg, under the title: RESEARCH ON THE COST OF NON-EUROPE, BASIC FINDINGS, ISBN 92-825-7946-7-8. This was underpinned by eighteen volumes of expert "research" (mostly by economic sector) performed by "independent consultants . . . supervised by commission officials." These were also published by the OOPEC, Luxembourg.

10. THE EUROPEAN CHALLENGE/1992, *op cit.*, p. 89 (emphasis added). The best single volume about the Single European Act is: N. GREEN, T.C. HARTLEY & J.A. USHER, THE LEGAL FOUNDATIONS OF THE SINGLE EUROPEAN MARKET (Oxford, 1991).

11. E.g., The Procurement Procedure of Entities Operating in the Water, Energy, Transport and Telecommunications Sector, 1990 O.J. 297/1 (October 29, 1990).

12. RALPH H. FOLSOM, ET AL., EUROPEAN COMMUNITY LAW AFTER 1992: A PRACTICAL GUIDE FOR LAWYERS OUTSIDE THE COMMON MARKET (Kluwer, 1993).

13. Many sources relate these facts. I have drawn from two core documents: Commission of the European Communities, WHITE PAPER ON GROWTH, COMPETITIVENESS, EMPLOYMENT: THE CHALLENGES AND WAYS FORWARD INTO THE 21ST CENTURY, E.C. Bulletin, Supp., June 1993, p. 10; Jacques Delors, "The White Pa-

per," in Commission of the European Communities, FRONTIER-FREE EUROPE, April 1994, p. 3.

14. Shawn Tully, "Now the new Europe," FORTUNE, December 2, 1991, p. 138.

15. David Marsh, "Balance of economic power begins to shift," FINANCIAL TIMES, March 9, 1994, p. 8.

16. For a brief treatment of this consult: THOMAS C. FISCHER, THE EUROPEANIZATION OF AMERICA: WHAT AMERICANS NEED TO KNOW ABOUT THE EUROPEAN UNION (Carolina Academic Press, 1995), pp. 139–147.

17. For its text, *see*: EUROPEAN UNION, SELECTED INSTRUMENTS TAKEN FROM THE TREATIES, (Vol. 1), pp. 15–89.

18. TEU, Article 3b, discussed earlier.

19. EC Bulletin 12–1978, pp. 10 *et seq. See also* Regulation 3320/94, [1994] O.J. L 350/27 (December 31, 1994). The value of an ecu at that time (the currency has since been named the "euro") was about $1.17.

20. For the full text regarding the EU's "economic/and monetary policy," *see*: Treaty articles 102(a)–109(m). The SEA had made a reference to "the progressive realization of Economic and Monetary Union" in its preamble, but that is not the same thing at all.

21. An excellent, brief (but thorough) overview of the plan is: Coopers & Lybrand, "Economic and Monetary Union," EC COMMENTARIES, February 11, 1993, Treaty article 4(a).

22. SEA, Title 111, article 30. The presidency of EPC was to be the same as the Council; has the duty of *initiating* action; and is to be assisted by a permanent Secretariat, in Brussels, guaranteeing some degree of continuity. SEA, Title 111, articles 30(10)(B) and (a).

23. TEU, Title V, article J.

24. TEU, article J.4(l).

25. Scott Sullivan, "Europe Takes a Giant Step," NEWSWEEK, December 23, 1991, p. 36.

26. TEU, Title VI, article K1 (a).

27. "European Police Force May Move a Step Closer," IRISH TIMES, June 1, 1993, p. 6.

28. TEU, Title VI.

29. Treaty, article 8–8e.

30. Treaty, articles 8b, c and d, respectively.

31. Neil Buckley, "EU north and south split on spending freeze," FINANCIAL TIMES, December 7, 1998, p. 3; "Eye on the EU," EUROPE, October 1998, p. 6; "The EU's coming wrangle for reform and spoils," THE ECONOMIST, January 2, 1999, p. 45; Peter Norman, "Bonn keen to rein in EU farm spending," FINANCIAL TIMES, December 9, 1998, p. 4; "Vienna Waltz: EU Summit Defers Tough Decisions," EURECOM, December 1998, p. 2; Peter Norman, "Leaders take first step in jobs pact," FINANCIAL TIMES, December 12–13, 1998, p. 2; Peter Norman, "Germany puts jobs at top of agenda," FINANCIAL TIMES, January 19, 1999, p. 3; "Restructuring corporate Germany," THE ECONOMIST, November 21, 1998, p. 63; "The changing face of German unions," THE ECONOMIST, December 5, 1998, p. 69; Neil Buckley, "EU mismanagement under fire," FINANCIAL TIMES, November 14–15, 1998, p. 2; "Parliament versus Commission," THE ECONOMIST, January 16, 1999, p. 45; "We will always have Paris," THE ECONOMIST, November 21, 1998,

p. 76; David Wighton & Neil Buckley, "EU shows broad consensus," FINANCIAL TIMES, October 26, 1998, p. 2. *See generally*, MICHAEL EMERSON, REDRAWING THE MAP OF EUROPE (St. Martin's Press, 1998); EU COMMISSION, AGENDA 2000: FOR A STRONGER AND WIDER UNION, COM (97) 2000 Final, vols. 1 and 2 (Brussels, July 15, 1997).

32. A decent, although selective, commentary on this process is: RANDALL HENNING ET AL., REVIVING THE EUROPEAN UNION (Institute for International Economics, Washington, D.C., 1994), particularly the first essay, "Prospects for Recovery and Renewed Integration," pp. 3–12. In general, books published by this Institute about international economics are quite good.

33. European Commission, EUROBAROMETER, Report No. 45, Spring 1996, p. iii.

34. "The Week in Europe: Leon Brittan in Morocco for Signing of Final GATT Act," Press Association Newsfile, Apr. 14,1994; Alex Brummer, "Saturday Notebook: Long Hard Road," THE GUARDIAN, April 16, 1994, p. 36.

35. The Community receives certain monies from the common customs tariff and a percentage of member state VAT income (currently set at 1.27%) and GNP. This income is referred to as the Community's "own resources." On the other hand, the Community cannot increase its revenues (except as a result of market forces) without a unanimous vote of the Council. That is not easy to get when national governments themselves are strapped for income.

36. These basic provisions of the EEC Treaty are now to be found in the *amended treaties* at Articles 9 *et seq.* (a customs union involving all trade in goods); 18 *et seq.* (providing for a common customs tariff), particularly articles 18 and 19; 30 *et seq.* (eliminating quantitative restrictions—quotas—between states); 37 (requiring "adjustment" of state monopolies of a commercial character); 48 *et seq.* (allowing for the free movement of workers and the right to "establish" cross-border businesses); 59 *et seq.* (allowing free movement of services in the Community); and 67 *et seq.* (allowing the same for capital and payments).

37. For example, case 41/74 Yvonne van Duyn v. Home Office [1974] ECR 1337. *Cf.* case 7/78 Regina v. Thompson [1978] ECR 2247.

38. In the amended treaties, these prohibitions appear at Article 91 and 92, respectively.

39. TEU, article 37.

40. Articles 9 to 34 make repeated reference to member state practices "having equivalent effect" to national tariffs and quotas.

41. Articles 210 and 211.

42. Articles 137 to 192, inclusive.

43. Article 201. See [1994] O.J. L-293 p. 9 *et seq.* (November 12, 1994) for the details of the plan through 1999.

44. Article 217 of the treaties addresses this problem.

45. Article 2, amended by TEU Article G(2).

46. New article 3b, added by TEU article G(5).

47. Treaty article 7c [based on TEU article G(a)].

48. Among the best sources for U.S. businessmen and lawyers are: AUDRY WINTER ET AL., EUROPE WITHOUT FRONTIERS: A LAWYER'S GUIDE (Bureau of National Affairs, 1989); FOLSOM ET AL., *op cit.*.

49. "Economic Watch: EU trade surplus widens," FINANCIAL TIMES, April 24,

1997, p. 2; "EU Economic Outlook for 1996–97," EURECOM, December 1995, p. 2; Treaty article 103(1).

50. COMMISSION OF THE EUROPEAN COMMUNITIES, THE BUDGET OF THE EUROPEAN COMMUNITY (1993), p. 3.

51. The aims of the CAP are set out in treaty article 39, but the program went far beyond that. A leading account is: FRANCIS G. SNYDER, LAW OF THE COMMON AGRICULTURAL POLICY (Sweet & Maxwell, 1985).

52. Francis Snyder, "Current Developments/European Community Law," 42 INTERNATIONAL AND COMPARATIVE LAW QUARTERLY 720 (1993).

53. "Reforming CAP," FINANCIAL TIMES, September 29, 1995, p. 17; Lionel Barber & Caroline Southey, "EU rejects farm budget targets," FINANCIAL TIMES, February 27, 1997, p. 2; "A Momentous Month of March for the Union," EURECOM, April 1999, p. 1.

54. Neil Buckley, "Heavy cuts demanded in EU fishing," FINANCIAL TIMES, April 23, 1996, p. 2.

55. Lionel Barber & others, "EU resolves crisis over exports of British beef," FINANCIAL TIMES, June 22–23, 1996, p. 1.

56. See treaty article 75(3). Article 37 obligates "Member States [to] progressively adjust any State monopolies of a commercial character [during the transitional period, ending in 1970]." This was probably done with respect to rates and conditions, but didn't provide competition to national networks. One typical commentary regarding the problems faced is: Charles Batchelor, "EU hopes to put [rail] freight back on track," FINANCIAL TIMES, April 22, 1997, p. 6.

57. Title XII, articles 129(b)-129(d), added by TEU G(38). "Trans-European Networks," FOCUS, Press Association Newsfile, April 14, 1994, p. 48; Lionel Barber, "Santer urges $1.2 bn. project spending," FINANCIAL TIMES, March 20, 1996, p. 2; Neil Buckley & Judy Dempsey, "Move to open EU's electricity markets," FINANCIAL TIMES, June 5, 1996, p. 2; Bruce Barnard, "Telecom Gold Rush: Hoping to Strike It Rich in Europe's Open Market," EUROPE, June 1996, p. 10.

58. Treaty articles 48 and 119. The treaties also provided the right to "establish" themselves and offer services cross-border (Articles 52 to 66).

59. The first large-scale effort at such a plan was a "white paper" (discussion draft) published in 1993: COMMISSION OF THE EUROPEAN COMMUNITIES, WHITE PAPER ON GROWTH, COMPETITIVENESS, EMPLOYMENT: THE CHALLENGES AND WAYS FORWARD INTO THE 21ST CENTURY, E.C. Bulletin, Supplement, June 1993. *See also*, David Goodhart, "Flexibility 'No answer to jobs crisis'," FINANCIAL TIMES, September 15, 1994, p. 2; Charles Lane & Theresa Waldrop, "Is Europe's Social-Welfare State Headed for the Deathbed?" NEWSWEEK, August 23, 1993, p. 37.

60. "Eye on the EU," EUROPE, April 1997, p. 4. *See also* "EU Economic outlook for 1996–97," EURECOM, December 1995, p. 2.

61. "The Commission's Programme for 1997," speech by Mr. Jacques Santer to the European Parliament, Stasbourg, 2 October 1996 [speech 196/260]; The Commission's Work Programme for 1997, COM (96) 507 final (October 17, 1996). The main Commission reports are: GROWTH, COMPETITIVENESS, EMPLOYMENT, *op cit.*; THE EUROPEAN EMPLOYMENT STRATEGY: RECENT PROGRESS AND PROSPECTS FOR THE FUTURE, COM (95) 465 final (November 10, 1995); and ACTION FOR EMPLOYMENT IN EUROPE: A CONFIDENCE PACT, CSE (96) 1 final (May 6, 1996).

62. Reginald Dale, "Germany: Europe's Reluctant Leader," EUROPE, May

1995, p. 16; Peter Norman, "Germany: Giant cloaked in uncertainty," FINANCIAL TIMES (SURVEY), October 23, 1995, p. 1; Judy Dempsey, "E. Germany still needs cash infusion," FINANCIAL TIMES, June 19, 1995, p. 2.

63. "1997 Annual Economic Report Released," EURECOM, March 1997, p. 2 (citing the Commission's 1997 Annual Economic Report).

64. Some representative articles are: "Glimpses of EU recovery," FINANCIAL TIMES, April 24, 1997, p. 31; Peter Norman, "A joyless recovery," FINANCIAL TIMES, April 14, 1997, p. 21; Peter Norman, "German reforms inch forward," FINANCIAL TIMES, April 21, 1997, p. 21; Gillian Tett, "OECD warns Europe on pensions and jobs," FINANCIAL TIMES, May 22, 1996, p. 4; "Plea for EU labor reform," FINANCIAL TIMES, March 31, 1995, p. 3; Robert Taylor, "Faced by more job losses, EU states look to U.S. flexibility," FINANCIAL TIMES, August 22, 1995, p. 2; Emma Tucker, "Pension regimes handicap worker mobility within EU," FINANCIAL TIMES, February 17–18, 1996, p. 2; Robert Taylor, "New realism dictates EU social policy," FINANCIAL TIMES, April 12, 1995, p. 2; Gillian Tett & Jim Kelly, "Brussels proposes to relaunch campaign to harmonize VAT," FINANCIAL TIMES, June 28, 1996, p. 1; "New Call for EU Approach to Taxation," EURECOM, April 1996, p. 1; "1997 Annual Economic Report Released," EURECOM, March 1997, p. 2.

65. Treaty article 118 a(2). Another good example is article 130 f(2), regarding research and technology, which reads, in relevant part: "For this purpose the Community shall . . . encourage undertakings, including small and medium-sized undertakings." In article 85(3), concerning competition, business ventures that "[promote] technical and economic progress, while allowing consumers a fair share of the resulting benefit" are broadly excluded from its anti-competitive prohibitions. SMEs are generally considered to fall into this excluded class.

66. The broad contours of the structural programs is in treaty title XIV (Economic and Social Cohesion), articles 130a–130e, as amended by TEU article G(38). The other two structural programs mentioned are the European Social Fund (articles 123–125, as amended by TEU G34 and 35) and the European Investment Bank (articles 198d and e and Protocol A). *See generally*, FISCHER, *op cit.*, pp. 223–238.

67. The Committee of the Regions [treaty articles 198a–198c], added by the Maastricht Treaty, is still too new to allow comment on its contribution to the Community political structure. However, the development of regional projects in the last few years makes this area of Community activity seem more and more vital to EU aims and an antidote to nationalism. *See*, for example, Axel Krause, "A Europe of Regions Becoming Reality," EUROPE, April 1994, p. 2; John Newhouse, "Europe's Rising Regionalism," FOREIGN AFFAIRS, January/February 1997, p. 67.

68. Treaty articles 198d–198e, and Protocol A, address the structure and function of the EIB.

69. Protocol A, article 18(1); "In Brief," EURECOM, March 1997, p. 4.

70. Robert Taylor, "EU report rejects [UK] social chapter fears," FINANCIAL TIMES, February 3, 1997, p. 8.

71. Treaty article 103(3) and (4).

72. 15 U.S. Code §1, *et seq.* (1988), as amended.

73. Article 85(3) provides the exception to 85(1) and (2); notably, beneficial

restraints "which [contribute] to improving the production or distribution of goods or . . . promoting technical or economic progress."

74. 15 U.S. Code §15 (1988).

75. "EU Launches Review of Vertical Restraints," EURECOM, February 1997, p. 2.

76. The main piece of Community anti-dumping legislation is Regulation 2423/88 (1988 O.J. §209; February 8, 1988). For typical reports of dumping tensions between Europe and Asia, *see*: Emma Tucker & Guy de Jonquières, "EU plans dumping duties on Asian TVs," FINANCIAL TIMES, September 16, 1994, p. 1; "Textiles: China may have to lay off thousands because of EU action," 13 ITR 1895 (December 11, 1996).

77. The exceptions to the general principle against state aid are in treaty article 92(2) and (3). The Commission's duties with respect to state aid are in article 93. The Council was given new powers by the Maastricht Treaty, G(18), to adopt regulations and determine conditions pertaining to state aid.

78. Just a few examples of many are: Neil Buckley, "Olympic Airways aid is halted," FINANCIAL TIMES, May 1, 1996, p. 3; Andrew Jack & Emma Tucker, "France in £3 bn bid to aid Credit Lyonnaise," FINANCIAL TIMES, February 21, 1997, p. 1.; Charles Bremner & Carl Mortished, "Airlines subsidy dispute reignites in Europe," LONDON TIMES, July 21, 1998, p. 23. *See also*, treaty article 37, addressing state monopolies of a commercial character.

79. Treaty articles 95 to 98.

80. Case /70/78 Commission v. United Kingdom (Wine and Beer) [1983] ECR 2265.

81. Treaty Article 99, added by TEU Article G(20).

82. *See*, for example, Lionel Barber, "EU ministers open fire on tax poachers; France and Germany believe it is time for Europe to curb beggar-my-neighbor tax rivalries," FINANCIAL TIMES, January 31, 1997, p. 2.

83. Emma Tucker, "Brussels move to shame EU states over single market," FINANCIAL TIMES, February 17,1997, p. 1.

84. These topics are dealt with in Title VI of the Treaty, articles K to K.9. The "areas . . . of common interest" are listed in article K.7.(1) to (9).

85. These provisions appear in articles K.3.(2); K.6.; K.4. and K.9., respectively.

86. TEU article K.1.(9) provides for "police cooperation for the purposes of preventing and combating terrorism, unlawful drug-trafficking and other serious forms of international crime, including if necessary certain aspects of customs cooperation in connection with the organization of a Union-wide system for exchanging information within a European Police Office (Europol).

87. Albrecht Funk, "Europeanization of Internal Security Policies in the Framework of the EU," ECSA Review, Winter 1997, p. 14; EUROBAROMETER, *op cit.*, pp. III and 54; "European police force may move a step closer," IRISH TIMES, June 1, 1993, p. 6.

88. *See*, for example, case C-17/93 J.J.J. Van der Veldt [1994] I ECR 3537 (July 14, 1994); case 178/84 Commission v. Germany (German Beer) [1988] 1 C.M.L.R. 780.

89. "EU Parliament approves new rules for labeling of food product imports," 13 ITR 1915 (December 11, 1996).

90. Frances Williams, "Call for stronger EU patent laws," FINANCIAL TIMES, May 22, 1976, p. 6.

91. Neil Buckley, "EU bid to break electricity deadlock," FINANCIAL TIMES, May 7, 1996, p. 2; Neil Buckley and Judy Dempsey, "Move to open EU's electricity markets," FINANCIAL TIMES, June 5, 1996, p. 2.

92. Damian Chalmers, "The Single Market: from Prima Donna to Journeyman," in: JO SHAW & GILLIAN MORE, NEW LEGAL DYNAMICS OF EUROPEAN UNION (Clarendon Press, 1995), p. 55.

93. For example, Martin Feldstein, "The case against EMU," THE ECONOMIST, June 13, 1992, p. 19; Robert J. Samuelson, "Europe's New Nutty Money," NEWSWEEK, January 13, 1997, p. 55; Peter Sutherland, "The Case for EMU," FOREIGN AFFAIRS, January/February 1997, p. 9; Peter Norman & Anaren Fisher, "Europe's realistic banker [Alexandre Lamfalussy, head of the European Monetary Institute]," FINANCIAL TIMES, October 24, 1994, p. 16.

94. C. Fred Bergsten, "The Dollar and the Euro," FOREIGN AFFAIRS, July/August 1997, p. 83. *See also*, C. RANDALL HENNING, COOPERATING WITH EUROPE'S MONETARY UNION (Institute for International Economics, Washington, D.C., 1997).

95. C. Fred Bergsten, *op. cit*; Peter Sutherland, *op. cit.*

96. The Exchange Rate Mechanism, or ERM. European Council resolution, reported in EC Bulletin 121, 1978, pp. 10 and following. This was not part of the EC Treaty, however.

97. An Ecu, still in use today, has a value that floats against the U.S. dollar, but has run from about $1.04 at the low end to about $1.25 at the high. The latest valuation of the basket is EC Regulation 3320/94, OJ L-350 (December 31, 1994) p. 27.

98. "In 1972 EC leaders airily announced that 'EU', including monetary union, would be completed by 1980. Nothing happened." "The History of the Maastricht Summit," THE ECONOMIST, November 30, 1991, p. 47.

99. The Report of the Committee for the Study of Economic and Monetary Union ("Delors Report") is summarized in EC BULLETIN 4/1989, p. 8. *See also*, Coopers & Lybrand, "Economic and Monetary Union," EC COMMENTARIES, February 11, 1993, p. 4.

100. I plan to address just the high points of the EMU program. For persons who are eager for more precise detail, I recommend that they read the relevant treaty sections: Articles 2, 3a, 4a, Title VI ("Economic and Monetary Policy"); articles 102a–109m, and Protocols No. 3 (Statute of the European System of Central Bank), No. 4 (Statute of the European Monetary Institute [precursor of the ECB]), No. 5 (the "excessive deficit procedure"), No. 6 (the "coverage criteria" referenced in treaty article 109j), No. 10 ("transition to the third state" of EMU) and Nos. 11 and 12 (giving "opt outs" from EMU to the United Kingdom and Denmark, respectively).

101. Treaty articles 104, 104a, and 109e. *See also* Regulations 3603/93 and 3604/93 (OJ L-332; December 31, 1993).

102. Treaty article 109f and Protocol No. 4 describe the responsibilities and functions of the European Monetary Institute. *See also*, Treaty articles 109e and 108.

103. Treaty article 109j (3) & (4) and Protocol No. 10.

104. The convergence criteria are meant to achieve "stable prices, sound public

finances and monetary conditions and a sustainable balance of payments," Treaty article 3a(3). The requirements on public debt are cited in Treaty article 104c, but the details given in Protocol No. 5. The requirements concerning price stability and inflation are cited in Treaty article 109, but the details found in Protocol No. 6.

105. PAUL KRUGMAN, PEDDLING PROSPERITY: ECONOMIC SENSE AND NON-SENSE IN THE AGE OF DIMINISHED EXPECTATIONS (Norton, 1994), p. 191.

106. COM (95) 503 final (Brussels October 31, 1995).

107. Frankfurt, November 1995. EMI reports should be ordered directly: Post-fach 10 20 31, D-60020 Frankfurt am Main, Germany.

108. Lionel Barber, "The long and bumpy road to Emu," FINANCIAL TIMES, September 29, 1995, p. 2.

109. Madrid European Council, Presidency Conclusions (December 15 & 16, 1995), SN 400195; and particularly Annex I (Part B).

110. "Launching the Euro," EUROPE (Inside), March 1996, p. 1; "The EU's feel-bad factor," THE ECONOMIST, September 30, 1995, p. 57; Gillian Tett, "Single currency position 'damaging'," FINANCIAL TIMES, July 30, 1996, p. 6; "Quest for an Emu without tears," FINANCIAL TIMES, July 3, 1996, p. 2; Wolfgang Münchau, "More companies switch on to euro," FINANCIAL TIMES, February 11, 1997, p. 3, citing IBM, COMPETING IN THE EURO-ZONE (London, 1997); Richard Lapper, "Markets start to believe the bird will fly," FINANCIAL TIMES, April 8, 1997, p. 3; David White, "Cost to banks of euro switch 'over-estimated'," FINANCIAL TIMES, June 10, 1997, p. 3; Wolfgang Münchau, "Emu 'D-Day scenario' provokes shud-ders: Consensus among large companies is that delay would be disastrous," FINAN-CIAL TIMES, March 11, 1997, p. 3.

111. Axel Krause, "No turning back: Chirac is determined to move France for-ward," EUROPE, April 1997, p. 8; David Buchan, "France tailors budget to meet Maastricht targets," FINANCIAL TIMES, September 19, 1996, p. 1; David Owen & Andrew Jack, "Arthuis holds firm in Emu faith," FINANCIAL TIMES, September 18, 1996, p. 2; Elizabeth Pond, "EMU: The Chancellor's Greatest Challenge," EUROPE, May 1997, p. 21; Ralph Atkins, "Germany's confidence in Emu grows," FINANCIAL TIMES, March 24, 1997, p. 3; Michael Lindemann, "Waigel's draft budget signals austerity drive," FINANCIAL TIMES, July 4, 1995, p. 2; Peter Norman, "Germany plans to curb public deficits to meet Emu criteria," FINANCIAL TIMES, June 13, 1996, p. 12; David Owen & Peter Norman, "German budget puts pressure on Paris," FINANCIAL TIMES, July 15, 1996, p. 2; Robert Chote, "Tietmeyer warns on one currency," FINANCIAL TIMES, February 3–4, 1996, p. 2; Robert Graham, "Ital-ians upset at Waigel remarks," FINANCIAL TIMES, September 22, 1995, p. 2; Lionel Barber & David White, "Italian PM fuels debate over future of Emu," FINANCIAL TIMES, September 25, 1995, p. 1; Robert Graham, "Italy gets the message on Emu criteria," FINANCIAL TIMES, September 27, 1996, p. 2; "Italy levies 'Euro-tax' in drive to meet Emu targets," FINANCIAL TIMES, November 20, 1996, p. 1; Robert Peston & James Blitz, "[U.K.] Labor party opts for a referendum on Emu," FINAN-CIAL TIMES, November 18, 1996, p. 8; Gillian Tett & George Graham, "City urged to speed up plans for Emu," FINANCIAL TIMES, August 9, 1996, p. 7; Lionel Barber, "UK Emu stance worries BT chief," FINANCIAL TIMES, July 10, 1996, p. 2; "UK on track to clear Emu hurdles," FINANCIAL TIMES, June 20, 1995, p. 2; John Mur-ray, "Emu would offer 'only modest gains' to Ireland," FINANCIAL TIMES, p. 16; Lionel Barber, "Row as France presses for Italy's early return to ERM," FINANCIAL

TIMES, March 18, 1996, p. 1; Robert Graham & David Buchan, "Italy calls for talks on ERM," FINANCIAL TIMES, October 5 & 6, 1996, p. 2; Simon Kuper & Richard Adams, "Lira rises on ERM return," FINANCIAL TIMES, November 26, 1996, p. 1; "Spain slashes spending plan by $6bn," FINANCIAL TIMES, September 28 & 29, 1996, p. 2; "Spanish PM pledges to meet Emu targets," FINANCIAL TIMES, September 30, 1996, p. 1; "Lisbon voices doubts on Emu," FINANCIAL TIMES, April 23, 1996, p. 2; Neil Buckley, "Belgium urges new debate on Emu sanctions," August 9, 1996, p.1; "Austria joins Exchange Rate Mechanism," EURECOM, January 1995, p. 1; Hugh Carnegy, "Finns aim to be there when Emu takes off," FINANCIAL TIMES, June 27, 1996, p. 2; Lionel Barber, "Euro plan gets boost as Finland joins ERM," FINANCIAL TIMES, November 25, 1996, p. 3; "Denmark begins to fuel Emu opt-out," FINANCIAL TIMES, November 27, 1995, p. 2; Kevin Hope, "Greece acts to keep on Emu track," FINANCIAL TIMES, November 20, 1996, p. 3.

112. Ecofin Council, "The Preparations for Stage 3 of EMU," Report . . . to the European Council, Dublin, December 13, 1996, SN 486213196 REV 3.

113. *Id.*, points 6–15. The operational details of ERM 2 were designed by the EMI and attached as an annex to the Ecofin report: European Commission, "Interim Report on Relations Between the Single Currency and Currencies of Countries Which Do Not Participate from the Start," Ref: IP/95/1316 (November 29, 1995). See also, Lionel Barber, "EU looks at multi-speed exchange rate system," FINANCIAL TIMES, February 21, 1996, p. 1; David Buchan, "Paris-Bonn accord on Emu 'ins' and 'outs'," FINANCIAL TIMES, March 27, 1996, p. 2; Andrew Fisher & Peter Norman, "Finding way through Emu ins and outs," FINANCIAL TIMES, April 11, 1996, p. 2. During 1996, the Austrian and Finish currencies join the ERM and Italy (forced out in 1992) rejoined. A House of Lords report in 1996 concluded the arrangements made for the Emu "ins" and "outs" were workable and sound. Select Committee on the European Communities, "An Emu of 'Ins' and 'Outs'," HL Report 86 (June 11, 1996).

114. Ecofin Report, *op cit.*, points 16–37. *See also*, Andrew Fischer & Peter Norman, "Bundesbank outlines plans for EU currency stability," FINANCIAL TIMES, April 11, 1996, p. 10; "Kohl insists on sticking to Emu criteria," FINANCIAL TIMES, September 25, 1996, p. 2.

115. Ecofin Report, *op cit.*, points 38–40. *See also*, "European Commission Proposes Rules for Contract, Bond Payments under Emu," 13 ITR 25 d32 (June 19, 1996).

116. Dublin European Council, Presidency Conclusions, December 13 & 14, 1996, pp. 2–3; Annex I. A report by the EMI on the "Monetary and Exchange Rate Policy Cooperation Between the Euro Area and Other EU Countries" (Dublin, December 13–14, 1996), is attached as Annex 2 to Annex 1. *See also*, "Dublin Summit Clears Path for Emu, Sets Table for IGC," EUROPE, January 1997, p. 1.

117. The Commission's convergence report and recommendation concurring the eleven countries is published at: European Commission, Euro 1999 (Parts 1 & 2), March 25, 1998. There are so many good commentaries on the history, structure, and prospects of EMU—including excellent *official* reports cited above and below—that I have selected just a few of the most informative and readable items to recommend here:

From Here to EMU: Milestones Along the Way," EURECOM, March 1998, p. 1; "Commission Recommends 11 Member States for EMU," EURECOM, April 1998,

p. 1; "EU Leaders Agree on EMU Countries and Central Bank President," EURE-COM, May 1998, p. 1; Lionel Barber, "Countdown to the EURO," EUROPE, April 1998, p. 8; Gillian Tett, "Emu, lies, damned lies and statistics," FINANCIAL TIMES, October 9, 1996, p. 2; "French budget measures criticized by Germany," FINANCIAL TIMES, November 2–3, 1996, p. 24; Ralph Atkins & Graham Bowley, "Germany gives nod to euro's first eleven," FINANCIAL TIMES, March 28–29, 1998, p. 2; Peter Norman & others, "Growth and rigour help clear the Emu hurdles," FINANCIAL TIMES, February 28–March 1, 1998, p. 2; Lionel Barber, "Point of no return," FINANCIAL TIMES, December 30, 1997, p. 9.

EUROPE magazine also published two informative reports: "Coming soon: the EURO," in September 1997, and "Euro sets sail," in June 1998.

For those who want a short, but detailed, overview, consult: European Commission, "The euro: Explanatory notes," EURO PAPERS, No. 17, February 1998.

118. Dublin European Council, *op cit.*, pp. 35–39; European Monetary Institute, Press Release, "Selection of the Euro Banknote Designs" (December 13, 1996); European Commission. "Denominations and Technical Specifications of Euro Coins: Proposal for a Council Regulation," COM (97) 247 final (Brussels, May 29, 1997) (It is estimated that 12 billion banknotes and 70 billion coins were in circulation in the EU Member States in 1994); EMI, "The Changeover to the Single Currency" November 1995, ANNEX 1: "Dialogue with the Banking Community on the Issue of the Changeover to the Single Currency"; European Commission, "The 24 Hour Global Financial Conference Video Conference from Brussels, 1 July 1997," especially speeches #97/148 and 149. *See also*, Andrew Fisher & Peter Norman, "Road to Monetary Union will be bumpy says EMI," FINANCIAL TIMES, April 3, 1996, p. 1: Bruce Clark & Gillian Tett, "Fall in EU Growth [rate] 'no threat' to single currency," FINANCIAL TIMES, May 16, 1996, p. 12; David Smith, "Demanding timetable may force EMU delay," LONDON TIMES, February 2, 1997, p. 3.9; Lionel Barber, "Threat of Emu delay haunts EU," FINANCIAL TIMES, February 24, 1997, p. 2; Lionel Barber & Wolfgang Münchau, "Brussels places its bets for Emu race," FINANCIAL TIMES, April 24, 1997, p. 2; "EMI Reveals Clues to Single Monetary Policy," EURECOM, February 1997, p. 1; Martin Wolf, "Emu's hidden strains," FINANCIAL TIMES, March 11, 1997, p. 18; Andrew Fisher, "US indifference to Emu deplored," FINANCIAL TIMES, August 6, 1996, p. 2.

119. European Council-Amsterdam, Presidency Conclusions, June 16 & 17, 1997 (TEXTE EN; SI (97) 500), pp. 4–7, and Annex I (European Council Resolutions on Stability, Growth and Employment [including the details of the Stability and Growth Pact]), pp. 23–31; and Annex II (Resolution of the European Council on the establishment of an exchange-rate mechanism and monetary union), pp. 32–36; Lionel Barber & Robert Preston, "Paris and Bonn heal rift that threatened Emu start," FINANCIAL TIMES, June 17, 1997, p. 1.

120. Lionel Barber, "Wim-Claude Trichenberg," FINANCIAL TIMES, May 4, 1998, p. 13; "EU Leaders Agree on EMU Countries and Central Bank President," *op cit.*; Wolfgang Münchau, "Central Bank board to make an early start," FINANCIAL TIMES, May 4, 1998, p. 2.

121. European Monetary Institute, "The Changeover to the Single Currency," November 1995 (especially pp. 7–21); Euopean Commission, "Economic and Monetary Union and Its Impact on the International Markets," April 1997 (especially

pp. 3–5 and 9–13). *See also*, European Monetary Institute, "The Single Monetary Policy in Stage Three; Specification of the Operational Framework," January 1997.

122. Wolfgang Münchau, "Encouraging start but problems loom," FINANCIAL TIMES, July 25–26, 1998, p. XXII; Wolfgang Münchau, "ECB must manage the mix," FINANCIAL TIMES, January 13, 1998, p. 2; "ECB board sees inflation as big threat," FINANCIAL TIMES, May 9–10, 1998, p. 2; Gordon Cramb, "ECB to try to avoid 'shocks'," FINANCIAL TIMES, June 29, 1998, p. 2; "Alarm bells ring over money supply," FINANCIAL TIMES, July 14, 1998, p. 3; James Blitz, "ECB warns euro-zone over deficit limits," FINANCIAL TIMES, April 16, 1999, p. 3.

123. EMI and Commission reports, cited above, especially the latter at pp. 1–3. *See also*, Bruce Barnard, "The EURO," EUROPE, November 1996, ESR 12; Stefan Wagstyl & Robert Preston, "Toyota Chief in Warning [to the U.K.] on EMU," FINANCIAL TIMES, January 30, 1997, p. 1.

124. EC, "Economic and Monetary Union . . . ," *op cit.*, pp. 3 & 14–15; Alan Beattle, "Currency star whose brightness has failed to dazzle," FINANCIAL TIMES, April 12, 1999, p. 6; Peter Norman, "Euro forecast to strengthen in the long term," FINANCIAL TIMES, April 20, 1999, p. 3.

125. Robert Graham & Andrew Jack, "Euro 'to speed French financial reshape'," FINANCIAL TIMES, July 4–5, 1998, p. 2; George Graham & Simon Davies, "London–Frankfurt link paves way for pan-Europe exchange," FINANCIAL TIMES, July 8, 1998, p. 1; Phillip Coggan, "Europe clambers to more peaks," FINANCIAL TIMES, July 15, 1998, p. 23; Barry Riley, "Aim for bourse without borders," FINANCIAL TIMES, May 18, 1998, p. 19; *cf.*, "The quick and the dead," THE ECONOMIST, September 18, 1999, p. 84.

126. Wolfgang Münchau, "Sturdy recovery eases ECB dilemmas," FINANCIAL TIMES, June 16, 1998, p. 3; Lionel Barber, "Europe looks to play wider role in global money system," FINANCIAL TIMES, January 20, 1998, p. 1; Simon Kuper & Gerard Baker, "End of strong dollar?", FINANCIAL TIMES, April 24, 1998, p. 13; Wolfgang Mnchau, "Dollar's domination could be ended by the euro," FINANCIAL TIMES, September 9, 1997, p. 3; James Harding & James Kynge, "China may use euro in reserves," FINANCIAL TIMES, May 6, 1998, p. 4; Vicki Barnett, "Watch out, dollar," FINANCIAL TIMES, April 23, 1998, p. 11; Gerard Baker, "The Emu has landed," FINANCIAL TIMES, May 5, 1998, p. 19.

127. "Europe's adventure begins," THE ECONOMIST, January 2, 1999, p. 16; George Graham, "A smooth conversion greets Europe's new currency," FINANCIAL TIMES, January 7, 1999, p. 21; "EU Finds Its Economic Voice," EUROPE (Inside), December/January 1998–1999, p. 1; Michael Smith, "Pressure builds on UK and Sweden to join ERM 2," FINANCIAL TIMES, September 28, 1998, p. 3; Kevin Brown & Robert Preston, "UK bosses call on government to give firm Yes to joining Emu," FINANCIAL TIMES, November 23, 1998, p. 18; Clare McCarthy, "Danish rates cut as poll backs the euro," FINANCIAL TIMES, January 8, 1999, p. 2; "Faster forward," THE ECONOMIST, November 28, 1998, p. 83; Robert Taylor, "Euro comparisons may bring new wage systems," FINANCIAL TIMES, October 13, 1998, p. 3.

128. "The world's new currency worries," THE ECONOMIST, January 9, 1999, p. 67; Martin Feldstein, "Emu and International Conflict," FOREIGN AFFAIRS, November/December 1997, p. 61.

129. Justin Fox, "Europe Is Heading for a Wild Ride," FORTUNE, August 17, 1998, p. 145; Yves-Thibault Silguy, "Now for the real test," FINANCIAL TIMES, May

4, 1998, p. 12; Martin Wolf, "Euro's world test," FINANCIAL TIMES, July 7, 1998, p. 16; Richard Portes & Helene Rey, "Struggle for world status starts," FINANCIAL TIMES, April 30, 1998, p. VIII (Birth of the euro); Henry Kissinger, "What price the euro for America?" THE DAILY TELEGRAPH, May 7, 1998, p. 19; George Graham, "IMF ponders monetary union," FINANCIAL TIMES, September 30, 1996, p. 6; Larry Summers, "American eyes on Emu," FINANCIAL TIMES, October 22, 1997, p. 14.

For persons looking for more complete exploration of this issue, consult: European Commission, "The Impact of the Introduction of the Euro on Capital Markets," Brussels, II/338/97–EN-2 (1997); European Commission, "The Legal Implications of the European Monetary Union under U.S. and New York Law," ECONOMIC PAPERS, No. 126 (January 1998); C. RANDALL HENNING, COOPERATING WITH EUROPE'S MONETARY UNION (Institute for International Economics, 1997).

130. Bruce Barnard, "Global Financial Crisis: Is Europe an Oasis of Stability?" EUROPE, November 1998, p. 16; "The merits of one money," THE ECONOMIST, October 24, 1998, p. 85; Robert Taylor, "Euro comparisons may bring new wage systems," *op cit.*, p. 3; Kevin Brown, "[UK] Business leaders give big boost to pro-euro lobby," FINANCIAL TIMES, November 23, 1998, p. 7; Edward Luce, "Fund managers predict euro will soon rival strength of dollar," FINANCIAL TIMES, November 10, 1998, p. 16; Richard Adams & Andew Balls, "Euro dawn promises challenge to mighty $," FINANCIAL TIMES, September 30, 1998, p. 6; Edward Luce, "Japanese investors switch to European bond markets," FINANCIAL TIMES, October 29, 1998, p. 17; James Kynge, "China to add the euro to its foreign currency reserves," FINANCIAL TIMES, October 31–November 1, 1998, p. 3.

131. Quentin Peel, "Ministers divided over voice for euro," FINANCIAL TIMES, September 25, 1998, p. 2; Neil Buckley, "Plan for euro-one 'trinity' to go to G-7," FINANCIAL TIMES, November 5, 1998, p. 3.

132. Irwin Stelzer, "Americans in a flap over Europe's EMU," LONDON TIMES, May 11, 1997, p. 3.11; Andrew Fischer, "European bourses may get left on back of EMU," FINANCIAL TIMES, April 15, 1997, p. 3; Fred Bergsten, "The dollar and the euro," FOREIGN AFFAIRS, July/August, p. 83; Robert Chote, "How the euro may fit in with the Fund," FINANCIAL TIMES, March 25, 1997, p. 3; Wolfgang Münchau, "Progress slow on external aspects of EMU," FINANCIAL TIMES, April 24, 1997, p. 2; C. RANDALL HENNING, *op cit.*; Rufus Olins, "Bankers warned of euro's impact," LONDON TIMES, March 2, 1997, p. 3.7; Jacques Santer (President of the European Commission), "The euro and international trade," in: speech to the Global 24 Conference (Frankfurt, July 1, 1997).

133. Opinion 1/94: opinion pursuant to Article 228 (6) of the European Community Treaty [1994] ECR 1–5267, see also [1996] ECR 1–1469.

134. Treaty article 113(3), part of the EU's "Common Commercial Policy" (Articles 110 to 116); Lionel Barber, "Brussels strive to call the tune on trade," FINANCIAL TIMES, March 12, 1997, p. 6.

135. "[EPC] has functioned like a private club between consenting foreign ministries." "A long march towards Euroarmy?," FINANCIAL TIMES, October 18, 1991, section I, p. 25.

136. A European foreign policy was given treaty status for the first time by TEU articles J to J(11). " 'Political unions aspirations are far-reaching and will demand leadership, a large measure of political will . . . and self-sacrifice. In times of recession and instability, such as [these], there are great pressures to renationalize policy.' "

Nicholas Doughty, "Plans to develop EU foreign policy promise turf battles," REU-
TER EUROPEAN COMMUNITY REPORT, March 3, 1993 (quoting Hans van de Broek,
Commissioner for External Relations).

137. The express language for this sketchy overview of the operation of the Union's (CFSP is found, respectively, at TEU, Articles J8(1)–(2), J3(3), J5(3), J7,
J8(1)–(2), J3(3), J5(3), J7, J8(5), J3(1), J1(4), J2(3), J4(2) & J4(4), J2(1) and
J4(1). *See generally,* "The EU's Common Foreign and Security Policy," brochure of
the European Commission (Luxembourg, 1996).

138. TEU article J5(1). *See also,* J5(4), concerning the obligations of EU members
of the UN Security Council. EC brochure, *op cit.*

139. Articles 210 and 240.

140. TEU article J1(3), J2(1), and J1(3), respectively.

141. Articles 229 to 230, the latter being added by TEU G(82). See also Articles
28 and 228(a), amended or superceded by TEU G(80) and G(81).

142. European Commission (Annual Report).

143. See, for example, EC article 109(3), TEU J5(4), and TEU J4(2).

144. These items are addressed in the treaties at articles 112, 113(3), 130u–1304
(added by TEU G(38) 131 to 136a, and Annex IV concerning the ACP). See also,
"Lomé 'will not survive the century'," FINANCIAL TIMES, November 3, 1994, p. 5.

145. The original EEA included Austria, Finland and Sweden, which have since
joined the EU. The agreement ([1994] OJL-1; January 3, 1994) needs to be revised
to reflect this, but has not been to date. A good short treatment of the EEA structure
and EA-EC relation will be found in Appendix I, EDWARD & LANE, *op cit.,* pp. 147–
152.

146. Lionel Barber, "The EU Institutions," EUROPE, November 1996, p. ESR
6.

147. Signed in December 1996 in Ottawa, the "EU and Canada have . . . a new
Political Declaration, together with an Action Plan, which will serve as a template
for closer political and economic ties." Similar to the EU–U.S. New Transatlantic
Agenda (NTA), "The EU–Canada agreement leaves open the possibility of cooperation between all three parties." The plan calls for a joint study to "lower trade
barriers, boost economic cooperation, intensify . . . links in [the areas of] foreign policy and security and give Europe and Canada an even more cohesive voice on the
international stage." "EU and Canada Sign Historic Agreement," EURECOM, January 1997, p. 2.

148. Council of the EU, THE NEW TRANSATLANTIC AGENDA, 12296195 (Presse
356). See also U.S. Mission to the EC (Brussels), Declaration on US–EC Relations,
signed November 23, 1990; Robert Guttman, "Interview: Jacques Santer," EUROPE,
February 1997, p. 12.

149. Selina Jackson, "The TABD: An Entrepreneurial Force behind the New
Transatlantic Agenda," ECSA REVIEW, Fall 1996, pp. 21–23, quoting Eizenstat from
a press briefing in Brussels, May 23, 1996.

150. "World Telecom Deal Clinched," EURECOM, March 1997, p. 1.

151. "New Nations Join U.S.–EU Info Tech Pact; Agreement Expected to Take
Effect Next Year," 12 ITR 1941 (December 18, 1996); "ITA Accord Advanced,"
EURECOM, March 1997, p. 2.

152. Nancy Dunne, "Battle to abolish 'redundant' rules," FINANCIAL TIMES, May

22, 1997, p. 6; "U.S. and EU to Complete Work on MRAs Next Month, Clinton Says," 13 ITR 1956 (December 18, 1996).

153. "U.S., EU Launch Broad Trade Initiative That Includes Services, Tariffs, E-Commerce," 15 ITR 856 (May 20, 1998); "U.S., EU Soon to Develop Plan for Implementing New Trade Initiative," 15 ITR 1320 (July 29, 1998); "U.S. Companies Urge USTR to Negotiate Removal of Existing Curbs on U.S.–EU Trade," 15 ITR 1214 (July 15, 1998); "U.S., EU to Sign a New MRAs This Month Facilitating Transatlantic Trade," 15 ITR 809 (May 13, 1998). The Text of the agreement: "U.S.–EU Summit Statement on New Transatlantic Agenda Projects," appears at http://www.usembassy.org.UK/potus 981 p.98 tnt 34.html.

154. THE NEW TRANSATLANTIC AGENDA, http://www.cec.lu/en/agenda/tr05.html; "18–05–98 Fact Sheet: The Trans-Atlantic Economic Partnership," MACROBUTTON HtmlResAnchor http://www.usembassy.org.uk/potus98/p.98tnt31.html; "U.S., EU Union Trans-Atlantic Partnership Action Plan," 15 ITR 1897 (November 11, 1998); "U.S., EU Will Need Additional Resources to Implement New Trade Plan," 12/17/1998 BTD d3; "U.S. Companies Urge USTR to Negotiate Removal of Existing Curbs on U.S.–EU Trade," 15 ITR 1214 (July 15, 1998); "TABD meets in Charlotte," EUROPE (Inside), December/January 1998–1999; "Administration Sees Little Support for U.S.–EU Free Trade Pact," 3/17/97 BTD d5.

155. Michael Skapinler, "Rival regulators in EU and U.S. air their differences," FINANCIAL TIMES, May 13, 1998, p. 6; "Meat Fight Looms over the Atlantic," EUROPE (Inside), April 1997, p. 3; "WTO Issues Ruling Backing U.S. Claim EU Ban on Beef Imports Violates Trade Rules," 5/9/97 BTD d3 (May 9, 1997); "Commission Clears Gene-Modified Corn," EURECOM, January 1997, p. 3; "EU–U.S. Banana Battle," 7/24/1998, BTD d5.

156. Axel Krause, "Looking South: Europe Proposes a New Initiative for Africa and the Middle East," EUROPE, December/January 1994–95, p. 18; "Euro-Med FTA by 2010?," EURECOM, October 1998, p. 1.

157. Owen Matthews & Bill Powell, "What Really Ails Russia," NEWSWEEK, June 8, 1998, p. 38; Chrystia Freeland & Others, "Russia wins more backing from IMF," FINANCIAL TIMES, May 30–31, 1998, p. 3; John Thornhill, "Crisis? What crisis? Asks the Russian in the street," FINANCIAL TIMES, June 10, 1998, p. 20.

158. Clifford Gaddy & Barry Ickes, "Russia's Virtual Economy," FOREIGN AFFAIRS, September/October 1998, p. 53; John Thornhill & Arkady Ostrovsky, "Sliding into chaos," FINANCIAL TIMES, October 21, 1998, p. 2; Stephen Fidler, "IMF faces dilemma on Russian loans," FINANCIAL TIMES, December 9, 1998, p. 3 [Russia is the IMF's largest debtor at $19 billion (one-fifth of outstanding IMF loans), with a total indebtedness of over $128 billion]; Bill Powell & Yeugenia Albats, "The End of the Miracle," NEWSWEEK, January 25, 1999, p. 37; "World Bank clears $400 million loan to Russia," FINANCIAL TIMES, November 7–8, 1998, p. 1; "IMF, Russia in high-stakes financial game," FINANCIAL TIMES, January 18, 1999.

159. "Clinton, G-7 Partners Give Russia 1997 Membership in Summit of Eight," 14 ITR 572 (March 26, 1997); Bruce Clark, "Yeltsin looks to Asia as G7 keeps him out of the club," FINANCIAL TIMES, April 23, 1996, p. 2; Lionel Barber, "Russia's New Role in Europe," EUROPE, March 1997, p. 15; Martin Walker, "EU Investing in Russia's Future," EUROPE, March 1997, p. 1; Dominique Moisi, "End of Age of Innocence," FINANCIAL TIMES, October 24, 1995, p. 16; "Russian OECD Appli-

cation Received; Reforms Needed to Join, Official Says," 13 ITR 22 d57 (May 29, 1996); Martin Walker, "Investing in Russia Not for the Weak at Heart," EUROPE, March 1997, p. 9; John Thornhill, "Russia moves to overhaul monopolies," FINAN-CIAL TIMES, April 29, 1997, p. 2; "Risks of Russian market exposed," FINANCIAL TIMES, March 25, 1997, p. 2; "Russian growth 'exaggerated'," FINANCIAL TIMES, March 25, 1997, p. 2; "Russia Sets Alcohol Import Quotas, Orders End to Exemptions from Duties," 13 ITR 1538 (October 2, 1996) (setting a quota on imported vodka to protect the local market, but lowering tariffs in imported salmon and caviar at the same time); "Adjustments to the bear: The troika at Russia's helm has made a promising start," FINANCIAL TIMES, April 28, 1997, p. 23; Chrystia Freeland, "Russian bond rules eased for foreign investors," FINANCIAL TIMES, July 20–21, 1996, p. 24; John Thornhill, "Russian court backs investors," FINANCIAL TIMES, May 22, 1997, p. 2; "Russia will protect Gazprom shareholders," FINANCIAL TIMES, May 27, 1997, p. 20; Chrystia Freeland, "IMF to resume [10 billion] Russian loans," FINANCIAL TIMES, April 4, 1997, p. 2; Bruce Clark & Chrystia Freeland, "$50 bn awaits Russian reform," FINANCIAL TIMES, February 27, 1997, p. 4.

160. "EU Sign Accords with Three Former Soviet Countries," 13 ITR 17 d51 (April 24, 1996); "Uzbekistan Business Center," 13 ITR 1575 (October 9, 1996); "IMF Approves $867 Million Loan to Ukraine for '96 Program," 13 ITR 21 d49 (May 22, 1996); "World Bank Oks $64 Million Loan for Turkmeninstan," 14 ITR 1008 (June 4, 1997).

161. FROM PLAN TO MARKET: WORLD DEVELOPMENT REPORT 1996, *op cit.*, pp. 85–132.

162. Neil Buckley, "EU urged to trade more in East Asia," FINANCIAL TIMES, November 12, 1996, p. 5; Lionel Barber, "EU agrees new Lomé blueprint," FI-NANCIAL TIMES, June 30, 1998, p. 5; "Divided EU Moves to Negotiate Pact with Mercosur," 15 ITR 1315 (July 29, 1998).

CHAPTER 10. WIDENING THE EUROPEAN COMMUNITY

1. The six states that founded the European Coal and Steel Community in 1951 and the European Economic Community in 1957 are: Belgium, France, Germany, Italy, Luxembourg and the Netherlands. They have since been joined by Denmark, Ireland and the United Kingdom (in 1973), Greece (1981); Spain and Portugal (1986), and Austria, Finland and Sweden (1995). Norway has twice turned down accession. As of 1999, the following countries had applied to join the EU: Bulgaria, Cyprus, the Czech Republic, Estonia, Hungary, Latvia, Lithuania, Malta, Poland, Romania, Slovakia, Slovenia, and Turkey.

2. A good, short article on the subject is: Per Magnus Wijkman, "EFTA Countries," in RANDALL HENNING AND OTHERS, EDS., REVIVING THE EUROPEAN UN-ION (Institute for International Economics, 1994), pp. 83–107. For a book-length treatment, *see*: THERESE BLANCHET & OTHERS, THE AGREEMENT ON THE EURO-PEAN ECONOMIC AREA (EEA) (Clarendon Press, 1994).

3. "Vienna Waltz: EU Summit Defers Tough Decisions," EURECOM, December 1998, p. 2; "A wider EU," THE ECONOMIST, November 7, 1998, p. 17; Michael Smith, "Eleven EU regions could lose aid," FINANCIAL TIMES, November 23, 1998,

p. 2; Eric Frey, "Austrians oppose EU enlargement," FINANCIAL TIMES, March 26, 1998, p. 3; Lionel Barber, "EU states in revolt over cost of admitting poorer nations," FINANCIAL TIMES, September 16, 1997, p. 16; "A most exclusive club," FINANCIAL TIMES, August 26, 1998, p. 8; Kevin Done, "East Europe trend 'slower, more erratic'," FINANCIAL TIMES, November 24, 1998, p. 3; "Widening the EU—but not too fast," THE ECONOMIST, November 7, 1998, p. 51; Quentin Peel & Stefan Wagstal, "Journey into the unknown," FINANCIAL TIMES, November 9, 1998, p. 15. *See generally,* EU COMMISSION, AGENDA 2000: FOR A STRONGER AND WIDER UNION, COM (97) 2000 final, vols. 1 and 2 (Brussels, July 15, 1997).

4. Anthony Robinson, "Investing in Central and Eastern Europe: Dawn of a more hopeful era," FINANCIAL TIMES, April 15, 1996, p. 1; Robinson, "Central Europe: Return to 'normality'," *op, cit.,* p. 2.

5. Anthony Robinson, "Painful adjustment for former Soviet empire," FINANCIAL TIMES, April 15, 1996, p. 2.

6. Caroline Southey, "EU to boost links with eastern bloc," FINANCIAL TIMES, March 1, 1996, p. 3; Anthony Robinson, "Mitteleuropa's leaders look to EU for security," FINANCIAL TIMES, December 15, 1995, p. 2; Barry Wood, "EU Eastward Expansion," EUROPE, May 1996, pp. 20–21. According to this account, "literally hundreds of civil servants are working full-time to bring national laws and regulations into conformity with EU standards. [Said] one diplomat, 'It is difficult for Western Europeans to comprehend the extent to which the desire to join the EU and NATO drives policy here in the East.' " Jonathan Kaufman, "Germany Cornering Markets," BOSTON GLOBE, February 24, 1992, p. 10.

7. Andre Fisher, "German exporters tap into E. Europe," FINANCIAL TIMES, July 19, 1996, p. 2; Manfred Wegner, "Trade, growth and industrial structure," *op cit.,* p. 29, in HENNING AND OTHERS, *op cit.*

8. Kevin Done, "Investors give Eastern Europe a miss," FINANCIAL TIMES, April 15, 1997, p. 2.

9. Manfred Wegner, *op cit.,* pp. 28–31.

10. Elizabeth Pond, "Germany's New Foreign Policy: Looking East & West," EUROPE, May 1996, p. 12; Lionel Barber, "Kohl draws line across Europe," FINANCIAL TIMES, December 14, 1995, p. 1; Jonathan Kaufman, "Germany Cornering Markets," BOSTON GLOBE, February 24, 1992, p. 1; Barry D. Wood, "Enlargement," EUROPE, October 1996, p. ESR 8.

11. Graham Bowley & Kevin Done, "Rapid reforms 'working for ex-communist states'," FINANCIAL TIMES, June 28, 1996, p. 16. The foregoing article was based on an information-rich book by the World Bank, FROM PLAN TO MARKET WORLD DEVELOPMENT REPORT (Oxford University Press, 1996), that studies state-managed economies that are now in transition; chiefly Central and Eastern Europe and the former Soviet bloc, but also including China, Mongolia and Vietnam. It examines intensively how one-third of the world population is faring now that communism has failed and market transition is proceeding. Only China, with its rigid governmental control of both micro- and macroeconomic policy and creative market opening has expanded without imploding first. For FDI figures, *see* Kevin Done, "Foreign investment in east Europe doubles," FINANCIAL TIMES, March 25, 1996, p. 3, *citing:* THE ECONOMIST INTELLIGENCE UNIT, ECONOMIES IN TRANSITION: FIRST QUARTER 1996. It calls "Germany . . . the dominant trader, investor aid donor and creditor for the transition economies [in eastern Europe]." More than 10 percent of

total German foreign investment is now directed at the most advanced transition economies.

12. Manfred Wegner, "Trade, Growth, and Industrial Structure," pp. 27–30, and Andras Inotai, "Central and Eastern Europe," pp. 139–164, both in HENNING AND OTHERS, *op cit.*; Caroline Southey, "EU to retain its current farm policies," FINANCIAL TIMES, September 27, 1995, p. 3; "EU farm aid for new members may be cut," FINANCIAL TIMES, March 4, 1996, p. 4; Stefan Wagstyl, "East European steel prices now match levels within EU," FINANCIAL TIMES, April 29, 1997, p. 24.

13. "Luxembourg Sets Stage for EU Enlargement," EURECOM, January 1998, p. 1; "EU to Begin Negotiations on Admitting East European Nations, Turkey Rejected," 14 ITR 2177 (December 17, 1997); Stefan Wagstyl, "EU hope Turks told talks will be tough," FINANCIAL TIMES, June 25, 1998, p. 3; Leyla Boulton, "Estonia counts the cost of cleaning up for the EU," FINANCIAL TIMES, March 3, 1998, p. 3; Eric Frey "Austrians oppose EU enlargement," FINANCIAL TIMES, March 26, 1998, p. 3; Quentin Peel, "SPD works on EU enlargement," FINANCIAL TIMES, June 2, 1998, p. 40. *See generally*, Reginald Dale, "Uniting the Continent: Europe's Greatest Challenge," EUROPE, December/January 1994–95, p. 13; "Survey: Business in Eastern Europe," THE ECONOMIST, November 22, 1997, p. 62.

14. "Associated Countries' Road Map to Single Market," EURECOM, May 1995, p. 1.

15. Barry Wood, "EU Eastward Expansion," EUROPE, May 1996, p. 20; "Enlargement," *op cit.*, p. ESR 8.

16. Caroline Southey, "EU funding for E. Europe under threat," FINANCIAL TIMES, November 27, 1995, p. 2; Coopers & Lybrand, "Trade Relations [with] Eastern Europe," EC Commentaries, September 29, 1994, section 12.4; Preliminary Draft, General Budget of the European Communities for the Fiscal year 1994. Overview, section (93) 800-EN, May 1993, p. 25.

17. "Essen Summit Endorses Eastern European Strategy," EURECOM, December 1994, p. 1; Axel Krause, "Looking South: Europe Proposes a New Initiative for Africa and the Middle East," EUROPE, December/January 1994–95.

18. Lionel Barber, "Larger EU at any price," FINANCIAL TIMES, November 30, 1995, p. 2; "Brussels sees EU expansion eastward without budget rise," FINANCIAL TIMES, June 26, 1996, p. 1; "EU: Finance—Eastward expansion, budget reform to limit funding," Economist Intelligence Unit, Business Europe, September 12, 1995; Lionel Barber, "Commissioners square upon regional aid fight," FINANCIAL TIMES, April 28, 1997, p. 2; "A Momentous Month of March for the Union," EURECOM, April 1999, p. 1.

19. Madrid European Council, 15 and 16 December 1995, Presidency Conclusions, Doc. SN 400195, III: "A Europe Open to the World, Enjoining Stability, Security, Freedom and Solidarity," pp. 22–23; Barry D. Wood, "Enlargement," *op cit.*; Lionel Barber, "Brussels sees E. European nations in EU from 2002," FINANCIAL TIMES June 17, 1996, p. 18; Caroline Southey, "EU farm aid for new members may be cut," *op cit.*; "The Commissions Work Programme for 1997: Political priorities," COM (96) 507 final (October 17, 1996), pp. 7–8; TEU Article O (accession provisions).

For comparison purposes, the two economically weakest EU member states, Portugal and Greece, have populations of 9.9 million and 10.4 million and per capita

GDPs of $9,370 and $7,710, respectively. The strongest candidates among the CEEs (Hungary, the Czech Republic and Poland) have populations of 10.25, 10.4 and 38.6 million, and per capita GDPs of $3,840; $3,210 and $2,470, respectively. However, the latter are twice the per capita GDP of other CEEs (Romania: 22.75 million, $1,230 per capita GDP; Bulgaria: 8.5 million, $1,160). All figures from: BRIAN HUNTER, ED., THE STATESMAN'S YEAR-BOOK, 133RD ED., 1996–97 (St. Martin's Press, 1996), pp. 245, 405, 580, 621, 720, 1042, 1050, 1064, 1177.

20. Gillian Tett, "Czech Republic set to be first ex-communist OECD member," FINANCIAL TIMES, September 12, 1995, p. 20; Vincent Boland, "Is the EU good enough for the Czechs?" FINANCIAL TIMES, August 2, 1995, p. 2; "Deutsche Telekom group wins Czech mobil phone bid," FINANCIAL TIMES, March 15, 1996, p. 19; Barry D. Wood, "Boom Time for the Czech Economy," EUROPE, May 1997, p. 9; Vincent Boland, "Czech currency abandons link to US dollar," FINANCIAL TIMES, May 27, 1997, p. 2; "Czechs find transition harder than they thought," FINANCIAL TIMES, April 3, 1997, p. 2.

21. Virginia Marsh, "Hungary knocks harder on EU door," FINANCIAL TIMES, July 19, 1995, p. 2; "Hungary joins OECD," 13 ITR 20 d52 (May 15, 1996); "Hungary lowers import surcharge," 13 ITR 1539 (October 2, 1996); Virginia Marsh, "Hungary sold short by black market," FINANCIAL TIMES, April 6–7, 1996, p. 2; Barry D. Wood, "Worrying About Hungary," EUROPE, May 1997, p. 12.

22. Lionel Barber, "Poland given trade warning by Brussels," FINANCIAL TIMES, July 17, 1996, p. 3; "Poland raises duties on barley," 14 ITR 1008 (June 4, 1997); "Poland sets up second free trade zone to offer investors tax, customs breaks," 13 ITR 26 d44 (June 26, 1996); Matthew Kaminski, "Poland offers Ukraine a view to the west," FINANCIAL TIMES, June 26, 1996, p. 3.

23. Barry D. Wood, "Don't Give Up on Slovakia," EUROPE, May 1995, p. 11; Hugh Carey, "Baltics seek stability of European fold," FINANCIAL TIMES, September 22, 1995, p. 3; "Foreign Investment: Bulgaria Picks 15 Competitive Firms for Quick Sales to Foreign Investors," 13 ITR 1572 (October 9, 1996); Anders Aslund, "Post-communist report card," FINANCIAL TIMES, August 5, 1998, p. 10.

24. The Commission's Work Programme for 1997; "Political priorities," *op cit.*, p. 6; David Gardner, "EU turns strategic eyes to South," FINANCIAL TIMES, May 17, 1995, p. 5; BARCELONA EURO-MEDITERRANEAN CONFERENCE (27–28 November 1995): DECLARATION AND WORK PROGRAMME, DOC/95/7 (December 4, 1995); James Whittington, "Chirac urges EU to boost Mideast role," FINANCIAL TIMES, April 9, 1996, p. 3; "EU–Israel Cooperation Pact," 13 ITR 20 d60 (May 15, 1996) (the EU has pacts with Tunisia and Morocco as well, and is in discussions with Syria); John Barham, "Treaty [customs union with EU] sends Turkey westwards," FINANCIAL TIMES, March 7, 1995, p. 4; "Turkey's new revenue-raising plan emphasizes widespread privatization," 13 ITR 1922 (December 11, 1996).

25. Bill Nichols, "Clinton turns his efforts to foreign policy; looks to future as he salutes Europe's past," USA TODAY, May 29, 1997, p. 10A.

CHAPTER 11. JAPAN: ASIA'S DISINTEGRATING COLOSSUS

1. See generally, LESTER THUROW, HEAD TO HEAD: THE COMING ECONOMIC BATTLE AMONG JAPAN, EUROPE AND AMERICA (Morrow & Co., 1992).

2. For example, CLYDE PRESTOWITZ, TRADING PLACES: HOW WE ALLOWED JAPAN TO TAKE THE LEAD (Basic Books, 1988); WILLIAM DIETRICH, IN THE SHADOW OF THE RISING SUN: THE POLITICAL ROOTS OF AMERICAN ECONOMIC DECLINE (Pennsylvania State University Press, 1991); JAMES FALLOWS, LOOKING AT THE SUN (Vintage, 1995). *Cf.* Stephen Fidler, "Might Asia lose a decade?" FINANCIAL TIMES, November 27, 1997, p. 13; James Fallows, "How the Far East Was Won," U.S. NEWS & WORLD REPORT, December 8, 1997, p. 110.

3. A review of Fred Bergsten and Marcus Noland's book, RECONCILABLE DIFFERENCES? U.S.–JAPAN ECONOMIC CONFLICT (Institute for International Economics, 1993), placed import penetration of the Japanese market at 5.9 percent, whereas that of the U.S. is nearly three times that (15.3 percent) and that of the EU even higher. Michael Prowse, "Strong-arm tactics," FINANCIAL TIMES, June 25, 1993, p. 12.

4. Michael Hirsh & Keith Henry, "The Unraveling of Japan Inc.," FOREIGN AFFAIRS (March/April 1997), p. 11; Michael Prowse, "Strong-arm tactics," *op cit.*

5. Peter Noonan, "World economy and finance," FINANCIAL TIMES, September 30, 1994, p. 1; International Monetary Fund, "World Economic Outlook," October 1995 (Washington, D.C., 1995), p. 15; Paul Krugman, "The Myth of Asia's Miracle," in POP INTERNATIONALISM (MIT Press, 1996), p. 167; Edward W. Desmond, "The Bottom Line on Japan," FORTUNE, July 21, 1997, p. 92; Michael Hirsh & Keith Henry, "The Unraveling of Japan, Inc.," *op cit.*

6. Robert J. Samuelson, "Global Boom and Bust?" NEWSWEEK, November 10, 1997, p. 35; Bill Powell, "Special Report: The Globe Shutters," NEWSWEEK, November 10, 1997, p. 32; Paul Abrahams, "On the brink of recession," FINANCIAL TIMES, October 7, 1997, p. 19; Gillian Tett, "Japan's stormy weather," FINANCIAL TIMES, August 22, 1997, p. 15.

7. William Dawkins, "Japan's economic recovery—a miracle or a mirage?" FINANCIAL TIMES, June 20, 1996, p. 6; Paul Abrahams, "Fears grow for Japan economy," FINANCIAL TIMES, October 1, 1997, p. 8.

8. Brenton Schlender, "Japan's White Collar Blues," FORTUNE, March 21, 1994, p. 97; Japanese felling pain of poverty," BOSTON GLOBE, January 31, 1994, p. 1; Michiyo Nakamoto, "Japanese salary men's jobs for life begin to unravel," FINANCIAL TIMES, January 16, 1996, p. 6 (the majority of Japanese businesses are overstaffed, particularly at the white-collar, senior level); William Dawkins, "Japanese jobless rate rises to [a post-war] record of 3.5%," FINANCIAL TIMES, June 29–30, 1996, p. 22; "U.S.–Japan Car Pact Report Due Out Nov. 12," 14 ITR 1899 (November 5, 1997); "U.S. Expresses Concern About Japan Computer Accord," 14 ITR 1900 (November 5, 1997); "One-Fifth of Japanese Imports Made by Overseas Subsidiaries, Report Says," 13 ITR 27 d15 (July 3, 1996); "Weakening of Japanese Keiretsu Offers Canada More Opportunities," 13 ITR 1412 (September 11, 1996); Karl Schoenberger, "Has Japan Changed?" FORTUNE, August 19, 1996, p. 72; Gillian Tett, "Policy holders desert Japan's life groups," FINANCIAL TIMES, August 6, 1997, p. 10; "Japan trade surplus doubles," FINANCIAL TIMES, September 18, 1997, p. 1 (a 113 percent rise year-on-year in August 1997).

9. Paul Abrahams, "Tokyo's mandarins fail to confront economic problems," FINANCIAL TIMES, October 31, 1997, p. 8; Stephanie Flanders, "IMF says 'wishful thinking' prolonged Japan's bank crisis," FINANCIAL TIMES, August 21, 1995, p. 1; Michiyo Nakamoto, "Japanese car group hit by scandal," FINANCIAL TIMES, Oc-

tober 24, 1997, p. 5; "Japan sokaiya scandal embroils more companies," FINANCIAL TIMES, October 28, 1997, p. 4; Gerard Baker, "Mob rule: Japan's mafia," FINANCIAL TIMES, March 16–17, 1996, p. 22; Gillian Tett, "Japanese business leaders aim to curb shareholder action," FINANCIAL TIMES, May 29, 1997, p. 12. A book that captures much of the chaos in the readjusting Japanese economy is BEN HILLS, JAPAN BEHIND THE LINES (Sceptre, 1996), but it is too sensational, too overstated.

10. Gerard Baker, "Collapse that may force Japan to put its house in order," FINANCIAL TIMES, March 19, 1996, p. 8; William Dawkins, "Japanese former housing loan chief arrested," FINANCIAL TIMES, June 27, 1996, p. 4; Gerard Baker, "Japan's banks report record loss," FINANCIAL TIMES, May 25–26, 1996, p. 1; Gillian Tett & David Wighton, "Japan Admits scale of bad loans," FINANCIAL TIMES, January 13, 1998, p. 7; Gillian Tett, "Illegal bond trade case worsens Japanese image," FINANCIAL TIMES, May 22, 1997, p. 1; Jeffrey Bartholet, "The Lost Decade," NEWSWEEK , July 27, 1998, p. 280.

11. "U.S. Calls on Japan to Make Auto Market Reforms," 15 ITR 1380 (August 12, 1998); "WTO Rules Against Japan in Dispute with U.S. over Curbs on Farm Imports," 15 ITR 1381 (August 12, 1998); Steven Butler & others, "Pacific Grim," U.S. NEWS & WORLD REPORT, December 8, 1997, p. 26; Robert Samuelson, "The Buyer of Last Resort," NEWSWEEK, August 24, 1998, p. 42; Dick Nanto, "U.S. International Trade Performance, 1970–95," Congressional Research Service 96–590 (June 28, 1996), Library of Congress; Nancy Dunne, "US deficit widens in wake of Asia crisis," FINANCIAL TIMES, July 18–19, 1998, p. 3; "U.S., EU Issue Warning . . . to Japan Not to Escalate Exports," 15 ITR 180 (February 4, 1998); Mark Suzman & others, "Asian crisis starts to take heavy toll on US exports," FINANCIAL TIMES, June 19, 1998, p. 10. *Cf.*, The Ministry of Foreign Affairs of Japan, "Downward Trend in Japan's Trade Surplus with the World," http://www.mofa.go.jp/jul/economy/01.html (November 12, 1997); "U.S. Increasingly Concerned over Trade Deficit with Japan," 14 ITR 1668 (October 1997); "Japan's Trade Surplus Surges on Exports of Computers, Automobiles," 14 ITR 1553 (September 17, 1997).

12. For example, U.S.T.R., "1998 National Trade Estimate," http://www.ustr.gov/reportsintel/1998/contents.html.

13. Rob Norton, "Japan's Failed Experiment," FORTUNE, October 30, 1995, p. 41; Carl Weinberg, "Tokyo is the real problem," FINANCIAL TIMES, November 17, 1997, p. 12; William Dawkins, "Driven by a force beyond its control," FINANCIAL TIMES, April 18, 1995, p. 16; "Cool response to Japanese package sends dollar down," FINANCIAL TIMES, April 18, 1995, p. 1; Gerard Baker, "Package falls short of modest expectations," FINANCIAL TIMES, April 15–16, 1995, p. 3; "Japan's new package only poses trouble farther down the line," FINANCIAL TIMES, September 20, 1995, p. 6; William Dawkins, "Cynicism grows over stimulus plan," FINANCIAL TIMES, September 21, 1995, p. 1; Gerard Baker, "Economic pessimism grips Japan," FINANCIAL TIMES, August 8, 1996, p. 4; Gwen Robinson, "Japanese public go bankrupt in record numbers," FINANCIAL TIMES, February 15–16, 1997, p. 3. In 1996, personal bankruptcies hit a record high of 50,615 cases, 17 percent higher than 1995. Corporate bankruptcies reached 1,204, 8 percent higher than the prior year.

14. "First Joint Status Report on the U.S.–Japan Enhanced Initiative on Deregulation and Competition Policy," Released at G-8 Summit, May 15, 1998, 15 ITR 891 (May 20, 1998).

15. Gerard Baker & Stephen Fidler, "U.S. eyes the Asian storm (interview with Robert Rubin)," FINANCIAL TIMES, July 13, 1998, p. 19; Taggart Murphy, "Don't Be Fooled by Japan's Big Bang," FORTUNE, December 29, 1997, p. 214.

16. Paul Abrahams & Gillian Tett, "Japanese exports down as sales to rest of Asia fall 18%," FINANCIAL TIMES, May 21, 1998, p. 8; Taggart Murphy, "Don't Be Fooled by Japan's Big Bang," *op cit.*

17. Paul Abrahams & others, "Hashimoto's day of reckoning," FINANCIAL TIMES, July 13, 1998, p. 2; Paul Abrahams & Mark Suzman, "Japan Launches $128bn package to lift economy," FINANCIAL TIMES, April 25–26, 1998, p. 1; Gillian Tett, "Tokyo markets begin to suffer 'package fatigue'," FINANCIAL TIMES, April 11–12, 1998, p. 3; Bill Powell, "More Woe from Asia," NEWSWEEK, August 17, 1998, p. 42; Fareed Zakaria, "Japan's American Problem," NEWSWEEK, August 3, 1998, p. 39.

18. Jeffrey Bartholet & others, "The Lost Decade," NEWSWEEK, July 27, 1998, p. 28; Fareed Zakaria, "Japan's American Problem," NEWSWEEK, August 3, 1998, p. 38; Gillian Tett, "Old traditions die hard," FINANCIAL TIMES, February 2, 1998, p. 9; "Japanese bank 'timebomb' strains market nerves," FINANCIAL TIMES, August 18, 1998, p. 4; "Foreign Acquisition of Japanese Firms a Record in Value, Volume in FY 1997," 15 ITR 788 (May 6, 1998); Gillian Tett, "Japanese in 'bridge bank' pledge to aid economic recovery," FINANCIAL TIMES, July 3, 1998, p. 1.

19. Michael Hirsch & Keith Henry, "The Unraveling of Japan, Inc.," FOREIGN AFFAIRS, March/April 1997, p. 1; U.S. Department of Commerce, Bureau of Economic Analysis, "International Accounts Data (November 5, 1997)," http://www.bea.doc.gov/bea/di/usadiad.html; Jim Rohwer, "The Dollar Rules," FORTUNE, November 24, 1997, p. 108.

20. Michiyo Nakamoto, "Revolution coming, ready or not," FINANCIAL TIMES, October 24, 1997, p. 14; William Dawkins, "Barriers fall to import invaders," FINANCIAL TIMES, March 19, 1996, p. 15; U.S. Bureau of the Census, "U.S.–Japan Merchandise Trade Data (1960–1996)," http:/www.ita.doc.gov/region/japan/usjnt.html.

21. Gillian Tett, "Big bang boosts foreign fund business," FINANCIAL TIMES, April 23, 1997, p. 22 ("Foreign investment advisers, . . . increased business by about 185 percent."); "U.S. banks [Merrill/Lynch and Morgan Stanley] lead Tokyo trading," FINANCIAL TIMES, November 6, 1997, p. 1; "Japan lifts Ban on Holding Companies, NTT Telecom Firm to Be First to Benefit," 14 ITR 1060 (June 18, 1997); "Foreign Acquisition of Japanese Firm up 68 percent," 14 ITR 1239 (July 16, 1997).

22. William Dawkins, "Japan starts to winnow out losers," FINANCIAL TIMES, February 17, 1997, p. 10; "Japanese finance: Ambitious plan for change takes shape," FINANCIAL TIMES, March 25, 1997, p. 1: Stephanie Strom, "Bailing Out of the Bailout Game," NEW YORK TIMES, November 8, 1997, p. D1; Michiyo Nakamoto, "Japan plans to sort out its property mess," FINANCIAL TIMES, October 17, 197, p. 6; "U.S., Foreign Business Propose 'Deregulations Checklist' for Japan," 14 ITR 1760 (October 15, 1997).

23. Neal Chowdhury and Anthony Paul, "Where Asia Goes from Here," FORTUNE, November 24, 1997, p. 96.

24. Michiyo Nakamoto, "Japan's GDP drops for fourth consecutive quarter," FINANCIAL TIMES, December 4, 1998, p. 22; "Still mired in the mud," THE ECON-

OMIST, November 28, 1998, p. 79; Naoko Nakamac, "Upturn likely for Japan next year," FINANCIAL TIMES, December 28, 1998, p. 1; Gerard Baker, "Clinton conjures up spectre for Obuchi," FINANCIAL TIMES, November 21–22, 1998, p. 4. *See also*: "Building the Financial System of the 21st Century: An Agenda for Japan and the U.S." (Harvard Law School and Japan Institute of International Affairs, 1998).

25. "U.S., Japan Strike Deal on Autos: Address Parts, Dealerships, Repairs," 12 ITR 27 d5 (July 5, 1995); "Adverse Impact of Japan Auto Deal on Other Trade Disputes Is Feared," 12 ITR 27 d3 (July 5, 1995); "Japanese Automakers Hail Trade Accord Plans Do Not Contain Numerical Targets," 12 ITR 27 d4 (July 5, 1995); "EU Slams US Tactics in US/Japan Auto Parts Row," EURECOM, June 1995, p. 1; Michiyo Nakamoto, "EU–Japan accord over car access," FINANCIAL TIMES, June 7, 1995, p. 7; "Europe turns out the victor in US–Japan car trade tussle," FINANCIAL TIMES, April 12, 1996, p. 6; "U.S. Officials Praise Progress Under U.S.–Japan Auto Accord," 13 ITR 1418 (September 11, 1996); "May Sales of U.S. Cars in Japan Drop 21 Percent from Last Year," 14 ITR 1023 (June 11, 1997); "U.S. Frustrated by Japan's Progress on Car Sales, Dealerships," 14 ITR 1759 (October 15, 1997); "Japan's U.S. Parts Import Set Record in 1996," 14 ITR 1197 (July 9, 1997); "Japan to Deregulate Law in January on Auto Repair," 14 ITR 1153 (July 2, 1997); John Griffiths, "Japan set for export drive: Car industry gears up for fresh assault on world markets," FINANCIAL TIMES, May 16, 1997, p. 8.

26. "U.S.–Japan Chip Accord Provides Boost to Market Penetration," 13 ITR 16 d16 (April 17, 1996); Michiyo Nakamoto, "Japan backs EU role in chip negotiations," FINANCIAL TIMES, June 4, 1996, p. 4; "U.S. and Japan agree outline for new semiconductor deal," FINANCIAL TIMES, August 2, 1996, p. 12 [The deal itself is at 13 ITR 1287 (August 7, 1996)]; "U.S. Will Take Action Against Japan If It Does Not Comply with Chip Pact," 13 ITR 1264 (August 7, 1996).

27. Tony Boyd, "Tokyo observed: Looser forex laws herald nation's Big Bang," AUSTRALIAN FINANCIAL REVIEW, November 25, 1996, p. 11; Gillian Tett, "Japan to open up corporate pension funds market," FINANCIAL TIMES, September 24, 1997, p. 1; "Foreign managers lift share of Japan funds," FINANCIAL TIMES, June 23, 1997, p. 16.

28. Gwen Robinson, "Tokyo exchange to relax rules," FINANCIAL TIMES, September 18, 1997, p. 15; Daniel Bogler & William Dawkins, "Japan plans financial deregulation by 2001," FINANCIAL TIMES, November 12, 1996, p. 1.

29. Michiyo Nakamoto, "Japan and US try to work out insurance against trade storm," FINANCIAL TIMES, May 29, 1996, p. 4; "Japan Commits to Insurance Deregulation," 13 ITR 1932 (December 18, 1996); "Little Progress Seen in Opening Japan Insurance Market to Foreigners," 14 ITR 1059 (June 18, 1997); "Foreign Insurers in Japan Propose Single, Streamlined Rate Organization," 14 ITR 1821 (October 22, 1997).

30. Michiyo Nakamoto, "Japan waits for the call," FINANCIAL TIMES, August 7, 1996, p. 9; "Japanese Reforms Seen Encouraging Foreign Telecom Firms to Enter Market," 14 ITR 1196 (July 9, 1997); "U.S. and Japan Agree on Renewal of NTT Accord," 14 ITR 1719 (October 8, 1997); "U.S. Asks Japan to Ensure NTT Rates for Interconnection at Market Prices," 14 ITR 1898 (November 5, 1997).

31. International Trade Daily, "U.S., Japan Seek Film Dispute Resolution Before More Friction Builds," 9/16/97 BTD d8; "U.S. Will Eye Implementation of WTO Ruling Against Japan," 10/7/96 BTD d2; "U.S. Says Japanese Plan to Cut Liquor

Taxes in 1998 Is Too Late," 14 ITR 1809 (October 2, 1997); "Japanese Firm Reaches Out-of-Court Settlement for Illegal Copying of Microsoft, Lotus Software," 13 ITR 1439 (September 18, 1996); Michiyo Nakamoto, "U.S. threatens Japan over music industry rights," FINANCIAL TIMES, November 1–2, 1997, p. 4; "U.S. Maritime Commission Hails Accord, Accepts Partial Fine from Japanese Shippers," 14 ITR 1851 (October 29, 1997).

32. Jim Rohwer, "Asia's Meltdown: It Ain't over Yet," FORTUNE, July 20, 1998, p. 93; Gillian Tett, "Japan offers $84 bn extra for economy," FINANCIAL TIMES, October 28, 1998, p. 1; "New Tokyo stimulus gets cold reception," FINANCIAL TIMES, November 17, 1998, p. 4; Martin Wolf, "Serious, yes. Hopeless, no," FINANCIAL TIMES, October 7, 1998, p. 15; Jim Rohwer, "Yikes! Japan's Bank Debt Bomb Is Scarier Than You Think," FORTUNE, November 9, 1998, p. 124.

33. Yoichi Fumabashi, "Tokyo's Depression Diplomacy," FOREIGN AFFAIRS, November/December 1998, p. 26.

CHAPTER 12. CHINA: THE MIDDLE KINGDOM IN THE MIDDLE

1. "China's Trade with Japan Slows Down Due to Asian Financial Crisis," 15 ITR 183 (February 4, 1998).

2. "Investment in Chinese Army-Run Firms More Than Four Times Previous Report," 15 ITR 161 (January 28, 1998).

3. STATISTICAL ABSTRACT OF THE UNITED STATES, 1996, 116th ED. (U.S. GPO, 1996), p. 835; WORLD BANK, FROM PLAN TO MARKET: WORLD DEVELOPMENT REPORT 1996 (Oxford University Press, 1996), pp. 132–135, 218, 220–221.

4. Paul Krugman, "The Myth of Asia's Miracle," in POP INTERNATIONALISM (MIT Press, 1996), pp. 181–182; Gillian Tett, "OECD seeks to set up [economic statistics] links with China," FINANCIAL TIMES, July 21, 1995, p. 4; WORLD BANK, FROM PLAN TO MARKET, *op cit.*, p. 208; "U.S. Total Trade Balances with Individual Countries, 1990–96," http://www.ita.doc. Gov/industry/otea/usfth/to8.prm (Table 8); Neal Chowdhury & Anthony Paul, "Where Asia Goes from Here," FORTUNE, November 24, 1997, p. 96; "Contractual Investment in China Continues to Decline," 14 ITR 2027 (November 26, 1997); Tony Walker & James Harding, "Chinese fears of slowdown gather pace," FINANCIAL TIMES, November 17, 1997, p. 4; Jim Rohwer, "China: The Real Economic Wildcard," FORTUNE, September 28, 1998, p. 106.

5. David Hale, "The challenge now is trade," FINANCIAL TIMES, November 7, 1997, p. 14.

6. Mortimer Zuckerman, "China's star is still rising," U.S. NEWS & WORLD REPORT, November 17, 1997, p. 84; James Kynge, "Zhu's popularity tested by Chinese suffering," FINANCIAL TIMES, March 17, 1999, p. 5; Tony Walker & others, "Jiang comes to town," FINANCIAL TIMES, October 27, 1997, p. 15. President Clinton said, "As always, America must be prepared to live and flourish in a world in which we are at odds with China. But that is not the world we want. Our objective is not containment and conflict; it is co-operation"; John Broder, "U.S. and China Reach Trade Pacts but Clash on Rights," NEW YORK TIMES, October 30, 1997, p. 1; Henry Kissinger, "Outrage Is Not a Policy," NEWSWEEK, November 10, 1997, p. 47; "How not to deal with China," THE ECONOMIST, March 20, 1999, p. 15.

7. MORTON ABRAMOWITZ, CHINA: CAN WE HAVE A POLICY? (Carnegie Endowment for International Peace: Brookings Institution, 1997).

8. Nancy Dunne, "Congress seeks to end China trade status battle," FINANCIAL TIMES, November 5, 1997, p. 1; "Air, auto executives urge permanent most favored nation status for China," 14 ITR 558 (March 26, 1997);"Lawmakers Say Congress Has Time to Vote on Permanent NTR for China," 16 ITR 1465 (September 15, 1999).

9. "China Willing to Work Harder to Meet U.S. Accession Conditions," 13 ITR 1808 (November 27, 1996); Guy de Jonquières & Tony Walker, "New Dawn in the east: Chinese membership of the World Trade Organization now looks closer," FINANCIAL TIMES, March 3, 1997, p. 21; Tony Walker, "Call to speed China WTO entry talks," FINANCIAL TIMES, April 24, 1997, p. 9.

10. "U.S. Wants China to Decide Now Whether It Will Open Markets Enough to Join WTO," 14 ITR 1617 (September 24, 1997); "U.S., EU Agree Progress Needed by China in WTO Accession Negotiations, Brittan Says," 14 ITR 1667 (October 1, 1997); "Daley Says China Will Never Enter WTO Without Submitting a Serious Proposal," 14 ITR 1755 (October 15, 1997); Paul Magnusson & Dexter Roberts, "Slow Boat to a Trade Deal," BUSINESS WEEK, April 12, 1999, p. 36; Joseph Kahn, "China's Premier Twice Voices Displeasure over Not Getting into the Club," NEW YORK TIMES, April 10, 1999, p. A5.

11. "Chinese Minister Blames U.S., Europeans for Failure to Join WTO," 15 ITR 1079 (June 24, 1998); James Harding, "Asian contagion may unnerve China," FINANCIAL TIMES, October 27, 1997, p. 3; "Chinese Minister Calls on U.S. to Accept Trade Imbalance, Help Nation Enter the WTO," 14 ITR 1717 (October 8, 1997).

12. Laura Tyson & James Harding, "Beijing's 'softly softly' overture strikes a flat note with Taipei," FINANCIAL TIMES, February 3, 1998, p. 6; Nick Gardner, "Hong Kong economy will boom even after they hand over to China," LONDON TIMES, February 16, 1997, p. Money 4.7; Laura Tyson, "China and Taiwan on brink of shipping link," FINANCIAL TIMES, April 17, 1997, p. 4; "Taiwan: Searching for a national identity," FINANCIAL TIMES, October 7, 1997, p. 1; "Pro-independence party wins local elections in Taiwan," BOSTON GLOBE, November 30, 1997, p. A23.

13. "China fears for its wild west," THE ECONOMIST, November 15, 1997, p. 40.

14. "Japan's 1995 Investment in China Tops U.S., Trails Taiwan, Hong Kong," 13 ITR 21 d10 (May 22, 1996). Hong Kong's investment stake is by far the largest ($60.1 billion), while Taiwan's is nearer that of Japan and the U.S.. William Dawkins, "Tokyo backs $300m loan for power plant in China," FINANCIAL TIMES, June 5, 1996, p. 16. *Cf.* Tony Walker & Michiyo Nakamoto, "Japanese companies take stock in investment in China," FINANCIAL TIMES, April 18, 1995, p. 5. For years, Japan has been China's largest trade partner, but in 1995 China became Japan's second largest trade partner, with a two-way trade of near $58 billion that is rising rapidly. Moreover, China enjoys the largest trade surplus with Japan, $14 billion in 1995.

15. Tony Walker, "EU's China strategy will aim to expand ties," FINANCIAL TIMES, July 3, 1995, p. 16; Sophie Roell, "China picks European group as partner for airliner project," FINANCIAL TIMES, July 11, 1996, p. 12; Lionel Barber, "China setback for EU foreign policy," FINANCIAL TIMES, April 7, 1997, p. 2; Tony Walker, "France forges ahead in trade with China," FINANCIAL TIMES, May 16, 1997, p. 7.

16. "Yeltsin backs ties with China," FINANCIAL TIMES, April 26, 1996, p. 8; Chrystia Freeland, "Jiang and Yeltsin warn U.S.," FINANCIAL TIMES, April 24, 1997, p. 8; Tony Walker, "Sino-Russian fuel deal close," FINANCIAL TIMES, June 19, 1997, p. 1; Tony Walker, "China pledges to continue Pakistan ties," FINANCIAL TIMES, December 3, 1996, p. 8.

17. "Trade Officials in Geneva Criticize China's Latest WTO Services Offer," 14 ITR 2124 (December 10, 1997). China's repeated, successive market-opening offers have routinely fallen short of "long-standing European and U.S. demands for more substantial and comprehensive trade liberalization."; "China to Be Called on to Further Open Its Services Market in WTO Accession Talks," 15 ITR 42 (January 14, 1998).

18. "China," CIA WORLD FACTBOOK 1995 (http://www.odci.gov/cia/publications/95 fac/ch.html). China is the third largest country in the world (after Russia and Canada) in terms of land mass, and the largest in terms of population. "The People's Republic of China," THE EUROPA WORLD YEAR BOOK 1996 (Europa Publications Limited, 1996), p. 834 *et seq.*

19. "China Falsifies Economic Statistics," 13 ITR 12 d26 (March 20, 1996); "China Enacts Legislation to Outlaw False Statistics," 13 ITR 22 d11 (May 29, 1996). "Chinese Officials Show Additional Concern over Drop in Foreign Investment This Year," 14 ITR 2093 (December 3, 1997); James Harding, "Three Gorges project faces $3 bn short fall," FINANCIAL TIMES, March 17, 1999, p. 1. *See generally,* Steven Butler & Brian Palmer, "Slow boat in China," U.S. NEWS & WORLD REPORT, December 15, 1997, p. 50.

20. "China–U.S. Trade Issues," CRS ISSUE BRIEF (Congressional Record Service, Library of Congress), May 3, 1996. From the time China opened its economy (based on a U.S. initiative in 1978), its real GDP has more than quadrupled and it has "become a major world trader and . . . recipient of foreign investment." From 1985 to 1995 China's GDP grew at an average rate of 9.6 percent annually.

21. Steven Radelet & Jeffrey Sacks, "Asia's Reemergence," FOREIGN AFFAIRS, November/December 1997, p. 56; Tony Walker, "China leads the pack—so far," FINANCIAL TIMES, June 28, 1996, p. 4.

22. "China–U.S. Trade Issues," CRS ISSUE BRIEF, *op cit.*

23. Tony Walker & James Harding, "Key stage on a long march to market," FINANCIAL TIMES, December 8, 1997 [Survey: China], p. 1; "Reforms lengthen job queues," *Id.*, p. 2; Tony Walker, "In China, economic growth is the way to win hearts and minds," THE AUSTRALIAN, November 25, 1996, p. 25.

24. "OECD Finds Chinese Data Distortions Much Bigger, Slow Growth," 14 ITR 1722 (October 8, 1997); James Kynge & James Harding, "China's bank shuts down debt-ridden institution," FINANCIAL TIMES, October 7, 1998, p. 1; Tony Walker, "Stockpiles disguise China's slowdown," FINANCIAL TIMES, March 21, 1997, p. 6 (estimating the surplus as about $64 billion, or 8 percent of GDP, cutting China's estimated growth by up to 2 percentage points); "Bicycles from China Are Being Dumped in U.S., Commerce Rules," 13 ITR 19 d41 (May 8, 1996).

25. Martin Wolf, "Picking up Deng's baton," FINANCIAL TIMES, February 25, 1997, p. 18; Simon Holberton, "Chinese expected to pursue annual growth rate of 8–9%" (the current five-year plan), FINANCIAL TIMES, September 26, 1995, p. 1; "China Seeks More Private Investment in State-owned Firms, Jiang Tells Congress," 14 ITR 1543 (September 17, 1997).

26. "Bribery, Corruption Still Rampant in China Despite Government Campaign," 13 ITR 1529 (October 2, 1996); "Auditors Find Misuse of World Bank Funds in China's Agricultural Projects," 14 ITR 2028 (November 26, 1997).

27. The intended pace may prove too slow, for Jiang envisions "[laying] a solid foundation for achieving basic modernization by the middle of the [21st] century." "Jiang Zemin's Report to the 15th Party Congress" (particularly Part V, "Economic Restructuring and Economic Development Strategy"), http://www.geocities.com/WallStreet/8038/jiang5.html.

Some commentators estimate that the state may retain as few as 1,000 of China's 370,000 state-run enterprises. The rest may be sold, privatized, merged or go bankrupt. About one-half run perpetually in the red. Their outstanding debt in 1994 was 800 billion yuan ($96.4 billion), "a colossal sum," and state businesses, which employ 100 million workers, are thought to be overstaffed by about one-third. Kathy Chen, "Jiang's Restructuring Plan Wins Praise," THE ASIAN WALL STREET JOURNAL, September 15, 1997, p. 1. *See also,* Tim Healy & David Hirsh, "Unleashing the People," ASIA WEEK, September 26, 1997.

28. Edward Mortimer, "Mirror, mirror on the wall," FINANCIAL TIMES, October 11, 1995, p. 13; "China and the world," FINANCIAL TIMES, March 19, 1996, p. 15; James Harding, "Beijing appeals for brake on sell-offs," FINANCIAL TIMES, August 6, 1998, p. 10.

29. "Europe and U.S. press Beijing on trade," FINANCIAL TIMES, May 6, 1996, p. 16; "Beijing directs fire at U.S. 'domination'," FINANCIAL TIMES, December 30, 1996, p. 3; "China Accuses U.S. of Conspiracy to Disrupt Country's Textile Trade," 13 ITR 1554 (October 9, 1996); "China to Require State Approval Before Local Staff Can Be Hired," 13 ITR 20 d14 (May 14, 1996).

30. Jonathan Mirsky & Peregrine Hodson, "China bows to U.S. and cuts import tariffs by a third," THE TIMES OF LONDON, November 20, 1995, p. 8; "Clinton plays China card," THE AUSTRALIAN FINANCIAL REVIEW, November 25, 1996, p. 14; Guy de Jonquières & Edward Luce, "Talks smooth China and U.S. relations," FINANCIAL TIMES, November 11, 1996, p. 1.

31. "China to Impose Regulation on Insurers in Competition with State-Owned Company," 14 ITR 1464 (September 3, 1997); "China to Keep Telecom Market Closed to Foreign Operators," 14 ITR 1460 (September 3, 1997); "China to Restrict Activity in Three Manufacturing Sectors,"13 ITR 27 d7 (July 3, 1996); "China Plans New Curbs on Foreign Firms Trying to Enter Pharmaceutical Market," 13 ITR 17 d15 (May 1, 1996); James Kynge, "Anti-western spirit," FINANCIAL TIMES, October 2, 1998, p. 13.

32. "Brake Drums and Rotors from China Subject of New ITC Dumping Probe," 13 ITR 12 d44 (March 20, 1996); James Kynge, "US warns China over trade barriers," FINANCIAL TIMES, September 24, 1998, p. 1.

33. "Customs Announces Crackdown on Transhipped China Apparel," 13 ITR 25 d14 (June 19, 1996); Tony Walker, "China and U.S. in textiles accord," FINANCIAL TIMES, February 3, 1997, p. 3; "China Cuts Rates on Imported Garments Despite Poor Performance of Home Industry," 14 ITR 1758 (October 15, 1997); "China to Raise Tax Rebates for Exporters of Textiles in Effort to Stop Industry Losses," 15 ITR 8 (January 7, 1998).

34. Tony Walker, "U.S. and China avert trade war over copyright privacy," FINANCIAL TIMES, February 27, 1995, p. 1; "U.S. Releases Sanctions List in Copyright

Dispute with China," 13 ITR 20 d2 (May 15, 1996); "U.S., China Agree on Copyright Shields; $2 Billion Sanction Threat Is Dropped," 13 ITR 25 d2 (June 19, 1996); "China Claims New Piracy Crackdown," 13 ITR 24 d15 (June 12, 1996); "China Sentences Three to Life in Prison for CD Piracy," 14 ITR 2171 (December 17, 1997).

35. "China Not 'Adequately' Controlling Some Exports to Iran, U.S. Official Says," 15 ITR 43 (January 14, 1998); "China Promises to Set Up System That Controls 'Dual-Use' Exports," 14 ITR 1901 (November 5, 1997); "China's Export Control Regime Has Been Upgraded But Still Needs Work," 14 ITR 2027 (November 26, 1997); "China Returns to U.S. Supercomputer That Was Being Used for Military Purposes," 14 ITR 1987 (November 19, 1997).

36. David Buchan, "Li plays Europe off against U.S.," FINANCIAL TIMES, April 13–14, 1996, p. 2; James Harding, "China promises to sign U.S. contracts," FINANCIAL TIMES, October 9, 1997, p. 6; Guy de Jonquières & James Harding, "Brittan in WTO deal with China," FINANCIAL TIMES, October 15, 1997, p. 8.

37. Peter Montagnon, "Recovery hangs on reform and refinancing," FINANCIAL TIMES, January 16, 1998, p. 8; "Workers clash with police in central China," AGENCE FRANCE, October 12, 1997.

38. "Severe Drought Conditions Force China to Lower 1997 Grain Harvest Forecasts," 14 ITR 1823 (October 22, 1997); "China Needs 'Breakthroughs' in Science to Meet Food Harvest Goals, Ministry Says," 14 ITR 1463 (September 3, 1997); CIA WORLD FACTBOOK 1995 (http://www.odci.gov/cia/publications/95fact/ch.html), p. 2.

39. James Harding, "China emerging as a bad boy in pollution stakes," FINANCIAL TIMES, December 9, 1997, p. 4; "China Environmental Market" (59-page booklet), 13 ITR 28 d88 (July 10, 1996); CIA WORLD FACTBOOK 1995, *op cit.*

40. *Id.*, p. 5; Tim Healy & David Hirsh, "The Economy: Unleashing The People," *op cit.*

41. "China Confirms Drop in 1997 Investment," 15 ITR 162 (January 28, 1998). However, bargain-hunting Western companies began to buy back into the more desirable emerging economies in Asia in the second half of 1997. Clay Harris & Jonathan Ford, "Asia-Pacific countries attract bargain hunters," FINANCIAL TIMES, January 19, 1998, p. 22; James Kynge, "China predicts slower growth as exports hit by Asian crisis," FINANCIAL TIMES, October 13, 1998, p. 18; Peter Montagnon, "China faces quandary over speed of reform," FINANCIAL TIMES, August 10, 1998, p. 4.

42. James Harding, "State companies on the rocks in China," FINANCIAL TIMES, October 3, 1997, p. 4; Joe McDonald, "Chinese Leader calls for Shake-up of State Industries," SEATTLE TIMES, September 12, 1997, p. A14; "China Will Be Cautious in Changing State Bank System, Bank Governor Says," 15 ITR 102 (January 21, 1998).

43. James Harding, "Chinese groups may issue bonds abroad; Foreigners to invest in state-owned enterprises," FINANCIAL TIMES, May 8, 1997, p. 5; "Lower-Than-Expected Investment Presents Opportunity for Foreign Firms, China Says," 14 ITR 2171 (December 17, 1997) (Foreign direct investment in China is expected to be $43 billion in 1997, 1.5 percent above 1996, but well below the $49.5 billion projected.); "U.S. investors learn lessons in China," FINANCIAL TIMES, October 29, 1997, p. 9; Simon Holberton, "Myths of business in China debunked," FINANCIAL

TIMES, September 22, 1995, p. 4 [noting that, of China's 1.2 billion "consumers" (about one-fifth of the world's population), 72 percent subsists on about $121 annually]; James Kynge, "Little profit in China for foreigners," FINANCIAL TIMES, October 2, 1998, p. 8.

44. "China to Lower Rates Only Slightly on Alcohol, Tobacco Products, Officials Say," 14 ITR 1668 (October 1, 1997); "China's Central Government Will Review Foreign-Financed Retail Firms," 14 ITR 1998 (November 19, 1997); "Foreign Investors in China Overpay Millions in Fraudulent Taxes, Fees," 13 ITR 21 d7 (May 22, 1996).

45. "Boeing Urges Full Normalization of Trade with China," 13 ITR 19 d25 (May 8, 1996); "China Approves Aetna Joint Venture in Shanghai," 14 ITR 1858 (October 29, 1997); Melanie Warner, "Motorola Bets Big on China," FORTUNE, May 27, 1996, p. 117; "U.S. Firms Need China Market Opening," 13 ITR 1241 (July 31, 1996).

46. "China's growth pains," FINANCIAL TIMES, January 27, 1998, p. 18; John Ridding & Tony Walker, "The long march to win investor's hearts," FINANCIAL TIMES, March 18, 1996, p. 17; "China Hopes Tariffs [*sic*] Cuts Will Generate 'Surge' in Foreign Investment," 14 ITR 1757 (October 15, 1997); "China Is Weighing Further Proposals on State Sector Investment," 14 ITR 1902 (November 5, 1997); "China to Extend Tax, Tariff Breaks for Foreign Firms," 14 ITR 2125 (December 10, 1997) (Asia's Little Tigers had a capital inflow of $93 billion in 1996, but a capital outflow of $12 billion in 1997. Capital flow to the rest of the region, however, rose from $202 billion in 1996 to $212 billion in 1997.) *Cf.*, John Ridding, "China Telecom offer has less lure than expected," FINANCIAL TIMES, October 17, 1997, p. 1; John Ridding & James Harding, "China share listings postponed," FINANCIAL TIMES, October 27, 1997, p. 18 (although this was at the heart of the Asian meltdown).

47. "China Expected to Expand Banks' Ability to Trade in Local Currency," 14 ITR 1671 (October 1, 1997); Tony Walker, "China wakes to need for banking reform," FINANCIAL TIMES, January 19, 1998, p. 18; Richard Tomlinson, "The Rise of China's Almost-Capitalist [Zhu]," FORTUNE, February 2, 1998, p. 42. *Cf.*, "China Will Be Cautious in Changing State Bank System," 15 ITR 102 (January 21, 1998).

48. "China Predicts Lower Summer Harvest," 15 ITR 958 (June 3, 1998); James Kynge, "China's growth target fades as focus is on floods," FINANCIAL TIMES, August 27, 1998, p. 3.

49. James Kynge, "Beijing to embrace Asia in pursuit of a new order," FINANCIAL TIMES, August 25, 1997, p. 3; James Harding & Tony Walker, "Beijing backs regional currency fund," FINANCIAL TIMES, November 18, 1997, p. 8; "U.S., China Agree to Discuss Standards; U.S. Weighs MRAs with APEC," 14 ITR 1817 (October 22, 1997); "Bilateral Agreements Signed During Chinese Presidents' Visit to Canada," 14 ITR 2083 (December 3, 1997);"U.S., China Resume WTO Accession Talks; Progress Cited, But More Work Is Needed," 16 ITR 1464 (September 15, 1999).

50. Jim Rohwer, "China: The Real Economic Wild Card," FORTUNE, September 28, 1998, p. 106; "Asia's Meltdown: It Ain't over Yet," FORTUNE, July 20, 1998, p. 93; James Kynge, "China imposes price curbs as deflation bites," FINANCIAL

TIMES, September 15, 1998, p. 6; Jonathan Alter, "Don't Break the China," NEWSWEEK, July 6, 1998, p. 31.

51. Tony Walker, "China spreads its wings," FINANCIAL TIMES, January 8, 1998, p. 20; Kent Jenkins & Others, "What's the BIG Deal?" U.S. NEWS & WORLD REPORT, November 24, 1997, p. 31; "Gilman Says State Department Report Politicizes Human Rights Situation in China," 15 ITR 183 (February 4, 1998).

52. James Kynge, "Beijing spurs drive for business 'divorce'," FINANCIAL TIMES, November 30, 1998, p. 6; Louise Lucas & James Harding, "Confidence in China suffers as full GITIC debt revealed," FINANCIAL TIMES, January 11, 1999, p. 1; "New Chinese Law Could Trigger Surge in Brokerage Mergers, Firm Collapses," 16 ITR 9 (January 6, 1999); James Kynge, "China plans to close down 25,800 coal mines this year," FINANCIAL TIMES, January 11, 1999, p. 5; "6,000 Chinese Manufacturers to Be Allowed to Trade Directly," 16 ITR 55 (January 13, 1999); James Harding, "China passes law to improve stock market regulation," FINANCIAL TIMES, December 30, 1998, p. 1; " 'No Room for Optimism' on Economy," 16 ITR 54 (January 13, 1999).

53. "Will China be next?" THE ECONOMIST, October 24, 1998, p. 23; "Beijing missing its target for growth," FINANCIAL TIMES, October 17–18, 1998, p. 4; "Losses in China's State Sector Reached $1 Billion in First Quarter," 15 ITR 998 (June 10, 1998); "Chinese Firms Suffering from Overcapacity," 15 ITR 1741 (October 21, 1998); "Chinese Economists See Substantial Gains from Liberalizing Trade," 15 ITR 2018 (December 2, 1998).

54. "China Seeks Overseas Funding for Transportation Infrastructure," 15 ITR 1886 (November 11, 1998); "China Plans Cooperative Efforts to Develop Coal Gas Industry," 15 ITR 1936 (November 18, 1998); James Harding & Peter Montagnon, "Investment distrust," FINANCIAL TIMES, October 29, 1998, p. 15; James Kynge, "China moves to reassure investors," FINANCIAL TIMES, November 5, 1998, p. 1.

55. "China to Separate Business Interests from Communist Party, State Entities," 15 ITR 2011 (December 2, 1998); James Harding, "The burden of change," FINANCIAL TIMES, December 8, 1997, Survey p. C; Neil Hughes, "Smashing the Iron Rice Bowl," FOREIGN AFFAIRS, July/August 1998, p. 67.

56. Peter Montagnon, "China faces quandary over speed of reform," FINANCIAL TIMES, August 10, 1998, p. 4; James Kynge & John Thornhill, "Beijing pledges $540m to help steady the trouble," FINANCIAL TIMES, September 2, 1998, p. 3; James Kynge, "China orders companies to repatriate dollar holdings," FINANCIAL TIMES, September 30, 1998, p. 1; "New Chinese curbs on foreign exchange," FINANCIAL TIMES, September 28, 1998, p. 4.

Two excellent articles that precisely state the conditions in China today and the problems facing the nation are: Neil Hughes, "Smashing the Iron Rice Bowl" and Nicholas Lardy, "China and the Asian Contagion." Both appear in FOREIGN AFFAIRS, July/August 1998, pp. 67 and 78, respectively. They note that, in a communist society, state-owned enterprises are more than just businesses. They are the "last bastion" of the community, responsible for the lives of its people even if they are out of work, laid-off or retired. They are the social security system of China. One can imagine the angst if they are under attack from the central government.

Another excellent source of information about China's present problems and future prospects is a series of reports by the World Bank, under the general title CHINA 2020, covering (in seven titles) issues such as developmental challenges, the environment, food supplies, health and elder care, capitalism and China's entry into the global economy.

CHAPTER 13. ASIA'S EMERGING ECONOMIES: "MIRACLE," MYTH OR NEITHER?

1. Robert A. Manning & Paula Stern, "The Myth of the Pacific Community," FOREIGN AFFAIRS, November/December 1994, p. 79.

2. JAMES FALLOWS, LOOKING AT THE SUN: THE RISE OF THE NEW EAST ASIAN ECONOMIC AND POLITICAL SYSTEM (Vintage Books, 1995).

3. Steven Radelet & Jeffrey Sacks, "Asia's Reemergence," FOREIGN AFFAIRS, November/December 1997, p. 44.

4. Manning & Stern, *op cit.*

5. Radelet & Sacks, *op cit.*, p. 52.

6. "A global deal," BOSTON GLOBE, September 21, 1997, D6.

7. "Investment in Korea," 13 ITR 25 d68 (June 19, 1996).

8. "Trade Policy: Countries of Pacific Region Seen Having Higher Growth, Lower Inflation," 13 ITR 24 d22 (June 12, 1996).

9. Paul Krugman, "The Myth of Asia's Miracle," FOREIGN AFFAIRS, November/December 1994, p. 62.

10. Manning & Stern, *op cit.*, pp. 80–81.

11. Michael Meyer, "Suharto Family Values," NEWSWEEK, January 26, 1998, p. 48. Although President Suharto described his country as a "rising Asian democracy," his family has been "showered with a veritable treasury of government concessions, tax breaks, monopolies and sweetheart financial deals" allowing them to amass a fortune estimated at $40 billion."

12. "TDA Lists Southeast Asia Projects," 13 ITR 25 d64 (June 19, 1996) (quoting TDA's report).

13. Manning & Stern, *op cit.*, pp. 81–83.

14. Paul Krugman, "The Myth of Asia's Miracle," in POP INTERNATIONALISM (MIT Press, 1996), p. 167.

15. Radelet & Sacks, *op cit.*, pp. 44–45; Paul Krugman, "Asia: What Went Wrong," FORTUNE, March 2, 1998, p. 32.

16. Paul Krugman, "Whatever happened to the Asian miracle?" FORTUNE, August 18, 1997, p. 26.

17. Paul Krugman, "The Myth of Asia's Miracle," *op cit.*

18. Paul Krugman, "Asia: What Went Wrong," *op cit.*, pp. 46–48.

19. Edward Lincoln, "Maybe it's the teacher's fault," U.S. NEWS & WORLD REPORT, December 15, 1997, p. 54; Peter Montagnon, "Governments 'behind Tiger success'," FINANCIAL TIMES, March 10, 1997, p. 4 (commenting on a British Overseas Development Institute Report); "Asian nations' growth 'likely to slow'," FINANCIAL TIMES, April 6, 1995, p. 6 (commenting on a report of the Asian Development Bank); Robert Samuelson, "Global Boom and Bust?" NEWSWEEK, November 10, 1997, p. 35; James Fallows, "How the Far East was Won," U.S. NEWS & WORLD REPORT, December 8, 1997, p. 11.

20. James Kynge, "Malaysian PM attacks IMF and currency speculators," FINANCIAL TIMES, September 1, 1997, p. 16.

21. James Kynge, "Malaysian disarray jolts world markets," FINANCIAL TIMES, August 29, 1997, p. 1; Paul Krugman, "Asia: What Went Wrong," *op cit.*, pp. 46–51.

22. Paul Krugman, "Whatever Happened to the Asian Miracle," *op cit.*

23. Neal Chowdhury & Anthony Paul, "Where Asia Goes from Here," FORTUNE, November 24, 1997, p. 96; Edward W. Desmond, "Japan: A Model for What *Not* to Do," FORTUNE, November 24, 1997, p. 98; Kimberly Blanton, "The perils of a fast buck," BOSTON GLOBE, September 6, 1998, p. E140.

24. James Kynge, "Mahathir woos America's IT giants," FINANCIAL TIMES, February 26, 1997, p. 4.

25. Rahul Jacob, "Where to Invest in Asia," FORTUNE, October 30, 1995, p. 162; Amy Kaslow, "Pacific Rim Beckons European Business," EUROPE, December/ January 1994–95, p. 21; Guy de Jonquières, "Asia set to become top investment target (displacing Western Europe)," FINANCIAL TIMES, February 6, 1996, p. 5.

26. Robert Chote, "IMF warning to members over corruption," FINANCIAL TIMES, August 6, 1997, p. 4; Justin Marozzi & Gerard Baker, "IMF upbeat over currency crises," FINANCIAL TIMES, July 22, 1997, p. 6; John Ridding & Paul Abrahams, "West talks down the effect of Asian crisis," FINANCIAL TIMES, November 21, 1997, p. 6; Ted Bardacke, "Asia in Crisis [series]: The day the miracle came to and end," FINANCIAL TIMES, January 12, 1998, p. 6 ("People thought raising capital every year was a substitute for cash flow"); Jonathan Fuerbringer, "Many Players, Many Losers: How and Why Asian Currencies Tumbled So Quickly," NEW YORK TIMES, December 10, 1997, p. D1.

27. Robert Chote & Mark Suzman, "Developing nations 'set to grow'," FINANCIAL TIMES, September 10, 1997, A 18.

28. Robert Chote, "Investors retreat from emerging markets," FINANCIAL TIMES, September 30, 1997, p. 6; Justin Fox, "The Great Emerging Markets Rip-Off," FORTUNE, May 11, 1998, p. 98.

29. John Ridding, "Financial turmoil will sort out Asia's sheep and goats," FINANCIAL TIMES, December 5, 1997, p. 5; John Burton, "Korea eases overseas borrowing curbs," FINANCIAL TIMES, July 25, 1997, p. 6; Ted Bardacke, "Thailand calls in IMF to discuss rehabilitation plan," FINANCIAL TIMES, July 29, 1997, p. 12; James Kynge & others, "Thai move lifts currencies," FINANCIAL TIMES, July 30, 1997, p. 1; Ted Bardacke, "Bangkok approves package of economic reforms [in return for a $16 billion IMF-led "bailout"]," FINANCIAL TIMES, August 6, 1997, p. 1; James Kynge & John Ridding, "Malaysian disarray jolts world markets," FINANCIAL TIMES, August 29, 1997, p. 1; John Burton, "Korea bankruptcies on rise [to an estimated 3,000 in January 1998 alone]," FINANCIAL TIMES, January 8, 1998, p. 3; "The Flexible Tiger [Taiwan]," THE ECONOMIST, January 3, 1998, p. 73.

30. Indira A.R. Lakshmanan, "Hong Kong market slip a challenge to China," BOSTON GLOBE, October 25, 1997, p. A2.

31. Aaron Zitner, " Assessing the damage," BOSTON GLOBE, October 24, 1997, p. E1; Robert Samuelson, "The Crash of '99?" NEWSWEEK, October 12, 1998, p. 260.

32. "How Far Is Down?" THE ECONOMIST, November 15, 1997, p. 19; Jim Rohwer, "Asia's Meltdown: It Ain't over Yet," FORTUNE, July 20, 1998, p. 93.

33. Jim Rohwer, "More Malaise in Malaysia," FORTUNE, November 24, 1997, p. 102; Bill Powell, "The Globe Shutters," NEWSWEEK, November 10, 1997, p. 30.

34. Michael Hirsh, "Into the Deep," NEWSWEEK, December 8, 1997, p. 46.

35. Philip Coggan & others, "Dow Tumbles 550 in Asia's wake," FINANCIAL TIMES, October 28, 1997, p. 1.

36. "Agony in October," BOSTON GLOBE, October 28, 1997, p. C1.

37. Jim Rohwer, "The Malaysian Contagion," FORTUNE, October 12, 1998, p. 141; Dorinda Elliott, "Sex Wars, Asian Style," NEWSWEEK, October 5, 1998, p. 48.

38. Ted Bardacke, "Thais agree on debt restructuring," FINANCIAL TIMES, September 11, 1998, p. 6; Peter Montagnon, "Wide-ranging reforms urged in E Asian financial systems," FINANCIAL TIMES, September 12, 1997, p. 6.

39. Guy de Jonquières and Frances Williams, "South-east Asian turmoil likely to hit WTO talks," FINANCIAL TIMES, September 15, 1997, p. 4.

40. Ted Bardacke, "Thailand calls in IMF to discuss rehabilitation plan," FINANCIAL TIMES, July 29, 1997, p. 12.

41. "APEC 97 Leaders Declaration," (November 25, 1997) http://www.APEC.org/html/ leaders declaration.html; Gillian Tett, "Idea whose time has come closer," FINANCIAL TIMES, October 9, 1997, p. 4.

42. Jim Rohwer, "Asia's meltdown: The risks are rising," FORTUNE, February 16, 1998, p. 84; "The Asian contagion," FINANCIAL TIMES, January 17–18, 1998, p. 6; Peter Montagnon & Justin Marozzi, "IMF moves to centre stage in Asia crisis," FINANCIAL TIMES, November 20, 1997, p. 4; Lionel Barber & Gerard Baker, "IMF seeks to calm Asia fears," FINANCIAL TIMES, January 22, 1998, p. 1; "Recovery hangs on reform and refinancing," FINANCIAL TIMES (Special Report), January 16, 1998, p. 8; Richard Waters & others, "Averting a global financial catastrophe was no holiday," FINANCIAL TIMES, January 7, 1998, p. 4; "IMF Funding Vital to Opening Trade in Asia, Eizensat Tells Finance Panel," 15 ITR 233 (February 11, 1998).

43. Michael Hirsh, "A High Flier Falls to Earth," NEWSWEEK, January 26, 1998, p. 46; "South Korea: The End of the Miracle," THE ECONOMIST, November 29, 1997, p. 21; Michael Hirsh, "And Now, It's Korea," NEWSWEEK, December 1, 1997, p. 46; John Burton, "South Korea agrees terms for IMF's rescue loan," FINANCIAL TIMES, December 1, 1997, p. 1; "Record $55 Billion Bailout Set for South Korea," NEW YORK TIMES, December 4, 1997, p. D1; "Centre-left wins narrow victory on South Korea," FINANCIAL TIMES, December 19, 1997, p. I; "Kim promises to implement IMF terms," FINANCIAL TIMES, December 20–21, 1997, p. 3.

44. "IMF warns Suharto it may cancel $43 bn rescue," FINANCIAL TIMES, February 16, 1998, p. 1; James Kynge & Shelia McNaulty, "Dissatisfaction with IMF dominates Asian Summit," FINANCIAL TIMES, December 15, 1997, p. 3; "The Asian Crash: Beggars and Choosers," THE ECONOMIST, December 6, 1997, p. 43; Sander Thoenes, "Indonesia seeks 'temporary pause' in debt repayment," FINANCIAL TIMES, January 28, 1998, p. 1; William Barnes, "Thai's press IMF to ease curbs," FINANCIAL TIMES, February 2, 1998, p. 3; Martin Wolf, "Same old IMF medicine," FINANCIAL TIMES, December 9, 1997, p. 12. Wolf points out that the ailing "Little Tigers" have neither "fiscal profligacy or high inflation." In 1995, one-third of Korea's GDP was attributable to exports. Despite this, the IMF has imposed a draconian program of higher interest rates, currency devaluation, and fiscal restraint. That may actually make the economies sicker longer and keep private investors (who would relieve the IMF) away longer. Richard Lambert, "Michel Camdessus: Defending the fund," FINANCIAL TIMES, February 9, 1998, p. 13; David Sanger, "As Economies Fail, the IMF Is Rife with Recriminations," NEW YORK TIMES, October 2, 1998, p. A1; Peter

Montagnon, "ADB warns of social turbulence in Asia," FINANCIAL TIMES, April 24, 1998, p. 6.

45. "Asian rally lifts stocks world-wide," FINANCIAL TIMES, February 3, 1998, p. 1; Sheila McNaulty, "Investors pour into Malaysia," FINANCIAL TIMES, February 4, 1998, p. 6 (a 23 percent rise in a key stock index in one day); John Burton, "Korea may ease [state-run companies'] sell-off terms," FINANCIAL TIMES, February 12, 1998, p. 6; John Ridding, "Hong Kong unveils $13 bn tax cuts to cushion Asia crisis," FINANCIAL TIMES, February 19, 1998, p. 1.

46. Gerard Baker, "U.S. looks to G7 backing on Asia crisis," FINANCIAL TIMES, February 20, 1998, p. 4; Gillian Tett & Gerard Baker, "U.S. hits at lack of tax cuts in Tokyo package to lift economy," FINANCIAL TIMES, February 21–22, 1998, p. 1.

47. Stephen Fidler, "Latin America scrambles for capital," FINANCIAL TIMES, February 10, 1998, p. 3.

48. Nancy Dunne, "Index shows Asia effect on U.S. economy," FINANCIAL TIMES, February 3, 1998, p. 4; "Asian turmoil threatens U.S. trade figures," FINANCIAL TIMES, January 22, 1998, p. 4; "U.S. fears of falling sales in Asia," FINANCIAL TIMES, February 21–22, 1998, p. 2; Gerard Baker, "Greenspan warns of effects of global crisis on U.S. economy," FINANCIAL TIMES, September 24, 1998, p. 1; Robert Samuelson, "The Crash of '99?" NEWSWEEK, October 12, 1998, p. 26.

49. Greg McIvor & Michiyo Nakamoto, "Fall-out from Asian turmoil starts to affect multinationals," FINANCIAL TIMES, January 14, 1998, p. 1; Shawn Tully, "Despite Asia's Woes, U.S. Banks Are Standing Tall," FORTUNE, February 16, 1998, p. 26; "Trade Deficit Widens in September; Japan, China Account for Half the Gap," 14 ITR 2040 (November 26, 1997).

50. "Changing the rules in Asia," FINANCIAL TIMES, January 7, 1998, p. 15; Peter Montagnon, "Recovery hangs on reform and refinancing," FINANCIAL TIMES, January 16, 1998, p. 8; Daniel Yergin & Joseph Stanislaw, "Sale of the century," FINANCIAL TIMES, January 24–25, 1998, p. 1.

51. "U.S., Other Nations Planning to Increase Export Insurance for Asia," 15 ITR 323 (February 25, 1998); Tony Walker & John Ridding, "Snapping up bargains," FINANCIAL TIMES, March 26, 1998, p. 11 (reporting on American investors such as George Soros and GM Capital, co-venturing with Thai and Japanese enterprises, respectively, including greater access, transparency, and even seats on boards); Ronald Henkoff, "Asia: Why Business Is Still Bullish," FORTUNE, October 27, 1997, p. 139. *Cf.*, Michael Hirsh, "An Asian Gold Rush? Maybe Not," NEWSWEEK, February 23, 1998, p. 42; Ellyn Spragins, "Don't Buy the Asian Dip," *id.*, p. 70; Jim Rohwer, "Asia's Meltdown: It Ain't over Yet," FORTUNE, July 20, 1998, p. 93.

52. "Asia Picks Up the Pieces," THE ECONOMIST, January 3, 1998, p. 69; "Malaysia to Halt Big Projects, Defer Decisions on Privatization," 14 ITR 1545 (September 17, 1997); Tony Walker, "Unbinding China," FINANCIAL TIMES, September 10, 1997, p. 17; "U.S., Taiwan Reach Market Access Pact; Accord Is Major Step Toward WTO Accession," 15 ITR 322 (February 25, 1998); Anthony Paul, "Indonesia: Life under the volcano," FORTUNE, April 13, 1998, p. 112.

53. "Hong Kong Government Working 'Very Hard' to Combat Copyright Piracy, Official Says," 15 ITR 329 (February 25, 1998); John Burton, "Korea to allow foreign takeover bids," FINANCIAL TIMES, February 5, 1998, p. 7; "South Korea unions accept job reforms," FINANCIAL TIMES, February 7–8, 1998, p. 4; Sheila McNulty, "Malaysia finds it difficult to swallow recovery's medicine," FINANCIAL

TIMES, March 6, 1998, p. 5; "Suharto finally caves in over currency board," FINAN-
CIAL TIMES, February 27, 1998, p. 6; "Domestic debt crisis mounts in Indonesia,"
FINANCIAL TIMES, March 6, 1998, p. 5.

54. "Japan Lacks Sense of Urgency About Asian Crisis," 15 ITR 381 (March 4,
1998); Michiyo Nakamoto & Gillian Tett, "Zen and the art of demand," FINANCIAL
TIMES, March 9, 1998, p. 15; "Japan Must Reform Economy to Aid Neighbors,
Eizenstat Says," 15 ITR 277 (February 18, 1998); Michael Hirsh, "More Hype Than
Bang," NEWSWEEK, March 30, 1998, p. 42.

55. Tony Walker & James Harding, "Pro-business reformers strengthen grip on
China," FINANCIAL TIMES, September 20–21, 1997, p. 4; James Kynge, "China acts
to meet target of 8% growth," FINANCIAL TIMES, March 9, 1993, p. 3 (but the
result could mean an additional 3.5 million unemployed, on top of the 11.5 million
laid-off workers at the end of 1997); "China plans to cut civil service in half," FI-
NANCIAL TIMES, March 7–8, 1998, p. 3. But *cf.*, "Chinese Stockpiles of Goods
Climbed Last Year [to $71 billion, or 19 percent of China's industrial output]," 15
ITR 436 (March 11, 1998); "China to Continue Limiting Investment by Foreigners
in Telecom, State Sectors," 15 ITR 380 (March 4, 1998).

56. Gerard Baker, "U.S. economy set to brush off effects of Asian crisis," FINAN-
CIAL TIMES, February 11, 1998, p. 1; Gerard Baker & Nancy Dunne, "Trillion-
dollar imports barely noticed," FINANCIAL TIMES, February 20, 1998, p. 6.

57. Nancy Dunne & Gillian Tett, "Shockwaves from Asian crisis hit U.S. and
Japanese trade," FINANCIAL TIMES, February 20, 1998, p. 1; Nancy Dunne, "Asian
fallout cranks up U.S. deficit," FINANCIAL TIMES, March 20, 1998, p. 4.

58. "December Trade Gap Soars 24%; 1997 Deficit Worst in Nine Years," 15
ITR 315 (February 25, 1998); "Senate Votes to Set Up Panel to Deal with Growing
Trade Deficit," 3/25/98 BTD d4; "Unilateral Sanctions Are Not Effective, Private
Sector Witnesses Tell Senate Panel," 15 ITR 387 (March 4, 1998).

59. Emiko Terazono & Philip Coggan, "High risk, low returns," FINANCIAL
TIMES, March 21–22, 1998, p. 6; Gillian Tett, "GE Capital ventures into Japanese
insurance market," FINANCIAL TIMES, February 19, 1998, p. 15; "Merrill Lynch
plans head-on challenge to Japan rivals," FINANCIAL TIMES, February 13, 1998, p.
1; Tony Walker & John Ridding, "Snapping up bargains," FINANCIAL TIMES, March
26, 1998, p. 11.

60. "Japan Lacks Sense of Urgency About Asian Crisis," 15 ITR 381 (March 4,
1998); "U.S. Anticipates Japanese Disputes; Asia-Pacific Rim Recovers From Crisis,"
1/27/98 BTD d14 (This is, bar none, *the* most-thorough account of U.S. engagement in the area); "Japanese Cabinet Approves New Three-Year Deregulation Policy," 15 ITR 574 (April 1, 1998); Gillian Tett, "Big Bang or just whimper?"
FINANCIAL TIMES, March 26, 1998, p. 1.

61. James Harding & James Kynge, "Deng's no-nonsense disciple," FINANCIAL
TIMES, March 18, 1998, p. 13; John Ridding, "Fittest survive in China's battle
against fall-out from east Asia's economic crisis," FINANCIAL TIMES, March 25,
1998, p. 4; James Kynge, "China breaks new ground as state companies go for a
song," FINANCIAL TIMES, March 23, 1998, p. 16.

62. The five countries most injured by the Asian crisis (Indonesia, Malaysia, the
Philippines, South Korea and Thailand), had net capital inflows of $93 billion in
1996, turning to an estimated outflow of $12 billion in 1997 (or about 10 percent
of their pre-crisis combined GDP). Martin Wolf, "Flows and blows," FINANCIAL

TIMES, March 3, 1998, p. 16; Richard Adams, "Growth picks up in East Europe," FINANCIAL TIMES, January 12, 1998, p. 3; Andrew Taylor, "Bankers face hard times as projects slip away," FINANCIAL TIMES, January 9, 1998, p. 7; Ramesh Thakur, "India in the World," FOREIGN AFFAIRS, July/August 1997, p. 15; Roula Khalaf, "Middle East & North Africa privatization: The pressure for change mounts," FINANCIAL TIMES, March 26, 1998, p. 1.

63. Peter Montagnon, "Goh warns on Asia's ties with the west," FINANCIAL TIMES, March 9, 1998, p. 3; Robert Chote, "IMF more vigilant after Asian failure," FINANCIAL TIMES, March 30, 1998, p. 1; Max Wilkinson, "A free market conspiracy theory," FINANCIAL TIMES, March 28–29, 1998, p. V [reviewing FALSE DAWN: THE DELUSIONS OF GLOBAL CAPITALISM, by JOHN GREY (Granta, 1998)].

64. Lionel Barber, "Seeking Closer Asian Ties," EUROPE, November 1997, p. 21; James Harding, "Europe 'overestimated' China's market," FINANCIAL TIMES, February 16, 1998, p. 2.

65. Martin Wolf, "Flows and blows," FINANCIAL TIMES, March 3, 1998, p. 16; Emiko Terazono & Philip Coggan, "High risk, low returns," FINANCIAL TIMES, March 21–22, 1998, p. 6; Asian Financial Crisis [Unless Cured Quickly] Could Weaken Support for Further Liberalization," 15 ITR 83 (January 21, 1998).

66. Tracy Corrigan, "Greenspan weighs up Asian crisis," FINANCIAL TIMES, February 28–March 1, 1998, p. 1; Robert Chote, "IMF more vigilant after Asian failure," *op cit*.; "Role of [IMF] surveillance and transparency underlined," FINANCIAL TIMES, March 30, 1998, p. 3.

67. "World Bank Urges East Asia to Strengthen Its Financial Systems," 14 ITR 1552 (September 17, 1997).

68. Seth Mydans, "An 'Asian Miracle' Now Seems Like a Mirage," NEW YORK TIMES, October 22, 1997, p. 1.

69. Robert Chote, "Poverty' coming back to E Asia,' " FINANCIAL TIMES, September 28, 1998, p. 4; Michael Hirsch, "Is Clinton Planning a Global New Deal?" NEWSWEEK, October 5, 1998, p. 46; David Wighton, "Blair urges radical IMF overhaul within a year," FINANCIAL TIMES, September 22, 1998, p. 9; Stephen Fidler, "In search of prevention rather than cure," FINANCIAL TIMES, October 5, 1998, p. 3.

70. Samuel Brittan, " 'Asian model,' R.I.P.," FINANCIAL TIMES, December 4, 1997, p. 10; "Asian models trip up," FINANCIAL TIMES, December 6–7, 1997, p. 6; Edward Lincoln, "Maybe it's the teacher's fault," U.S. NEWS & WORLD REPORT, December 15, 1997, p. 54.

71. Tony Tassell, "Worst of Asia's crisis 'may be over,' " FINANCIAL TIMES, November 24, 1998, p. 8; "WTO Praises Indonesia for Trade Reforms," 12/7/1998 BTD d6; Tony Tassell, "Manila economy beats market forecasts," FINANCIAL TIMES, November 30, 1998, p. 6; "South Korea Sees Record Year for Foreign Direct Investment," 16 ITR 53 (January 13, 1999); Joseph Stiglitz, "Lessons of the Asia crisis," FINANCIAL TIMES, December 3, 1998, p. 14.

72. "APEC's Family Feud," THE ECONOMIST, November 21, 1998, p. 41; "ASEAN Looks to the New Year," THE ECONOMIST, December 19, 1998, p. 47.

73. "Asia's nascent recovery," FINANCIAL TIMES, October 24, 1998, p. 6; Ted Bardacke, "Asia leaders in rates cut plea," FINANCIAL TIMES, October 14, 1998, p. 6; Fred Bergsten, "APEC to the Rescue," THE ECONOMIST, November 7, 1998, p. 21; "ASEAN Finance Ministers Approve Investment Pact, 'Surveillance Mecha-

nism'," 15 ITR 1716 (October 14, 1998); Richard Adams, "OECD warns of the perils of further economic turbulence," FINANCIAL TIMES, November 18, 1998, p. 4.

CHAPTER 14. METAMORPHOSING THE GATT: THE WORLD TRADE ORGANIZATION (WTO)

1. LESTER THUROW, HEAD TO HEAD: THE COMING BATTLE AMONG JAPAN, EUROPE AND AMERICA (Morrow & Co., 1992), p. 279.

2. "45 years of doing the rounds," FINANCIAL TIMES, December 16, 1993, pp. 4–5. The full text of the 1993 GATT/WTO agreement can be found at 33 INTERNATIONAL LEGAL MATERIALS 1125.

3. "The Impact of the WTO and NAFTA on U.S. Law," 46 J. LEGAL EDUC. 569, December 1996.

4. "How the WTO Works," http://www.unicc.org/wtoworkswpf.html#WTO's.

5. *Id.*

6. Neil Buckley, "EU split on response to WTO banana ruling," FINANCIAL TIMES, September 10, 1997, p. 4.

7. Frances Williams, "EU appeals against WTO banana ruling," FINANCIAL TIMES, June 12, 1997, p. 8.

8. "EU Offers Vague Pledge to Implement WTO Ruling on Banana Import Regime," 14 ITR 1835 (October 22, 1997).

9. "EU Lashes Out at U.S. Proposal to Retaliate Against EU over Banana, Beef Trade Practices," 15 ITR 1781 (October 28, 1998); "U.S. 'Tired' of WTO Banana Talks, Retains Right to Retaliate," 11/9/1998 BTD d7; "U.S., EU Head Off Showdown on Bananas as Europe Agrees to New Procedural Twist," 2/1/1999 BTD d2; "WTO Formally Adopts EU Banana Ruling," 5/7/1999 BTD d2; "EU Changes to Banana Import Regime Will Take More Time," 16 ITR 776 (May 5, 1999).

10. "WTO Will Be Challenged by Increasingly Complex Cases, Lawyer Predicts," 1/15/98 BTD d4.

11. *Id.*

12. Andrew W. Shoyer, "The First Three Years of WTO Dispute Settlement: Observations and Suggestions," speech before Economic Strategy Institute, January 14, 1998.

13. Judith Bello & Alan Holmer, " 'Special 301': Its Requirements, Implementation and Significance," 13 FORDHAM INT'L L. J. 259. "USTR Announces Results of 'Out-Of-Cycle' Special 301 Reviews of Five Countries," 14 ITR 1864 (October 29, 1997); Nancy Dunne, "Not so Super 301 after all," FINANCIAL TIMES, October 16, 1994, p. 6. The statute is 19 U.S.C. §2411, as amended. Special 301 is a spin-off of Super 301. It also required the USTR to identify and negotiate the removal of offensive trade practices, while holding the threat of retaliation over the offending country's head. With the emergence of the WTO, Super 301 was to be phased out, since it was retaliatory.

14. "Options to Meet Clean Air, WTO Goals Sought by EPA After Gas Decision Rule," 13 ITR 28 (July 10, 1996).

15. "Brazil, Venezuela Claim U.S. Slow to Implement WTO Ruling on Gasoline," 1/23/97 BTD d5 (January 23, 1997).

16. "EPA Meets WTO Fuel Regulation Deadline; Foreign Refiners Get Individual Baseline," 14 ITR 1474 (September 3, 1997).

17. Neil Buckley, "Brussels to appeal over hormones," FINANCIAL TIMES, July 2, 1997, p. 6.

18. "WTO Decision on EU Beef Imports to Have Impact Beyond Hormones," 15 ITR 142 (January 28, 1998); "WTO Makes Final Ruling Against Japan on Restrictions of U.S. Farm Imports," 10/29/1998 BTD d7.

19. "WTO DSB Accepts Ruling Against EU Ban on Importing Hormone-Treated Beef," 15 ITR 268 (February 18, 1998); "EU to Conduct New Beef Hormone Studies While Keeping Ban," 15 ITR 454 (March 18, 1998); "Salmon Decision Clarifies Conditions for Banning Food Imports," 15 ITR 1808 (October 28, 1998). *Cf.*, Michael Smith, "US promises better health checks on meat," FINANCIAL TIMES, November 2, 1998, p. 4.

20. "Barshefsky Warns U.S. Will Go to WTO If EU Labeling Plan Disrupts Farm Exports," 14 ITR 1115 (June 25, 1997); "U.S. Reiterates Complaint to WTO on EU Labeling of Genetically Modified Foods," 15 ITR 1572 (September 23, 1998).

21. "U.S. Submits Opening Brief to WTO in Japan Film Complaint," 2/21/97 BTD d2.

22. "Japan Rebuts U.S. Film Complaint; Denies WTO Violations, Trade Barriers," 4/4/97 BTD d6.

23. "Interagency Committee Will Test Japan's Claims on Film Market," 2/5/98 BTD d8; *See also*, "JFTC Warns Photo Film Group to Stop Exchange of Information," 15 ITR 1497 (September 9, 1998).

24. "U.S. Making 'Mockery' of WTO Appeal on Bananas Through Timetable Demand," 12/7/1998 BTD d5; "Hitting Back at U.S. Banana Retaliation, EU Seeks Panels to Block List, Kill Section 301," 12/22/1998 BTD d3; "U.S. to Push Ahead for WTO Approval on Banana Trade Sanctions Against EU," 1/13/1999 BTD d3; "U.S. Foiled in Attempt to Get WTO Nod to Retaliate Against EU in Banana Dispute," 1/26/1999 BTD d2; "U.S., EU Agree to Hold Talks in Effort to Reach Compromise on Banana Split," 1/27/1999 BTD d7; "EU to Outline Compliance with WTO Hormone Ruling," 1/19/1999 BTD d6; "Clinton Extends Waiver of Helms-Burton Provision," 16 ITR 96 (January 20, 1999); "U.S. Awaits Coming of 'Millennium Round' of WTO Negotiations," 16 ITR 103 (January 20, 1999).

25. "EU Suggests Improvements to WTO Dispute Settlement," EURECOM, November 1998, p. 2; "WTO Dispute Settlement Review Playing Out amid Increasing Number of Conflicts," 11/23/1998 BTD d8; "WTO Dispute Settlement Review to Continue into Next Year," 12/4/1998 BTD d10.

26. "WTO Members Say They Will Not Meet Ratification Deadline for Financial Services," 16 ITR 72 (January 20, 1999); "WTO Members to Meet Feb. 11 to Decide When to Implement Financial Services Pact," 2/5/1999 BTD d3; "WTO Members Call for Fast Action in Agriculture, Services in '99 Talks," 11/24/1998 BTD d6; "EU, U.S. Bicker on Particulars, But Harmonize on Principles," 1/26/1999 BTD d7.

27. "EU, Japan Agree to Urge Launching of New Global Round of Trade Negotiations," 16 ITR 57 (January 13, 1999); "Clinton Calls for New Global Trade Round Including Intellectual Property, Procurement," 16 ITR 72 (January 20, 1999); "Trade Deals in Agriculture and Services Should Top U.S. Agenda," 16 ITR

205 (February 3, 1999); "U.S. Will Press Labor, Environment at WTO Ministerial," 16 ITR 204 (February 3, 1999); "Developing Country Groups Urge Narrow WTO Trade Round," 16 ITR 73 (January 20, 1999). *See generally* (for the U.S. position on the Millennium Round), "U.S. Awaits Coming of Millennium Round' of WTO Negotiations," 16 ITR 103 (January 20, 1999).

28. "Latvia to Become Second Ex-Soviet State, 134th Member of World Trade Organization," 16 ITR 101 (January 20, 1999); "WTO Urged by Some Members to Speed Up Accession Process," 15 ITR 2086 (December 16, 1998).

29. "Ten Countries to Submit Lists of Products to Include," 14 ITR 2115 (December 10, 1997).

30. "Industrialized Nations Urge Negotiations to Expand Tech Products Covered by WTO," 14 ITR 1657 (October 1, 1997); "U.S. High-Tech Firms Suggest Expanding ITA to Include Hundreds of New Products," 14 ITR 1746 (October 15, 1997); "Deadline on ITA-II Talks Pushed Back Again," 15 ITR 1784 (October, 1998).

31. "WTO Members Reach Agreement on Telecommunications Pact Date," 15 ITR 139 (January 28, 1998); "World Telecom Deal Clinched . . . ," EURECOM, March 1997, p. 1.

32. "Statement by Treasury Secretary Rubin, USTR Barshefsky Regarding Conclusion of WTO Financial Services Talks with Charts Indicating Improved Commitments from 70 Countries, Released by the White House Dec. 13, 1997," 14 ITR 2181 (December 17, 1997); "Ratification of WTO Financial Services Pact Lags as Only 22 Signatories Complete Work," 15 ITR 1748 (October 21, 1998).

33. "U.S. Ditches World Maritime Talks," EURECOM, June 1996, p. 3; "WTO Maritime Committee Puts Talks on Hold Until 2000, at U.S. Request," 13 ITR 27 d22 (July 3, 1996).

34. "Canada Backs Labor, Environment Provisions in Global Investment Accord, Marchi Says," 14 ITR 1862 (October 29, 1997).

35. "Canadian Government Rejects Proposal to Shift Investment Agreement to WTO," 13 ITR d33 (June 26, 1996).

36. "NGO Coalition, Environmentalists Vow Campaign Against OECD'S MAI," 14 ITR 1861 (October 29, 1997).

37. "U.S. Negotiators See No Chance MAI Can Be Signed at OECD April Ministerial," 15 ITR 256 (February 18, 1998); "WTO Seeks to Extend Deadline for Completion of Investment Talks," 15 ITR 2022 (December 2, 1998).

38. "U.S. May Press EU to Eliminate Domestic Farm Support Program in WTO," 15 ITR 40 (January 14, 1998); "EU Requests WTO Panel On US Export Subsidies," EURECOM, July/August 1998, p. 2.

39. "WTO to Establish Dispute Panel on Canadian Dairy Trade Regime," 15 ITR 569 (April 1, 1998).

40. "New Zealand Threatens WTO Action Against Canadian Dairy Marketing System," 14 ITR 1203 (July 9, 1997); "WTO Feud over Agriculture Subsidies Pits Cairns Group Against U.S., Europe," 15 ITR 1677 (October 7, 1998); "Gore Lays Out U.S. Agenda for WTO Talks," 16 ITR 201 (February 3, 1999). *See also*, OPEN MARKETS MATTER (OECD, 1998), pp. 39–55, 139–150.

41. "EU Challenges U.S. Textile Origin Rules in WTO Dispute Settlement Proceeding," 14 ITR 999 (June 4, 1997).

42. "WTO Committee Makes Slow Progress Reaching Comprehensive Rules of

Origin," 15 ITR 222 (February 11, 1998); "U.S. Official Downplays Delay in WTO Rules of Origin Talks," 15 ITR 1839 (November 4, 1998).

43. "WTO Panel Sides with U.S. in Case on Argentine Tariffs," 24 ITR 2083 (December 3, 1997).

44. Nancy Dunne, "Korea takes US dumping row to WTO," FINANCIAL TIMES, June 11, 1997, p. 4.

45. "South Korea Drops Complaint Against U.S. on TV Imports," 1/16/98 BTD d5; "WTO Sets Up Dispute Panel on U.S. Autidumping Act of 1916," 16 ITR 192 (February 3, 1999).

46. " WTO to Establish Panel to Settle U.S.-Korea Dispute," 1/20/98 BTD d5, "Against anti-dumping," THE ECONOMIST, November 7, 1998.

47. "TBT Harmonization" http://www.wto.org/eol/e/wto03/cont3.htm; Claire Gooding, "Standardize and deliver," FINANCIAL TIMES, October 13, 1995, p. 1.

48. "Nations Conclude Financial Services Pact; Lang Calls Accord First Step in Process," 14 ITR 2155 (December 17, 1997).

49. "WTO Chief Says Body Will Not Impinge on Members' Rights to Protect Environment," 14 ITR 2222 (December 24, 1997) (quoting World Trade Organization Director General Renato Ruggiero). *See also*, OPEN MARKETS MATTER, *op cit.*, pp. 105–110.

50. "Options for Resolving the WTO Shrimp-Turtle Case," 15 ITR 294 (February 18, 1998).

51. "WTO Panel Rules Against U.S. in Case Challenging Shrimp Import Ban," 3/17/98 BTD d4; "U.S. Examining Ways to Make Shrimp Restrictions More Transparent," 2/18/1999 BTD d2.

52. "WTO Cannot be 'Judge, Jury, Police' on Environment Issues, Ruggiero Says," 3/18/98 BTD d2; "Turtle Soup," THE ECONOMIST, October 17, 1998.

53. "EU to Appeal WTO Ruling on U.S. Computer Networking Equipment," 3/25/1998 BTD d8; "WTO Appellate Body Overturns Panel, Rule Against U.S. in Computer Tariff Row," 6/5/1998 BTD d2; W.T.O., Report of the Appellate Body, Customs Classification of Certain Computer Equipment, AB-1998–2 (June 5, 1998), 1998 WL 295540.

54. THOMAS C. FISCHER, THE EUROPEANIZATION OF AMERICA: WHAT AMERICANS NEED TO KNOW ABOUT THE EUROPEAN UNION (Carolina Academic Press, 1995), pp. 291–292.

55. Frances Williams, "Open race for the world's top trade job," FINANCIAL TIMES, October 2, 1998, p. 8; "Who now?" THE ECONOMIST, October 24, 1998, p. 80; Bruce Barnard, "The World Trade Watchdog Has a Big Bark," EUROPE, September 1995, p. 28; "No Retreat from Trade Globalization, Ruggiero Warns," 13 ITR 20 d28 (May 15, 1996); "WTO Paper Argues Dispute Rulings Recognize Environmental Policy Goals," 11/5/1998 BTD d7; "WTO, Other Groups Pledge to Coordinate Assistance to Least Developed Countries," 14 ITR 1920 (November 5, 1997); "Ruggiero Meets with NGOs in Effort to Broaden WTO Transparency," 11/10/1998 BTD d12; Guy de Jonquieres, "Trading places [Moore]," FINANCIAL TIMES, September 3, 1999, p. 12; "Future WTO Head [Supachai] Calls for Equity in Trade Benefits for Developing Nations," 16 ITR 1441 (September 8, 1999).

56. "Experts Complain WTO Dispute Settlement Is Slow, Ill-Defined, and Often Unsuccessful," 15 ITR 1840 (November 4, 1998); "WTO Begins Contentious Talks

on Reform of Dispute Resolution Rules; Delays Expected," 15 ITR 1788 (October 28, 1998); "U.S. Directs Focus to Compliance, Transparency in WTO Dispute Reform," 11/4/1998 BTD d5.

57. "Thailand's Panitchpakdi Urges Speeding Up Talks on Chinese, Russian Accession to WTO," 15 ITR 1792 (October 28, 1998); "China Shows 'Marked Reluctance' to Take Steps Necessary to Join WTO, Brittan Says," 15 ITR 1648 (September 30, 1998); "China's Export Subsidies, Trade Policies Threaten U.S. Relations," 15 ITR 1824 (November 4, 1998); Clifford Gaddy & Barry Ickes, "Russia's Virtual Economy," FOREIGN AFFAIRS, September/October 1998, p. 53; "Ruggiero Calls for Accelerated Talks, Open Markets," 15 ITR 1592 (September 23, 1998).

58. WORLD TRADE SURVEY: "Seconds out," THE ECONOMIST, October 3, 1998, p. 37; "Chances Good for a 'Millennium Round,' Brittan Says," 14 ITR 2038 (November 26, 1997); "WTO Member States Stake Out Positions on Scope, Duration of Future Trade Talks," 15 ITR 1625 (September 30, 1998); "U.S. Firms Prefer 'Focused' Trade Talks to New Global Round," 15 ITR 1785 (October 28, 1998); Guy de Jonquières, "U.S. may favor widening trade talks," FINANCIAL TIMES, October 19, 1998, p. 3; "U.S., EU Looking into Ways to Achieve 'Early Harvest' in New WTO Trade Talks," 15 ITR 1636 (September 30, 1998).

59. "Developing Countries Now Prime Users of WTO Dispute Procedures," 13 ITR 15d6 (April 10, 1996); "Developing Countries Want WTO to Focus on Fairness of Existing Trade Agreements," 15 ITR 600 (April 8, 1998); Clive Cookson, "WHO warns of jump in infectious disease," FINANCIAL TIMES, May 20, 1996, p. 5; "WTO Chides Mexico for Preferring Regional Trade Pacts over Multilateralism," 14 ITR 1771 (October 15, 1997).

CHAPTER 15. A NEW ERA IN WORLD TRADE

1. *See generally*, "Where Next?" (A Survey of World Trade), THE ECONOMIST, October 3, 1998.

2. *See generally*, Robert Samuelson, "God Is in the Details," NEWSWEEK, April 20, 1998, p. 47 [stating that macroeconomic (global) policy can't succeed without good microeconomic (national) policy]; "The Continent's Jubilant Left Breaks Free," THE ECONOMIST, October 3, 1998, p. 51.

3. Martin Wolf, "The heart of the new world economy," FINANCIAL TIMES, October 1, 1997, p. 12; Jane Martinson & William Lewis, "OECD urged to set governance standard," FINANCIAL TIMES, April 2, 1998, p. 1; Fareed Zakaria, "So Much for Globalization," NEWSWEEK, September 7, 1998, p. 36; Arthur Schlesinger, Jr., "Has Democracy a Future?" FOREIGN AFFAIRS, September/October 1997, p. 2.

4. ORGANIZATION for ECONOMIC COOPERATION AND DEVELOPMENT, OPEN MARKETS MATTER: THE BENEFITS OF TRADE AND INVESTMENT LIBERALIZATION (OECD, 1998).

5. Robert Taylor, "Globalization is on trial, say union leaders," FINANCIAL TIMES, October 29, 1998, p. 10; "UNCTAD Urges Poor Countries to Focus on Existing Protections in Future WTO Talks," 15 ITR 1755 (October 21, 1998).

6. Samuel Brittan, "Who's afraid of globalization," FINANCIAL TIMES, January 8, 1998, p. 21; William Dawkins & Guy de Jonquières, "Quad nations seek unity on telecoms," FINANCIAL TIMES, April 19, 1996, p. 4; Frances Williams, "Business

leaders urge WTO to push for simpler customs methods," FINANCIAL TIMES, March 11, 1998, p. 9; Wolfgang Reinicke, "Global Public Policy," FOREIGN AFFAIRS, November/December 1997, p. 127; Peter Drucher, "The Global Economy and the Nation-State," FOREIGN AFFAIRS, September/October 1997, p. 159.

7. *See generally*, WORLD DEVELOPMENT REPORT 1997 (Oxford University Press, 1997), particularly "Overview" and chapters 1 and 9; David Buchan & Peter Norman, "IMF urges close watch on weaker economies," FINANCIAL TIMES, February 8, 1995, p. 1; Canute Jones, "Caribbean angry at 'big brother' U.S.," FINANCIAL TIMES, May 22, 1997, p. 4; "World Bank Says Despite Good Prospects, Too Many Developing Countries Lag," 13 ITR 19 d11 (May 8, 1996); Jeffrey Sachs, "Peace & Prosperity at Hand," MICHIGAN LAW QUADRANGLE NOTES, Spring 1995, p. 3.

8. Stephen Fidler & Max Wilkinson, "World leaders back joint action in face of financial turmoil," FINANCIAL TIMES, September 15, 1998, p. 1; Robert Chote, "Struggle is on to fit the pieces together again," FINANCIAL TIMES, October 2, 1998, p. 1; "Missing the Point," THE ECONOMIST, October 10, 1998, p. 15; Simon Kuper, "World Bank builds link with business," FINANCIAL TIMES, January 19, 1998, p. 6; Guy de Jonquières, "Poorest nations urged to adopt market reform," FINANCIAL TIMES, April 16, 1996, p. 5; Judy Dempsey, "Liberalization key to growth, says IMF," FINANCIAL TIMES, November 17, 1997, p. 5; "U.N., International Chamber of Commerce to Prepare Investment Guides to LDCs [less-developed countries]," 15 ITR 319 (February 25, 1998). *Cf.*, JOHN GRAY, FALSE DAWN: THE DELUSIONS OF GLOBAL CAPITALISM (Granta, 1998).

9. Martin Wolf, "The heart of the new world economy," FINANCIAL TIMES, October 1, 1997, p. 12; Paul Krugman, "Challenging Conventional Wisdom" and "The Localization of the World Economy," in POP INTERNATIONALISM, pp. 130 and 205, respectively.

10. Denver Summit of the Eight, "Promoting Financial Stability," June 20–22, 1997 (http://www.library.utoronto.ca/www/G-7/denverexec.htm); Robert Taylor & others, "G8 takes up fight against unemployment," FINANCIAL TIMES, February 23, 1998, p. 1; FRED BERGSTEN & RANDALL HENNING, GLOBAL ECONOMIC LEADERSHIP AND THE GROUP OF SEVEN (Institute for International Economics, 1996); Robert Taylor, "Social clauses divide G-7," FINANCIAL TIMES, April 2, 1996, p. 3; "WTO Chief Cites Challenges to Multilateral Trading System," 15 ITR 366 (March 4, 1998); "APEC Forest Products Accord May Become International Pact," 15 ITR 607 (April 8, 1998).

11. Guy de Jonquières, "Rules for the regulators," FINANCIAL TIMES, March 2, 1998, p. 19; "WTO Negotiators Cite Progress in ITA-II Talks," 15 ITR 553 (April 1, 1998); Robert Samuelson, "Global Boom and Bust?" NEWSWEEK, November 10, 1997, p. 35; Edward Alden, "G7 close to setting up developing nations forum," FINANCIAL TIMES, September 20, 1999, p. 16.

12. MADE IN AMERICA (MIT Press, 1987); Wolfgang Münchau, "U.S. tops entrepreneurs' league," FINANCIAL TIMES, November 25, 1997, p. 6; David Whitford, "The Party Keeps Cooking," FORTUNE, March 16, 1998, p. 24; Richard Waters, "America finds its customer is the world," FINANCIAL TIMES, October 10, 1997, p. 14. *See generally*, LEA BRILMAYER, AMERICAN HEGEMONY (Yale University Press, 1994).

13. "APEC Telecom MRA Almost Done," 15 ITR 672 (April 22, 1998); "U.S.

Urges APEC Members to Accept Harmonization of Standards in Auto Sector," 15 ITR 676 (April 22, 1998).

14. "Asia, Fast Track Overshadow U.S. Agenda as World Trading System Turns 50," 15 ITR 110 (January 21, 1998); "Slow Road to Fast-Track," THE ECONOMIST (World Trade Survey), October 3, 1998, p. 32.

15. "USTR Barshefsky Sets Out Trade Agenda for 1998, But Fails to Mention Fast Track," 15 ITR 360 (March 4, 1998); "U.S. Trade Report Cites Barriers in Japan, EU, Korea," 15 ITR 552 (April 1, 1998). The full report (Office of the U.S. Trade Representative), entitled 1998 NATIONAL TRADE ESTIMATE, can be found at: http://www.ustr.gov/reports/nte/1998.html.

16. Martin Wolf, "Serious, yes. Hopeless, no," FINANCIAL TIMES, October 7, 1998, p. 15; Japan Rebuts U.S. Criticism by Listing WTO-Inconsistent U.S. Trade Measures," 15 ITR 677 (April 22, 1998); "Trade Deficit Widens to $12.1 Billion as Gap with Japan Reaches $1 Billion," 15 ITR 690 (April 22, 1998).

17. Murray Weidenbaum, "American Isolationism versus the Global Economy," EXECUTIVE SPEECHES, February/March 1996; Lee Hamilton, "Trade on a fast track," FINANCIAL TIMES, October 23, 1997, p. 14; Ed Brown, "It's Put Up or Shut Up Time for U.S. Trade Policy," FORTUNE, October 27, 1997, p. 34.

18. "Commission Releases 1997 Report on U.S. Trade Barriers," EURECOM, September 1997, p. 1; "EU Unveils Draft Proposal for Trade Liberalization with U.S.," 15 ITR 370 (March 4, 1998); "Canada Considers Helms-Burton Law to Be a Deal Breaker in MAI Negotiations," 14 ITR 1681 (October 1, 1997); Fareed Zakaria, "Loves Me, Loves Me Not," NEWSWEEK, October 5, 1998, p. 55.

19. Willard Berry, "Why sanctions don't work," FINANCIAL TIMES, December 1, 1997, p. 14; "Unilateral Sanctions Are Not Effective, Private Sector Witness Tells Senate Panel," 15 ITR 387 (March 4, 1998); "Curb Unilateral Sanctions, Lawmakers Urge Colleagues," 15 ITR 553 (April 1, 1998); "Implementation of U.S. Encryption Policy a 'Failure,' U.S. Exports Harmed, Daley Says," 15 ITR 687 (April 22, 1998); "EU Supplants U.S. in Directing WTO Agenda," 15 ITR 468 (March 18, 1998); Imogen Mark, "U.S. sidelined as Mercosur power grows," FINANCIAL TIMES, April 20, 1998, p. 3; Gerard Baker, "Clinton fails to win over doubters [at the Summit of the Americas]," FINANCIAL TIMES, April 20, 1998, p. 3.

20. Nancy Dunne, "U.S. trade figures fall further into red," FINANCIAL TIMES, October 21, 1998, p. 8; "Trade Gap Leaped to Record $16.8 Billion in August; Exports Slumped for Fifth Month," 15 ITR 1753 (October 21, 1998); Nancy Dunne, "Output drops as U.S. industry begins to lose steam," FINANCIAL TIMES, October 17/18, 1998, p. 3.

21. Nancy Dunne & Mark Suzman, "U.S. trade deficit hits $12.1 billion, the highest since 1992," FINANCIAL TIMES, April 18–19, 1998, p. 1; Robert Kuther, "The battle over trade policy," BOSTON GLOBE, September 14, 1997, p. D7; "Crowded International Agenda May Derail Fast-Track Measure," 15 ITR 221 (February 11, 1998); "U.S. Seen Unlikely to Persuade EU to Enter New NTO Farm Talks Without Fast Track," 14 ITR 1991 (November 19, 1997); "Rubin: Fast Track May Boost Exports by $200 Billion," 14 ITR 1924 (November 5, 1997); "Survey Finds Business Support for Fast Track," 14 ITR 1926 (November 5, 1997); Mark Suzman, "Fears grow that US tariff benefits for poor countries may fall foul of Congress antagonism on trade issues," FINANCIAL TIMES, September 1, 1999, p. 8.

22. Robert Chote, "Wanna be in my gang, my gang . . . [the IMF]," FINANCIAL

TIMES, April 17, 1998, p. 5; Ken Warn, "Brittan seeks backing for millennium round," FINANCIAL TIMES, April 15, 1998, p. 8; "U.S. Calls Proposal for WTO Round Beginning in 2000 'Largely Premature'," 15 ITR 689 (April 22, 1998); "Quad Ministers Split on Multilateral 'Millennium Round' for Trade Liberalization," 5/1/98 BTD d7.

23. *See generally*, DAVID VOGEL, BARRIERS OR BENEFITS? REGULATION IN TRANSATLANTIC TRADE (Brookings Institution Press, 1997); MILES KAHLER, REGIONAL FUTURES AND TRANSATLANTIC ECONOMIC RELATIONS (Council on Foreign Relations Press, 1995); THE LIMITS OF LIBERALIZATION: REGULATORY COOPERATION AND THE NEW TRANSATLANTIC AGENDA (John Hopkins University Press, 1997); ELLEN FROST, TRANSATLANTIC TRADE: A STRATEGIC AGENDA (Institute for International Economics, 1997); "Brittan in Boston: The Case for the [New Transatlantic Market] NTM," EURECOM, April 1998, p. 2; "EU Unveils Draft Proposal for Trade Liberalization with U.S.," 15 ITR 370 (March 4, 1998); Nancy Dunne, "Barshefsky studies plan for transatlantic talks," FINANCIAL TIMES, March 5, 1998, p. 8; "U.S., EU Business Leaders to Urge Trade," 14 ITR 1909 (November 5, 1997); "Jobs in Foreign-Owned Subsidiaries Rose," 15 ITR 731 (April 29, 1998).

24. "New U.S.–EU Trade Initiatives Possible at 2000 Talks," 4/28/98 BTD d8; Guy de Jonquières, "U.S. may favor widening trade talks," FINANCIAL TIMES, October 19, 1998, p. 3; Haig Simonian, "Daimler Chrysler deal in final stages," FINANCIAL TIMES, September 19/20, 1998, p. 23; Richard Stevenson, "Europeans Challenge U.S. in Economic Crisis," NEW YORK TIMES, October 7, 1998, p. 1; "Who Sets Internet Rules? Not Just U.S., Says EU," EURECOM, March 1998, p. 2.

25. "U.S., EU Agree on Mutual Recognition of Electronic Products," 13 ITR 25 d30 (June 19, 1996); "EU, US Near Accord on MRA Agreements," EURECOM, June 1997, p. 1; "EU Ministers Approve Trade Framework with U.S. on Veterinary Equivalency," 15 ITR 455 (March 18, 1998); "FDA Proposes Rule to Implement Last Year's Pharmaceutical MRA with EU," 15 ITR 649 (April 15, 1998); "EU, US Sign Accord on Science and Technology," EURECOM, December 1997, p. 3; Nikki Tait & Samer Iskandar, "Chicago board of trade links up with European exchange," FINANCIAL TIMES, March 19, 1998, p. 1.

26. U.S. Official Urges Close Cooperation with Europe on Food Safety Disputes," 15 ITR 148 (January 28, 1998); "EU May Need 15 Months or More to Study Growth Hormones Before Lifting Import Ban," 15 ITR 220 (February 11, 1998); "U.S. Bans Imports of Cattle, Sheep from Europe, Citing Possible BSE Disease," 14 ITR 2177 (December 17, 1997); "U.S. Threatens Retaliation Against EU over Beef Import Ban," 3/19/98 BTD d2; Guy de Jonquières, "Nerves are taut as leaders hint at an EU–US trade war," FINANCIAL TIMES, November 9, 1998, p. 3.

27. "United States May Press to Eliminate Domestic Farm Support Program in WTO," 15 ITR 40 (January 14, 1998); Michael Smith, "Farmers uneasy at CAP reform plan," FINANCIAL TIMES, February 19, 1998, p. 2.

28. "A 'total' EU–US Row on the Horizon," EURECOM, October 1997, p. 1; "U.S. Asks for Industry Help in Averting Trade War with EU over Electronic Data," 15 ITR 310 (February 25, 1998); "U.S., Europe at Loggerheads over Talks to End Bribery in International Transactions," 14 ITR 1985 (November 19, 1997); Neil Buckley, "EU Warns US on reshaping Internet," FINANCIAL TIMES, February 27, 1997, p. 7; Michael Smith, "Brussels may sue EU states over US aviation deals," FINANCIAL TIMES, March 11, 1998, p. 1.

29. "France Announces New Privatizations of Steel Company USINOR, Air France," 14 ITR 1911 (November 5, 1997); Emma Tucker, "Employers say EU state aid reform 'weak'," FINANCIAL TIMES, February 18, 1998, p. 2; Andrew Jack & Emma Tucker, "Tensions grow on French bank rescue," FINANCIAL TIMES, April 2, 1998, p. 2; Henri Marte, "Europe's counter-attack [in aerospace]," FINANCIAL TIMES, March 23, 1998, p. 14; "EU, US Hold WTO Talks on [Foreign Sales Corporations] FSC Export Subsidies," EURECOM, January 1998, p. 3; "Welcome, whoever you are [Schröder]," THE ECONOMIST, October 3, 1998, p. 56.

30. Lionel Barber, "Europe looks to play wider role in global money system," FINANCIAL TIMES, January 21, 1998, p. 1; Vicki Barnett, "Watch out, dollar; EMU's capital consequences," FINANCIAL TIMES, April 30, 1998, p. 12; Liam Halligan, "Dollar may seek revenge on euro," FINANCIAL TIMES, April 30, 1998, p. 8; "Europe and the Global Economic Downturn," EUROPE (Inside), October 1998; Martin Wolf, "Europe's tug-of-war," FINANCIAL TIMES, October 28, 1998, p. 13; Gillian Tett & Edward Luce, "Yen deposit rates fall below zero," FINANCIAL TIMES, November 6, 1998, p. 1; Edward Luce, "Japanese investors switch to European bond markets," FINANCIAL TIMES, October 29, 1998, p. 17.

31. In early 1998, Europe's chronic unemployment rate finally began to shrink, although still far higher than ours. Some of this can be laid to restructuring European businesses, and some to economic growth. "In Brief," EURECOM, April 1998, p. 4; Chan Kim & Renée Mauborgne, "Opportunity beckons," FINANCIAL TIMES, August 18, 1998, p. 8.

32. "Luxembourg [Summit] Sets Stage for EU Enlargement," EURECOM, January 1998, p. 1; "Business in Eastern Europe: The Next Revolution," THE ECONOMIST, November 22, 1997, Survey, p. 1; "Widening the EU—but not too fast," THE ECONOMIST, November 7, 1998, p. 51; Quinten Peel & Stefan Wagstyl, "Journey into the unknown," FINANCIAL TIMES, November 9, 1998, p. 15.

33. *See generally* (pamphlet), European Commission, "How Does the EU Relate to the World?" (1996); "Europe and Asia: Forging Closer Ties," EURECOM, April 1998, p. 2; Alan Cane, "Euro-Japanese deal brings global mobile phones closer," FINANCIAL TIMES, May 1, 1998, p. 1; "EU Backs Japan's Rejection of U.S. Demands in Chip Talks," 13 ITR 28 d2 (July 10, 1996); Tim Burt, "Canada in talks on EFTA entry," FINANCIAL TIMES, March 26, 1998, p. 3; "EU Foreign Ministers Back Proposal to Treat Russia, China as Market Economies," 15 ITR 738 (April 29, 1998); "EU Supplants U.S. in Directing WTO Agenda," 15 ITR 468 (March 18, 1998).

34. Gerard Baker, "Clinton considers a new economic order," FINANCIAL TIMES, November 24, 1998, p. 1.

35. Paul Krugman, "Challenging Conventional Wisdom," in POP INTERNATIONALISM (MIT Press, 1996), pp. 131–154.

36. Paul Krugman, "Technology's Revenge," in POP INTERNATIONALISM, pp. 191–203; Paul Krugman, "Is Capitalism Too Productive?" FOREIGN AFFAIRS, September/October, 1997, pp. 79–94; "Deflation and All That," THE ECONOMIST, November 15, 1997, p. 77.

37. "One World?" THE ECONOMIST, October 18, 1997, p. 79; "Trade Winds," THE ECONOMIST, November 8, 1997.

38. "Germany, Japan, and U.S. Lead Industrial Nations in Productivity Growth," 14 ITR 1427 (August 20, 1997); "EU Ministers Will Back New Round of Multi-

lateral Trade Negotiations in 2000," 15 ITR 565 (April 1, 1998); Robert Samuelson, "The Loss of Confidence," NEWSWEEK, October 19, 1998, p. 60; Henry Kaufman, "A lack of leadership," FINANCIAL TIMES, October 7, 1998, p. 11.

39. James Harding & Chrystina Freeland, "In search of a multi-polar world," FINANCIAL TIMES, November 8–9, 1997, p. 4; "EU Foreign Ministers Back Proposal to Treat Russia, China as Market Economies," 15 ITR 738 (April 29, 1998); "U.S., China Making 'Steady' Progress in WTO Accession Talks," 15 ITR 783 (May 6, 1998); "Chinese Progress on Human Rights Needed if U.S. Is to Ease Sanctions," 15 ITR 785 (May 6, 1998); "India Has 'Ways to Go' on Economic Reform, U.S. Says," 14 ITR 2128 (December 10, 1997); "President Urges Congress to Approve Bill with Africa," 15 ITR 19 (January 7, 1998); *See generally*, ROBERT LAWRENCE & OTHERS, EMERGING AGENDA FOR GLOBAL TRADE: HIGH STAKES FOR DEVELOPING COUNTRIES (Johns Hopkins Press, 1996).

40. "Expert Warns of Burden to WTO Dispute System," 15 ITR 778 (May 6, 1998); "WTO Reaches Agreement on Procedure for Arbitration of Disputes over Subsidies," 15 ITR 737 (April 29, 1998); "WTO Chief Floats Solutions to Problem of Leaked Reports," 4/28/98 BTD d6.

41. "New Zealand Nominates Mike Moore, Morocco Pushes Abouyoub to Head WTO," 15 ITR 1593 (September 23, 1998); "WTO Leadership Crisis Continues," 5/5/1999 BTD d2; "Compromise Splits Six-Year Term Between Moore and Supachai," 16 ITR 1200 (July 21, 1999); "W.T.O. deadlock officially ends," NEW YORK TIMES, July 23, 1999, p. C 4.

42. Richard Wolffe, "US anti-trust chief [FTC] warns of strangle hold on new technology," FINANCIAL TIMES, April 27, 1998, p. 1; "Technical Barriers to U.S. Trade a Growing Problem," 15 ITR 726 (April 29, 1998); "OECD Ministers Say E-Commerce, Deregulation, Trade Top Agenda," 15 ITR 727 (April 29, 1998); "Canada Proposes Tariff Standstill for Electronic Commerce Until 2000," 15 ITR 725 (April 29, 1998).

43. "Capital Goes Global," THE ECONOMIST, October 25, 1997, p. 87; Robert Chote, "Wanna be in my gang, my gang . . . ," FINANCIAL TIMES, April 17, 1998, p. 5; "Fund urged to be harder task master," FINANCIAL TIMES, April 18–19, 1998, p. 3; "OECD Investment Talks Remain on Track Despite Some Concerns," 15 ITR 773 (May 6, 1998); "France Pulls Out of OECD Talks on Multilateral Investment Treaty," 15 ITR 1750 (October 21, 1998); Martin Wolf, "Flows and blows," FINANCIAL TIMES, March 3, 1998, p. 16; "Pangloss on globalization," FINANCIAL TIMES, March 7–8, 1998, p. 6; Robert Samuelson, "Global Capitalism, R.I.P.?" NEWSWEEK, September 14, 1998, p. 41; Paul Krugman, "Soros' Plea: Stop Me!" FORTUNE, November 23, 1998, p. 36; John Plender, "Taming wild money,"FINANCIAL TIMES, October 20, 1998, p. 17.

44. Henry Kaufman, "A lack of leadership," *op cit.*; John Authers & Richard Waters, "Markets, not banks, call the shots," FINANCIAL TIMES, October 12, 1998, p. 3; Stephen Fidler & Andrew Balls, "Feast or famine: Are controls the answer?" FINANCIAL TIMES, October 6, 1998, p. 13; Paul Krugman, "Saving Asia: It's time to get radical," FORTUNE, September 7, 1998, p. 75.

45. "Prime Minister's Speech at the New York Stock Exchange," British Information Services, September 21, 1998; "Clinton Calls for New Economic Mechanism," 15 ITR 1676 (October 7, 1998); Aaron Zither, "G-7 Forum Eyes Global Loan Plan," BOSTON GLOBE, October 4, 1998, p. 1; "Declaration of G-7 Finance

Ministers and Central Bank Governors," October 30, 1998, http://www.library.utoronto.ca/www97/finance/sn103098.htm; "G-7 Leaders Statement on the World Economy," October 30, 1998, http://www.library.utoronto.ca/www97/finance/sn103098.html.

46. Robert Chote, "A world in the woods," FINANCIAL TIMES, November 2, 1998, p. 16; "Transparent Hype," THE ECONOMIST, November 7, 1998, p. 14; Jim Rohwer, "Capital Controls Done Right," FORTUNE, November 9, 1998, p. 32; George Graham, "Supervisors seek better banking loan standards," FINANCIAL TIMES, October 15, 1998, p. 8.

47. "Trade by Any Other Name," THE ECONOMIST, October 3, 1998 (Trade Survey), p. 10; Jim Kelly, "World Bank warns Big Five over global audit standards," FINANCIAL TIMES, October 19, 1998, p. 1; "Here Come the Good Guys," THE ECONOMIST, November 7, 1998, p. 79.

48. "OECD Nations Agree to Eliminate Tax Deductibility for Foreign Bribes," 13 ITR 16d3 (April 17, 1996); "Treaty to Outlaw Bribery Is Signed Without Accord on Tax Deduction Ban," 14 ITR 2220 (December 24, 1997); "Clinton Sends Anti-Bribery Document to Senate for 'Early' Approval," 15 ITR 774 (May 6, 1998); Thomas Omestad, "Bye-bye to Bribes," NEWSWEEK, December 22, 1997, p. 390.

49. Andrew Jack & Emma Tucker, "Tensions grow on French bank rescue," FINANCIAL TIMES, April 2, 1998, p. 2; "Boeing, Airbus Industries Trade Charges over Government Subsidies," 15 ITR 455 (March 18, 1998); Samer Iskander, "Credit Lyonnais rescue costs soaring," FINANCIAL TIMES, November 3, 1998, p. 2.

50. *See generally*, THOMAS C. FISCHER, "Chapter 12: Competing Competition Laws and Policy," in THE EUROPEANIZATION OF AMERICA: WHAT AMERICANS NEED TO KNOW ABOUT THE EUROPEAN UNION (Carolina Academic Press, 1995), pp. 177–202; David Henderson, "The Case Against Antitrust," FORTUNE, April 27, 1998, p. 40; Robert Rice, "[U.S. Antitrust] Guidelines meet a cold front [in Europe]," FINANCIAL TIMES, March 7, 1995, p. 12; "Boeing/MDC Merger Cleared [by EU] (with notable Conditions)," EURECOM, September 1997, p. 1; Nicholas Timmins, "OECD set to step up attack on cartels," FINANCIAL TIMES, March 2, 1998, p. 4; Guy de Jonquières, "Van Miert seeks global competition rules accord," FINANCIAL TIMES, January 31–February 1, 1998, p. 4; "WTO Not Likely to Tackle Competition Rules in the Next Trade Round," 15 ITR 1627 (September 30, 1998); "Business Groups Say Too Early for WTO to Set Framework for Competition Policy," 16 ITR 1484 (September 15, 1999).

51. "No Breakthrough at WTO in Textile Rules of Origin Talks," 15 ITR 775 (May 6, 1998); "[U.S.] Customs Wants Comments on Changed Interpretation Affecting Origin Rulings," 15 ITR 582 (April 1, 1998); "Commerce Attorney Sees Delay in Harmonization of Origin Rules," 15 ITR 1589 (September 23, 1998).

52. "USTR Official Says Dumping Complaints May Spread Beyond Steel to Other Sectors," 15 ITR 1790 (October 28, 1998); "World Trade Survey," THE ECONOMIST, October 3, 1998, p. 17.

53. "ITA Finds That Japan Dumps Supercomputers in U.S.," 14 ITR 1457 (September 3, 1997); "ITC Investigates Imports of Steel Plate from Six Countries," 15 ITR 624 (April 8, 1998); "EC Imposes Provisional Dumping Duties on Cotton," 15 ITR 583 (April 1, 1998); "Strength of U.S. Economy Seen as Restraint on Dumping Cases," 15 ITR 622 (April 8, 1998); "Dumped Semiconductors from Taiwan Injure U.S. Industry," 15 ITR 623 (April 8, 1998); "Economists Find An-

tidumping Duties on Rise, Unsound Method of Protection," 15 ITR 1462 (August 26, 1998).

54. "The Wages of Fear," World Trade Survey, THE ECONOMIST, October 3, 1998, p. 28; "Schools Brief: Workers of the World," THE ECONOMIST, November 1, 1997, p. 81; "EU's Employment Summit Does the Job," EURECOM, December 1997, p. 1; Robert Taylor, "Asia crisis will add to jobless total," FINANCIAL TIMES, September 24, 1998, p. 5.

55. Stephen Golub, "Are international labor standards needed to prevent social dumping?" 12/1/97 (IMF) Finance & Development, p. 20; Anthony Freeman, "Child Labor's Impact on Free Trade," Congressional Testimony, October 22, 1997 (1997 WL 14152423); Michel Hansenne, "One Set of Elemental Labor Standards for All the World," INTERNATIONAL HERALD TRIBUNE, June 4, 1998, p. 10.

56. "Union Advisory Committee Urges Labor Standards in OECD Investment Act," 14 ITR 995 (June 4, 1997); "EU/US Symposium on Int'l Labor Standards," EURECOM, March 1998, p. 3; "ILO Ducks Formal Trade/Labor Link, Leaving Many, Including U.S., Unhappy," 14 ITR 1112 (June 25, 1997).

57. "Ruggiero Defends WTO Environment Record Following Preliminary Shrimp/Turtle Decision," 15 ITR 465 (March 18, 1998); "WTO Cannot Be 'Judge, Jury, Police' on Environment Issues," 3/18/98 BTD d2; "State Department Makes Decisions on Shrimp Imports Despite WTO Ruling,"15 ITR 772 (May 6, 1998); "Environmental Discussions Top Agenda of OECD Investment Treaty Negotiations," 14 ITR 1918 (November 5, 1997); Gregg Easterbrook, "Hot Air Treaty," U.S. NEWS & WORLD REPORT, December 22, 1997; "World Trade Groups Urged to Do More to Address Trade/Environment Nexus," 15 ITR 1682 (October 7, 1998); Frances Williams, "Rich and poor clash over trade and environment," FINANCIAL TIMES, September 9, 1999, p. 4.

58. "Changes Proposed for EU's Banana Policy," EURECOM, February 1998, p. 3; "Cairns Group Leader Praises U.S. Focus on Liberalization of Agricultural Trade," 15 ITR 596 (April 8, 1998); "Agricultural Subsidies Down 8 Percent," 14 ITR 1030 (June 11, 1997); "Agricultural Ministers Meet at OECD, Agree That Liberalization Must Go Farther," 15 ITR 408 (March 11, 1998).

59. Alexander Nicoll, "Globalization 'makes the world less safe'," FINANCIAL TIMES, April 24, 1998, p. 5; Andrew Jack, "Euro's creation raises money laundering fears," FINANCIAL TIMES, February 10, 1997, p. 4. A task force (now involving about 26 nations) of the G-7 nations, the European Commission and Gulf Co-operation Council, has explored ways to deal with money laundering since 1989. It is estimated that criminal elements launder "hundreds of billions of dollars a year." "Nuclear Complacency," THE ECONOMIST, October 17, 1998, p. 20.

60. "Remaking NATO," FINANCIAL TIMES, June 7, 1996, p. 13; Bruce Clark, "NATO drafts its rules for entry," FINANCIAL TIMES, August 22, 1995, p. 2; "NATO: The Price of Expansion," THE ECONOMIST, November 15, 1997, p. 53; Lionel Barber, "Building the New NATO for the 21st Century," EUROPE, March 1988, p. 13.

The Maastricht Treaty calls for the "eventual framing of a common defense policy [for the EU], which might in time lead to a common defense," [TEU, title V, art. J.4(1)]. *See also*, Scott Sullivan, "Europe Takes a Giant Step," NEWSWEEK, December 23, 1991, p. 36; Bernard Gray, "U.S. seeks more European defense partners," FINANCIAL TIMES, May 29, 1996, p. 4; Alexander Nicoll, "European defense industries move closer to consolidation," FINANCIAL TIMES, April 21, 1998, p. 28. *See generally*, PHILIP GORDON (ED.), NATO'S TRANSFORMATION (Rowman & Littlefield, 1996); SEAN KAY, NATO AND THE FUTURE OF EUROPEAN SECURITY (Rowman & Littlefield, 1988).

61. "Liberalization May Aid Growth [International Trade Commission] Finds," 14 ITR 1995 (November 1997), *citing* its study: THE DYNAMIC EFFECTS OF TRADE LIBERALIZATION: AN EMPIRICAL ANALYSIS ["Every 1 percent in real global income induces an estimated 1.8 percent increase in global trade, with transportation equipment, capital goods (particularly electronic equipment), and apparel [being] some of the most rapidly increasing components of trade"]; Caspar Henderson, "National step to sustainability," FINANCIAL TIMES, January 7, 1998, p. 12; DANIEL YERGIN & JOSEPH STANISLAW, THE COMMANDING HEIGHTS: THE BATTLE BETWEEN GOVERNMENT AND THE MARKETPLACE THAT IS REMAKING THE MODERN WORLD (Simon & Schuster, 1998). In general, *see* OECD, OPEN MARKETS MATTER (1998), pp. 17, 105–110, 139–150.

62. In his program, "A Prairie Home Companion," radio personality Garrison Keillor reports on a fictitious Midwestern town named Lake Wobegon. He says that in Lake Wobegon "the women are strong, the men are good looking, and all the children are above average." The latter may be true of a small part of the world, but it cannot be true of the world as a whole. For every one of the world's economies to be "above average" is a vain hope. An equitable sharing out of opportunity and/or resources is the best that can be expected. The hostilities that persist in the world because all peoples and all nations believe that they deserve to be "above average" must be put to rest.

Selected Bibliography

U.S. ECONOMY

U.S. Law

CUMULATIVE DIGEST OF UNITED STATES PRACTICES IN INTERNATIONAL LAW (Dept. of State, 1998).

J. MICHAEL FINGER, ANTIDUMPING: HOW IT WORKS AND WHO GETS HURT (University of Michigan Press, 1993).

General U.S. Trade

C. FRED BERGSTEN & MARCUS NOLAND, RECONCILABLE DIFFERENCES? UNITED STATES–JAPAN ECONOMIC CONFLICT (Institute for International Economics, 1993).

LEA BRILMAYER, AMERICAN HEGEMONY: POLITICAL MORALITY IN A ONE-SUPERPOWER WORLD (Yale University Press, 1995).

WILLIAM DIETRICH, IN THE SHADOW OF THE RISING SUN: THE POLITICAL ROOTS OF AMERICAN ECONOMIC DECLINE (Pennsylvania State University Press, 1991).

EDWARD M. GRAHAM & PAUL R. KRUGMAN, FOREIGN DIRECT INVESTMENT IN THE UNITED STATES, 3RD ED. (Institute for International Economics, 1994).

GARY HUFBAUER & KIMBERLY ANN ELLIOTT, MEASURING THE COSTS OF PROTECTION IN THE UNITED STATES (Institute for International Economics, 1994).

MELVYN KRAUSS, HOW NATIONS GROW RICH: THE CASE FOR FREE TRADE (Oxford Univesity Press, 1997).

NAFTA

BARRY APPLETON, NAVIGATING NAFTA: A CONCISE USER'S GUIDE TO THE NORTH AMERICAN FREE TRADE AGREEMENT (Carswell, 1994).

RICHARD FEINBERG, SUMMITRY IN THE AMERICAS: A PROGRESS REPORT (Institute for International Economics, 1997).

RALPH FOLSOM & DAVIS W. FOLSOM, UNDERSTANDING NAFTA AND ITS INTERNATIONAL BUSINESS IMPLICATIONS (Matthew Bender, 1997).

RALPH H. FOLSOM, NAFTA IN A NUTSHELL (West Publishing Co., 1999).

RALPH H. FOLSOM, MICHAEL W. GORDON & JOHN A. SPANOGLE, HANDBOOK OF NAFTA DISPUTE SETTLEMENT (Transnational Publishers, 1998).

RAUL OJEDA ET AL., NORTH AMERICAN INTEGRATION THREE YEARS AFTER NAFTA (North American Integration and Development Center, 1996).

U.S. CONGRESS, OFFICE OF TECHNOLOGY ASSESSMENT, U.S.–MEXICO TRADE: PULLING TOGETHER OR PULLING APART? (U.S. GPO, 1992).

FTAA

GARY CLYDE HAUFBAUER & JEFFREY J. SCHOTT, WESTERN HEMISPHERE ECONOMIC INTEGRATION (Institute for International Economics, 1994).

EU GENERALLY

COMMISSION OF THE EUROPEAN COMMUNITIES, THE BUDGET OF THE EUROPEAN COMMUNITY (Annual).

EURECOM: MONTHLY BULLETIN OF EUROPEAN UNION ECONOMIC AND FINANCIAL NEWS (UN Delegation, New York).

EUROPE: MAGAZINE OF THE EUROPEAN UNION (Delegation of the European Commission, Washington, D.C.).

EUROPEAN UNION: SELECTED INSTRUMENTS TAKEN FROM THE TREATIES, VOLS. 1–2 (Office for the Publications of the European Communities, 1995).

THE EUROPEAN UNION AND THE REGIONS (Oxford University Press, 1995).

MAKING SENSE OF SUBSIDIARITY: HOW MUCH CENTRALIZATION FOR EUROPE? (Centre for Economic Policy Research, 1993).

LEON BRITTAN, GLOBALIZATION VS. SOVEREIGNTY? THE EUROPEAN RESPONSE (Cambridge University Press, 1998).

MICHELLE CINI, THE EUROPEAN COMMISSION: LEADERSHIP, ORGANIZATION, AND CULTURE IN THE EU ADMINISTRATION (Manchester University Press, 1998).

BERNARD CONNOLLY, THE ROTTEN HEART OF EUROPE (Faber and Faber, 1995).

RENAUD DEHOUSSE, EUROPE: THE IMPOSSIBLE STATUS QUO (St. Martin's Press, 1997).

JACQUES DELORS, OUR EUROPE: THE COMMUNITY AND NATIONAL DEVELOPMENT (Verso, 1992).

JAAP W. DEZWAAN, THE PERMANENT REPRESENTATIVES COMMITTEE: ITS ROLE IN EUROPEAN UNION DECISION-MAKING (Cartermill, 1995).

DESMOND DINAN, EVER CLOSER UNION? AN INTRODUCTION TO THE EUROPEAN COMMUNITY, 2ND ED. (Lynne Rienner, 1998).

DAVID A. EDWARD & ROBERT C. LANE, EUROPEAN COMMUNITY LAW: AN INTRODUCTION, 2ND ED. (Butterworths, 1995).

GEOFFREY EDWARDS & DAVID SPENCE, THE EUROPEAN COMMISSION (Cartermill, 1994).

MICHAEL EMERSON, REDRAWING THE MAP OF EUROPE (St. Martin's Press, 1998).

EUROSTAT, EUROPE IN FIGURES, 4TH ED. (Brussels, Annual).

ROMAN FRYDMAN & ANDRZEJ RAPACZYNSKI, PRIVATIZATION IN EASTERN EUROPE: IS THE STATE WITHERING AWAY? (Oxford University Press, 1994).

CHARLIE JEFFERY, THE REGIONAL DIMENSION OF THE EUROPEAN UNION: TOWARDS A "THIRD LEVEL" IN EUROPE? (European Studies, 1996).

BARRY JONES AND MICHAEL KEATING, THE EUROPEAN UNION AND THE REGIONS (Clarendon Press, 1995).

E.J. KIRCHNER, DECISION MAKING IN THE EUROPEAN COMMUITY (St. Martin's Press, 1992).

D. LASOK & K.P.E. LASOK, LAW & INSTITUTIONS OF THE EUROPEAN UNION, 7TH ED. (Butterworths, forthcoming).

PIERRE-HENRI LAURENT & MARC MARESCEAU, THE STATE OF THE EUROPEAN UNION, VOL. 4: DEEPENING AND WIDENING (Lynne Rienner, 1997).

P.S.R.F. MATHIJSEN, A GUIDE TO EUROPEAN UNION LAW, 7TH ED. (Sweet & Maxwell, 1999).

PHILIP NORTON, NATIONAL PARLIAMENTS AND THE EUROPEAN UNION (European Studies, 1996).

JOHN PINDER, EUROPEAN COMMUNITY: THE BUILDING OF A UNION (Oxford University Press, 1995).

CAROLYN RHODES & SONIA MAZEY, THE STATE OF THE EUROPEAN UNION, VOL. 3: BUILDING A EUROPEAN POLITY (Lynne Reinner, 1995).

SINGLE MARKET

PAOLO CECCHINI, THE EUROPEAN CHALLENGE, 1992: THE BENEFITS OF A SINGLE MARKET (Gower, 1998).

COMMISSION OF THE EUROPEAN COMMUNITIES, AGENDA 2000, COM (97) 2000 FINAL (Brussels, 15/07/1997).

COMMISSION OF THE EUROPEAN COMMUNITIES, WHITE PAPER ON GROWTH, COMPETITIVENESS, EMPLOYMENT: THE CHALLENGES AND WAYS FORWARD INTO THE 21ST CENTURY, E.C. BULL., Supp., June 1993.

COOPERS & LYBRAND, A GUIDE TO VAT IN THE EU: 1996–1997 (Kluwer, 1997).

RALPH H. FOLSOM ET AL., EUROPEAN COMMUNITY LAW AFTER 1992: A PRACTICAL GUIDE FOR LAWYERS OUTSIDE THE COMMON MARKET (Kluwer, 1993).

JOHN NEWHOUSE, EUROPE ADRIFT (Pantheon, 1998).

AUDRY WINTER ET AL., EUROPE WITHOUT FRONTIERS: A LAWYER'S GUIDE (Bureau of National Affairs, 1989).

EU LAW

THE LEGAL PROFESSION IN THE NEW EUROPE: A HANDBOOK FOR PRACTITIONERS (Blackwell Business, 1993).

LORD SLYNN OF HADLEY, THE ROLE AND FUTURE OF THE EUROPEAN COURT OF JUSTICE (British Institute of International and Comparative Law, 1996).

JACK BEATSON & TAKIS TRIDMAS, NEW DIRECTIONS IN EUROPEAN PUBLIC LAW (Hart Publishing, 1998).

L. NEVILLE BROWN & TOM KENNEDY, THE COURT OF JUSTICE OF THE EUROPEAN COMMUNITIES (Sweet & Maxwell, 1994).

RENAUD DEHOUSSE, THE EUROPEAN COURT OF JUSTICE (St. Martin's Press, 1998).

ROBERT R. DRURY & PETER G. XUERRB, EUROPEAN COMPANY LAW (Dartmouth, 1991).

MICHAEL A. EPSTEIN, INTERNATIONAL INTELLECTUAL PROPERTY: THE EUROPEAN COMMUNITY AND EASTERN EUROPE (Prentice Hall, 1992).

RALPH H. FOLSOM, EUROPEAN UNION LAW IN A NUTSHELL, 3RD ED. (West Publishing Co., 1999).

TREVOR C. HARTLEY, THE FOUNDATIONS OF EUROPEAN COMMUNITY LAW: AN INTRODUCTION TO THE CONSTITUTIONAL AND ADMINISTRATIVE LAW OF THE EUROPEAN COMMUNITY (Clarendon Press, 1994).

K.P.E. LASOK, THE EUROPEAN COURT OF JUSTICE: PRACTICE AND PROCEDURE (Butterworths, 1994).

DAVID MEDHURST, A BRIEF AND PRACTICAL GUIDE TO EC LAW (Blackwell Scientific Publications, 1994).

RICHARD PLENDER, EUROPEAN COURTS AND PRECEDENTS (Sweet & Maxwell, 1997).

SACHA PRECHAL, DIRECTIVES IN EUROPEAN COMMUNITY LAW: A STUDY OF DIRECTIVES AND THEIR ENFORCEMENT IN NATIONAL COURTS (Clarendon Press, 1995).

JO SHAW & GILLIAN MORE, NEW LEGAL DYNAMICS OF EUROPEAN UNION (Clarendon Press, 1995).

JOSEPHINE STEINER, ENFORCING EC LAW (Blackstone Press Limited, 1995).

JOHN A. USHER, EUROPEAN COURT PRACTICE (Oceana, 1983).

MAASTRICHT

MICHALE J. BAUN, AN IMPERFECT UNION: THE MAASTRICHT TREATY AND THE NEW POLITICS OF THE EUROPEAN INTEGRATION (Westview Press, 1996).

RENAUD DEHOUSSE, EUROPE AFTER MAASTRICHT: AN EVEN CLOSER UNION? (Law Books in Europe, 1994).

EMU

EURO 1999, PART 1 & 2 (European Commission, 1998).

EUROPEAN MONETARY INSTITUTE, PROGRESS TOWARDS CONVERGENCE 1996 (Frankfurt, 1996).

REPORT BY THE ECOFIN COUNCIL TO THE EUROPEAN COUNCIL, THE PREPARATIONS FOR STAGE 3 OF EMU, SN 4863/3/96, REV 3.

GREEN PAPER ON THE PRACTICAL ARRANGEMENTS FOR THE INTRODUCTION OF THE SINGLE MARKET CURRENCY, COM(95) 333.

C. RANDALL HENNING, GLOBAL IMPACT OF MONETARY UNION IN EUROPE (Institute for International Economics, forthcoming).

C. RANDALL HENNING, COOPERATING WITH EUROPE'S MONETARY UNION (Institute for International Economics, 1997).

WOLFGANG MÜNCHAU, THE FINANCIAL TIMES GUIDE TO ECONOMIC & MONE-
TARY UNION (FT Publications, 1998).

EU EXPANSION

GRAHAM AVERY & FRASER CAMERON, THE ENLARGEMENT OF THE EUROPEAN
UNION (Sheffield Academic Press, 1998).
MARC MARESCEAU, ENLARGING THE EUROPEAN UNION: RELATIONS BETWEEN
THE EU AND CENTRAL AND WESTERN EUROPE (Longman, 1997).
JOHN REDMOND & GLENDA G. ROSENTAHL, THE EXPANDING EUROPEAN UNION:
PAST, PRESENT, FUTURE (Lynne Rienner, 1997).

EU TRADE

EU-US Trade

European Commission, *Progress Report on EU/US Relations*, No. 7, December 1995.
THE LIMITS OF LIBERALIZATION: REGULATORY COOPERATION AND THE NEW
TRANSATLANTIC AGENDA (Johns Hopkins University Press, 1997).
THE NEW TRANSATLANTIC AGENDA (http://www.cec./u/eu/agenda/tr05.html).
A TRANSATLANTIC BLUEPRINT (The European Institute, November 1995).
"U.S., EU Trans-Atlantic Economic Partnership Action Plan," 15 ITR 1897 (No-
vember 11, 1998).
MATTHEW CANZNONERI, WILFRED J. ETHIER & VITTORIO GRILLI, THE NEW
TRANSATLANTIC ECONOMY (Cambridge University Press, 1996).
KEVIN FEATHERSTONE & RAY H. GINSBERG, THE UNITED STATES AND THE EU-
ROPEAN UNION IN THE 1990S: PARTNERS IN TRANSITION, 2ND ED. (St.
Martin's Press, 1996).
THOMAS C. FISCHER, THE EUROPEANIZATION OF AMERICA: WHAT AMERICANS
NEED TO KNOW ABOUT THE EUROPEAN UNION (Carolina Academic Press,
1995).
ELLEN L. FROST, THE NEW TRANSATLANTIC MARKETPLACE (Institute for Interna-
tional Economics, forthcoming).
MILES KAHLER, REGIONAL FUTURES AND TRANSATLANTIC ECONOMIC RELATIONS
(Brookings Institution, 1995).
BRUCE STOKES, OPEN FOR BUSINESS: CREATING A TRANSATLANTIC MARKETPLACE
(Council on Foreign Relations, 1996).
DAVID VOGEL, BARRIERS OR BENEFITS? REGULATION IN TRANSATLANTIC TRADE
(Brookings Institution, 1997).

EU Trade Generally

"World Business, Playing the New Europe: A Guide to Understanding and Profiting
from the Latest Investment Hot Spot." NEW YORK TIMES, September 28,
1998, pp. R1, R29.
EUROPEAN UNION TRADE WITH EASTERN EUROPE: ADJUSTMENT AND OPPORTU-
NITIES (Center for Economic Policy Research, 1995).

THERESE BLANCHET ET AL., THE AGREEMENT ON THE EUROPEAN ECONOMIC
    AREA (EEA) (Clarendon Press, 1994).
CHRISTOPHER PIENING, GLOBAL EUROPE: THE EUROPEAN UNION IN WORLD AF-
    FAIRS (Lynne Rienner, 1997).

ASIAN ECONOMY

APEC ADVISORY COUNCIL, APEC MEANS BUSINESS: BUILDING PROSPERITY FOR
    OUR COMMUNITY (APEC Secretariat, 1996).
IMPLEMENTING THE APEC BOGOR DECLARATION, AUSTRALIA-JAPAN RESEARCH
    CENTRE (The Australian National University, Canaberra ACT 0200, Austra-
    lia).
FREDERICK M. ABBOTT, CHINA IN THE WORLD SYSTEM: DEFINING THE PRINCIPLES
    OF ENGAGEMENT (Kluwer Law International, 1998).
C. FRED BERGSTEN, WHITHER APEC? THE PROGRESS TO DATE AND AGENDA FOR
    THE FUTURE (Institute for International Economics, October 1997).
PETER DRYSDALE & DAVID VINES, EUROPE, EAST ASIA AND APEC: A SHARED
    GLOBAL AGENDA? (Australia-Japan Research Centre).
PACIFIC ECONOMIC COOPERATION COUNCIL (PECC), MILESTONES IN APEC LIB-
    ERALIZATION: A MAP OF MARKET OPENING MEASURES BY APEC ECONO-
    MIES (P. Drysdale, 1996).
ARVIND PANAGARIYA ET AL., THE GLOBAL TRADING SYSTEM AND DEVELOPING
    ASIA (Oxford University Press, 1997).
PAUL SHEARD, "*Keiretsu*, Competition, and Market Access," IN GLOBAL COMPE-
    TITION POLICY (Institute for International Economics, 1997).
WORLD BANK, CHINA 2020 (7-Part Series) (Washington, D.C., 1997).
WORLD BANK, INFRASTRUCTURE DEVELOPMENT IN EAST ASIA AND PACIFIC: TO-
    WARDS A NEW PUBLIC-PRIVATE PARTNERSHIP (World Bank, 1996).

WORLD ECONOMY

JAMES ATWOOD, ANTITRUST AND AMERICAN BUSINESS ABROAD (McGraw-Hill,
    1981).
RICHARD BLACKHURST, ALICE ENDERS & JOSEPH FRANCOIS, THE URUGUAY
    ROUND AND MARKET ACCESS: OPPORTUNITIES AND CHALLENGES FOR DE-
    VELOPING COUNTRIES (World Bank, 1995).
BARRY EICHENGREEN, GLOBALIZING CAPITAL (Princeton University Press, 1998).
MORRIS GOLDSTEIN & CARMEN REINHART, FORECASTING FINANCIAL CRISES:
    EARLY WARNING SIGNALS FOR EMERGING MARKETS (Institute for Interna-
    tional Economics, forthcoming).
EDWARD M. GRAHAM, GLOBAL CORPORATIONS AND NATIONAL GOVERNMENTS
    (Institute for International Economics, 1996).
EDWARD M. GRAHAM & J. DAVID RICHARDSON, GLOBAL COMPETITION POLICY
    (Institute for International Economics, 1997).
JOHN GRAY, FALSE DAWN—THE DELUSION OF GLOBAL CAPITALISM (Granta,
    1998).
PAUL KRUGMAN, POP INTERNATIONALISM (MIT Press, 1996).

ANDREAS F. LOWENFELD, INTERNATIONAL PRIVATE TRADE, 3RD ED., VOL. 1 (Matthew Bender, 1996).

OECD ECONOMIC OUTLOOK, MULTINATIONAL COMPANIES AND INTERNATIONAL TRADE DEVELOPMENTS (December 1996).

DANI RODIK, HAS GLOBALIZATION GONE TOO FAR? (Institute for International Economics, 1997).

JEFFREY J. SCHOTT, THE WORLD TRADING SYSTEM: CHALLENGES AHEAD (Institute for International Economics, December 1996).

LESTER THUROW, THE FUTURE OF CAPITALISM (Morrow & Co., 1996).

THE WORLD BANK, WORLD DEVELOPMENT REPORT 1997: THE STATE IN A CHANGING WORLD (Oxford University Press, 1997).

DANIEL YERGIN & JOSEPH STANISLAW, THE COMMANDING HEIGHTS: THE BATTLE BETWEEN GOVERNMENT AND THE MARKETPLACE THAT IS REMAKING THE MODERN WORLD (Simon & Schuster, 1998).

JACOB ZIEGEL, NEW DEVELOPMENTS IN INTERNATIONAL COMMERCIAL AND CONSUMER LAW: PROCEEDINGS OF THE 8TH BIENNIAL CONFERENCE OF THE INTERNATIONAL ACADEMY OF COMMERCIAL AND CONSUMER LAW (Hart Publishing, 1998).

WORLD TRADE/WTO

GUIDE TO GATT LAW AND PRACTICE: ANALYTICAL INDEX, 6TH ED. (GATT, 1994).

OPEN MARKETS MATTER: THE BENEFITS OF TRADE AND INVESTMENT LIBERALIZATION (Organisation for Economic Co-Operation and Development, 1998).

REGIONALISM AND THE WORLD TRADING SYSTEM (WTO, 1995).

"U.S. Awaits Coming of 'Millennium Round' of WTO Negotiations (The U.S. Position in a Nutshell)," 16 ITR 103 (January 20, 1999).

DALE E. HATHAWAY & MERLINDA D. INGCO, AGRICULTURAL TRADE LIBERALIZATION IN THE URUGUAY ROUND, SESSION I (World Bank, 1995).

ANNE O. KRUEGER, THE WTO AS AN INTERNATIONAL ORGANIZATION (University of Chicago Press, 1998).

ERNST-ULRICH PETERSMANN, THE GATT/WTO DISPUTE SETTLEMENT SYSTEM (Kluwer Law International, 1998).

ERNEST H. PREEG, FROM HERE TO FREE TRADE: ESSAYS IN POST-URUGUAY ROUND TRADE STRATEGY (University of Chicago Press, 1998).

JEFFREY J. SCHOTT, WTO 2000: SETTING THE COURSE FOR WORLD TRADE (Institute for International Economics, September 1996).

Index

Accession, of new members to the European Union, 126, 136–137, 140–141
Action, Community, 82–85
  attacks on, 85–88
  See also Decisions; Directives; Opinions; Recommendations; Regulations
Advisory rulings. *See* Preliminary rulings, of European Court
Africa, 55–56, 233
African, Caribbean and Pacific Countries (ACP) (former colonies of EC nations, parties to the Lomé Convention), 55–56, 77, 127, 203–204
Agenda 2000, 91, 99
Agricultural Guidance and Guarantee Fund. *See* European Agricultural Guidance and Guarantee Fund
Agriculture, Common Policy. *See* Common Agricultural Policy
Agriculture, trade rules regarding, 226, 240–241
Allies/adversaries, 27, 115, 228–231
Andean Pact, 66, 72
Annulment actions, 85–86
Antitrust

EC policy, 110–111, 237 (*see also* Articles 85–86)
  international, 37, 237–238
  U.S.–EC cooperation, 111, 237–238
  U.S. policy (Sherman Act), 110–111, 237
  See also Competition law
Approximation, of laws, 93
Argentina, 70
Article 85 (EC competition law), 110–111, 237
Article 86 (EC competition law), 108, 110–111, 237
Asia
  collapse of economy, 182–188
  foreign direct investment, 183, 184, 185–186, 194, 196
  in general, 9, 20, 28, 178–179, 186–187, 193–194, 233, 235
  market structure, 176–181, 183–187
  recovery, 189–191, 192–197
  sudden growth of, 178–180
  See also Asian "ladder"; Asian "miracle"; Asian model
Asia Pacific Economic Cooperation Forum (APEC), 45, 170, 175, 176, 178, 190, 198, 227
Asia Pacific Fund, 175, 190

Asian "crisis," 184–188, 235
Asian "ladder," 146, 179, 180, 182, 193
Asian "miracle," 178–179
Asian model, 146, 148, 154, 167, 179, 182, 185, 193, 197–198
Assembly. *See* European Parliament
Association of Southeast Asian Nations (ASEAN), 120, 175, 198, 227
Automobiles, 154–155

Banana dispute (U.S. and EU), 105, 203–204, 221
Barshefsky, Charlene, 45, 126, 206, 208
Beef, 207–208, 209
Blair, Tony, 103, 110, 197, 235
Bloc, trading. *See* Trading bloc
Block exemptions, 111
Brazil, 68–69, 73, 223
Bribery, 236–237
Brittan, Sir Leon, 102, 126, 229
Budget, Community, 99, 104, 135, 137, 142
Bulgaria, 127, 140, 143

Canada, 59, 71, 126, 128
Capital, movement of, 80, 82, 93, 117, 139, 173, 185–186, 235–236
    See also Free movement
Central and East European States (CEES), 127–128, 134, 136–143
Chile, 55, 68, 70
China
    economic structure, 160–162, 168
    and the EU, 165–166
    foreign direct investment, 173–174, 177, 187
    future of, 175–177
    Hong Kong and Taiwan, relations with, 164, 165, 187
    infrastructure problems, 163, 167–170, 172–173, 177
    and Japan, 165
    membership in the WTO, 164, 166, 170, 175, 210

most-favored-nation status, 163–164, 171, 173
    opening and reform, 162, 164–165, 167, 169, 173–176, 195–196, 233
    role in Asia, 161–162, 163, 175–177, 187, 194
    and Russia, 166, 176
    U.S. policy toward, 154, 162–163, 164, 166, 170, 171, 173, 176
Chirac, Jacques, 103
Citizenship, in the Community, 97, 98–99, 101
Civil law, 86
Clinton, William
    and Asia, 178
    and China, 163, 164, 166, 170
    and domestic issues, 10, 45
    and the EU, 127, 129
    and "fast track" negotiating authority, 11, 72–73, 227–228
    and international trade, 10–11, 33, 45, 197, 210, 228, 235
    and Mexico, 60–61
    and NAFTA, 59
    and Russia, 128, 144
    and South Africa, 28
    and South America, 65, 67–70, 72
Coal and steel (ECSC). *See* Treaty
Co-decision procedure (Council and Parliament), 83
Cohesion fund/policy, Community, 108, 141–142
Commission, European. *See* European Commission
Committee, Economic and Social. *See* Economic and Social Committee
Committee of the Regions, 108
Common Agricultural Policy (CAP), 104–105, 137, 142, 230
Common currency. *See* Euro
Common Customs Tariff (CCT), 93
Common defense policy, 98
Common Fisheries Policy (CFP), 104–105
Common Foreign and Security Policy (CFSP), 76, 91, 97–98, 126

See also Common defense policy
Common Market, 93, 94, 96–101
See also Single market
Common transport policy, 105–106
See also Trans-European Networks
Community actions. *See* Actions, Community
Community Budget. *See* Budget, Community
Community institutions
  in general, 81–82, 126
  reform of, 76–77, 78, 89–92, 99, 137–138
Community legislation. *See* Legislation, Community
Community's own resources. *See* Budget
Company law, 80, 87
Competence, to act, 82–83, 86
Competition law, 37, 110–111, 226, 233, 237–238
See also Antitrust
Competitiveness
  of Asia, 179–180, 187–188, 193–196
  of China, 163–165, 169, 176–177
  of the EU, 78, 79, 95–96
  in general, 13–14, 32, 47–48, 50–51, 225–232, 242–243
  of Japan, 145–146, 147–148, 156
Concentrations. *See* Article 86
Concerted practices. *See* Article 85
Conciliation Committee (Council and Parliament), 83, 115
Consultation procedure (Council and Parliament), 83
Convergence criteria, to adopt a single currency, 117, 118, 119–120, 122, 123
Cooperation procedure (Council and Parliament), 83
Council
  European, 94, 103, 117, 118, 121, 126, 130, 131, 137
  of ministers, 81, 83, 85, 86, 90–91, 112, 113, 127, 137
  president of, 127

Council of Ministers for Economic and Financial Affairs. *See* Ecofin Council
Court of First Instance (CFI), 81, 93
Court of Justice, European (ECJ), 80, 81, 85–88, 93
Crime, international, 36, 82, 98, 241–242
Customs Union, 75, 93
Czech Republic, 127, 138–141, 142, 143

Deepen, the European Community, 76, 80–81, 89–92, 94–102, 104, 116
Defense, common policy. *See* Common Defense Policy
Delors, Jacques, 79, 97, 117
Derogation, from Community legal requirements, 85, 102
Deutsche mark (DM), 79, 116, 119, 123, 124
Developing countries, 127, 179–181, 186, 187–188, 210, 214–218, 220, 225
Directives, 84–85, 95
Disparity, Member States, 131, 136, 138, 140, 141
Dispute settlement. See World Trade Organization
Dominant position, 111. *See also* Article 86
Drug trade, 60
Dumping, of goods, 111–112, 215, 238–239

Eastern Europe. *See* Central and Eastern Europe
Ecofin Council (Council of Ministers for Economic and Financial Affairs), 118, 119, 120, 123
E-commerce, 230
Economic and Monetary Union (EMU)
  convergence criteria, 118–119, 122
  Delors plan, 97, 117–118
  in general, 97, 109–110, 116–119
  members of, 119, 121

"opt-outs," 118, 120, 121, 122, 124
stability pact, 120
time line for, 117–118, 121–122
Economic and Social Committee
(ESC), 109
Economic models
capitalistic, 30, 45–46, 128–129, 133–135
communistic, 31, 133–134, 136, 160
in general, 8, 30–31, 51–53, 224, 232, 235–236, 242–243
micro-managed, 30–31, 145–146, 147–148
socialistic (macro-managed), 30, 90, 106–107, 134–135
Edinburgh Summit, 122
EEC Treaty (of Rome). *See* Treaty
"Effects" test, antitrust, 238
Employment, 90, 97, 106–107, 121, 231
Energy, 115
Enforcement, of Community law, 85–89
Enlargement, of the Community. *See* Widening the European Community
Environment, 37, 210, 213, 217–219, 226, 233, 240
Establishment, freedom of. *See* Free movement
Estonia, 140–141
Euratom Treaty (EAEC). *See* Treaty
Euro (common EU currency), 117–125, 231
See also Ecu
EUROBAROMETER, 100
Europe, in general, 10, 12–13, 75–78, 93–102
Europe agreements, 127, 137–138
European Agricultural Guidance and Guarantee Fund (EAGGF), 108
European Atomic Energy Community (Euratom). *See* Treaty
European Bank for Reconstruction and Development (EBRD), 138
European Central Bank (ECB), 87, 97, 117, 120, 121–123, 125

European Coal and Steel Community (ECSC). *See* Treaty
European Commission, 79, 80, 81, 83, 85, 86, 90–91, 111, 112
European Community (EC). *See* European Economic Community
European Council. *See* Council
European Court of Justice. *See* Court of Justice, European
European currency unit (ecu), 94, 97, 100, 116–117, 120
See also Euro
European Economic Area, 127, 137
European Economic Community (EEC), 76–84, 89, 93–102
European Exchange Rate Mechanism. *See* Exchange Rate Mechanism
European foreign policy. *See* Common Foreign and Security Policy
European Free Trade Association (EFTA), 127, 137
European Investment Bank (EIB), 109, 128, 131–132
European Monetary Institute (EMI), 97, 117–118, 120–121
European Monetary System (EMS), 94, 97, 116–117
European networks. *See* Trans-European Networks
European Parliament (EP), 81, 83, 87, 90, 95
European police office. *See* Europol
European political cooperation (EPC), 95, 98
European Regional Development Fund (ERDF), 108
European Social Fund (ESF), 109
European System of Central Banks (ESCB), 117, 122, 123
European Union (EU), in general, 7, 76, 89, 91, 93, 227, 233
See also Agenda 2000
Europol, 98, 114, 241
Exchange Rate Mechanism, European (ERM), 94, 97, 117, 118, 119–120
Expansion, of the Community. *See*

Widening the European Community

Export
in general, 6, 10–11, 13, 19–27, 215
to restore economy, 145, 147, 152, 161–162, 179–180, 182–183, 187, 193, 195
See also Trade
Extraterritorial jurisdiction, antitrust, 238

"Fast track" (negotiating authority), 11, 45, 67, 72, 227–228
"Federalism," 75, 83, 91, 92, 101, 114–115
Financial services, 77, 122–125, 156–157, 189, 190, 210, 212, 213, 216, 228
Fines
EU, 87
WTO, 205
Fisheries, Common Policy (CFP). *See* Common Fisheries Policy
Flexibility. *See* "Two-speed" Europe
Foreign aid, 13, 37–38, 239–240
Foreign direct investment (FDI)
and Asia, 162, 181, 183–186, 195–196
and China, 173
and Europe, 31, 39, 80, 139, 140
flight of, 9, 36, 74, 186, 235–236
in general, 6, 19, 36, 46, 50
and growth, 224–225
and India, 27, 28
and Japan, 24, 148, 153
and South America, 67, 68, 70
Foreign policy, common. *See* Common Foreign and Security Policy
"Fortress Europe," 30, 77, 128
"Four freedoms," 82, 93–94, 102. *See also* Free movement
"Franco-German bargain," 79, 102
Free movement
of capital, 82, 85, 97, 109–110, 117
of goods, 82, 85, 93–94, 104–105
of persons, 82, 85, 93–94
of services, 82, 85, 93–94
of workers, 82, 85, 93–94, 106–107

Free Trade Area of the Americas (FTAA), 58–59, 65–67, 71–74, 128, 231
Freedom, of establishment. *See* Free movement
Fuji Film case, 208, 221
Full faith and credit. *See* Mutual Recognition of National Judgments

General Agreement on Tariffs and Trade (GATT)
creation of, 201
enforcement of, 43, 54, 56–57, 202–203
miscellaneous issues
computers, 219
dumping, 215
environment, 217–219
harmonization, 215–216
labor, 216–217
mutual recognition agreements, 215
non-governmental organizations (NGOs), 213, 220
origin, 214
other initiatives
maritime, 212–213
mutual agreement, investment, 213
public procurement, 213–214
rounds, generally, 102, 201–202, 225
Millennium Round, 210, 211, 221–222, 229, 240
Uruguay Round, 102, 202, 209, 221, 229
sectoral agreements, 35, 210–211, 229
financial services, 209, 212, 216
Information Technology Agreement (ITA), 211
telecommunications, 211–212
See also World Trade Organization
General Agreement on Trade in Services (GATS), 212
Germany, reunification of, 25, 79, 96, 106
Globalization
defined, 4–7

effect on trade, 46–48, 51–52, 154,
   226–233, 235–236, 241–242
in general, 33–38, 54, 209–210,
   223, 224–226
problems of, 11–15, 75, 134, 160,
   186–188, 192–193, 231–242
Goods, free movement of. *See* Free
   movement
"Green paper," 111
Gross domestic product (GDP)
   Asia, 178
   Central and East European States,
      133
   China, 160, 161
   comparison of, 9–10
   EU, 74, 104, 105
   India, 27
   Japan, 23–24, 153
   Russia, 132
   U.S., 13, 19, 22, 150
Grounds, to annul Community acts. *See*
   Annulment
Group exemptions, competition law.
   See Block exemptions
Group of Seven (G-7) (Canada, France,
   Germany, Italy, Japan, the UK
   and the U.S., now sometimes in-
   cluding Russia), 5, 9, 36, 38,
   127, 132–133, 165, 226, 231,
   235–236

Harmonization, of laws, 93, 112–113,
   215–216, 219, 233–236
Helms-Burton Act (U.S. boycott of
   Cuba), 53–54, 209, 228
Hong Kong, 162, 164, 165, 178, 184,
   185–188, 191
Human rights, 163, 176, 216–217,
   231–232
Hungary, 127, 133–141, 143

Implied powers, 82–83
India, 27–28, 132, 233
Individual exemptions, from competi-
   tion law. *See* Negative clearance
Indonesia, 181, 183–184
Information Technology Agreement
   (ITA), 34–35, 129–130, 211

Institutional reform. *See* Community in-
   stitutions, reform of
Institutions, of the European Community, 81–82. *See also* Commission;
   Council; Court; European Parliament
Insurance (Japanese market), 156–157,
   212, 216
Intellectual property rights, 36, 38,
   171, 206
Intergovernmental conference (IGC),
   76–78, 89–92
Internal market. *See* Single market
International Labor Organization
   (ILO), 216–217, 239–240
International law (public versus private),
   4, 6
International Monetary Fund (IMF)
   and Asia, 186, 188–189, 190–192,
      194, 197
   and Brazil, 69
   in general, 3, 38, 196, 231, 235–235
   and Mexico, 60–61
   and Russia, 133, 134, 166
International trade, 3–4, 32–38, 223–
   226
Investment, Multilateral Agreement on
   (MAI), 213
Iran, 163, 166, 228

Japan
   in general, 7, 145–147, 154, 158–
      159, 233
   market structure, 147–148, 151,
      155, 156–158
   recession, 147–149, 152, 154, 157,
      159, 223
   recovery, 153–154, 159, 194
   reform, failure of, 147, 148, 149,
      151–152, 158, 159, 195
   reform, market access, 151–152, 153–
      154, 155, 159, 195
   role in Asia, 152, 154, 194
   See also Trade, Japan
Jiang Zemin, President of China, 163,
   166, 167–168, 169, 170, 176

Kantor, Mickey, 45, 126
Kohl, Helmut, 103

Korea (South), 10, 178, 179, 184, 186, 187, 188, 191, 197, 215, 227

Labor standards, 37, 48–49, 77, 210, 216–217, 226, 233, 239–240
Languages, of the European Community, 101, 103
Latvia, 140
Lithuania, 140
Law, Community
  application of, 82–89
  attacks against, 85–88
  derogation from, 85, 102
  direct applicability, 84, 85
  direct effect, 84
  making of, 83–85, 93
  supremacy of (*see* Supremacy, of Community law)
  transposition of (*see* Transposition, of Community law to member State law)
Leadership, in world trade, 8, 32–33, 38–40, 219–220, 225–231, 232–233
Legislation, Community, 82–85
Legislative initiative, 83
Less-developed countries, 48, 161, 164
"Little Tigers" (fastest-developing Asian economies), 145, 162, 164, 178–179, 184, 185, 186, 188
Lomé Convention (ACP), 55–56, 77, 203

Maastricht Treaty
  on European Union (TEU), 76, 87, 90–92, 97–99, 113–114, 135
  "opt-outs," 118, 121–122
  ratification of, 90, 97
Major, John, 90, 102, 103
Malaysia, 181, 182, 184, 185
Maritime trade, 212–213
Marshall Plan, 43, 75
Mediterranean policy, Community, 131–132
Member States
  in Council, 78, 83–84, 90

disparity, 91–92, 95, 103, 104–105, 108–109, 119–120
  in general, 76, 77, 79–80, 92
Mercosur, 66, 71–72, 73, 128, 223
Mexican peso, devaluation of, 35, 60–61, 66, 235
Mexico, 20, 59–66, 71, 74, 128
Merger Treaty. *See* Treaty
Models, economic. *See* Economic models
Monetary stability, 35–36, 133–135, 189–193, 213, 235–236
Monetary Union, European. *See* Economic and Monetary Union
Monopoly. *See* Antitrust; Article 85; Article 86
Most-favored-nation (MFN) status, 163–164, 171, 173
Multilateral Agreement on Investment (MAI), 213, 235
Mutual recognition agreements (MRAs), 114, 130, 215, 229–230
Mutual Recognition of National Judgments (Brussels Convention), 88–89

National courts, enforce EU law, 87–88
"Necessary and proper" power, 82
Negative clearance, 110–111
Networks, Trans-European. *See* Trans-European Networks
New Transatlantic Agenda (NTA), 129
Newly Independent States (NIS) (former states of the Soviet Union), 134
Non-governmental organizations (NGOs), 209, 213, 220
Non-tariff barriers (NTBs), 34, 37, 103, 207–209
Normal trade relations (NTRs). *See* Most-favored-nation status
North American Free Trade Agreement (NAFTA), 21, 45, 54–56, 58–66, 70, 71, 225–227, 231
North Atlantic Treaty Organization (NATO), 98, 126, 127, 132, 133, 142, 143, 231, 241

North-south policy, Community, 131–
    132, 140, 141
Norway, 76, 141

Official Journal (O.J.), of the European
    Communities, 93
Opinions, 84–85
"Opt-outs," Denmark, U.K., 118, 121–
    122
Organization for Economic Coopera-
    tion and Development (OECD),
    39, 127, 133, 213, 235, 236
Origin, rules of, 214, 238
Own resources, Community's. *See*
    Budget

Pacific Economic Cooperation Council
    (PECC), 179
Pacific Rim, 33, 178
Parliament, European. *See* European
    Parliament
Patent protection, 115
Penalties, for violation of EU law, 87
Peso "crisis" (Mexico), 35, 60–61, 66,
    235
PHARE, 142
Philippines, 184, 187, 194
PILLAR II. *See* Common Foreign and
    Security Policy
PILLAR III (Common Justice and
    Home Affairs Policy), 76, 91, 97–
    98, 113–114, 241
Plea, of illegality. *See* Annulment
Poland, 127, 133, 139–141, 143–144
Poland and Hungary: Aid for Economic
    Restructuring. *See* PHARE
Policy, Common Foreign and Security
    Monetary (*see* Economic and Mone-
        tary Union; European Monetary
        System; Exchange Rate
        Mechanism)
    Social (*see* Social policy)
    See also Common Foreign and Secu-
        rity Policy
Political union. *See* European political
    cooperation
Precedence. *See* Supremacy

Preliminary rulings, of European Court,
    87–88
Procurement, public, 210, 213–214
Professionals, free movement of, 82
Programme, Work (of Commission),
    79, 93, 95, 99, 131
    See also Agenda 2000
Protectionism, 12, 33–34, 64, 67, 77,
    130–131, 141–151, 160, 193,
    195

Quad Four (Canada, the EU, Japan
    and the U.S.), 5, 36, 38, 125,
    165, 235
Qualified majority voting, in Council,
    78, 83, 90, 95

Recommendations, 84, 85
References, for preliminary rulings. *See*
    Preliminary rulings
Reform, institutional. *See* Community
    institutions, reform of
Regional Development Fund, European
    (ERDF). *See* European Regional
    Development Fund
Regionalism, 5, 7, 38, 58, 77, 190–
    191, 198, 225–227, 233, 235–
    241
Regions, Committee of. *See* Committee
    of the Regions
Regulations, 84–85
Research and development (R & D),
    48, 129, 230
Reunification, German. *See* Germany,
    reunification of
Revenue, Community. *See* Budget
Romania, 127, 140, 141, 143
Rome, Treaty of (EEC). *See* Treaty
Ruggiero, Renato, 217, 219, 220, 222
Rulings, preliminary. *See* Preliminary
    rulings
Russia, 128, 131, 132–134, 138, 140,
    144, 160, 166, 167, 221

Santer, Jacques, 79, 106
Section 301 (U.S. trade retaliation),
    156, 206, 208
Security, global, 7, 9, 36, 241–242

Services, freedom to provide. *See* Free movement
Sherman Act (U.S. antitrust), 110–111, 237–238
"Shrimp/turtle" dispute (WTO), 218–219
Singapore, 10, 178, 180, 182–183, 187
Single currency, Community. *See* Euro
Single European Act (SEA). *See* Treaty
Single market, 12, 76–77, 84, 92, 93–97, 100
Slovakia, 127, 140, 143
Small and medium-sized [business] enterprises (SMEs), 47, 48–49, 107–108
Social policy, European, 78, 90, 98–99, 106–107, 109, 230–231
South America, 66–68, 70, 71–72, 73–74. *See also individual countries*
South Korea, 10, 178, 179, 184, 186, 187, 188, 191, 197, 215, 227
Southern Common Market. *See* Mercosur
"Stability Pact," common currency, 120
Standing, to sue, 86–87
State aid. *See* Subsidies
Structural funds, 104–106, 108–109
Subsidiarity, principle of, 82
Subsidies, state, 112, 237
Super 301, 228. *See* also Section 301
Supranational institutions, 75, 76, 77, 81, 83
Supremacy (Precedence), of Community law, 85–86

Taiwan, 162, 165, 176, 178, 180, 182, 186–187, 194, 210
Tariffs, 3, 37, 93
Tax harmonization, EU, 112–113
Telecommunications, 158, 211–213
Trade
  Canada, 20, 21, 55, 59, 128
  China, 160–161, 170–172, 173–176, 195–196, 227
  EU, 24–27, 127–129, 131–135, 136–138, 165, 227

Japan, 21, 23–25, 32, 145–146, 154–157, 165, 195, 227
Mexico, 20, 21, 55, 59–65, 128
Pacific Rim, 20, 178–180, 195–196
U.S., 19–21, 22–23, 33, 43–57, 149–151, 162–163, 164, 226–228
U.S.–EC, 21, 26–27, 32–34, 39–40, 50–51, 77, 80–81, 128–131, 165–166, 203–204, 228–231
world, 8–15, 21–22, 28, 34–36, 38–39, 44, 47–48, 128, 145–146, 160, 201–202, 214–215, 219, 223, 224–225, 231–232
Trade-related aspects of intellectual property rights (TRIPs), 38
Trade Related Investment Measures Agreement (TRIMs). *See* Investment, Multilateral Agreement on
Trade surplus (or deficit), 48–50, 195, 243
Trading bloc, 21–22, 58–59, 67, 71–72, 75, 233
Transatlantic Business Dialogue (TABD), 129–130
Transatlantic Economic Partnership (TEP) (U.S. and EU), 130, 227
Trans-European Networks, 105–106
Transport policy. *See* Common transport policy
Transposition, of Community law to Member State law, 80, 84, 95
Treaty
  of Amsterdam, 76, 89–92
  Coal and Steel, 76, 81, 89, 94
  Euratom, 76, 89
  of European Union (TEU) (*see* Maastricht Treaty)
  in general, 76, 82–83, 88–89
  of Lomé (*see* Lomé)
  of Maastricht (*see* Maastricht Treaty)
  Merger, 76
  of Rome (EEC), 76, 89, 94, 102
  Single European Act (SEA), 76, 89, 95–97
Turkey, 141
"Two-speed" Europe, 75, 78, 80, 89, 91–92, 99–100, 121

Unanimous voting, Council, 82, 101, 113
Unemployment, in general, 44, 64, 95–96, 106–107, 147–148, 153, 168, 232
Unification, Germany. *See* Germany, reunification of
United Kingdom (U.K.), 79, 80, 90, 94, 102, 109, 120, 125
United Nations (UN), 3, 38, 43, 127, 225
United States (U.S.)
  consumption, 10
  EC antitrust cooperation (*see* Antitrust)
  EC trade cooperation (*see* New Transatlantic Agenda and Transatlantic Economic Partnership)
  in general, 8, 10–15, 128–131, 226–228
  trade with Canada, Mexico, the EC, the Pacific Rim and the World (*see* Trade)
"United States of Europe," 77, 81–82, 92
U.S. Trade Representative (or Office of the U.S. Trade Representative) (USTR), 45, 53, 126, 149–150, 151, 155, 206, 208, 227
Uruguay Round, of GATT. *See* General Agreement on Tariffs and Trade

Value-added tax (VAT), 113
"Variable-speed" Europe. *See* "Two-speed" Europe
Venezuela, 69

Western European Union (WEU) (EU military alliance), 98, 126, 241–242

White paper
  Agenda 2000, 99
  on employment, 106
  on expansion of the Community, 141
Widening the European Community, 76, 81, 136–144, 231
Work Program, EU, 79, 93, 95, 99, 131
  See also Agenda 2000
World Bank, 3, 38, 43, 127, 134, 135, 189, 197, 236
World "Government," 5, 38–39, 225–226
World trade. *See* Trade, world
World Trade Organization (WTO)
  dispute settlement process, 202–206, 218, 220–221
  enforcement of decisions, 12, 205–206
  expansion, of membership, 210, 221
  future of, 6, 8, 12, 15, 219–222, 233–235
  in general, 38, 133, 150, 175, 189, 201–202, 220–222, 225
  miscellaneous issues, 213–219
  review and reform, 208–209, 220–221, 234
  side and sectoral agreements, 210–213
  structure and operation, 202–206
  U.S. experience with, 53–54, 56–57, 201, 206–210, 218–219
  See also General Agreement on Tariffs and Trade

Yaoundé Convention. *See* Lomé
Yeltsin, Boris, 132, 133
Yen, 124, 154, 156

About the Author

THOMAS C. FISCHER is Professor of Law and Dean Emeritus, New England School of Law, Boston. Formerly Professor of Law and Associate Dean of the University of Dayton School of Law, he has been a visiting scholar or fellow at numerous universities here and abroad, including Cambridge, Exeter, Edinburgh, Münster, Konstanz (Germany) and Auckland (New Zealand). In 1997 he held the coveted Inns of Court Fellowship (London). His most recent book, *The Europeanization of America*, was nominated for the American Bar Association's Gavel Award.